THE DISPOSITION OF NATURE

The Disposition of Nature

ENVIRONMENTAL CRISIS AND

WORLD LITERATURE

JENNIFER WENZEL

FORDHAM UNIVERSITY PRESS

New York 2020

Fordham University Press gratefully acknowledges financial assistance and support provided for the publication of this book by Columbia University.

Visit us online at www.fordhampress.com.

Library of Congress Cataloging-in-Publication Data available online at http://catalog.loc.gov.

Printed in the United States of America

22 21 20 5 4 3 2 1

First edition

in memory of Barbara Harlow

CONTENTS

This European opulence is literally scandalous, as it has been founded on slavery, it has been nourished with the blood of slaves and it comes directly from the soil and subsoil of that underdeveloped world. . . . Perhaps it is necessary to begin everything all over again . . . to re-examine the soil and mineral resources, the rivers, and—why not?—the sun's productivity.
—Frantz Fanon, *The Wretched of the Earth*

INTRODUCTION

Reading for the Planet

Reading for the planet?

How nonsensical is it to think that reading might help "save the earth"? Or that literature can address the many environmental challenges confronting the world today?

Narratives of limitless growth, premised upon access to cheap energy and inexhaustible resources, underwrite the predicaments of the present. As an alternative to such obsolete futures, new modes of imagining might begin to chart a path beyond impasse and inertia. This book considers the role that literature and other kinds of cultural imagining play in shaping our understanding of the world and the planet, with a view toward forging new modes of relation among humans and with nonhuman nature. My guiding assumption in *The Disposition of Nature* is that things like climate change, fossil-fuel dependence, and resource depletion are not merely technological, economic, or political problems but also narrative problems and problems of the imagination. Beyond "literature" as conventionally defined, I attend to other media like film and photography and to the broader workings of the imagination, for better and for worse, in and on the world. This book traces notions of *world-imagining*, by which I mean imagining

I

a world and one's place in it, at scales ranging from the cells of our bodies to the earth as a whole.

I write as both a citizen of the United States and a literary critic trained in postcolonial studies. While the forms of intelligence and habits of mind that shape this book are informed by that scholarly training, my fundamental affiliation is as a human animal concerned about my planetary home and the fates and futures of my fellow creatures. With "reading for the planet," I have several things in mind. One is to consider whether and how the literary can be part of an environmentalist praxis: reading for the sake of the earth. Another is to understand "the planet" (or world or globe) as an interpretive rubric that raises questions of totality and scale. This means reading for images of the world entire: as a conceptual, social, or planetary whole. But it also means reading for traffic lines of power and modes of inequality that conjoin and divide those wholes. It means charting a moral economy of distance that can obscure relationships between sites and subjects thousands of miles apart. Reading for the planet is not disembodied "global," cosmopolitan, or universalist reading from nowhere, as in the bird's-eye view or "God trick" (Haraway 1988, 582), but reading from near to there: between specific sites, across multiple divides, at more than one scale. This multiscalar reading practice shuttles between the microscopically specific and the world-historical, in four dimensions, across space and time—reading (and rereading) as a dynamic process of *rescaling.*

I will say more about reading, but I want to observe now how suddenly the humanities have embraced thinking at the totalizing scale of the world, globe, or planet. The arguments and speculations in this book are located at the intersections of several academic disciplines. With regard to literary studies, this book thinks together two recent developments: first, the rise of environmental humanities, Anthropocene anxiety, and the material turn that thinks in new ways about matter, things, and objects, and about nature and the human; and second, the rivalry between postcolonial studies and world literature as frameworks for literary analysis. In the twenty-first century, a revived conversation about world literature seeks to reframe literary comparison in terms of the globe rather than the nation-state, at the same time that scholars are beginning to understand modernity and European imperialism as a radical (and radically uneven) remaking of nature and the planet itself. At a moment when literary studies dares to envision a "world literature" capacious enough to be worthy of the name, environmental studies sees a planet in crisis. Yet, this new conversation about world literature has said relatively little about the earth or the planet.[1] How, then, can we understand contemporary concerns about planetary environmental crisis in terms of postcolonial studies' interest in histories of political, economic, social, and epistemological inequality, as well as world literature's interest in readers without borders? How can we think among these terms—globe, world, earth, and planet—to calibrate the *globe* in globalization with the *world* in world literature or the earth/planet at risk in environmental crisis?

These expansive questions indicate that the disciplinary questions in literary studies outlined earlier are *only one instance* of the dynamic of world-imagining that is the central concern of this book. Such imagining is at work everywhere, all the time: beyond narrow disciplinary debates, yet informed by modes of thought and cultural logics that the tools of literary analysis can elucidate. To answer these questions also demands engagement with other disciplines—including history, anthropology, geography, political ecology, science and technology studies, and law—for their insights about colonialism and imperialism, globalization, and struggles among humans over nonhuman nature. In turn, this book demonstrates how a supple understanding of cultural imagining and narrative logics—a facility with the literary—has import beyond the discipline of literary studies, to foster more robust accounts of the past, present, and future of global inequality, in order to energize movements for justice and livable futures. This multivalent traffic between matter and ideas is the crux of *the disposition of nature*, by which I mean both what kind of thing nature is or is understood to be, and how humans arrange, control, and distribute nonhuman nature, often as "natural resources." This book traces relationships between these two senses of disposition: assumptions about what nature is are mutually constituted with contests over how it is used.

Anthropologist Anna Tsing observes that, as with any scale, the global is not simply out there, preformed and available to thought, but must be constructed in particular situations (2005, 57–58). We are living through one such situation now. The premise of Ursula Heise's *Sense of Place and Sense of Planet: The Environmental Imagination of the Global* (2008) was that environmental thought since the mid-twentieth century had been so invested in the local and place-based as to obstruct analysis at the global scale Heise dubbed "eco-cosmopolitanism." Over the past decade, *environmental* and *planetary* have come to function as near synonyms; it is easy to forget that ecology was not long ago taken to task for having no account of the global. This shift is due partly to looming challenges posed by global warming: both the rapid dissemination of Anthropocene talk across the disciplines, in the wake of interventions like Dipesh Chakrabarty's 2009 essay "The Climate of History," as well as the increasing frequency of extreme droughts, storms, and floods that used to be called once-in-a-century events.[2] (By "Anthropocene talk," I mean both the proposed new epoch in geological history, characterized by the effects of human actions on the Earth system, and reflections on its implications for various disciplines.) As elaborated later, climate change and the Anthropocene could be understood to demand the ultimate rescaling of attention and concern: beyond the local or national, beyond the human or anthropocentric, and beyond modernity itself.

The Disposition of Nature is not about the Anthropocene per se but has been written under its ever-expanding shadow. One aim of this book is to situate this paradigm shift (and epochal transition) in terms of genealogies of environmental concern and instances of environmental injustice that precede or exceed this emergent framework. Not every environmental crisis is most intelligible or tractable through the Anthropocene lens, and *Anthropocene* is not a synonym for global warming. Instead, the Anthropocene involves multiple, human-induced changes to the Earth system resulting from rearrangements of molecules and life forms across the planet, associated with the burning of wood and fossil fuels, industrial chemistry, planned and accidental discharges of nuclear material, and global trade and migration.[3]

In one sense, this book is about what contemporary neoliberal globalization means for literary and environmental studies and for imagining a more just future for all in the face of deepening inequalities, old and new. In a broader sense, this book is about what *globalization* means, period. How do we understand the continuities and disjunctures between "globalization" as an account of the present, on the one hand, and the earth-spanning, globe-mapping, world-creating, lifeworld-destroying effects of European imperialism and the transatlantic slave trade over the past five hundred years, on the other? The textures and tempos of lived experience tell us that the present world is unrecognizable when viewed through the lens of shipborne empires and their rise and fall, even as the traffic lines of power, plenty, and privilege in the twenty-first century reinscribe many of the same old divisions and debts from centuries past, albeit sometimes in new forms.

For example, climate injustice—the unevenly distributed causes and effects of global warming—is the most recent example of the Global South subsidizing the development of the Global North.[4] For decades, we have heard that the nation-state is withering away, while in many countries the state has been *repurposed* to facilitate intensified extraction of natural resources by multinational corporations and the diversion of wealth to national and international elites. The nation-state plays a crucial role in this contemporary version of what anthropologist Fernando Coronil called the "international division of nature," which he saw Marxian analysis having neglected in its attention to the international division of labor (1997, 29). Tracking continuities and shifts in this disposition of nature over the past half millennium, Coronil argued, can clarify what is new, and what is quite old, in contemporary neoliberal globalization. But it is not only the nature, labor, and markets of the formerly colonized world that subsidized the development of Europe and the United States. Industrialization and consumer capitalism in the Global North have made outsized use of the earth's atmosphere and oceans as "sinks" for waste products like carbon dioxide (CO_2).

This disproportionate using up of the planet's capacity to regulate itself within the biophysical parameters that support human life is a borrowing against—even theft of—other people's futures. These uneven histories of extraction, combustion, and emission shape the present and future in *material* form, and these processes have intensified since World War II.[5] Indeed, if globalization is construed in molecular terms, something qualitatively new happens when wartime advances in chemistry and nuclear technology rearrange the postwar world at a molecular level, along with the Great Acceleration in CO_2 emissions associated with the energy intensification of agricultural and manufacturing supply chains and transport. Like persistent organic pollutants (POPs)—synthetic chemicals that do not easily break down into less toxic compounds but disperse and accumulate in the food chain—the effects of such histories persist in bodies, biomes, and built environments, not to mention cultural imaginaries and horizons of expectation.

The implications of this perspective are twofold. First, one cannot tell this expanded story of globalization without acknowledging the environment as its condition of possibility and its product. Second, the formerly colonized world is indispensable, not marginal, to this history. Notice how words mislead, how *marginal* or *peripheral* in a geographic sense comes to mean *unimportant* or even *immaterial*, when precisely these flows of valuable or harmful matter are at stake. This occlusion is the logic of what economists call *externalization*—displacing costs (and acknowledgment of costs) elsewhere in space or time. In the history of European colonialism, this logic works partly through diffusionist narratives that posit the West as the origin from which all blessings flow toward the rest of the world. These narratives transpose and redescribe Europe's material debts to and dependencies upon the colonized world as beneficent "gifts" of civilization, Christianity, modernity—or environmental concern. The urgent challenge that postcolonial studies poses in the twenty-first century is this: how to understand the import of imperialism for the present, with regard to these histories and ideologies of exploiting humans and nonhuman nature? To that end, each chapter of this book juxtaposes different historical moments to consider how capitalism/colonialism and globalization function through continuity and rupture.

This intertwined sense of old and new ways of imagining and acting upon the world also underwrites the account of world literature in Aamir Mufti's *Forget English!* (2016). Mufti observes that the revival of interest in World Literature began during the years of this new century preceding the 2008 financial crisis and the subsequent Great Recession (6–7). (I use the capitalized form World Literature to mark the twenty-first century scholarly, curricular, and publishing project.) Indeed, one can draw a sharp dividing line in the new World Literature scholarship. Consider its seminal statements: David Damrosch's *What Is World Literature?* (2003), Franco Moretti's *Maps, Graphs, and Trees* (2007) and "Conjectures" and "More Conjectures" on World Literature (2000, 2003), and Pascale Casanova's *The World Republic of Letters* (2004). These texts are enthusiastic about taking the transnational movement of texts and genres as a framework for literary analysis. Monographs published after the economic crash and the disappointments following the Arab Spring—for example, Emily Apter's *Against World Literature* (2013), the Warwick Research Collective's (WReC) *Combined and Uneven Development: Towards a New Theory of World-Literature* (2015), and Pheng Cheah's *What Is a World?* (2016)—are more skeptical of the World Literature project.

This trajectory indicates that World Literature's turn toward the global slightly predates the shift toward the planetary in environmental humanities discourse.[6] And yet, as with climate justice and the international division of nature, everything old is new again, or at least still with us; here too, the specter of empires past haunts the horizon of the present. Among scholars of World Literature, Mufti is peerless in tracing historical continuities and complicities between, on the one hand, the acquisitive impulses of European imperialism and its Orientalist literary projects, and on the other hand, the recent rush to remap (and reanthologize) the world according to World Literature. Instead of positing World Literature as an arriviste claimant to the intellectual and curricular space claimed by postcolonial studies in the late twentieth century, Mufti makes it possible to understand this enterprise as the work of latter-day emperors in new clothes. He connects the historical dots between nineteenth-century Orientalists dreaming of a world library and the World Literature impresarios Emily Apter derides for their "entrepreneurial, bulimic drive to anthologize and curricularize the world's cultural resources" (2013, 3). Troping on Marx's classic formulation, we might say that the tragedy of Orientalism repeats as the farce of World Literature. The Orientalist knowledge/power project and the broader history of European imperialism are World Literature's condition of possibility. Yet the disciplinary push to claim the world for World Literature maintains that empire and postcoloniality are "over": outmoded and inadequate to make sense of world literary space. Thus, many influential voices on both environmental and literary questions assert that it's high time to *forget empire* (to trope on Mufti's title) while having forgotten (or never recognized to begin with) their imbrication within its enduring histories.

There are urgent reasons to be able to think at a planetary scale and to read any version of "the world" in terms of its historical conditions of possibility. As Lee Medovoi wrote in 2009, "What the media typically call the 'environmental crisis' is better understood as the current face of politics itself, namely the many different kinds of geopolitical struggle to reshape the circuits of power that flow between planetary life and accumulation on a global scale" (123–24). This connection between environment and geopolitics makes the discipline of political ecology relevant to *The Disposition of Nature*. By "political ecology," I mean not only (and not even primarily) the "new materialist" speculations of theorists like Bruno Latour, Michel Serres, and Jane Bennett about what a more-than-human politics might look like, but also (and more pointedly) the analysis of particular social movements and political struggles whose contested terrain is nature itself: how nature is understood, valued, inhabited, and distributed among humans. Both versions of political ecology inform this study. The new materialists taught me to be alert to the constitutive, coproducing role of nonhuman entities and forces, while the radical geographers and anthropologists make me wary that such notions of distributed agency will give cover to humans and corporations seeking to evade responsibility for harm. David Harvey (2003) describes the accumulation of capital—often by force or other means of dispossession—as an ongoing project, not merely a catalyzing (or "primitive") moment at the birth of capitalism when laborers were first alienated (or "freed") from their means of livelihood. The Anthropocene paradigm demands that we understand how this ongoing accumulation of capital is entangled with the accumulation of CO_2 in the earth's atmosphere and oceans (Anderson 2012). At its most incisive, literary criticism can demonstrate how the accumulation of capital and carbon is entangled with the accumulation of cultural capital. Literary imagining can make legible the discrepancies between statist, gridded "abstract space" and "lived space" that political ecologists Peter Vandergeest and Nancy Peluso identify as a major source of conflict and instability as states seek to manage territorial relations between people and natural resources (1995, 387–89). The rivalry between postcolonial theory and World Literature is legible, in Medovoi's terms, as part of a geopolitical struggle to reshape circuits of power at a global scale.

This book puts into productive tension the relationships through which writers, readers, and literary infrastructures constitute World Literature and those through which human actions are imbricated with nonhuman nature at scales ranging from the body and the household to the planet. The chapters frame "world literature" capaciously—juxtaposing global bestsellers (often dismissed as "airport literature") and visual culture with more conventionally literary texts from Africa, the Caribbean, Europe, India, and the United States—to consider how different kinds of texts foster and complicate the work of world-imagining and reading across geographic and experiential divides. This approach is contrapuntal, seeing one place always as imbricated with another. It involves *distant reading* of another sort than the computer-assisted quantitative approach spearheaded by Franco Moretti—but also *close reading* attentive to form, rhetoric, and mediation. While I draw on World Literature's interest in world-systems, transnational circulation, translatability, and the politics of literary prestige (or "consecration"), I also confront the limits of these approaches: They often imagine a world of circulation without friction, where unresolved histories of economic, ecological, and epistemological violence are elided, naturalized, or euphemized.

I understand literature and cultural imagining as a mesh of relations in which the liberatory and immiserating implications of globalizations—old and new—are knit and can be laid bare. The excavation of the politics of knowledge that is among postcolonial theory's most transformative achievements can reveal the lines of force that shape what counts as literature, nature, or crisis. (This line of analysis is among the signal contributions of postcolonial ecocriticism, discussed later.) Reading for the planet undertakes a mapping of difference and distance, even within a single site: People can inhabit the same space without living in the same world. As the feminist philosopher Kelly Oliver asks, "Can we learn to share the earth with those with whom we do not even share a world?" (2015, 206).

Several concerns and concepts recur throughout this book. One is the multinational corporation and its predecessor, the colonial charter company. Each chapter considers the corporation from some angle: as a vector of globalization; a legal person desirous of the rights of citizenship without the responsibilities; a distributor of wealth, risk, and responsibility; a beneficiary of state violence and a proto-state; a producer of knowledge and culture; or a major source of both world imaginings and planetary harm. What is the shape of the world that corporations imagine, and how do those imaginings shape the world we inhabit? This line of analysis extends work in critical corporate studies by scholars like Purnima Bose and Laura Lyons, who take the corporation as a cultural object to be read (2010). It recognizes the importance of the multinational corporation in disposing the postwar, postcolonial world: as Antony Anghie shows, the prospect of newly sovereign nation-states nationalizing (i.e., claiming the right to "dispose freely") their natural resources in the wake of mid-twentieth-century decolonization movements catalyzed a new realm of "transnational" law for arbitrating disputes between postcolonial states and nonstate actors like private companies. Instead of being subject only to national laws, the multinational corporation was elevated to a kind of sovereign status: able to make "'treaties' whose terms were sacrosanct," much as colonial charter companies like the East India Company or Royal Niger Company had done (Anghie 2015, 152). Another reckoning of the force of the multinational corporation as an actor in and on the world is the tabulation of the ninety corporations and municipal entities—not an undifferentiated "humanity" or even the Global North—responsible for the vast majority of greenhouse gas emissions over the past two centuries (Heede 2014). As literary studies confronts the Anthropocene and looks beyond the nation as an organizing framework, the multinational corporation must be an important object, rubric, and scale of analysis.

Another thread woven through this book is the idea that vulnerability to environmental harm is, to borrow postcolonial ecocritic Rob Nixon's phrase, "unevenly universal" (2011, 65): conditioned by biological parameters at a species level, yet inflected by social inequalities. I am concerned with imagining across social divides and breaking through what I call *quarantines of the imagination*. However, gestures toward universality or planetary community that do not grapple with this unevenness can effect a *gentrification* of the imagination, displacing communities and epistemologies in the name of breaking down barriers. Therefore, each chapter of this book considers scenes of *world-imagining from below*, where marginalized characters or documentary subjects situate their precarious local condition within a transnational context. The anthropologist James Ferguson is right to read such moments as urgent appeals for inclusion in modern world society (2006, 174).

For readers and viewers, these claims for inclusion can both elicit and
interrupt the readymade responses of uncritical paternalist sympathy or a
too-easy sense of solidarity or shared vulnerability. A final recurrent concern, therefore, are *formal strategies that invite reflexivity* from the audience,
including scenes of documentary subjects watching film or TV. These
scenes of looking and reading are another form of reading for the planet.
When texts use reflexive strategies to connect sites of representation with
sites of reception, they facilitate transfers of readers' awareness between
texts' thematic concerns with environmental crisis or complicity and the
range of rhetorical and sociological relationships implied by the consumption of text or image. These moments articulate the unevenness and the
universality of environmental vulnerability *at the level of literary form.*

Every Good Thing

> It's like every good thing in the world is dying and the people of the
> world, they see but do not care.
>
> —INDRA SINHA, *Animal's People*

> I only mind the absence of this admission, this contradiction: perhaps
> every good thing that stands before us comes at a great cost to
> someone else.
>
> —JAMAICA KINCAID, *My Garden (Book)*

My approach to these issues of universality, unevenness, and interpretation is crystallized in the juxtaposition of the preceding sentences. The first
reads as a lament of an ailing planet and an indifferent populace. Read aph-
oristically and through the lens of eco-apocalypse, Indra Sinha's sentence
expresses the impasse of the Anthropocene: inadequate action in the face
of mounting evidence of an increasingly inhospitable planet. The second
sentence traces an unacknowledged economy of gain and loss: the hidden
subsidies, paid by other people, that underwrite every pleasure, marvel,
achievement, necessity, sustenance. Jamaica Kincaid resituates at the scale
of individual experience Walter Benjamin's dictum: "There is no document of civilization that is not at the same time a document of barbarism"
(1969, 256).[7]

Both accounts of "every good thing" are gestures toward reading for
the planet; they imagine and make claims about the world entire. The in-
exact echoes between them reflect divergent accounts of relations among
humans, and between humans and nonhuman nature, that are indispensable to my approach in this book. Each is necessary, yet incomplete with-

out the other. By pitting "the people of the world" against "every good thing in the world," Sinha laments a shared human indifference to other life forms and the environmental enmeshment of human life itself. By contrast, Kincaid depicts a dual economy that differentiates among humans by distributing "good things" and "great costs" unevenly among them. Rather than the familiar notion of trade as giving something to get something, Kincaid's account of circulation sounds like theft. She places at the center of exchange the externalities—costs and effects, often negative—which conventional economics deems "external" or irrelevant to the marketplace. Kincaid traces how these costs are displaced elsewhere, to someone other than the recipient or beholder of "every good thing." I understand both forms of harm and disregard—environmental and economic—to be at work in the threat environmental injustice poses to "every good thing" and to those who pay their costs, even as I reckon with the contested modes of valuation through which things are designated as good (or "goods") to begin with.[8]

Reading between these sentences, one can recognize the concerns of each implicit in the other. The good things in the world that are dying could be social or cultural rather than natural or organic; the "someone else" who pays for them could be other-than-human. (Attentive to the legal and ethical distinctions between *human* and *person*, this book contemplates who or what can be regarded as a person—particularly the multinational corporation in Chapters I and 4 and nonhuman nature and literary personification in Chapters 2 and 3.) My guiding assumption is that such juxtapositions can yield unexpected insights—here about relations that Nixon has taught us to recognize as forms of violence (2011). Yet the resonances between environmental and economic harm that emerge from juxtaposing these accounts of "every good thing" entail costs of their own, involving a form of force—perhaps even violence—that wrests them from their contexts. What is an epigraph, if not a bon mot: a "good thing that stands before us" on the page, at the risk of being read without regard to, or against the grain of, its textual matrix—the discursive lifeworld where it first emerged?

Within these sentences from Sinha and Kincaid, those prefatory words "It's like" and "perhaps" invoke the metaphorical, the provisional, the possible. They are portals to the realm of the imaginary or counterfactual: the literary. In Sinha's *Animal's People*, "It's like every good thing in the world is dying" is an analogy the protagonist-narrator Animal offers to describe the feeling evoked by *marsiyas*, poetic laments chanted by worshippers during Muharram, which marks the unjust slaying of Imam Hussain, grandson of the Prophet Muhammad. What Animal appreciates about *marsiyas* is their expression of the mourners' defiance of the indifference to evil evinced by "people of the world" who "see but do not care." As discussed in Chapter 4, Animal is not a Muslim; a survivor of the 1984 Union Carbide disaster in Bhopal still awaiting justice decades later, he finds in *marsiyas* an approximation of what his predicament feels like. Animal's attentiveness to the form of *marsiyas* and the context and effects of their performance finds insights about planetary environmental injustice and its cultural expression in an unlikely place: in texts that aren't "about" the environment at all.

This scene of reading within Sinha's novel encapsulates several aspects of my approach to interpretation and the literary. First, this book builds upon and pushes beyond the first waves of scholarship in postcolonial ecocriticism. As with many emergent fields, one important task for postcolonial ecocritics has been assembling a repertoire (one need not call it a canon) of primary texts in which nature, the environment, and environmental crisis are salient concerns.[9] Reading for the planet is after something more: to attend to subtle aspects of environmental imagining that are occluded when one reads thematically—for the nature bits. This book attends to how literary form, rhetorical address, and (drawing on World Literature studies) the circulation of texts are implicated in the politics and disposition of nature, even in texts ostensibly not "about" environmental crisis—as with Animal's account of *marsiyas*. A text need not announce concerns with the environment in its theme and plot to illuminate relationships among nature, culture, and power. How can we understand the capitalist logic of externalities in relation to aesthetic representation and its fugitive politics: what remains "external" to representation, just outside the frame, or difficult to recognize within it? This mode of analysis depends upon a twofold, reflexive approach to reading and imagination: examining acts of interpretation, spectatorship, and world-imagining undertaken by characters and narrators that are staged diegetically as scenes of reading *within* texts (such as Animal's reading of *marsiyas*), as well as formal and sociological questions of genre, narration, intertextuality, and other aspects of literary mediation that shape how readers like you and me make sense of these texts, the worlds they imagine, and their relation to the worlds we inhabit and those we desire.

This approach to the literary is germane to Kincaid's *My Garden (Book)* (1999), whose title plays upon processes of germination, transplantation, hybridization, cultivation, culling, creative arrangement, and juxtaposition at work in both gardening and writing. A garden can be something like a commonplace book; a sentence reads and means differently when inscribed in someone else's book than for the person who first wrote it. Kincaid's hypothesis about the uneven distribution of good things and great costs concludes "The Glasshouse," a chapter about the eighteenth-century emergence of modern botany and a worldwide imperial network of botanical gardens—one part of a European-controlled global traffic in plants and people, knowledge and ideas, and money and power. Kincaid shows how commercial imperatives and Linnaean taxonomical classification intertwined in this process, which sorted lifeforms according to their appearance and deemed that "people who look like me" (1999, 157) were lesser humans who could be bought and sold. Kincaid describes being bowled over by "the most beautiful hollyhock I had ever seen" (149) at Kew Gardens, metropolitan anchor of the British empire's garden network. With a Benjaminian jolt, she recognizes that this gorgeous flower standing before her is *Gossypium*, the Linnaean genus name for cotton, the epitome of a good thing that comes at great cost to someone else.

In a startlingly compact series of rhetorical moves, Kincaid uses the history of imperial gardening to articulate an ambivalent stance regarding colonialism, slavery, and their largely unacknowledged presence in the present. Her statement about "every good thing" takes on its full weight in relation to what precedes it:

> I do not mind the glasshouse; I do not mind the botanical garden. This is not so grand a gesture on my part; it is mostly an admission of defeat: to mind it would be completely futile, I cannot do anything about it anyway. I only mind the absence of this admission, this contradiction: perhaps every good thing that stands before us comes at great cost to someone else. (1999, 152)

Kincaid distinguishes the history of empire as fait accompli from the reckoning of the economic, historiographical, and epistemological terms of that "defeat"—the afterlives of its costs and injustices—which has yet to happen. Kincaid's hypothesis about the distribution of good things and great costs aligns with familiar divisions between colonizer and colonized, free and enslaved. But with *Gossypium* standing before her, Kincaid implicates herself within this history of acquisitiveness; she contemplates how her own passion for gardening reflects the desire for possession driving that imperial traffic. It is difficult to decide whether such imperious desire for nature, internalized by those who historically paid its costs, is an additional, ironic aspect of "defeat," or in defiance of it. Kincaid's ambivalence and her staging of it epitomize the capacity of narrative intelligence to tease out the intersubjective and transhistorical complexities of how "people like me" come to love plants like cotton.[10]

With exquisite, excruciating precision, Kincaid sorts out what she does and does not "mind" about the history and legacy of imperial traffic. She situates her individual reckoning in a broader historical context and its attendant politics of acknowledgement and disregard. The "absence of this admission" regarding the contradictory economy of good things and great costs resonates with the disjuncture between seeing and (not) caring in *Animal's People*. This lack of acknowledgment remarked in both accounts of "every good thing" indexes another important concern in this book: the problematic assumptions that *seeing* is *knowing* and that *knowing* is a catalyst for *caring, acknowledging*, or *acting* to rectify suffering or injustice. So much humanities thinking is premised on "the relay of media → empathy → action," in Stephanie LeMenager's formulation (2013, 17), and I share her skepticism about whether narratives and images work in such straight lines.[11] I want to trouble the notion that environmental injustice is best understood as a problem of invisibility, which is premised upon the Enlightenment ideal of bringing things to light as a catalyst for change.

Among the things concealed by the visibility/invisibility dyad are the subtle interplay of invisibility and hypervisibility. Some things that seem invisible are actually hiding in plain sight (or even subject to surveillance); other things that seem spectacularly hypervisible remain for all practical (and political) purposes unregarded and unapprehended. (For Nixon, *apprehension* names the aim of making violence perceptible to the senses so as to be amenable to political action, intervention, and interruption [2011, 14–16].) This book attends to modes of spectatorship where knowledge doesn't necessarily translate into action. Social inequality can manifest as scopic asymmetry: differences of power in relation to seeing and being seen. Looking and seeing are never neutral or innocent. As Nixon asks, "Who gets to see, and from where? When and how does such empowered seeing become normative?" (15). And what does this normative vision obscure or erase? The well-meaning exposure *of* harm can cause additional exposure *to* harm—an unintended precipitate of the uncritical, sympathetic benevolence that often attends the act of looking upon suffering, even and especially through the representational prostheses of photography, film, and print. Nonetheless, a returned gaze can be an invitation to reflexivity and solidarity.

This approach has important implications for literary and cultural texts as technologies of world-imagining, and it entails "reading for the planet" in another sense: thinking in terms of *legibility* and *intelligibility* rather than visibility. The salient question is not whether environmental injustice can be seen, but under what conditions it can be *read*, understood, and apprehended. (Attentive to modes of interpretation beyond literacy's decoding of letters, I consider how illiterate humans—and nonhuman animals— "read" texts and the world.) This is not to say that visibility and visuality have no place in this book. Photographs and film, along with prose and poetry that confront the politics and costs of looking, are important objects of analysis, in order to tease out what visual culture, as well as literature as conventionally defined, can tell us about imagining, reading, and the work they do in the world.

The Content of the Form

The literary is always-already at work in making sense of the environment, even if unpredictably or unhelpfully so. Just as surely as a walk in the woods, nature becomes known to us in large part through narrative and other patterns of imagining. That is to say, particular literary genres, aesthetic modes, and narrative templates provide the forms through which human understandings of nonhuman nature and its dispositions are forged. Paradoxically, these cultural forms shape our sense of what is natural, or just: these human constructs naturalize nature and its relation to the social. Consider, for example, the casual use of the word *tragedy* to describe an event like the deadly release of poisonous gas at the Union Carbide pesticide factory in Bhopal, India, in 1984. The literary sense of tragedy, with its plot logic of accident intermingled with inevitability, hovers ambiguously over the discussion, further clouding the assessment and adjudication of responsibility that keeps Bhopal survivors waiting for justice.

Many of the words commonly used to describe the environment as problem—not only *tragedy*, but also *crisis* and *catastrophe*—are borrowed from the domain of the literary. As terms for dramatic genres (tragedy) or pivotal moments within the arc of a plot (crisis and catastrophe), they imply particular narrative templates and assume particular modes of causation and relationships between character and setting. These literary implications and assumptions are often of little help, however, in making sense of the environmental problem at hand: The plot logics they entail are not necessarily congruent with the forces (human and nonhuman) at work in the phenomena they are enlisted to describe. "Catastrophe" and "tragedy" are rarely invoked in their technical literary sense; instead, they colloquially name a situation that is *bad*, and extremely so, often for humans who had little role in causing the problem. One partial exception is the "tragedy of the commons," theorized by ecologist Garrett Hardin, who took his model of tragedy—as the "remorseless working of things" (1968, 1244)—not from Aristotle's anatomy of dramatic plots but from philosopher Alfred North Whitehead. Chapter 3 examines Hardin's faulty assumptions about protagonists, causes, and effects. Of the three terms, *crisis* has been most robustly taken up by other discourses and adapted as a technical term in its own right. Crisis is indispensable to the workings of capitalism and narrative alike; in medicine, *crisis* names a turning point in the course of a disease (Cazdyn 2007).

The broader point is that nature is mediated by the literary in a way that precedes and exceeds representation in any particular text. Rather than positing nature or environmental crisis as "out there" in the world, available to and in need of literary representation (and rescue), I understand cultural logics to be already at work in nature or crisis. This distinction is important for several reasons. It troubles the common sense that takes environmental crisis as "the problem" and literature or ecocriticism as "the solution," as in Richard Kerridge's definition of ecocriticism as an interpretive approach that "evaluates texts and ideas in terms of their coherence and usefulness as responses to environmental crisis" (Kerridge and Sammells 1998, 5). This desire for utility and responsiveness is compelling, as the ground for an ethic of environmental responsibility. Indeed, to the extent that I identify as an ecocritic, it is not merely intellectual curiosity but also civic concern that motivates my work: the hope that my readerly intelligence might *do something* in the world, as a "force of nature," in Ian Baucom's bold formulation of the postcolonial humanities (2012, 18). "How to offer *one's self*," as Nadine Gordimer wrote about the antiapartheid struggle (1989, 264). The problem, however, is that such commitment and urgency can misrecognize both nature and literature.

We want literature to be on the side of the angels—or on the side of nature.[12] But if literary imagining informs what we talk about when we talk about nature, it also shapes what we don't talk about, and the forms those silences take. There is probably more evidence that literary imagining has been *complicit* in environmental crisis than that it offers robust solutions; this is particularly true with regard to environmental injustice as the uneven distribution of benefits and burdens, the "good things" of nature as well as their "great costs." Drawing on Said's *Orientalism*, David Mazel observes that "what comes to count as the environment is that which matters to the culturally dominant" (1996, 142). Likewise, unequal power relations shape what "comes to count" as environmental crisis: "if we believe that environmental and social justice are intertwined, we need to adjust our understanding of what an environmental problem is," Deane Curtin writes (2005, 114). This emphasis on how unequal relations among humans intersect with nonhuman nature is fundamental to the environmental justice perspective. The urgent task, then, is not to look to literature as a "solution" but to understand its role in calculating what counts as "nature," "environment," "crisis," or even "human": the social dynamics and cultural logics that not only *cause* crises but also inflect how crises are experienced and recognized as such, by whom. This means recognizing the work that literature and cultural imagining do *all the time* in naturalizing ideas about nature and shaping constituencies of caring and regimes of visibility, as well as their exclusions and occlusions.

In other words, *what counts?* and *who cares?* are environmental questions for which literature provides tacit answers we don't even seek. Global warming, in Medovoi's counterintuitive insight, is occurring not "because capitalism has *ignored* the environment or because nobody *cares* about nature. On the contrary, the point is to stress just *how much* the environment has mattered to capitalism throughout its history, how central a role it has played, precisely because 'environmentality' is the mechanism through which the milieus of life are assessed and transformed, and rendered more productive" (2009, 136–37). An imperative for cultural analysis is probing how this transformation of nature in economic production intersects with the *aesthetic* assessment and transformation of nature in cultural production. These discordant senses of "caring" about nature and how nature "matters" work in tandem, even if they seem to point in opposite directions.

Indeed, capitalism works partly by loosening the relationship between "caring" in the realms of affect and the imaginary and "mattering" in the material sense. The founding myth of capitalist modernity—human liberation from nature—is underwritten by ever more intensive and geographically expansive modes of capturing nature in the form of "natural resources," to keep the engine of this freedom running. Chapter 3 posits nineteenth-century debates about the pathetic fallacy as a cultural "mechanism" for managing the aesthetic and economic rendering of nature at a moment of industrialization and imperial expansion of private property and resource extraction regimes. Both Romantic poetry and Whole Foods demonstrate that sentimental relationships to nature are compatible, even complicit, with ruthless extractivism; like everything else, empathy and "caring" about nature can be commodified. Another powerful example of literature's complicity in modernity's myth of human autonomy from nature is the observation by petro-critic Imre Szeman that literary fiction in the era of fossil fuels has abetted an ideological "fiction of surplus": the idea that seemingly unlimited access to cheap and easy energy is anything other than an unrepeatable historical accident (Yaeger et al. 2011, 324). By not reckoning with this historical anomaly of abundant energy—not deigning to care about how energy matters or counts as a historical condition of possibility—literature helps entrench the image of fossil-fueled modernity as freedom rather than constraint.

As I wrote this book, I came to understand that one could not grasp the work of imagining in the world without acknowledging its inverse, shadow self: the work of *unimagining*. I noticed that accounts of environmental injustice use the word "unimaginable" to describe suffering or harm so great as to evoke a sense of the sublime; confronting the unimaginable, thought ceases and words fail. But how does a situation *become* unimaginable, beyond the capacity to be imagined? What historical processes *create* situations described as unimaginable? What representational processes, through which images are framed and stories get told, shape and limit the capacity to imagine? What is at stake in describing a situation as "unimaginable" are these transitive acts of unmaking. *Unimagining*, then, names the processes through which something becomes unimaginable. In terms of what "counts" as nature or crisis, we might say that the remainder—that which doesn't count—is *unimagined* in this active, if tacit, sense.

The ethical stakes of unimagining involve the withdrawal of attention that occurs in the guise of paying attention to injustice, harm, and suffering. To label something *unimaginable* is to contain it: to draw a comforting line of distance and difference around it, to pull back from the work of engagement and understanding, of disentangling and finding oneself entangled, that might implicate a person in the network of relations and processes that produced the situation deemed *unimaginable*. This containment effects a quarantine of the imagination: an inability or refusal to imagine across geographic, temporal, or experiential divides. I take such imaginative failures not as an end to thinking, but as a point of departure. How do literature and the intelligence at work in literary imagining make environmental crisis legible, or reinforce habits of mind that render distant crises unimaginable? Unimagining tends to effect its exclusions and immiserations transitively—as an active mode of imagining, not merely as a lack for which *imagining*, or *more imagining*, is the remedy.

This perspective has important implications for the claims one can make about literature and reading for the planet as doing something in the world. The texts we read make their most powerful interventions not as empirical evidence of environmental crisis or as ready-made blueprints for action, but through their literary mediations and the forms of their imagining. The literary does not offer a transparent window on the world; it frames particular views through artifice and convention, not least the conventions that underwrite realism's sly illusion of offering access to reality without mediation. Form has and is content: To grapple with the literary is to recognize that what is said cannot be separated from how it is said. An attentiveness to such mediations (and an awareness of the contested status of "the literary" itself) is an intervention literary critics are uniquely suited to make—while learning from the work of scientists, historians, anthropologists, policymakers, and activists. A desire for critical intervention is best realized by embracing, not disavowing, a concern with literary convention.[13] This concern can be worldly and engaged rather than hygienically formalist: not "close reading" in the New Critics' sense, which invoked the poem's autonomy as a quarantine against Cold War–era politics, but instead a practice of paying careful attention, to measure distances and mark complicities among the world, the text, and the critic.[14]

Attending to literary mediation and formal convention becomes only more important when nature and the planet are behaving in unfamiliar ways. Consider the pressures on representation and interpretation posed not only by phenomena like climate change, but also by influential explanatory rubrics like new materialism's lively objects and hyperobjects, Rob Nixon's slow violence, or Ulrich Beck's risk society. What these analyses share is a potential to disrupt basic assumptions about the building blocks of narrative: plot, character, and setting. What happens to narrative when setting becomes character, plot becomes setting, objects become subjects, and part becomes whole? When agency (the capacity to be a protagonist) is distributed across human and nonhuman entities? When the relationship between cause and effect (the foundation of plot) is dilated across vast spans of space and time (the dimensions of setting)?

Writing in the wake of industrial and nuclear accidents at Seveso, Three Mile Island, Bhopal, and Chernobyl, German sociologist Ulrich Beck theorized forms of harm "no longer tied to their place of origin" that have the potential to "endanger *all* forms of life on this planet" (1992, 22). Particularly confounding for Beck was risk's invisibility: "Those who simply use things, take them as they appear, who only breathe and eat, without an inquiry into the background of the toxic reality, are not only naïve but they also misunderstand the hazards that threaten them, and thus expose themselves to such hazards with no protection" (73). This analysis of the permeation of risk throughout modern industrial society inverts conventional notions of agency. Imperceptible dangers lurk within seemingly inert and inanimate objects; conversely, human agency dissolves into a "general complicity" of institutions and systems in which "everyone is cause *and* effect, and thus *non*-cause . . . as if one were acting while being personally absent" (33). This account of agentive things and absent people is perhaps akin to Marx's tale of the upside-down world of the commodity fetish; modern spirits are also afoot in Beck's description of an emergent "shadow kingdom" of malignant imperceptible forces "comparable to the realm of the gods and demons in antiquity" (72). Risk therefore disrupts realism, which had displaced the machinations of gods, monsters, spirits, and kings in favor of ordinary human protagonists and plots that obey the laws of physics. In the shadow kingdom of risk, those who accept things in their ordinary appearance are naïve; only those capable of imagining the unseen can understand what may really be going on. This oscillation between the matter-of-fact and the occult feels new, but in a familiar way. It is another chapter in the story of modernity and modernism; as Fredric Jameson writes, "genuine realism . . . is a discovery process" that attends to "the hitherto unreported, unrepresented, and unseen," thereby (like modernism) "subvert[ing] inherited ideas and genres" (2012, 476). The broader point, as explored in Chapters 2 and 3, is that the conventions of literary realism and poetic propriety are contingent upon assumptions about what the "real" is and how it works. Such assumptions are being overwhelmed by new and newly recognized facts on the ground in a world that isn't quite what we thought, which demands, in turn, new narrative templates and modes of imagining.

At the heart of these challenges to narration, representation, and interpretation are dizzying questions of scale. Slow violence only registers as violence from a vantage that considers years, decades, centuries, or even millennia of accretion and persistence, at odds with the default perspective that measures cause and effect, harm and injury, in more direct and proximate terms (Nixon 2011). Writing in the wake of the postwar chemicalization of agriculture, Rachel Carson observed in *Silent Spring* (1962) that "it is not possible to add pesticides to water anywhere without threatening the purity of water everywhere" (42). This "toxic discourse," eco-critic Lawrence Buell observes, must be understood within a longer history of "totalizing images of a world without refuge" dating back to early nineteenth century fears about human-induced climate change (2001, 38–39). (Chapter 3 examines the global network of colonial scientists who observed these changes.) Part dissolves into whole; totalization is back with a vengeance, translated into a register of the everyday. Climate change is the kind of change that changes everything, Naomi Klein (2014) and others tell us. It "affects everything that rests on that substrate [of modern civilization]: agriculture, land use, transportation, energy, politics, behavior . . . everything. Climate change is not 'a story,' but a background condition for *all future stories*," observes journalist David Roberts (2013, ellipses in original). In other words, climate is fundamental to narrative—and to life. Were "fundamentalism" not an even more troubled word than "totality," one could argue for a climate fundamentalism that could reckon with its bedrock importance for this everything: for every good thing. Unlike the rigid adherence to inerrant and unchanging sacred texts or doctrine in religious or market fundamentalism, climate fundamentalism would grapple with the fragile mutability of its foundation. Indeed, the Anthropocene spells the very erasure of the fundament itself, at least in the geographical sense of *fundament* as "the face of the earth as it existed before the entrance of man into the scene."[15]

What Is the Shape of the World?

The prevailing world lexicon is incapable of naming and bearing all of our immense nows . . .

—YVONNE OWUOR, "READING OUR RUINS"

World, globe, planet, earth: This book is about big things. It's also about the tricky relay from part to whole, and the partiality, positionality, and provisionality of any version of totality. This is what I mean when I say that reading for the planet involves rescaling: mapping the elastic geographies that shape proximity and distance, reading from near to there. Totality got a bad name in the late twentieth century for its hubris: flying too close to the sun. Indeed, the fate of Icarus on wings of wax offers an apt metaphor for the hegemonic perspective from which the total globe is visualized: not upon the earth, but flying high above it. While the iconic photographs taken by US Apollo missions in the 1960s and '70s now epitomize this mode of world imagining, the Apollonian view emerged as hegemonic long before it became technologically possible to produce images from above the earth.[16] One underremarked aspect of the Apollo 17 *Blue Marble* image—the first photograph of the entire Earth—is that it features the African continent, rather than Europe or North America. Ethnocentrism—putting one's own culture, continent, or worldview at the center of the world—is among the things that gave totality a bad name. Another was the presumption that one aspect of human life and society (say, modes of economic production) was fundamental to all others. One risks mistaking the shape of the world by misunderstanding relationships between parts and wholes.

What interests me about projects of world-imagining is the shape of the worlds they imagine, which is bound up with the positions of power and interest from which they imagine. One paradox of planetarity is that claims to global community or world citizenship can sound radically different depending on the position from which they are articulated. Salutary though they may be, new imperatives of world-imagining may replicate and reinforce the inequalities and exclusions of earlier universalist projects that posited a unitary globe, from the Roman and British empires to Pax Americana. This is why Mufti asks *"at which locations in the world exactly such perceptions of the worldwide acquire their aura of transparency,"* and why he worries that "the ability to think 'the world' itself . . . is hardly distributed evenly across the world" (2016, 8, 10). To pinpoint just where the idea of the "worldwide" becomes self-evident involves a counterintuitive thinking between scales, to map the unevenness and partiality of world-imagining. Notice the contradictions in *partial*, which can mean either incomplete or interested and biased: A partial view in the former sense becomes partial in the latter sense by not recognizing itself as such. It is another quarantine of the imagination, an act of unimagining operating "upon the body, the imagination, and the self," but also in "the way academic disciplines constitute their objects of inquiry." "Without even necessarily knowing it," David Harvey observes, "acceptance of a conventional spatiotemporal frame then amounts to acceptance of existing patterns of social relations" (1996, 290, 266).

Such concerns spurred my interest in scenes of world-imagining from below. These imaginative gestures across geographic borders and experiential divides are staked upon an elastic geography, teasing out multiple answers to the question, how far is a place like Bhopal, or the Niger Delta? What do promises of development and modernization look like from different temporal, geographical, and experiential angles and scales? Belowness involves not only *class position*, in the familiar idiom of subalternity, but *spatial position*: perspective and altitude in a literal sense. Both subaltern and subatmospheric, scenes of world-imagining from below offer glimpses of a counterintuitive planetary subjectivity—grittier than the Apollonian view from high above the earth and the high-minded elite cosmopolitanism associated with that perspective. Privilege tends to be conflated with a capacity for farseeing and perspicacity, as opposed to the "limited horizons" attributed to those who experience and imagine the world from some local, rooted position below, thought to be unable to perceive the whole. The novels, films, and other texts examined in this book reveal some of the problems with that hegemonic view; not only is seeing not necessarily knowing, but it can entail its own forms of blindness in how "big people" see (or don't see) the world, as Bhopal survivor Sajiba Bano wrote in a 1996 letter to Union Carbide CEO Warren Anderson (Hanna, Morehouse, and Sarangi 2005, 115).

World-imagining from below can challenge the reflex suspicion that thinking the world entire necessarily erases difference and elides local agency. It refuses a quarantine to the local. Even if the capacity for world imagining is unevenly distributed, it would be a mistake to cede to capitalism the impulse toward totality or, as Mary Louise Pratt writes, to assume that ideas of the human or universal were "invented only once," in Enlightenment Europe: "Humanity can be totalized from anywhere" (and people do it all the time) (2008, 219). Joseph Slaughter makes a similar point when he upends not only conventional, paternalist notions about reading as training the moral imagination but also the liberal, Eurocentric cartographies of power those models of reading assume. He observes that the seminal act of generous imagining in narratives of suffering is undertaken not by the reader, but by the narrator, who "imagines a reader or listener who will respond to both the injustice of the appellant's suffering and his or her shared humanity" (2008, 105). Slaughter identifies in the rhetoric of humanitarian narratives the sort of gesture I have in mind with world-imagining from below. Rather than conventional notions of sympathy generated by the imaginative identification of reader with sufferer (a metaphoric substitution between otherwise unrelated entities), Slaughter articulates a metonymic relation of "contiguity between one part of humanity and another" from which narratives activate a "claim of belonging to a common community . . . [and] membership in the universal class of humanity from which their suffering has effectively excluded them" (93, 105). Instead of metaphoric sympathy premised on difference, this mode of narrative generates metonymic solidarity—a horizontal or lateral relation appropriate to world-imagining from below.

The uneven universality of vulnerability to environmental harm involves both metonymic contiguity and relative proximity to danger, a relation both spatial and temporal. To assume a map of the world with "strict longitudinal and latitudinal lines of suffering and safety" is to disregard time and history, Slaughter observes, quoting Red Cross founder Henry Dunant: "No man can say with certainty that he is forever safe from the possibility of war" (2008, 104). This perspective on vulnerability across time resonates with Beck's risk category of those "not-yet-affected":

"freedom from risk can turn overnight into irreversible affliction" (1999, 40).
For Slaughter, awareness of metonymic contiguity and historical contin-
gency can prompt claims for inclusion in a common human community.
In a different political vein, Beck recognizes shared (if unevenly distributed) risk as a ground for "a solidarity of all living things" (74) that may
nonetheless be unwanted—a "like-it-or-not interdependence," in Buell's
gloss (2001, 54).[17] These notions of unwilling solidarity barely conceal
a grimace at the leveling and prospective loss of privilege implicit in
metonymy.

How, then, to apprehend the join between unevenness and universality
in Nixon's "unevenly universal" vulnerability—the treacherous relay from
part to whole, or world to planet? Keeping these tensions in play, Kelly
Oliver articulates an "earthbound ethics" that "perhaps" might recognize
that "even if we do not share a world, we do share a planet" (2015, 206).
This ethics of cohabitation hinges upon a self-consciously literary shuttling
between parts and wholes: on the one hand, a sense of "singular ethical
responsibility to every living creature *as if* to the world itself—*as if* to the
very earth itself," so that the death of any being would be something like
"the end of not just *a* world, but of *the* world"; on the other hand, a recognition of the Earth's singularity, as "the only planet that sustains us and
every living being." As with Sinha's and Kincaid's accounts of "every good
thing," ethical force resides in the capacity to imagine and reimagine.
"Perhaps" and "as-if" join a shuttling dance with the hard fact of Earth as
the only home to us all. Oliver imagines replacing the will-to-mastery of
"political sovereignty" with "poetic sovereignty": a fluid, provisional, and
relational "power of interpretation" alive to the "poetry in the codes,
rituals, and tracks of each singular living being" (206). This model of interpretation is another way of describing reading for the planet.

It seems to me that projects of world-imagining run aground when they
forget this as-if and confuse *a* world for *the* world. This tendency has long
been the error of the instance of world-imagining that is world literature,
even in the recent endeavor to expand its world beyond Europe. "Efforts
to rethink the study of world literature will continue . . . as long as there
is a discrepancy between the lively expectations generated by the term
'world' and the pinched reality elicited by conventional approaches": Sarah
Lawall's observation from 1994 still rings true (45). What is the shape of
the world that World Literature imagines? This question is not new.[18] I
concur with recent critics who observe that World Literature's world looks
like a market, but I would add that this market-world is nothing like a
planet.

The influential trio of critics who relaunched World Literature for the twenty-first century—Pascale Casanova, David Damrosch, and Franco Moretti—imagine the world in terms of "circulatory movements that cut across national-territorial borders"; their analyses trace "the impact of these spatial movements on the production, reception, and interpretation of literary texts" (Cheah 2016, 3). Damrosch (2003) defines world literature as that which gains in translation; in economic terms, the circulation of texts is a value-adding activity. Casanova (2004) charts "world literary space" by tracing the movement of literary texts from "peripheral countries" toward the center, which she locates in Paris. Franco Moretti (2000, 2003, 2007) identifies in literary macrohistory an inverse movement of genres, from Europe out into the world. World Literature's world, Pheng Cheah observes, is conflated with "the globe made by economic globalization" (2016, 37).

Cheah's observation about economic globalization should be read in the historically expansive sense detailed earlier, not least because the "new" World Literature studies grounds itself in seminal nineteenth-century statements by Goethe and Marx and Engels about what the emergent world (market) means for the prospect of a world literature. Goethe envisioned the broader circulation of texts as enabling "universal spiritual commerce," a metaphor that inscribed the market into the logic and landscape of world literature. Marx and Engels address world literature in the *Communist Manifesto* (pause to think on that!), but Casanova, Damrosch, and Moretti tend toward a view of capitalism, markets, and world literature that is more Goethean than Marxian. Because Goethe has no real critique of capitalism, Cheah argues, World Literature offers little more than an uncritical, liberal reflection of global capitalism, vitiating its "worldly force . . . in relation to the world globalization creates" (2016, 43, 28). The bourgeois liberal idealization of the market as a site of free exchange—"the all-too-common assumption of a 'level playing field'" (WReC 2015, 22)—posits a world that's flat and frictionless, *innocent and equal*; anything distasteful or violent is dubbed an externality and dispatched and quarantined elsewhere. Marx and Engels, by contrast, not only understood world literature (in Mufti's phrase) as a "product of the Western European bourgeoisie's drive to create a world market"; they understood that drive to be transforming the colonized world, in Marx's phrase, into "a heap of ruins" (Mufti 2016, 87). World literature is another good thing that comes at great cost to someone else.

One might object that the cheerful account of the world-as-friendly-market underwrites only Damrosch's version of World Literature, since

Moretti takes a Darwinian view of how the "fittest" texts and genres survive and propagate themselves, and Casanova attends in her peculiar way
to "violence" and inequality in world literary space (2004, 43). Admittedly,
their world may not be quite flat and friendly; nonetheless, its center is un-
ambiguously in Europe and its traffic lines congruent with those of global
capitalism. Although the movements they trace run in opposite directions
(Moretti tracking centrifugal movements from Europe, Casanova centripetal ones toward Paris), these cartographies are center-centric. Even as
they seek a World Literature encompassing a world beyond the European
continent, their models reinscribe the familiar centers of European
empire.

The forms of agency propelling these movements are also troublesome.
Moretti invokes waves and trees as models for the "organic" dissemination of genres; he borrows the evolutionary trees Charles Darwin used to
diagram the origin and divergence of species. Natural selection becomes
an analogy for "cultural selection"; this literary Darwinism naturalizes the
market by construing it as a force of nature.[19] Moretti's evolutionary tree
assumes the one-way diffusion of forms from a common origin; the shadow
title of his argument could be "a tree grows in Europe." Consider an earlier
precedent for Moretti's trees: the family tree that early nineteenth-century
British comparative linguists used to map the relationships among Indo-
European languages. The family tree visualizes "linear directionality" de-
riving from a single source, as with Moretti's genres. Anthropologist
Bernard Cohn remarks that the Orientalists' "trees always seemed to be
northern European ones, like oaks and maples [that branch from a single
trunk], and the British never seemed to think of using the most typical
South Asian tree, the banyan, which grows up, out, and down at the same
time" (1996, 55). The shape of the world reflects the perspective from which
it is imagined.

The role of nature in Casanova's account of world literary space is no less
problematic. Literature is a "resource" with which regions are "endowed"
to a greater or lesser extent; these natural resources flow from "peripheral"
countries toward the center (2004). In effect, her model of literary production and consecration is premised upon an extractivist logic that overlaps
remarkably with the international division of nature charted by Coronil
and Fanon before him. (As I will elaborate, it is a world-systems analysis of
World Literature.) Yet the force of her recognition of the "struggle" and
"violence" in this process is blunted by her insistence on the "autonomy"
of world literary space from geopolitics and the nonidentity between
the "independent laws of literature" and political economy (or political

ecology) (86).[20] Consequently, her "international literary law" (12) cannot account for the more troubling reasons why (in Matthew Arnold's phrase) "the best that has been thought and said" by Nigerian writers flows toward European and American literary capitals, like so much sweet and light crude.

Connecting the causal dots between this literary traffic and European empire, Mufti analyzes what we might call (continuing the conjunct Arnoldian/oil metaphor) a process of refinement, where Orientalists transformed "vastly dispersed and heterogeneous writing practices and traditions" from around the world into something called "literature." Mufti names this process "assimilation," which is *"ongoing . . . repeated constantly in the very forms of circulation that constitute world literature"* (2016, 57). He does not note the parallel with Marxian notions of the "primitive" accumulation of capital as an ongoing process, but the point is implicit in his analysis of Orientalism as the condition of possibility for world literature, and European colonialism as the condition of possibility for Orientalism (80). Mufti's account of world literature is therefore more satisfyingly capacious than WReC's demarcation of "world-literature" as literature that "registers" the contradictions of the "modern capitalist world-system": a subset of literary texts from the past two centuries whose "substrate" is capitalism and whose "subject and form" is modernity (2015, 15). These texts (and WReC's readings) are important and instructive, but Mufti makes legible how tales spun across vast spans of time and space—including, say, those about Śakuntalā, Šahrāzād, and Sundiata (or Son-Jara), as well as those by Shakespeare and Spenser—come to register as "literature" in the first place. Mufti closes the circle on this textual traffic by observing that traditions repackaged as "literature" by Orientalists were often exported back to their original sites of production as the foundation for emergent "national" traditions (2016, 102). This counterintuitive insight about the disposition of literature is important for several reasons, among them the implicit parallel with the evangelizing/entrepreneurial projects of twenty-first-century "impresarios" (Apter 2013, 3) who trade upon the cultural capital of elite American universities while spreading the good news of World Literature to rest of the world. More broadly, this long view underscores that nation and world/globe are not in a stadial relation, in which national concerns and literatures give way to globalization and world literature; these scales emerge in dynamic, mutually constitutive relationship to one another.

At stake in these models of world literature is that tricky relay between *a* world and *the* world. The terminology of centers and peripheries

borrows (with varying degrees of explicitness) from sociologist Immanuel Wallerstein's world-systems analysis. For Wallerstein, "world-systems"
are historical networks of socioeconomic relation among geographically
dispersed sites that forge "worlds" beyond a single state. Among these is
the modern capitalist world-system, whose unceasing expansionist drive
allows us to forget that a world-system is not (necessarily) a system of the
world: "we are not talking about the (whole) world, but about systems, economies, empires *that are* a world (but quite possibly, and indeed usually, not
encompassing the entire globe)" (Wallerstein 2004, 15–16). The "maxi-
mally encompassing project" (WReC 2015, 5) of World Literature forges
a world-system that mistakes itself for the world.

For me, the urgent question remains how to calibrate the world-system
of World Literature with the Earth system remade in the Anthropocene—
as well as other vectors of environmental injustice. In his demur to the hegemonic World Literature project, Cheah insists that "the globe is not a
world," by which he means a Heideggerian *Welt* of becoming and belonging; the uncritical liberalism of World Literature as world market construes
literature as a commodity like any other, rather than a mode of worlding
that might (following Goethe and Auerbach) spur the emergence of a "universal humanity" (2016, 42). My concern is that the globe is not a planet.
World Literature's "trees" and "natural resources" are metaphors drawn
from nature without regard for the living substrate and political ecology
of its world, whatever kind of world that might be. Although one could ask
why environmentalism's earth should accord with World Literature's world,
they do share one important commonality. Maps of both—at least as drawn
in the United States and Europe—tend to replicate the Eurocentric dis-
tortions of a Mercator projection. In hegemonic strands of Anthropocene
discourse, the undifferentiated human species posited as a force in geological history occupies the position of "universal humanity" in Cheah's
normative tradition. WReC's historical delimitation of "world-literature"
as that which registers the modern capitalist world-system overlaps with
one proposed periodization of the Anthropocene that dates its onset to
James Watt's 1784 refinement of the steam engine. Both phenomena involve an intensification of fossil energy inputs necessary for economic
production. Some critics argue that the Anthropocene is better understood as the "Capitalocene," whose protagonist is not an undifferentiated
"human" but the stratifications engendered by capital.

The chief promulgator of the Capitalocene idea, environmental historian Jason W. Moore, returns to key figures in the Marxian tradition to
theorize "world-ecology." Following Wallerstein, Moore's world-ecology

is not the ecology of the whole world—not a single planetary ecosystem—but the mutual interpenetration of global capitalism with discrete sites and the increasingly world-historical aspect of so many socioecological situations. Critics including Graeme Macdonald, Sharae Deckard, and Michael Niblett (the first two are members of WReC) have examined the import of Moore's world-ecology for World Literature. Although not as single-mindedly as some of them, I find "world-ecology" helpful for understanding the uneven, unpredictable ways that transnational forces shape local places and for thinking between, say, the Niger Delta and Detroit, North Dakota, or the Mississippi Delta: sites profoundly but disparately shaped by (and indispensable to) oil extraction and hydrocarbon-fueled global capitalism. This is the multiscalar work of reading for the planet, imagining from near to there.

The nagging question I have had to answer for myself in writing this book, given these pitfalls, is: Why write about world literature at all? "The idea of world literature seems to exercise a strange gravitational force on all students of literature, even on those whose primary impulse is to avoid or bypass it entirely, forcing on them involuntary and unwanted changes of course and direction," Mufti writes in his preface, without specifying whether this observation is also a confession (2016, x). One answer is that I became a student of literature *because* of world literature. The most transformative experiences in my undergraduate literary education at Austin College align with the two poles that long characterized world literature pedagogy: appreciating a shared humanity and acquiring knowledge about a particular tradition. The grief of Gilgamesh became my grief, while I took apprentice-expert pleasure in reading Chinese poetry (in translation) in terms of its own poetics. In my first tenure-track position, at Stonehill College, I loved teaching "Introduction to World Literature" for the liberating challenge of not possibly being an expert on everything, and for the strange solace of teaching Paul Celan in the weeks after 9/11.

When the new World Literature project gathered steam in scholarly conversation, however, and when "World Literature in English" and "Global Anglophone" emerged in English departments as hiring and curricular categories to designate literatures other than British or American, my graduate school training as a scholar of Third World literatures and postcolonial theory made me suspicious about this disciplinary landgrab. (In US universities, the World Literature project is something of a hot potato between comparative literature and English.) After the radical epistemological challenge of postcolonial studies in the 1980s and its institutional consolidation in the 1990s, the rise of World Literature augured how quickly the hegemonic shape of the world could snap right back into place. It is unsurprising that most of the recent skeptical critics of World Literature— WReC, Cheah, Mufti—trained as postcolonialists or built the field, even if through the robust practice of postcolonial autocritique.

Rather than ignore the conversation on World Literature, I engage with it in order to challenge the quarantines of the imagination that deform its ambitious attempt to rechart the grounds of literary comparison. This task is all the more urgent now, in seeking ways to construe the worldwide, the global, and the planetary with an eye toward environmental justice. I am inspired by the similar conclusions reached by Mary Louise Pratt (2008) and Fernando Coronil (2001) in essays that are touchstones in my think- ing. Having been fierce critics of neoliberal globalization, they each point to globalization's utopian strains and emancipatory promises as a project for the future, to be realized by those who would imagine the world other- wise. Reading for the planet is reading in four dimensions, across both space and time. At a moment of authoritarianism ascending, inequality ex- ploding, and oceans rising, what does the future look like? The next sec- tion scrutinizes the temporal politics and generic constraints at work in the shapes of the futures we imagine—as a case study for what reading for the planet can do. Because most of the texts examined in this book aren't "about" the Anthropocene per se, here I contemplate some of the pitfalls of its planetary consciousness.

Evicted from the Future: On Ending Otherwise

Overcoming the concept of "progress" and overcoming the concept of "period of decline" are two sides of one and the same thing.
                                    —WALTER BENJAMIN, *The Arcades Project*

I begin by discussing fictions of the end . . . so we begin with apocalypse . . . .
                                    —FRANK KERMODE, *The Sense of an Ending*

The end of the world as we know it offers an obvious point of departure for thinking about environmental crisis on a planetary scale. Global warm- ing and the attendant transformations of the Anthropocene estrange time by destabilizing the straightforward, secular assumption that pasts and pre- sents *have* futures; that things just keep on going; that time and history keep unfolding, for better or worse. As I argue elsewhere with regard to anticolonial movements, one way that history comes to be imbued with meaning is by understanding it as the working out of "past's futures": the temporal unfolding of dynamic projects of anticipation, which may be re-fashioned or renounced when the future turns out to be other than what was imagined in the past (Wenzel 2009). This mode of expectation is con-founded by the past's future inscribed in carbon, the not yet fully realized effects upon the Earth system of burning fuels that fossilized over mil-lions of years. These effects are expected to endure thousands of years into the future, as the harm the body of the planet remembers. This inexorable past's future of climate change seems to jeopardize, at the scale of human experience, the inexorability of futurity itself. This reconfiguration of past and future posits modernity's progress narratives as confounded once and for all by a future utterly different from that which fossil fuels once promised.

The narrative genre and critical register commonly enlisted to make sense of this unthinkable predicament is eco-apocalypse. Like utopia, eco-apocalypse is premised upon imagining alternative worlds radically dif-ferent from our own: it aims to imagine the unimaginable. Writing amidst Cold War nuclear anxiety, the escalation of the Vietnam War, and racial strife in the United States, the narrative theorist Frank Kermode observed that every era believes its relationship to futurity to be unique—an obser-vation that begs to be juxtaposed with Edward Said's remark that "every single empire in its official discourse has said that it is not like all the others" (Kermode 1967, 94–96; Said 2003, xxi). One remarkable aspect of the pre-sent moment is the imaginative *inertia* of its utopias—or at least those vi-sions of a better world imagined from within what Niger Delta poet Ogaga Ifowodo calls the petroleum-fueled "chain of ease" (2005, 5). Such half-hearted utopianism dreams of nothing so much as a familiar future: life continuing basically as it is now, with all the costs (still) externalized, dis-placed outside the frame of the narrative, the predicaments of the present transformed only in so far as we won't have had to change very much after all. We don't like thinking about climate change, British novelist John Lanchester wrote in 2007, "because we're worried that if we start we will have no choice but to think about nothing else"; this *not thinking* is con-nected to the weak, passive utopianism of living as if somehow everything will be fine.

This cognitive inertia is the shadow or leeward side of "ecocatastrophe"—a recurrent motif that Medovoi traces throughout the history of capitalism, from Malthus to the neoliberal present—which "serves as a mechanism for insisting upon biopolitical reform, calculated change to the environment (and/or to the population) before it is too late," and thereby "facilitates some kind of regulatory transition between accumulation regimes" (2009, 136).

As a mode of riding out the periodic waves of crisis and contradiction upon which capitalism thrives, passive utopianism doesn't so much deny the need for reform as imagine that such transitions can be effected without really changing anything (Bellamy and Szeman 2014). Within this banal unthinkingness lurks a horror nonetheless: a "desire for capitalism itself when faced with what this damage portends"—the ominous recognition that we might actually choose the death of nature over the death of capitalism (Medovoi 2010, 143). Such not-thinking is the ultimate externalization.

Either not-thinking, or "think[ing] of nothing else." The latter response aptly describes eco-apocalypse, a narrative form with pitfalls of its own. In a more spectacular way, eco-apocalypse can also shut down the hard work of imagining futurity meaningfully and making the future *apprehensible*, in Nixon's sense. By seizing the imagination, eco-apocalypse can be another mode of unimagining the future, rendering it *still* unimaginable. Both environmentalists and their opponents have worried about the limits of using apocalyptic fears to mobilize change (Enzensberger 1974). Images of our own destruction can generate denial or a literary pleasure of catharsis, neither of which does much to loosen attachments to the status quo. As Frederick Buell remarks, "apocalypse . . . almost seems too easy; with a big bang . . . it and we are over and done with" (2003, 70). I have a different concern about the political liabilities of eco-apocalypse: As the narrative expression of a crisis of futurity, eco-apocalypse can misrecognize the present.

The imaginative lure of eco-apocalypse can obscure attention to the mundane loss of futurity theorized by James Ferguson, who observes that mid-twentieth-century promises of modernization in Africa have been abandoned, and narratives of development disavowed. The industrialized, affluent West was once construed as a possible future for the rest of the world, but now, he argues, the progress narrative of "history" reverts to the stasis of "hierarchy," "behind" returns to "beneath" (2006, 177–93). Inequality endures into an indefinite future of longing for infrastructure. This "crisis of futurity," Pratt writes in a similar vein, looms "all over the planet," among people who "live conscious of their redundancy to a global economic order which is able to make them aware of its existence and their superfluity . . . expelled from [its] narratives of futurity" (2008, 210–11). What does it mean to be evicted from the future in this way: to confront not the "end" of the world, but having been shut out of the temporal horizon of its desires and ends? In Sinha's and Kincaid's terms, it is not that "every good thing in the world is dying," but that the costs of those things, paid by others, have robbed them of a future. A Niger Delta activist interviewed in Sandy Cioffi's documentary *Sweet Crude* (2010) describes the predicament of underdevelopment in terms of its contrast with the good life—that is, American life as depicted on TV. This scene, which I examine Chapter 2, underlines a contradiction of contemporary globalization: The global culture industry circulates images of affluence more effectively than global capitalism distributes wealth. (Or, as Crystal Bartolovich observes, "the relative balance in today's technological advancements make it far easier for images of hunger to be displayed . . . in the North than for starvation in the South to be obliterated" [2010, 56].) What is distinctive about the unevenness of world-imagining in the era of satellite TV, social media, and the Internet is that the excluded tend to have vivid images of what they are excluded from.

How to calibrate these crises of futurity—the future lost to climate change as the belated cost of modernity's chain of ease, as opposed to never having enjoyed the benefits of modernity to begin with? Recall the relation between "accumulating-capital and accumulating-carbon" (Anderson 2012, 6). To understand vulnerability to environmental harm as unevenly universal is to recognize its inflection by histories of unequal relation to both capital and carbon accumulation, in which economic and ecological modes of harm intersect. To focus on the universality of vulnerability at the expense of the unevenness—to move too quickly to ideas of the human as species, or community as planetary—is not so much a quarantine as a gentrification of the imagination, a gesture toward new forms of community that is blind to the displacements it causes. Narratives of eco-apocalypse can effect a gentrification of the imagination, if time and futurity become an axis of difference that displaces or disguises the socioeconomic axis of inequality in the present. The weak utopianism of a future all but unchanged is also a desire for privilege intact. In literary terms, the predominant narrative forms for imagining futurity are inadequate for apprehending the challenges of the present. The shapes of the future imagined in eco-apocalypse can serve as an alibi for persistent histories of inequality, thereby leaving other futures—what the theorist of utopia Ernst Bloch called "real" futures (1986, 1:75)—still unimagined.

As an example of the multiple crises of futurity and histories of accumulation at work in environmental imagining, consider "Postcards from the Future," a photographic collaboration by visual artists Robert Graves and Didier Madoc-Jones. This series of images, exhibited at the Museum of London and the National Theatre in 2010 and 2011, features iconic London views typically featured on postcards but reimagines them as proleptic Kodak moments from a future where the most spectacular effects of climate change no longer exist solely in the imagination.[21] An aerial view of a watery cityscape visualizes London as Venice. Camels replace horses at the Horse Guards Parade. Rice paddies and water buffaloes appear in front of Parliament Square. Monkeys surveil the city from St. Paul's Cathedral, and laundry hangs from the Gherkin, the financial services skyscraper repurposed as an apartment block for climate migrants who flood the city. Wind turbines and water lilies sprout from an inundated Piccadilly Circus.

These arresting images are not merely memories, but *mementoes* of the future. "Postcards from the Future" recasts the generic conventions of the postcard, which effects a twofold transmission of memory: "wish you were here" consolidates one's memories in the act of sharing them with other people, while reassuring the faraway recipient, "I haven't forgotten you." As a mass-produced cultural form that conveys personal messages through the medium of an open letter, postcards are more effective at the second task of memory than the first; they aren't a great technology for transmitting other people's vacation memories, but they do let us know we haven't been forgotten.

Graves and Madoc-Jones (2010) explain that they seek to "create illusory spaces in which people can explore the issues of a changed world and not reject them as 'stuff that happens to other people.'" But postcards are, by definition, documents of stuff that happens to other people! The power of "Postcards from the Future" must lie in that second task of memory, reminding people that they haven't been forgotten. If we take the project's title literally, "Postcards *from* the Future"—with the Future as sender rather than temporal location—then these postcards are the Future's way of saying to the viewer, "I haven't forgotten you." The implicit, reciprocal question—have you forgotten me? —is explicit in the project's tagline, which transforms the conventional postcard sentiment, "wish you were here," into a question: "wish you were *here*?" And if not, what are you going to do to make sure that you don't arrive here, or that "here" never arrives, that London never becomes what you see here? This recasting of the postcard genre intersects with the rhetorical premise of apocalyptic narratives, whose vivid depictions of grim trajectories aim to inspire change and effect a plot twist, in which their anticipated futures never will have arrived.

What is most disturbing about the eco-apocalyptic aspect of "Postcards from the Future" is its conflation of time and space as axes of difference. In addition to "wish you were *here*?" some of these images also seem to ask, "don't you wish *they* weren't here?"—where "they" are hordes of climate refugees. In an aerial view of Buckingham Palace hemmed in by thousands of shanties, or a street-level view of Trafalgar Square as crowded bazaar, the density of improvised habitation suggests an Orientalized "Third World" (in the unfortunate, vulgar sense of overpopulation, corruption, and state failure) scaling the white cliffs of Dover that tower a bit less over rising, uncalm seas. These images from 2010–11 are eerily prescient of subsequent climate and migration pressures, yet they are also stubborn vestiges of imperialist temporal imaginaries. The xenophobia unleashed by recent desperate waves of migration to Europe only underscores the racial anxiety at work in "Postcards from the Future," in which the environment is both narrative protagonist and geopolitical threat.

Similar anxieties suffuse "The Coming Anarchy," Robert Kaplan's warning about threats that environmental degradation and resource wars in West Africa and beyond could pose to US national security. The recurrent motif in Kaplan's 1994 *Atlantic Monthly* essay, widely cited during the Clinton years, is a stretch limo gliding through the potholed streets of New York, whose passengers are the United States and Europe. Outside the stretch limo is the "rest of mankind . . . a rundown, crowded planet of skinhead Cossacks and juju warriors, . . . battling over scraps of overused earth in guerrilla conflicts that ripple across continents" (8). (These fevered images, Somali novelist Nuruddin Farah [1996] astutely observes, resemble nothing so much as a mefloquine dream.) Kaplan's coming eco-anarchy is supposed to frighten because, far from progress narratives' certitudes about the developed world offering "to the less developed, the image of its own future," as Marx wrote (1967, 9), Kaplan imagines a dark future anterior, *a future inferior*, in which "Third World problems" (and people) will have arrived in the First World, pounding on the tinted windows of the stretch limo. (Imagine a menacing mob of squeegee men and women, or worse.) Kaplan inverts assumptions about the shape of the future that underwrote developmentalist impulses during and after the era of high imperialism. Despite his travel "by foot, bus, and bush taxi in more than sixty countries" (1994, 13), Kaplan's remains a quarantined imagination: He drums up fears of "Third World" scarcity, disease, and overpopulation as the anarchy coming to America, with hardly a glance at their relationship to the history of European imperialism or the pressures of First World overconsumption.[22] For Kaplan, colonialism was little more than a mapmaking enterprise. Forget empire, indeed.

In this context, "Postcards from the Future" read as souvenirs of their own obsolescence, when leisure tourism is overshadowed by forced and uncontrolled migration. What is strange about the artists' stated desire to move past thinking about climate change as "stuff that happens to other people" is that their postcards depict a future where Londoners will live like, and London will look like, people and places in the Global South. Domesticating climate change, the artists Orientalize London—in a way different from, yet related to, colonial-inspired fashions like paisley or peacock feathers, or earlier waves of migration spurred by European imperialism and its afterlives. When time and space as axes of difference merge like this, latitude, not longitude, determines Greenwich Mean Time. The world-imagining in these images plays upon a reverse colonial fear: that the Third World present offers an image of the First World's future.

This dynamic is at work in the production of these images. Photographs from Kenya and Morocco were superimposed over a photo of Trafalgar Square; photographs of ninety shanty homes in Kenya were digitally multiplied to 20 million dwellings and superimposed over an aerial view of Buckingham Palace. This digital superimposition of images of the Third World visualizes the future imposition of climate refugees. These images address global warming's derangement of time through a politically freighted scrambling of space. Depicting London as displaced from its proper latitude, home to populations displaced from elsewhere, it looks like the empire blights back. But as with Kaplan's stretch limo, these images do not necessarily convey the unevenness in the history, present, and projected future of climate injustice, where the effects of emissions by the industrial North will be felt disproportionately by those in in the Global South. To revise the slogan of postcolonial migrants to Britain—"We are here because you were there"—the slogan of climate migrants could be "we are here because your emissions are everywhere." *Like so much else, the future will be unevenly distributed.*

The fears these apocalyptic narratives trade upon aren't just about nature-becoming-unfriendly. They project into the future histories of inequality that remain unacknowledged and unresolved. They offer a fraught version of reading for the planet, described above as reading from near to there, tracing lines of risk and responsibility that link and divide specific sites. But these images depict here *as* there. Their defamiliarizing surprise might elicit aversion and disavowal, solidarity, or something else entirely. Perhaps they reveal that an apocalyptic future is already here, but unevenly distributed, being lived by other people. They also risk naturalizing the privilege of not having to live apocalyptically, yet. In other words, no single politics attaches to the insight that others inhabit a degraded future that has already arrived, that one person's apocalyptic future is another's precarious present. (Every good thing in this world that is dying has come at a great cost to someone else.) One could read that difference historically and confront the injustice of the present, but one could also see it as natural, civilizational, menacing, and in need of quarantine—a coming anarchy.

This apocalyptic inversion of progress narratives, which posits the Third World as the frightening future of the First, turns upside down the old imperial habit of Europeans denying the coevalness of the colonized, refusing to recognize that everyone inhabits the same moment in time. In the colonial era, European perceptions of people as "backward," "behind" or "beneath" were invoked to justify conquest and civilizing projects. Europe's others were once seen as inhabiting a lesser past; here they are seen as inhabiting its projected future inferior. Temporality again functions as a mode of othering, but the order is reversed.

This new denial of coevalness conjoins the two crises of futurity enumerated earlier: The consequences of carbon accumulation in the future are imagined to look a lot like being on the wrong end of capital accumulation in the present, with little acknowledgment of the shared but uneven history that joins them. This temporal imaginary, newly emergent yet drawing upon longstanding Eurocentric habits of mind, illustrates the necessity of a long view of capitalism's expansion *through the production of inequality and unevenness on a global scale*—a perspective largely elided from World Literature discourse in the Damrosch-Moretti-Casanova vein. It also demonstrates the pertinence of postcolonial critique in the shadow of the Anthropocene. Beginning with "The Climate of History" (2009), Dipesh Chakrabarty's provocations on the Anthropocene broke new discursive ground while effecting foreclosures of their own. The political/postcolonial perspective of his previous historiographical work has given way to a planetary/parametric concern with the boundary conditions within which (human) life is possible—a shift that risks euphemizing the differentiated, yet conjoined histories of carbon and capital. As Anthropocene species-talk gains ground in public conversation, this approach is analogous to seeking explanations for postcolonial misery anywhere but in the history of imperialism and underdevelopment. Climate change becomes one more opportunity to forget colonialism and empire.

One additional example illustrates the brittleness of extant modes of world-imagining in the future tense. "Poison," a short story by Henrietta Rose-Innes, won the Caine Prize for African Writing in 2008; it appeared in *African Pens: New Writing from Southern Africa* (2007), a collection featuring the winners of a competition judged by J. M. Coetzee. "Poison" stands apart from the other stories in *African Pens*, many of them documentary/realist accounts of HIV/AIDS or crime as challenges confronting

South African society in the new century. In a more speculative vein, "Poison" is an eco-apocalypse set in an imagined present, a few days after a massive chemical explosion causes a mass exodus from Cape Town. Its protagonist, Lynn, is a young white woman belatedly fleeing the city who runs out of gas just short of a highway travel stop. The tensions in the story—between the apocalyptic and the ordinary, and between the global and the South African–inflected—are pertinent to the challenge of imagining futurity without reinscribing troubled histories, and to the concerns of World Literature with texts circulating beyond their sites of writing and representation. "Poison" can be read as a generic running-out-of-gas story,[23] its roadside travel stop full of junk food familiar to any driver or passenger who inhabits the consumer end of corporate globalization, encircled within petromodernity's chain of ease. The dead birds and mysterious oily rain falling from the sky are stock images of eco-apocalypse, as are the infrastructural failures following the explosion: The gas station runs out of gas, the electric grid and cell network fizzle out, the toilet stops flushing. The story offers hints of a Robinsonade, when the shipwrecked protagonist at the deserted petrol-pump island takes an inventory of food, potable liquid, and potential tools.

In this generic, could-happen-anywhere-within-a-certain-class-stratum reading of the story, what is striking is the inertia with which Lynn confronts eco-apocalypse. She waits too long to leave the city; she passes up a seat in a gassed-up vehicle because she's certain "rescue services" will arrive, and, besides, where is there to go? (2007, 4). She kicks off her high heels and untucks her tailored shirt, fighting the impulse to curl up and sleep, "nothing . . . required of her except to wait" (4). The only imaginative resources she has to confront the menacing contaminated future, now looming in her car's rearview mirror like the storm of progress that blasts Walter Benjamin's angel of history, are those of an individualized bourgeois discipline and her failings in that regard: "It was typical; she struggled to get things together. . . . She should have kept things cleaner, looked after things better. . . . When this was all over, she was definitely going on a proper detox. Give up all junk food, alcohol. Some time soon" (2, 9, 10). So she resolves at the story's end, opening another bag of chips after three days with no help in sight. Even the comically inadequate gesture of a "proper detox" as a response to a poisoned city is voiced in the indefinite, never-to-arrive future of resolutions not meant to be kept: contained—safely, yet precariously—within the horizon and habits of ordinary time.

This dual sense of the ordinary—as both comforting and discomfiting in its inadequacy—is crucial to the story. The absurdity of wearing high heels to a mass evacuation verges on parody, but the story aims beyond caricature toward a broader crisis of futurity, where people cling to a life they know is unsustainable because there seem to be no alternatives on offer—along the lines of Lauren Berlant's "cruel optimism" (2011).[24] Lynn's body plays a contradictory role in the plot: The disaster's extremity registers physiologically rather than cognitively. At pivotal moments, bouts of nausea and diarrhea conspire with indecisiveness ("delivered her from decision" [5]) and get in the way of her ability to act. This is inertia in both the colloquial sense of immobility and the Newtonian sense of resistance to change in an object's state, even a state of motion: the difficulty of changing the environmental order of things and slowing the momentum of harm.

Lynn could be a surrogate for the rapt but ultimately unmoved reader of apocalyptic narratives, where the future is so unthinkable that the thought grooves of the status quo are impossible to escape. Lynn confronts disaster by not thinking about it, lest she think of nothing else, as Lanchester (2007) fears. "Poison" offers a richly imagined, gently satirical account of a particular quarantine of the imagination: the "gap between knowing and doing, evidence and action" that shapes the impasses of the present (Szeman 2012, 435). This predicament demonstrates the need to shift the terms of engagement from seeing and caring to reading and apprehending. Rose-Innes shows what the inability to act in the face of disaster looks and feels like—even while living and breathing through it, the pores of one's skin seeping its oily black residue, which, Lynn observes, "show[s] up worse" on white people (2).

Indeed, this place being South Africa, other narratives are at work, among them the racialized polarities of automobility, where white people tend to drive passenger cars and black people tend to walk or take minibus taxis. The geographic and historical specificity of this running-out-gas narrative comes into focus when Lynn's "unnerving" sensations of standing on a "road surface not meant to be touched with hands or feet, to be examined too closely or in stillness" give way to "thoughts of the people she'd seen so many times on the side of the highway, walking along verges not designed for human passage, covering incomprehensible distances" (5–6). In a racially charged moment, she declines a seat on a minibus taxi—"it's not that," she insists, refusing to voice the unspoken assumption that middle-class white women don't ride in such vaguely dangerous vehicles, the transport network of the poor and carless (4).

Juxtaposing Kaplan's creepy stretch limo with this minibus taxi, I understand Rose-Innes to be cognizant of histories of social division that inform the experience and imagination of eco-apocalypse, in a way that "The Coming Anarchy" and "Postcards from the Future" are not. The "throat-slitting gesture" (2007, 1) of the gas station attendant signals that the station has run out of gas, but it also evokes white fears of racial apocalypse: white South Africans running out of time. In the explosion's aftermath, clinging to the broken chain of ease, Lynn is uncertainly poised between longing for infrastructure and her previous privileged position of taking infrastructure for granted. Except for Lynn, everyone manages to leave the station in one vehicular arrangement or another; no one else waits for rescue by the state, perhaps because so many South Africans have gotten by *in spite of* the state.

"Poison" is punctuated by a series of grim postcards from the future. Lynn glances back repeatedly at Devil's Peak—a quintessential Cape Town postcard site since the genre's earliest days. The mountain is enshrouded in a terrifying new weather system (some of the most vivid writing in the story): an "oily cloud . . . [its] plume twice as high as the mountain," the air an "alien gel," the "tainted sun . . . a pink bleached disk, like the moon of a different planet" (1, 6). This alien sky offers an Anthropocene imaginary in its multiple aspects, fusing this strange weather with industrial chemistry's rearrangement of molecules across bodies and biomes: these anthropogenic changes have unpredictable, uncontrollable effects that render Earth unhomely. The counterpart to the sinister weather looming over the city behind Lynn is the pastoral promise of the rural landscape before her, "an old two-wire fence . . . holding back the veld," a "stringy cow [with] grassy breath," an avid goat (7). Another intertextual modulation is at work here: a shift from Maureen Smales's embrace of the vast unknown of the bush, at the end of the revolutionary apocalypse imagined in Nadine Gordimer's *July's People* (1981),[25] to the South African pastoral of which Coetzee (Rose-Innes's professor at the University of Cape Town) is the Anglophone critic and practitioner par excellence. The will-to-innocence in this variant of the pastoral wishes away the harms of history and the centuries of struggle over land whose trace remains in fences running over the veld like scars (Coetzee 1988; Barnard 2007). Rose-Innes's Anthropocene imaginary broadens the scope and the *kinds* of history the pastoral holds at bay. At the story's end, Lynn turns her back on the catastrophe hanging over Table Mountain: "She wanted to face clear skies, sweet-smelling veld." The sound she longs to hear is no longer the blaring sirens and reassuring bullhorns of first responders, but the croak of a frog, "just one, starting its evening song beyond the fence" (10).

Rose-Innes offers a new variation on the South African pastoral as an escape from history: not merely colonial conquest and racialized exploitation (which neither protagonist nor author can escape), but also unevenly universal vulnerability to environmental harm. While it is impossible not to want the future Lynn wants—clear skies, frog songs, and better living "when this is all over"—this imagined future bears the poisonous traces of a South African literary history that reveal it to be a retreat into an idealized past. That future is rusted out, like the broken-down car Lynn nests herself into at the story's end, when automobility has run out of gas. She notices that it's the same model as her car, but twenty years older— literalizing almost too neatly the structure of another's degraded past becoming one's degraded future.

The shapes of the futures imagined in "Postcards from the Future" and "Poison" are only fully legible in relation to *histories* of exploitation that endure into the present. These histories are thickly mediated through literary traditions, itineraries of reading, and narrative forms (like eco-apocalypse and pastoral) that accrete in world-ecological, world-systemic fashion; that is, both "global" and national, but also more local than that— as in iconic London sites, or the distinctive topography of the Cape, with which these examples are enmeshed in webs of intertextual relation. Neither World Literature nor Anthropocene discourse can do without postcolonial studies' attention to these multiscalar histories.

In temporal terms, the melancholy lure of eco-apocalypse can be far too easy; the desire to imagine our own destruction, or living on in the aftermath of collapse, distracts attention from the collapse and the alternatives already at work in the present. (In "Poison," Lynn notes that the sunlight is "an end-of-the-world shade of pewter," which "had always been the color of the light in places like this" [2007, 3]). Rather than eco-apocalypse or desires for ending otherwise in the face of a future inferior, we need to cultivate desires for something other than an ending. To imagine change under the sign of hope, or at least something other than apocalypse or business as usual—even while acknowledging the constraints upon life in a more-than-human world. This means being alert and alive to "zones of exclusion" as "social spaces where life is being *lived* otherwise" (Pratt 2008, 212) and to what Frederick Buell describes as "living on through loss . . . ways of living in nature as it is now . . . [with] love of what remains" (2003, 290). Such a capacity to reimagine alternative possibility in the present, beyond the terms of a postcard politics, might be able to grapple more meaningfully with pasts that aren't even past, and futures—both imagined and unimagined—that may never arrive.

The Shape of Things to Come: Notes for Reading This Book

This book is divided into two parts, "Citizens and Consumers" and "Resource Logics and Risk Logics." The two chapters in the first part examine issues of "choice," agency, and complicity entailed in citizenship and consumerism. They resituate this familiar dyad within a transnational framework to consider the ethical and environmental predicaments of contemporary consumer capitalism as well as ongoing struggles to define and claim the prerogatives of citizenship (whether national or planetary) in sites of resource extraction like the Niger Delta. When these versions of citizenship and consumerism are juxtaposed, world-imaginings and scenes of reading (or spectatorship) begin to limn alternative forms of polity and modes of solidarity. In the book's second section, "Resource Logics and Risk Logics," the two chapters consider forms of world-imagining inherent to global capitalism's disposition of nature, people, and power. By *resource logics*, I mean habits of mind that understand nature as other than human, disposed as a resource for human use, and subject to human control. Resource logic is centripetal, the appropriative dynamic by which capital draws the world to itself, as in processes of enclosure. Risk logic is centrifugal, displacing costs and harms elsewhere in space and time, beyond the pale of responsibility. In risk logics, this externalization can involve *internalization*: the traffic, transit, and trespass of hazardous substances across national borders and the semipermeable membranes of living bodies. Globalization often works through *localizing* risk, harm, or profit—a spatial corollary of neoliberalism's tendency to socialize risk while privatizing profit.

This book also works through localization. Mindful of the danger of mistaking *a* world for *the* world, I do not understand this book as an encyclopedic, exhaustive account of environmental crisis or world literature— or even world literature "about" environmental crisis. Part I draws on African (and Caribbean) examples, while Part II is grounded in India, with contrapuntal gestures toward North America, the United Kingdom, and Vietnam. (This neat geographic division is not entirely by design; citizenship and consumption are obviously pertinent beyond Africa, and resource and risk logics are not unique to India.) The geographic emphases of this study reflect my scholarly expertise and the locations from which I am best able to read for the planet: to understand how relations of position and power shape *specific* instances and modes of world-imagining. There is a lot of world left out of this book, but its insights are ready to travel.

Another important localization (and limitation) concerns language. Most of the texts examined here were written in English. This is hardly an innocent position, but it is a world-historical one. The disjunctive affinities between the maximalist ambition of the World Literature project and the hegemony of the English language (within World Literature and beyond) only seem ironic or contradictory if one neglects their historical mediation through a third discursive field: Orientalism and empire (Mufti 2016, 158). In its expansiveness, Anglophonia risks forgetting the Babel upon (and within) its borders, the imperial history of its dissemination, and its relations with myriad vernacular traditions. While the textual corpus of this book is largely Anglophone, I seek to undermine Anglocentrism (even in its own language) by insisting that English is not a neutral, transparent medium whose global reach is an ahistorical given. Throughout this book, I attend to instances where inequality and violence manifest as conflicts among multiple languages, stratified registers of language, and the ability to "speak grammar" (Nigerian parlance for Standard English, often connoting obfuscation), in order to demonstrate the cosmopolitan provincialism and political inadequacy of a world (and a world literature) where English is favored as a language of convenience without regard for its multifarious roles in histories of conquest. This line of inquiry is most extensive in Chapter 4, which shows that one cannot make legal or literary sense of Bhopal if one works only in English, even as the inequalities (within literary studies, the law, and beyond) between places like the United States and India foster such monolingual parochialism among the powerful.

Localization is also at work in the varied methodological approaches across the four chapters—a reflection of the problems posed by imagining a world and one's place in it. In two chapters, a specific site of environmental crisis offers a point of entry and organizing logic (the Niger Delta in Chapter 2; Bhopal in Chapter 4). Other chapters focus on a particular genre (documentary film in Chapter 1) or socioecological relation (the enclosure of "waste" land in Chapter 3). Chapters 3 and 4 each constellate their inquiry around a single literary text, but they aim beyond practical criticism or *explication de texte* by shuttling between multiple geographic sites, historical moments, scales, and discourses. Throughout this book, close readings are interwoven with several modes of thick contextualization in order to work out questions of method and articulate concepts whose import reaches beyond the text at hand. This is what it means to connect the dots from near to there. Attentive to literature's staging of intersubjective encounters (not always between humans) and its singular intelligence, I tease out its capacity for imaginative and political work in the world. The shape of this teasing-out is more looping than linear; the arguments proceed cumulatively, pursuing unexpected associations and insights of the sort opened up by the juxtaposition of Sinha and Kincaid, then circling back to reflect anew on the central questions. Chapter subsections give shape to these constellating arguments, which may veer in surprising directions—a trace of my own reading, and rereading, for the planet. These chapters record what it means to be troubled by a text, with an eye toward making trouble.

Chapter 1, "Consumption for the Common Good? Commodity Biography in an Era of Postconsumerism," considers the limits of disseminating knowledge about the harms of economic globalization as a strategy for creating change. The chapter identifies an emergent genre of world-imagining: documentary films that trace biographies of specific commodities (Jamaican tourism in *Life and Debt*, Nile perch in *Darwin's Nightmare*, and Ethiopian coffee in *Black Gold*). These films aim to change viewers' behavior by implicating them in distant environmental crises, as consumers and citizens. Offering an alternative to the predicament of complicit consumption (where one's life is subsidized by others' suffering), these films urge a shift from overconsumption to green consumption—what I call *postconsumerism*, which privileges products that dare to tell their stories. Imagining itself as capitalism with a difference, postconsumerism works through value-adding narratives that function less as defetishizing knowledge than as new objects of consumerist desire. Nevertheless, moments of reflexivity, in which documentary subjects are depicted as consumers of commodities and/or film, disrupt too-easy binaries of First World consumption vs. Third World production. The chapter situates these films within longer histories of consumption and its ethical conundrums, including the nexus of commodity knowledge and desire in *Moby-Dick*, and lessons in ethical consumption and viewership in Dziga Vertov's experimental films of the 1920s.

Chapter 2, "Hijacking the Imagination: How to Tell the Story of the Niger Delta," constellates texts from a range of genres (Ogaga Ifowodo's poem *The Oil Lamp*; prose fictions by Uwem Akpan, Helon Habila, and Ben Okri; the photo-essay anthology *Curse of the Black Gold*; Sandy Cioffi's documentary film *Sweet Crude*) around a particular site of environmental crisis, the Niger Delta, arguably the most polluted place on earth. Juxtaposing political ecology's analysis of natural resource conflicts with

Benedict Anderson's account of nations as imagined communities, I consider how oil fuels the unimagining of Nigeria and the Niger Delta, and how such quarantines of the imagination might be overcome. What is the state for? To whom do natural resources belong? These questions bear upon national and planetary citizenship in Nigeria and beyond, joining political representation to aesthetic representation. Oil hijacks the imagination, promising wealth without work, progress without the passage of time—a dynamic whose literary manifestation is the mode I call petromagic-realism. The execution of Ken Saro-Wiwa in 1995 galvanized world attention, but I trace the pitfalls of reading across historical, geographical, and experiential distance when Saro-Wiwa's martyrdom continues to hijack the imagination and obstructs understanding the complexity of the Niger Delta today.

Chapter 3, "From Waste Lands to Wasted Lives: Enclosure as Aesthetic Regime and Property Regime," traces relationships between material processes and cultural logics of enclosure. Waste land—land not under cultivation, producing no revenue for the state—was the original raw material of colonial capitalism. *Waste* also names the troublesome byproducts of such transformation: *wasted lands* and *wasted lives*, the waste of the world laid waste. These processes entail ways of seeing and knowing; aesthetic regimes help to naturalize and manufacture consent for property regimes, bringing the beautiful and the profitable into alignment. The personification of nature (as in the pathetic fallacy) is bound up with the objectification of humans: aesthetic renderings of landscape draw upon and reinforce the dehumanizing, anti-commons common sense forged by resource logics. I consider the role of European imperialism in consolidating hegemonic notions about the disposition of nature, thereby situating new materialist attempts to recognize nonhuman agency within a broader historical context. "Dhowli," a short story by the Bengali writer-activist Mahasweta Devi, anchors this chapter's examination of a worldwide history of waste and wasting, which begins (if we follow John Locke) when "all the world was America" and ends (if we follow Devi) at the margins of a remote forest in rural Bihar. "Dhowli" represents forests as sites of imagination, inscription, and interpretation, as well as resource extraction and exploitation; the story offers a counterintuitive, scandalous account of violence, waged against people *through* an indifferent nature, as normative and thus largely invisible, at least at a distance. At a different scale, the depiction of indifferent nature in "Dhowli" offers an Anthropocene allegory *avant la lettre*.

Chapter 4, "How Far Is Bhopal? Inconvenient Forums and Corporate Comparison," considers what it would mean to take the multinational corporation (rather than the nation-state or empire) as an axis for literary comparison. Charting Dow Chemical's global history of harm, I link Indra Sinha's Bhopal novel *Animal's People* to Agent Orange and the acute silicosis epidemic resulting from Union Carbide's excavation of the Hawk's Nest Tunnel in West Virginia, memorialized in Muriel Rukeyser's book-length poem *The Book of the Dead*. In their decades-long effort to avoid liability for Bhopal, Union Carbide and Dow have invoked the legal doctrine of *forum non conveniens* (or "inconvenient forum"), an inherently comparative doctrine concerned with language, location, and the difficulty of interpreting across geographical and experiential divides, which I juxtapose with the concerns and methods of comparative literature. *Animal's People*'s exuberant multilingualism and dizzying array of intertextual allusions derive from its ambivalence about the possibility of environmental justice and planetary solidarity. Aware of its own circulation in the uneven landscape of world literature, *Animal's People* is caught between the conventionality of a bourgeois marriage plot and a revolutionary, eco-apocalyptic sublime. This formal tension is the novel's solution to the challenge of imagining justice for Bhopal without ignoring the historical fact of justice still undone. The novel reveals the pitfalls of bourgeois sympathy and radical solidarity as responses to the calculations of risk logic and the contradictions among toxic, financial, and media exposure: Universal vulnerability to corporate poisons means "we all live in Bhopal," yet that predicament remains highly uneven.

An epilogue, "Fixing the World," pivots from the 2009 documentary film *The Yes Men Fix the World* (on the culture-jamming satirical pranksters the Yes Men) to Nigerian novelist Chinua Achebe's reflections on the difference between "beneficent" and "malignant" fiction in order to reflect upon the kinds of remedy and redress that literature and other counterfactual imagining can offer in the face of environmental injustice. I argue that we should understand all such fictions as *risky*: unpredictable in the workings of cause and effect across time and space. Such risks entail not only exposure to the possibility of harm but also leaps of faith into the unknown and the as yet unrealized, as well as the prospect that the "touch of innocence" (Zinn 1967) that we tend to imagine about ourselves might be countered with a newfound sense of complicity, entanglement, or even self-reflexive solidarity.

PART I

Citizens and Consumers

CHAPTER I

Consumption for the Common Good? Commodity Biography in an Era of Postconsumerism

In bourgeois society the legal fiction prevails, that each person,
as a buyer, has an encyclopedic knowledge of commodities.

—KARL MARX, *Capital*

It is a matter of great astonishment that the consideration of the habits
of so interesting, and, in a commercial point of view, of so important an
animal [as the Sperm Whale] should have been entirely neglected, or
should have excited so little curiosity among . . . [those who] of late
years must have possessed the most abundant and the most convenient opportunities of witnessing their habitudes.

—THOMAS BEALE, *History of the Sperm Whale*

Taken together, these remarks of Karl Marx and Thomas Beale suggest that consumers and producers *should* know a lot about commodities and where they come from, but neither actually do. Herman Melville cites Beale in the "Extracts" chapter of *Moby-Dick*, one of several chapters in which Melville's own encyclopedic knowledge of whales and whaling—gathered through reading and observation—overtakes the novel's narrative thrust. What meaning can be found in a whale is one question that drives the novel, and Melville is canny about the similarities between whales and books. In terms of present-day concerns, particularly signifi-cant is the whaler-narrator Ishmael's disclosure to his readers (who con-sume whale oil in order to consume books) this bit of knowledge about whaling: "Upon one particular voyage which I made to the Pacific, among many others we spoke thirty different ships [*sic*], every one of which had had a death by a whale, some of them more than one, and three that had each lost a boat's crew. For God's sake, be economical with your lamps and candles! Not a gallon you burn, but at least one man's blood was spilled for it" (Melville [1851] 1993, 171). For Ishmael, the exchange of blood for oil is an unfortunate necessity that demands mindful consumption, rather

49

than a moral horror that necessitates a different geopolitics, as with the "No Blood for Oil" slogan inspired by the Gulf Wars of the late twentieth and early twenty-first centuries. Ishmael's direct address to the reader momentarily narrows the gap between nineteenth- and twenty-first-century modes of combustion and their costs in human lives. His uncertainty elsewhere in the novel about whether whale populations are threatened by whaling invites a certain pathos today: Not only are whales now regarded sympathetically as endangered fellow mammals rather than as diabolical resource-fish, but the dominant fuel of our own phase of modernity is also finite and entails costs that jeopardize the oceans' (and thus the planet's) capacity to support cetacean and human life.[1] For his own part, Melville seems not to have heeded this call to parsimony in calculating the ratios among gallons of ink, oil, and blood spilled for the sake of *Moby-Dick*.

Moby-Dick would have been impossible to write or decipher in the absence of a global—or at least oceanic/littoral—capitalism. Tracing the "devious zigzag world-circle of the *Pequod*'s circumnavigating wake," Melville pushes the novel form to its limits to tell a tale of whaling, a global industry he posits as the vanguard of imperialism's maps, markets and missionaries ([1851] 1993, 167). *Moby-Dick* is a prodigious feat of world-imagining, in which Nantucket figures not as quaint summer retreat on the margins of US territory (nor as inspiration for ribald rhymes) but as the center of a world-system and world-ecology in which the real action is at its furthest reaches: "Ah, the world! Oh, the world!," Ishmael exclaims, remarking on whaling's largely unwritten history (92). "Ah, the whale! Oh, the whale!" is the novel's implicit alternating refrain. The relationship between world and whale is captured in the image of the *Pequod*, bedecked in whale ivory and bone, as a "cannibal of a craft, tricking herself forth in the chased bones of her enemies" (59). Captain Ahab's "barbaric white leg," the whalebone prosthesis he adopted after having been "dismasted" along with his ship, echoes this murderous incorporation of a vanquished antagonist (103). Described as "cannibal" and "barbaric," on the wrong side of the civilization binary, these expropriations of whales' body parts effect a reverse totemism, pledging enmity rather than affiliation. They are perhaps even fetishistic, a variant on the process of reduction by which, "however peculiar . . . any chance whale may be, they soon put an end to his peculiarities by killing him, and boiling him down into a peculiarly valuable oil" (170).

Moby-Dick peers into the mist and mystery of the commodity fetish, as it restores to view not only the human social relations that underwrite a cask of whale oil, but also the singularity of one whale whose peculiarities cannot be boiled off when he is quite literally rendered into a commodity, no matter how peculiar—or, as Marx might say, "very strange" (1977, 1:163)—its value may be. Unlike whale oil, *Moby-Dick*'s value as *cultural* commodity depends precisely upon the metaphysical singularity of its namesake whale. Ishmael's description of whale oil production as the elimination of individual whales' peculiarities resonates ironically with his dismissal of the threat posed by whaling: "we account the whale immortal in his species, however perishable in his individuality" (Melville [1851] 1993, 381). In these respects, *Moby-Dick* differs from a novel like *Heart of Darkness*, which tallies the costs of the ivory trade in terms that also broach the metaphysical but says not a word about elephants. For that, we must let the commodity do the talking.

Could elephant tusks themselves speak, what would they say? As if rewriting Marx's scenario from the "Commodities" chapter of *Capital*, ivory tusks carved on the Loango coast of central Africa in the late nineteenth century seem to speak not of their "natural intercourse as commodities," where "in the eyes of each other we are nothing but exchange-values," as Marx ventriloquizes (1967, 1:83), but the *unnatural*—and brutal—history of European trade and its disposition of nature, in which human beings, elephants, palm trees, and other flora were *reduced* to nothing but exchange-values (see Figure 1). With human and animal figures relief-carved in an ascending spiral, the violence of the African/European trade in palm wine and palm oil, rubber, ivory, and humans is on full view. Images of chained gangs of slaves and forced laborers insist upon the continuities among these forms of trade, despite the official British suppression of the transatlantic slave trade and its ostensible replacement by a "legitimate commerce" in nonhuman products.[2] The sociocultural effects of African and European encounters are legible in images of Africans in European dress. Elephants, elephant hunts, and human porters bearing ivory tusks are depicted within these narratives, in which the commodity tells its own story, inscribed upon its body (see Figure 2).

It is, of course, not the ivory nor the elephants that craft this narrative, but the ivory carvers of Loango for whom the tusks are the medium on which the history of Euro-African trade can be inscribed. Whereas the Loango tusks bear a narrative of their history, the whale parts on the *Pequod* are "trophies" that begin to turn the ship into a whale and are implied to have some relation to narrative and the ship's history. Ahab's whale prosthesis and the tattoos of Queequeg and Ishmael extend the metonymic slippages of inscription among whale, ship, whaler's bodies, and narrative.[3] The novel form (and his own leviathan ambitions) afforded Melville nearly

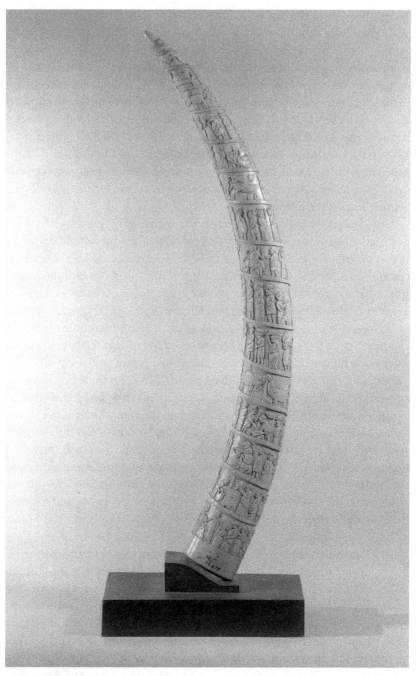

Figure 1. Elephant tusk carved with figures in relief, Kongo (Vili), late nineteenth century. A. August Healy Fund. Courtesy of the Brooklyn Museum.

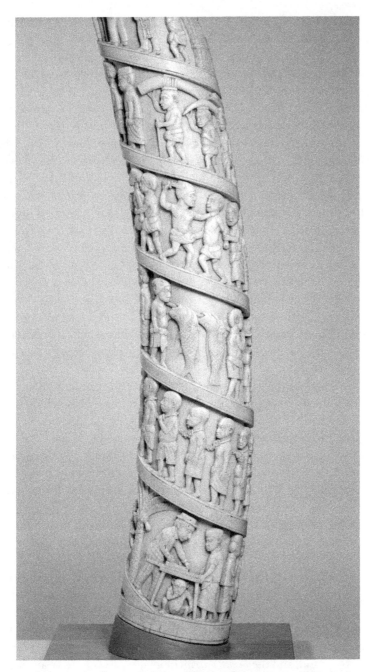

Figure 2. Elephant tusk with scenes of African life (detail), Anonymous (Congolese), c. 1850–60. Acquired by Henry Walters, ca. 1910. 71.586. Courtesy of The Walters Art Museum, Baltimore.

endless possibilities for constellating meaning and matter; as a medium, the Loango tusks are less malleable.

What is perhaps most remarkable about the Loango tusks is the audience to whom they and their carvers spoke: they were produced for European traders, as souvenirs of their African sojourns.[4] The tusks were mnemonic devices that supplemented the tales with which returned traders regaled family and friends (Bridges 2009). They were not unlike the nineteenth-century stereoscope, or twentieth-century View-Master, which disseminated mass-produced photographic image of exotic places. With the tusks, images were inscribed by local artists onto a medium of trade; the increasing scarcity of ivory in the late nineteenth century bears witness to that trade's rapacity. And yet, the knowledge inscribed onto the tusks seems distinct from the knowledge read off of them; we can only surmise that the carvers' sly incivility in depicting some of the horrors of trade with Europeans may have been read by their intended audience under the sign of adventure, or along the lines of the unfortunate necessity that Ishmael sees in the human blood distilled in whale oil, or as Marx's "intercourse" between commodities. If anyone could be expected to know that "commodities cannot themselves go to market and perform exchanges in their own right," as Marx writes, it would be "their guardians": the traders themselves (1977, 1:178).

Marx's insight is that the commodity fetish remains under its own thrall; could they speak, he implies, commodities would not necessarily tell a de-fetishizing truth. They are as "in love with money" as anyone else (1977, 1:202). Or, as with *Moby-Dick* and the Loango tusks, knowledge about human and animal suffering obscured by the mystique of the commodity does not necessarily interrupt exchange; indeed, in the case of the tusks, trade depends precisely upon the exchange of such knowledge, which, nonetheless, may not have the same *meaning* on either side of the exchange. Art historian Zoë Strother argues that the carved tusks should be read not as a continuous narrative, following around the spiral, but instead according to a discontinuous logic of juxtaposition, along the vertical axis: The most skilled carvers aligned these juxtapositions in particularly meaningful ways, and large tusks are too unwieldy to have been intended to be viewed by moving (around) them (2010, 52). The carved tusks pose an interpretive problem because of the tension between a *narrative* history of violent exploitation that the carvers inscribed as they worked their way around the spiral, and the *juxtapositions* of images, abstracted from this history, that are available to the stationary viewer.[5] The problem of viewing the tusks approximates the consumer's predicament: limited knowledge of the commodity, even if its story is writ large upon its surface.

Moby-Dick and the Loango tusks can be read as narratives that disseminate knowledge about commodities: texts that tell commodity stories—or commodities that tell their own stories—and thereby implicate consumers in the forms of violence that surround them. My concern in this chapter is with consumption, consumerism, and a more recent cultural form that confronts their attendant social and environmental harms: documentary films that I read as *commodity biographies*. These narratives of the life-stories of commodities trace global networks—Melville's "devious zigzag world-circles"—linking (mostly Third World) producers and (mostly First World) consumers. Such films might be seen to remedy the lack of knowledge about commodities that Marx and Beale remark upon in my epigraphs. Although these documentary films are in many ways far removed from the nineteenth-century examples with which I began, these "texts" each contemplate what medium or form is adequate to both the commodity stories they want to tell and the worlds they want viewers to imagine. In this, they offer instructive allegories for versions of world literature modeled on itineraries of worldwide commerce, whether in the nineteenth-century era of whaling and Melville's seminal world novel or the present era of resource exhaustion and documentary film. Asking viewers to connect the dots between their consumption habits and the lives of distant producers, commodity biography film is a genre premised upon reading for the planet.

This chapter considers three examples of commodity biography film: *Life and Debt* (2001), *Darwin's Nightmare* (2004), and *Black Gold* (2006). *Moby-Dick* and the Loango tusks bring into relief a crucial paradox by offering a longer historical trajectory for these films—that, say, of capitalism, rather than merely late capitalism's postmodernism. The paradox is this: While we might want to read these films as defetishizing their commodities—breaking the spell of enchantment that obscures the social relationships constituted by the movement and exchange of matter and labor—the films generate not only knowledge of the commodities' life stories but also desire for the commodities themselves. This is particularly true—as with the Loango tusks—when knowledge about a commodity, even horrific knowledge, becomes part of its appeal. In other words, commodity defetishization is a classic gesture of the sort I consider in *The Disposition of Nature*: making legible the obscured histories and geographies that generate pleasure and privilege for some, immiseration for others, a fragile planet for everyone. Yet the knowledge project of rendering things visible collides with questions of aesthetic form—in this case, cinematic structures of scopic desire. Images of others' suffering on screen somehow generate another kind of pleasure for those who watch.

Knowledge, then, has its limits. The echoes between exchanges of blood for oil in *Moby-Dick* and in Iraq indicate that US citizens have long known that their energy consumption habits have consequences for people in distant places. As *Darwin's Nightmare* director Hubert Sauper remarks, his film merely connects the dots among discrete facts that "everyone knows" (Sauper 2004). The injustices of contemporary globalization do not stem from a simple lack of knowledge. Even as these films seek to move viewers, as consumers and citizens, along that media relay from knowledge to understanding to action, knowledge itself becomes part of the problem, rather than the solution.[6] In terms of the tension between narrative and juxtaposition noted above, these commodity biography films might offer consciousness-raising narratives of suffering and exploitation. Yet they can also be read in terms of juxtaposed figures of knowledge that are themselves a source of consumerist pleasure.

In what follows, I read each film in turn, examining how it narrates the life-story of its respective commodity: Jamaican tourism in *Life and Debt*, Nile perch in *Darwin's Nightmare*, Ethiopian fair trade coffee in *Black Gold*. These films aim to change consumer behavior by charting complex, transnational networks that implicate viewers in distant economic and ecological crises. They appeal to viewers as consumers and citizens by engaging the tangled webs of ideology, moral responsibility, and desire that shape their relationships to commodities and polities. Each film's commodity biography constructs a different relationship between consumption and knowledge, and I am interested in how this nexus generates its own form of consumerism that obstructs the imagining of new modes of citizenship.

Commodity biography films aim to transform consumer behavior even as they elicit consumerist desire. This tension belies an important predicament involved in reading for the planet. I understand consumerism as central to the project of environmental justice, in a world where some people consume too much, others arguably consume too little, and it is difficult to imagine either the planet or politics as capable of sustaining a more equitable arrangement. These films reflect an emergent shift from an ethos of overconsumption to a putative ethics of consumption—from consumerism to postconsumerism. Postconsumerism posits mindful consumption as an altruistic act whose benefits accrue not immediately (or not only) to the consumer but to the producers (as in fair trade), the planet (as in green consumerism), or to others in need (as in "portion of the profits" donation). Postconsumerism aims to bridge the classic consumer/citizen divide, so that acting upon individual desires within the marketplace is congruent with working for the common good in the polis, or on the planet. Postconsumerism privileges the consumption of seemingly defetishized commodities that dare to tell their stories; such narratives, however, evoke new forms of desire that threaten to leave untouched (even as they are thought to address) the relations of inequality obscured by the commodity form. The change they effect may occur solely in the realm of the imaginary—a powerful instance of what I call the gentrification of the imagination.

Everyone's a Tourist: Life and Debt

Stephanie Black's 2001 film *Life and Debt* offers a valuable primer on both the impossible economic choices facing newly independent nation-states and the experience of contemporary globalization as an unjust loss or lack of opportunity for millions around the world. Global trade and aid policies shape the daily struggles of Jamaicans, as the film demonstrates by tracing not only the fate of commodities such as green onions, potatoes, bananas, chicken, beef, and milk, but also the fiscal pressures of structural adjustment and debt servicing. *Life and Debt* tells a similar story about each commodity, whose production has been crippled by US trade policies that eliminate domestic and international markets. Subsidized US produce floods Jamaican markets; multinational firms (including McDonald's) promise to source local beef and potatoes but never find them up to standard, and US-based Chiquita protests the sale of Jamaican bananas in the European Union—an arrangement described as a postcolonial gesture of reparation.[7] The one "commodity" spared this fate is Jamaica itself, reduced to an object of consumption by foreign tourists; *Life and Debt* warns that the social unrest provoked by the suppression of nearly every other sector of Jamaica's economy threatens the tourist experience. To revise Dean MacCannell's classic account of tourism as commodification, "modern workers, on vacation" can hardly make "a fetish of the work of others," when those others are put out of work (1976, 6).

Life and Debt argues that tourism in Jamaica quarantines what Mac-Cannell calls "the alienation of the sightseer" from the "alienation of the worker" (1976, 6). "If you come to Jamaica, this is what you will see," the voiceover narration begins (Black 2001); the opening scenes establish an unbreachable visual divide between an idyllic tourist retreat and an underdeveloped British postcolony confronting new threats from the

United States. Interviews with Jamaican producers, politicians, and economists are interspersed with observational scenes from a middlebrow tourist
package, arranged chronologically from arrival to departure. The film
constructs a *narrative* about the pressures of neoliberal globalization on
small economies through this logic of *juxtaposition* in which the experiences
of tourist and Jamaican seem—as on the glossy surface of a tourism
brochure—distinct and discontinuous. The voiceover looks beneath the
surface to reveal what "you" (the tourist) will and will not see, or will not
want to see, "if you come to Jamaica." David Harvey argues that the "geographical ignorance that arises out of the fetishism of commodities" emerges
from a separation of the "space horizons" of production and consumption
(1990, 423). One task of commodity biography, then, is to bring into relation
the lives of producers and consumers, which are usually (and paradoxically)
disjoined by the global circulation of commodities. *Life and Debt* offers a
site where the disjunct "space horizons" of Jamaican producer and foreign
tourist finally meet. Their everyday incommensurability is more poignant
for being located geographically in the same, small place.

The voiceover narration of *Life and Debt* was written by Jamaica Kincaid
and adapted from her nonfiction book, *A Small Place* (1988), whose lyrical
and biting analysis offers a *longue durée* commodity history, mercilessly
historicizing the "native"/foreign tourism dynamic in terms of the transatlantic slave trade and settler/plantation colonialism: The lives of island-
ers and tourists were intertwined long before the tourist's arrival. The
book-to-film adaptation of the voiceover partakes of the commodity logic
of substitution, replacing one island economy with another: the Antigua
of *A Small Place* becomes the Jamaica of *Life and Debt*. Daring to project
what "you"—the tourist—will perceive during a visit to Antigua, the rhetorical structure of *A Small Place* risks alienating the reader who must
inhabit the position of the "you." The intimate encounter (not quite a
dialogue) between this tourist/reader "you" and the first-person Antiguan
narrator (not quite Jamaica Kincaid) expands to a world-historical encounter between colonizer and colonized, master and slave. *A Small Place*
builds to a climax of dialectical, decolonizing transformation, in which
both the "human rubbish" masters who came to Antigua to "satisfy their
desire for wealth and power," and their "noble and exalted" slaves, cease to
be master and slave, cease to be "human rubbish" or "noble and exalted,"
and become "just human beings" (1988, 80–81). This climax echoes the
dialectical movement toward revolutionary humanism in Fanon's *The
Wretched of the Earth*.

Life and Debt's voiceover also concludes with the dialectical transformation of slaves and masters into human beings, yet the film's assemblage of interviews, observational scenes, and a chorus of Rasta elders dilutes the intensity of the book's encounter between *I* and *you*. The film gestures only briefly toward a longer Caribbean history. Its target is contemporary US-driven neoimperialism rather than the European imperialism of previous centuries. Consequently, when the film (drawing from the book) mentions the "number of African slaves the ocean swallowed up," in the context of the Atlantic now having to absorb Jamaica's unprocessed sewage, the analogy is so jarring as to seem cheap. Moreover, the concluding dialectical turn of the voiceover—in which victim and villain in this palimpsestic history become "just human beings"—is undermined by the visual rhetoric of tourists serenaded by obliging, uniformed Jamaican musicians as they board the shuttle bus to the airport. The tourists are presumably none the wiser, still "human rubbish" being washed back to their own shores.

This contrast between sound and image derives from a crucial difference between prose and film. The "you" of the voiceover has both an aural and a visual addressee: the viewer of the film, and the tourists it depicts. These tourists remain fat, pink, and obliviously happy. Unlike the trade officials and Jamaican producers, they are never interviewed or shown to reflect about their experience; they are only observed—unflatteringly, undisturbed in their natural habitat. While this unobtrusive observational style might evoke cinema verité's will to documentary transparency and immediacy (in only one scene does a tourist acknowledge the camera, to wave goodbye as he departs), *Life and Debt*'s omniscient voiceover ironizes and directs viewers' interpretation, a method harking back to the paternalist mode of early documentary film.[8] The tourists are the only subjects in the film with no voice; their thoughts and perceptions are coercively represented through the voiceover. They are paradoxical hegemonic subalterns, who cannot speak but must be spoken for, not only by the voiceover but also by their governments, which impose policies from which the tourists benefit but do not understand. (To the extent that *Life and Debt* is an allegory of globalization, it depicts the nation-state not as withering away, but instead becoming more explicitly an instrument of capital, as I discuss in Chapter 2.) The tourists remain isolated in their own "space horizon," quarantined from the commodity knowledge about the relations between production and consumption that the film offers.

Much of that knowledge comes in the form of interviews with Jamaicans, including former statesmen (Michael Manley), economists, trade

officials, and displaced producers, who echo the refrain that globalization
has targeted and destroyed their capacity for self-reliance. In the segment
on garment factories in Kingston's international zone, workers lament that
they are not protected by local (Jamaican, "Third World") labor regulations, but are instead at the mercy of international ("First World") practices. Jamaican beef producers cite the same dynamic in environmental
terms, as Jamaican law (unlike US law) prohibits the use of "antibiotic in-
jections, cancer-causing agents." The Jamaican producers are would-be
capitalists and free-traders unable to compete with US agricultural subsidies. "Give us back our market," one interviewee demands, as viewers
cringe at repeated shots of milk poured out from storage vats onto the
ground because it cannot be sold at a price competitive with milk powder
from the United States, subsidized at a rate of 137 percent.

In *Life and Debt*, these displaced producers are also knowledge producers, savvy "native informants" who both appeal to and challenge mainstream US assumptions about how the world works. In the colonial era,
the perceived naïveté of local informants was exploited to shed light on cultures and lifeways perceived as bounded; here, by contrast, local voices
offer detailed knowledge and sophisticated analyses of the broadest reaches
of globalization. Although unnamed—credited only through a blanket
acknowledgment of "gratitude to the interviewees who share the truth with
such eloquence"—these proud but desperate Jamaicans offer incisive analyses of their place in a world-system. Despite their foreign travel, it is the
tourists who are the naïfs. They have not even begun to begin unlearning
their privilege as their loss.[9]

Life and Debt's construal of Jamaican workers as knowledge producers
is an important challenge to what Priti Ramamurthy calls "master narratives of globalization that naturalize gendered and racialized constructions
of difference and reproduce binaries between First and Third World"
(2004, 741). One binary that troubles Ramamurthy is producer/consumer,
in which the Third World makes and the First World takes.[10] Here, too,
Life and Debt challenges received notions by emphasizing the consumerist
desires of those whom conventional commodity chain analysis posits solely
as producers.[11] Its voiceover remarks that "every native of every place is a
potential tourist"; most "natives," however, can afford neither to "escape"
their own habitation nor "to live properly" within it. Consequently, they
"envy your ability to leave, to make their burden a source of pleasure." Ex-
ploding the tourist/native and consumption/production binaries by uni-
versalizing them as potential aspects of everyone's experience, *Life and Debt*
insists that what distinguishes natives-who-become-tourists from natives-

who-remain-natives is class, rather than race or nationality. Everyone wants to be a tourist; those who cannot afford to become tourists, the film implies, may become migrants seeking economic opportunities foreclosed at home.

As it ironizes tourism's consumerist pleasure, *Life and Debt* also invokes xenophobic fears of the uncontrollable movement of human beings. Shots of Jamaicans lined up outside the US embassy in Kingston make an implicit threat compatible with the rhetoric of the War on Terrorism: redress the effects of US trade policies for those "over there," or they will come "over here." Even as it makes important interventions in commodity biography's nexus of knowledge and consumption by depicting Jamaicans as knowledgeable, would-be consumers, *Life and Debt* takes them away again by implying that the pressures of globalization may force these formidable agents to leave their "proper" place. A viewer's possible identification with these hardworking, would-be free-traders is undermined when they are posited as a threat, either as perpetrators of petty crime or social unrest that mars the tourist experience, or as unwanted migrants washing up on First World shores. Here it is the descendants of enslaved people who are implicitly figured as "human rubbish," echoing the startling analogy between drowned slaves and unprocessed tourist sewage as forms of pollution in the Atlantic Ocean. The film's visual rhetoric means that viewers can hardly identify with the oblivious tourists either: compared to *A Small Place*'s almost claustrophobic dialectic of decolonizing dis/identification between the reader and the "you," *Life and Debt* offers a static position of too-easy disidentification between the viewer and the tourists onscreen, who remain ugly from start to finish. The film constructs no space where transformation of the viewer can take place. In *Life and Debt*'s contradictions, the lineaments of postconsumerism begin to emerge: both the bourgeois-liberal commingling of altruism and self-interest and the self-conscious, elitist sense of consumption-with-a-difference that allows viewers to distinguish themselves from mindless tourists on cheap package tours.

Part of the Big System: Darwin's Nightmare

Whereas *Life and Debt* is structured around the juxtaposition of knowledgeable Jamaicans and ignorant tourists, Hubert Sauper's *Darwin's Nightmare* (2004) takes a form predicted by vernacular, butterfly-wing versions of chaos theory: Dump a bucket of fish into a lake, wait forty years, and then trace as many consequences as you can, no matter how improbable or unrelated they may seem. *Darwin's Nightmare* narrates a fish tale in which the Nile perch was introduced into Lake Victoria in the 1950s to boost fishing yields; with no natural predators, the fish upset the lake's food chain, and the subsequent industrialization of Nile perch profoundly transformed the region. The film constellates numerous local problems around Nile perch, including the lake's ecological collapse, the reorientation of fishing from subsistence to cash crop, shifts in labor patterns and family structures as men are drawn away from farms and families to urban fish factories or fishermen's "work colonies," orphaned children, prostitution and an explosion of HIV/AIDS, and famine. Of the films discussed in this chapter, *Darwin's Nightmare* is most explicitly concerned with environmental crisis in the conventional sense, but also most profoundly troubled by how to narrate that crisis, not least since it construes the social and the ecological as inextricably related.

Nile perch are processed for export to Europe in the Tanzanian city of Mwanza, the nexus of multiple fallen empires and superseded trading routes. Indeed, the film's treatment of Nile perch traces global relations through time and space. The contemporary transnational networks that intersect in Mwanza are depicted in relation to overlapping histories: the Indian Ocean trade, the European colonization of Africa, and the aftermaths of decolonization and the Cold War. The factory owners and suppliers are Tanzanians of Indian descent. The pilots who transport the fillets are disaffected former Soviets. While the planes' cargo holds are ostensibly empty when they arrive in Mwanza, the film insinuates that they carry illicit arms for the war in the Democratic Republic of the Congo that destabilized much of the African continent at the turn of the twenty-first century. Sauper locates the impetus for *Darwin's Nightmare* in a 1997 trip to eastern Zaïre during the filming of *Kisangani Diary*, a documentary on refugees from the Rwandan genocide. The United Nations High Commission for Refugees organized humanitarian relief flights using former Soviet planes. Talking with the pilots, Sauper learned that these flights were involved in illicit arms trafficking to supply the struggle for control of Zaïre (renamed Democratic Republic of the Congo in 1998) that killed several million people in central Africa. Sauper was struck by the paradox of planes that brought "hope and destruction in the same airplane": guns *and* butter, swords *and* ploughshares, "landmines and wooden legs" (2004). *Darwin's Nightmare* alleges that the arms trade that began with humanitarian relief was adapted to the transnational pathways of the Nile perch industry.[12]

The illicit weapons traffic that the film posits as the verso of the "legitimate commerce" in Nile perch epitomizes what Sauper calls the "back-

Figure 3. Frame enlargement from *Darwin's Nightmare*, scene in fish-frame village.

side" of the "miracle" of globalization lurking "behind the curtain" (2004). He aims to excavate the "quintessence of the madness of our time— globalization—North/South traffic." The motto of a corporate calendar glimpsed in one scene—"You're part of the big system"—functions as a mise-en-abyme. The film constructs this "big system" through interviews with and observations of players on the ground in Mwanza: fishermen, factory workers and owners, sex workers, street children, Soviet pilots, and European trade officials. Another visual emblem of Sauper's method appears when the camera, in a wide shot, lingers on a young man who turns to reveal his skeleton T-shirt, black with white bones: documentary film, according to Sauper, offers an "x-ray of reality" (see Figure 3). Connecting the dots among what "everyone knows" (even if no one in Mwanza wants to talk about the guns), documentaries make visible the hidden structures that give shape and solidity to experience.

An "x-ray of reality" is a technology uniquely suited to apprehending commodities as "social things whose qualities are at the same time perceptible and imperceptible by the senses" (Marx 1967, 1:72): it renders invisibility visible. It aims to break the spell of the commodity's enchantment and right its upside-down world. Indeed, the man in the skeleton T-shirt appears in one of the most visually stunning and rhetorically forceful sequences in *Darwin's Nightmare*, in which truckloads of filleted Nile perch carcasses are transported from gleaming, sterile factories in Mwanza to a "fish-frame village" where they are salvaged for local consumption: dried in the sun and fried as food. In this apocalyptic landscape, female workers are mired in mud and maggots and maimed by their exposure to ammoniac gas exuded by rotting fish. One woman pulls back the cloth that cushions the basket on her head to reveal a scarred-over eye socket. This harrowing sequence, in which the man in the skeleton T-shirt suddenly appears (the skeleton on his shirt echoing the fish-frames at his feet), offers a visual approximation of Marx's vivid tableaux. "Capital comes [into the world] dripping from head to toe, from every pore, with blood and dirt," Marx wrote; "It is an enchanted, perverted, topsy-turvy world, in which Monsieur le Capital and Madame la Terre do their ghost-walking as social characters and at the same time directly as mere things" (1967, 1:760, 3:830).

The fish-frame village sequence depicts the rotten underbelly of Nile perch production, an abject echo of the automated assembly line under the fillet factory's fluorescent lights. While the fillets are neatly packed, frozen, and flown away, locals salvage and eat what the film depicts as the rotting, maggot-filled refuse of Europe: "a few million Africans eat what the big planes would not carry," reads an intertitle at the beginning of this sequence.[13] Nile perch is a "big system" comprising multiple modes of production and geographies of consumption. The misery of the mise-en-scène means that the difficulty of *watching* this sequence (not to mention *listening* to it—the squish of a foot in mud in extreme close-up, the gelatinous crunch of carcasses over which flies hover and buzz) allows viewers to imagine being (and breathing) on the underside of this stratified production-consumption network: Viewers are made to look upon processes that cost others their vision. Film posters for the French, German, Spanish releases of *Darwin's Nightmare* use a sequence of images—fish, fish-frame, gun— to visualize Sauper's defetishizing claims: the illicit transnational trade transforms fish into guns, yet another source of misery.

Like *Life and Debt*, *Darwin's Nightmare* portrays the producers of commodities as prospective consumers, but its implicit link between the aversiveness of viewing the fish-frame sequence and that of processing or consuming fish-frames is only one instance where *Darwin's Nightmare* constructs a relay between fish and film. Indeed, the most interesting scenes of local consumption are of film rather than fish. Attendees at a fisheries management workshop watch a documentary about Nile perch's harm to Lake Victoria, which eutrophied without the cichlids that consume algae and other waste.[14] Yet another mise-en-abyme, this is the film Sauper could have made: a monologic ecodisaster pic shot mostly underwater, a simple fish tale with dominating voiceover and horror film music. In another scene of spectatorship, Mwanza street children gather on a beach around an old-fashioned projector and bedsheet to watch an evangelical film about Jesus, fisher of men, setting out in a boat from a beach. Another sequence in *Darwin's Nightmare* about impending famine in Tanzania contrasts shots of a family watching a TV news report about UN food aid with shots of former Soviet pilots watching (but changing the channel on) coverage of the Nile perch industry featuring footage from factories and press conferences similar to what the film's viewers have already seen. (The scenes in the pilots' residence are oddly full of fish—small fish are strung on lines to dry in the living room; one pilot talks of previous trips to African war zones while he cleans and cooks a foot-long fish.)

These scenes of spectatorship conjoin fish and film in ironic ways, evoking a reflexive sense of the documentary itself as a commodity that is produced and consumed, and whose character-producers are also viewer-consumers. Sauper takes this postconsumerist reflexivity to an extreme in a complex, elegiac scene prompted by the murder of the prostitute Eliza by an Australian client. The surviving "girls in the bar" watch Sauper's unedited footage of interviews with Eliza (which we have previously seen) on the tiny flip-screen of a handheld camera. The emotional charge of this scene, in which raw footage evokes raw emotion, puts the camera into the characters' hands at the same time that it turns them into spectators of the same intimate footage that viewers watch. Unlike the other scenes of spectatorship, this one does not involve fish, but Eliza's murder by a john emphasizes the risk inherent in sex work, in which "selling oneself," commodifying one's body, is taken to its limit. That the surviving women watch the same footage viewers have *already* seen—but *before* the footage has become a film—amplifies the solidarity-through-spectatorship offered by scenes of watching the films' subjects watch film and TV; both literally and figuratively, they flip the screen. In this sense, they differ from scenes in *Life and Debt* where Jamaicans watch local TV news coverage of civil disturbances, factory closings, and other signs of economic distress analyzed more expansively in the film. The implication is that tourists never watch the news, and Jamaicans will never watch the film. Nonetheless, such scenes invite viewers to become self-conscious of themselves as spectators and to imagine the films' subjects in terms beyond the commodity networks that join them as consumers and producers.

One of the most striking characters in *Darwin's Nightmare* theorizes this expansive view. Jonathan, a former street child and artist who paints scenes of life in Mwanza, declares himself a "citizen of the world." This world-imagining from below reverses the relations between worldliness and naïveté at work in conventional assumptions about cosmopolitanism as a stance dependent upon class privilege; it echoes the counterhegemonic economy of knowledge and ignorance in *Life and Debt*. As film scholar Ruby Rich observes (somewhat patronizingly), Sauper shows how "even African villagers can be worldclass experts on their own society, life, and fate" (2006, 112). Both films work against sanctioned ignorance as a luxury of the affluent; that the "unworldly" poor might understand the far-flung reasons for their poverty remains difficult to imagine for many First World beneficiaries at the other end. Jonathan invites viewers to rethink not only consumerism, but, more importantly, citizenship and the forms of knowledge it demands: to recognize themselves as "part of the big system" of markets, states, and communities.

In one important respect, however, *Darwin's Nightmare* reinforces hegemonic habits of mind: It reprises images of Africa of the sort that Chinua Achebe condemned in Joseph Conrad's *Heart of Darkness*. One critic describes the film's "dreamlike style" as "a succession of shocking scenes that are all allegorical, haunting, combined into meaningful puzzles" (Bartlet 2006): in a word, Conradian. In "Filming in the Heart of Darkness," Sauper recounts the ordeal of shooting in Mwanza. Like a modern-day Marlow waiting for rivets to repair his steamship, Sauper writes, "Forced idleness became a dull routine. We would sit in the merciless equatorial sun surrounded by a million Nile Perch skeletons . . . trying not to go mad." Sauper's homage to *Heart of Darkness* is evident in shots of wrecked airplanes littering the shores of Lake Victoria, and of unconscious glue-sniffing children: these images evoke a scene in the novel that depicts "decaying machinery," looking "as dead as the carcass of some animal," and "dark things [that] seemed to stir feebly" while lying under the trees at the outer station (Conrad [1902] 2006, 15). *Darwin's Nightmare* closes with a shot of a silent African woman watching over the plane's departure, not unlike the "wild and gorgeous apparition of a woman" who sends Kurtz off in Marlow's steamer (60). The camera at her back, she turns to face it, confronting the viewer rather than Marlow (or both, if we take the camera's perspective as that of Marlow).

Although filming *Darwin's Nightmare* took several months, the film's narrative—like Marlow's—is structured around the few days between the arrival and departure of the Ilyushin flown by the former Soviet pilots, who work on their aging plane with astonishingly crude tools while they wait, not for rivets, but for their cargo of Nile perch. Dima, a Ukrainian pilot, is a strangely sympathetic figure who, like Kurtz, partakes in nighttime revels with "natives"—the "girls at the bar" who service foreign men. Dima confronts the horror of the global system that brings, he says, bombs to African children and grapes to European ones. We know, from the first scene with Dima, why he flies weapons to Africa even though he wants "all the children of the world [to] be happy": because he, like people "in every country," must feed his family, whom we meet in digital photos the pilots show each other on their cameras (Sauper 2004). He is, like Marlow, "loyal to the nightmare of my choice" (Conrad [1902] 2006, 64). Indeed, Marlow's loyalty is tested when he returns from the Congo to tell Kurtz's "Intended"—who is willfully blind to the true character of her beloved and the trade that took his life—that "The last word he pronounced was—your name" (77). For Dima, "the horror" (Kurtz's actual expiring whisper) and the name of his Intended are the truth and the lie of globalization spoken in one breath.

Read from a certain angle, Kurtz's indictment of "the horror" in *Heart of Darkness* refers to European imperialism and the "idea at the back of it" rather than African depravity and European susceptibility to it (Conrad [1902] 2006, 7). Its early readers would have understood Conrad's novella in the context of the Congo Reform Association's exposés of King Leopold's horrific system; only later could *Heart of Darkness* become the ethereal masterpiece of modernist stylistics and the ahistorical study of psychological breakdown derided by Achebe in his 1975 "An Image of Africa" lecture. So, too, with Sauper's Conradian flourishes: They signify unpredictably, yet threaten to reinforce the hegemonic worldview the film ostensibly aims to undermine. For it is not only Conrad whom Sauper echoes, but also E. D. Morel, the Elder Dempster shipping clerk who uncovered the horrors of Leopold's Congo in the 1890s by examining the company's account logs, which indicated that boats went out to Africa containing only weapons and chains and returned to Brussels full of ivory and raw rubber. Morel turned to journalism, founded the Congo Reform Association, and sought Conrad's support; Sauper cites an analogous revelation as the seed for *Darwin's Nightmare*. Yet Sauper's reprise of Conradian images of Africa might direct viewers' interpretation of the film as a stylized lament over yet another African basket case, thereby reinscribing the master narrative of globalization within the fraught history of representing Africa from outside.

Perhaps what is most startling about the skeleton T-shirt is how vivid it is: the fabric jet black, the printed skeleton crisp white. It shows no sign of the wear that one might expect from the used clothing trade that brings T-shirts to the Global South bearing unlikely messages from afar.[15] It "pops" against the smoky haze of the fish-frame village and the grainy, underlit digital video in which *Darwin's Nightmare* is shot. It might lead us to believe that documentary film's "x-ray of reality" reveals how things really are. But x-rays, like the treacherous Congo river that Marlow navigates, are composed in shades of gray: sometimes cloudy, "inscrutable," filled with ghost images that may or may not be signs of trouble (Conrad [1902] 2006, 34). Marlow explains the challenges of navigation: "When you have to attend to . . . the mere incidents of the surface, the reality—the reality, I tell you—fades. The inner truth is hidden—luckily, luckily" (34). While he acknowledges that reality and truth may lie beneath external appearances, Marlow prefers such visible invisibilities to the intervention proffered by an "x-ray of reality." Despite its reflexivity about consumption, Sauper's anatomy of the "big system" asks viewers to consider something so big, complex, and chaotic (i.e., unsystematic) that it is perhaps too much knowledge to understand, let alone act upon: postconsumerism as anomie rather than self-satisfaction.

Monsieur le Coffee: Black Gold

The cast of characters in *Black Gold*, Marc and Nick Francis's 2006 documentary about Ethiopian coffee, is probably as large as that in *Darwin's Nightmare*, and its geographical itinerary ranges across a broader terrain. Compared to the brooding chaos of *Darwin's Nightmare*, however, *Black Gold* seems positively cheery and simple, its narrative structured around a single protagonist, Tadesse Meskela, general manager of the Oromia Coffee Farmers Cooperative Union. The film follows him as he meets with growers and auctioneers in Ethiopia, and buyers, roasters, and retailers in Europe and the United States, to advocate for the collective's 74,000 farmers by seeking fair trade markets for their coffee. Like *Darwin's Nightmare* and *Life and Debt*, *Black Gold* links its commodity biography to the history of global capitalism: It posits the fate of Ethiopian coffee on the world market as a case study in contemporary neoliberalism.[16]

Black Gold echoes and updates *Life and Debt*'s argument for free trade over coercive, self-perpetuating foreign aid; it links Meskela's story to a critique of the structural inequalities of the international trade and finance regime comprising the World Trade Organization (WTO), the World Bank, and the International Monetary Fund. The film closes with the WTO's 2003 negotiations in Cancún, which collapsed when the divide between poor and rich nation-states regarding agricultural subsidies could not be bridged. The story of Ethiopian fair trade coffee becomes an emblem for what Hubert Sauper might call the "big system," as *Black Gold* broadens its focus to argue that fair trade policies could eliminate (or at least mitigate) the need for international aid in the form of development loans and humanitarian relief.

The film's unforgettable final sequence depicts a cargo ship with piles of grain being processed by African workers on a mechanized assembly line. These images echo an earlier sequence in which coffee beans are loaded into burlap sacks and onto ships for export. But as the final sequence continues, viewers recognize that the grain is American wheat brought to Ethiopia as food aid. The assembly line workers, in a choking, blinding whirl of chaff, pack the wheat into white sacks bearing a red and blue "USA" logo; they also fashion the sacks into protective head and face gear.[17] The frame widens to reveal countless ships in the harbor, waiting to be unloaded. The final shot is a close-up of an empty sack floating in the sea like flotsam, its USA logo visible. This visual trade-not-aid appeal to American viewers signifies just as powerfully as the intertitle statistics punctuating this sequence: Foreign aid and unequal trade not only choke and starve Africa to death, but they also "trash" Brand USA. If you don't want to see the "USA" label on the bags of grain rubbished this way, *Black Gold* suggests, look for the "fair trade" label on your next bag of coffee. (An earlier scene at a UN feeding site documents the 2002 famine in Ethiopia, whose immediate cause was extreme drought; the international trade and aid policies analyzed in the film generate suffering in their own right and structure the emergence of and response to "natural" disasters like drought.) This consumerist appeal to American self-interest is perhaps not as sinister as *Life and Debt*'s shot of Jamaicans lined up outside the US embassy. However, *Black Gold*'s indictment of humanitarian aid is even more forceful than that in *Darwin's Nightmare*, which examines the illicit arms trade's cooptation of aid and legitimate trade, rather than aid or trade policies themselves.

Black Gold's argument for fair trade is formulated most simply in Meskela's arithmetic lesson for his coffee farmers. He quizzes them about the price of a cup of coffee in the United States; having revealed the correct (if seemingly incredible) answer, he has them extrapolate the profit on a kilo of beans, whose low price in the local market they know too well. Fair trade, then, offers an alternative arithmetic that would pay the growers more and circumvent the middlemen who interpose themselves between Ethiopian coffee farms and European cafés. This scene implies a knowledge divide between Meskela and his farmers: they are not the worldly, subaltern analysts of globalization in *Life and Debt* and *Darwin's Nightmare*.

What redeems this scene is its double pedagogy: the ultimate audience for the arithmetic lesson is *Black Gold*'s viewers, who are equally ignorant on their side of the production/consumption divide. They know how many dollars they pay for a cup of coffee; when they learn how many cents the farmers are paid for a kilo of beans, they are meant to be as aghast as the farmers. Viewers are invited to make their own calculations that would radically redefine surplus value: what little difference paying a few cents more would make in their household economies, as opposed to the world of difference it would make for the farmers.

The subtle reflexivity of this scene is reinforced in *Black Gold*'s treatment of coffee consumption. Scenes of Ethiopian coffee growers preparing and drinking coffee together are juxtaposed with scenes of customers at European and American cafés. The visual contrast between the rustic implements and picturesque green highlands of Ethiopia and the gleaming espresso machines and tasteful tableware of sleek Italian coffeehouses could not be more stark. But unlike *Life and Debt* and *Darwin's Nightmare*, *Black Gold* not only acknowledges the possibility that "poor producers should desire the products of their labor" (Ramamurthy 2004, 742), but it also depicts those desires as fully realized, in circumstances different from, but not inferior to, First World consumption. Some viewers are doubtless unable to stomach watching the fish-frame village sequence in *Darwin's Nightmare*, let alone thinking of eating the food produced there; by contrast, more than a few viewers likely find themselves fantasizing about drinking coffee brewed by actual Ethiopian coffee growers, with the green hills of Africa rolling behind them.[18] The juxtaposed scenes of coffee drinking in *Black Gold* prod viewers to remap their assumptions about demand, desire, and the sociality of consumption.

Given the time he spends onscreen, it is curious that we never see Meskela drinking the coffee he is so passionate about. The reason, I think, is that in the film's logic, he *is* coffee. He represents Ethiopian coffee as both advocate and metonym. He travels through the global networks in which coffee circulates on its journeys from field to cup; his conversations with people at various points in the process restore to view the social relations of production. Translating knowledge across the production/ consumption divide, Meskela's work for the cooperative, and its dissemination in *Black Gold*, seem poised to undo the contradiction "between the conversion of things into persons and . . . persons into things" that Marx observes in the commodity fetish as a relay between personification and objectification (1977, 1:209). Meskela's story is the story of coffee.

Yet the commodity fetish is not susceptible to such simple reversal. Replacing a mysterious, seemingly self-propelled socializing thing with a human person who acts on behalf of that thing might begin to right the upside-down world and make legible the layers of congealed human labor that the thing, as commodity, (mis)understands and (mis)presents to the world as an aspect of its own being. *Black Gold*'s substitution of coffee with Meskela could prompt viewers to decode the commodity's "social hieroglyphic," to "get behind the secret of our own social products . . . the mist through which the social character of labor appears as an objective character of the products themselves" and "a relation between persons" appears to us solely as a "relation between things" (Marx 1967, 1:74). But Meskela-as-coffee seems to complete, not reverse, this strange process of personification/objectification. The defetishizing gesture in *Black Gold*'s commodity biography is overtaken by a further symbolic turn in which coffee-become-man becomes coffee again, with a human face.

To state this dynamic in terms of commodity biography's economy of narrative, knowledge, and desire: Narrative can elicit, rather than neutralize, consumerist desire. Like *Darwin's Nightmare*, *Black Gold* outlines a stratified production process, divided between the global, corporate-dominated coffee market and those seeking fair trade alternatives. Neither layer of production in *Darwin's Nightmare* is depicted as sensuously appealing; in *Black Gold*, both are. The scene at an Illy coffee factory could be straight from a mid-twentieth-century industrial film's paean to automated production, without a worker in sight: all gleaming metal and controlled motion, whose visual rhythm is echoed in a jaunty, percussive score. Unlike the fish-frame village of *Darwin's Nightmare*, the less capital-intensive production alternative Meskela represents is portrayed sympathetically—indeed, so sympathetically that viewers likely share Meskela's heartbreak when he cannot find any Ethiopian coffees at a London Sainsbury's supermarket. When Meskela finally locates a bag of fair trade Sidamo on the shelf, the implication is clear: equally relieved viewers are invited to shift their affiliation from one production stream to the other. Both streams, after all, end at Sainsbury's, or the local equivalent. But whether or not a fair trade option is available, few viewers could watch *Black Gold* without hankering for a cup of joe.

In his own person and as the Marxian "guardian" of Ethiopian fair trade coffee, Tadesse Meskela is a profoundly sympathetic character. He is the kind of "underdog" Bruce Robbins finds in popular histories of commodities like sugar, tea, and tobacco: protagonists who overcome the villains

standing in the way of their democratizing dissemination. These protagonists are the commodities themselves. Robbins dubs these popular histories "effective capitalist propaganda" that tends "to leave out anything that
might make the consumer feel guilty," including the darker aspects of the
history of colonialism (2005, 455–56). Meskela-as-coffee is the protagonist
of what might seem a more critical kind of defetishization narrative, what
Michael Pollan calls "food that comes with a story" that "represents a not-
so-implicit challenge to every other product in the supermarket that dares
not narrate its path from farm to table" (2001). But the effects of what Pollan calls the "radical" act of commodity narration are arguably rather
limited. Commodity biographies with sympathetic underdog protagonists
(whether commodities, guardians, or their hybrids) may simply invert the
relationship between the commodity and the narrative of its production.
Whereas the conventional commodity keeps the story of its production
hidden,[19] here the commodity shouts its story to the world: The story becomes its friendly face, not its forgotten secret. As Peter Hitchcock writes,
"commodity desire is not more inevitable than responsibility—both desire and responsibility are produced within regimes of truth that are
irreconcilable—their contradictions are themselves an index of the world
system" (2003, 119).

In the era of postconsumerism, the "supermarket narratives" Pollan
dubbed radical are business as usual—marketing by other means, value-
added activity, in the updated idiom of enlightened globalization. Multinational corporations targeted by anti-globalization campaigns write their
own commodity biographies: Starbucks offers "stories" about coffee from
Ethiopia, Kenya, Sumatra, Java, and Guatemala. Commodity biographies
can generate a "'double' commodity fetishism" in which the story of production "reenchants" the consumer (Cook and Crang 1996, 132). I think
fondly of Tadesse Meskela every time I buy Ethiopian coffee. Pollan describes "the kinds of pleasure that are only deepened by knowing" (2006,
11), but it is important to spell out the social stakes of such pleasure. The
world of commodities becomes divided between those who tell their
stories and those who don't; this narrative differentiation between
things is entangled with a social differentiation between people. Some
consumers will pay a premium for products that dare to tell their stories, yet the effect of this shift in consumption (and narrative) habits
might be less a change in production conditions than a democratization
of connoisseurship: new stories, not new histories. For elite consumers,
some commodities have always been unfetishized, enveloped in an aura
of artisanal or otherwise exclusive production. In postconsumerism, such

values appeal to a broader demographic, who become connoisseurs of narrative too.

Postconsumerist commodity biographies proffer stories of uplift and beneficence toward producers that can mask consumers' own upwardly mobile desires. They appeal to affluent or aspiring consumers' desire to have only the best—valorizing hierarchies of taste that assume and obscure economic hierarchies. Even as viewers are soberly urged toward buying fair trade coffee, they are tantalizingly enticed through appeals to what Robbins calls "the connoisseur's pleasure in expert acquisition" (2005, 455). The message of *Black Gold* is this: If you want to drink the good stuff while doing good, buy fair trade coffee grown by friendly, hardworking Ethiopian coffee growers who want to build schools for their children and would prefer not to have to uproot their coffee plants to grow the illicit but lucrative stimulant *qat*. Valorizing connoisseurship (of the right kind of stimulants) as a means to self-affirmation and social status, the film argues not only *against* the injustice of the world coffee market but also *for* the unrivalled superiority of Ethiopian regional coffee varieties. *Black Gold* opens with the near-comical slurping and expectoration of professional coffee tasters in London, who proclaim the exceptional quality of Ethiopian Harar. *Black Gold*'s defetishizing narrative functions equally as product placement in the service of aspirational consumerism. That *Black Gold* is less reflexive about its relationship to consumerist desire than *Darwin's Nightmare* is evident in the fact that we don't see Tadessa Meskela, or anyone else, watching film.

Postconsumerism: New and Improved

This is not an argument against fair trade. Rather, it is a demur at a structure of feeling evoked by discourses of enlightened consumerism that promise to help the poor or save the planet by buying things: this emergent ethos I call postconsumerism. Its underlying assumption is homologous with that of commodity biography film: contemporary neoliberal globalization generates injustices that can be addressed by knowledge that inspires action. Knowledge about consumption can spur producers to demand their fair share, while knowledge about production can lead consumers to change their behavior, as well as broader terms of demand and modes of citizenship.

Yet the economies of knowledge and desire at work in these films suggest that globalization is not merely a problem of knowledge, or, rather, that knowledge alone is not the solution to globalization. The challenge is less to make things visible than to understand how they become legible and what can be read out of them. In *Black Gold, Life and Debt*, and *Darwin's Nightmare*, knowledge is not necessarily power for Ethiopian or Jamaican farmers, who are shown to be no match for the institutional power of the North enshrined in the World Trade Organization, World Bank, and International Monetary Fund; nor for the workers constellated around Nile perch in Mwanza, who are depicted as hopelessly ensnared in the "big system." On the consumption side, the problem of knowledge is more complex. Having watched *Darwin's Nightmare*, one couldn't begin to know what to do about Nile perch. But this problem is not new. Even as he implores them to be economical, Ishmael knows that his readers know that men shed blood to fill their lamps, in whose glow they turn page after page of *Moby-Dick*.

Such knowledge generates a predicament of complicitous consumption, in which consumers know about the harm caused by their actions but cannot (or will not) do anything to prevent it. American conservationist Aldo Leopold famously wrote in 1932, "When I go birding in my Ford, I am devastating an oil field, and reelecting an imperialist to get me rubber" (1991, 165). Leopold's awareness of complicitous consumption reveals an additional layer of reflexive complexity, however, in the less-often cited sentence preceding this one: "When I submit these thoughts to a printing press, I am helping to cut down the woods." "Have we not already compromised ourselves?" (165), Leopold asks as he articulates the unavoidability of consumption that generates some form of harm; more pointedly, he acknowledges that efforts to confront or disseminate awareness of the harm of complicitous consumption can themselves generate harm. A variant of this predicament hovers around commodity biography film: viewers' self-consciousness about themselves as consumers of film can both foster and obstruct the films' rerouting of consumer desire.

This predicament is evident in what may be the earliest use of film to narrate commodity biographies, Dziga Vertov's *Kino-Glaz* (Film-Eye, 1924), in which Vertov exploits a singular capacity of the medium—that it can be run backward—to narrate commodity biographies of beef and bread. Vertov begins with the commodity and traces back the story of its production: Running the film backward, he is able to turn back time, raise the dead, rejoin the country with the city, invert the laws of nature so that gravity lightens the load of labor, and offer second chances to consumers who make the mistake of not buying from the socialist collective. In his masterpiece *Man with a Movie Camera* (1929), Vertov submits his own film to an analysis of production, by juxtaposing filmed scenes, freeze-frames, and scenes of his wife, Yelizaveta Svilova, at work in the editing booth, with the same frames that viewers have seen now held in her hands or on the cutting table. His pedagogical aim to create critical viewers, aware of their spectatorship and the film's constructedness, is evident in scenes of a cinema hall filling with spectators. Yet Vertov is in love with his own technical prowess. The lesson on "the correct way to dive" in *Kino-Glaz*, which uses reverse and slow motion to gaze upon the beautiful bodies of competitive divers, inadvertently reveals that the magic of film technics has no necessary ideological valence, in terms of the production of knowledge and desire. Why else would the Young Pioneers of *Kino-Glaz* need to constantly post scolding signs, which double as diegetic, didactic film intertitles, urging comrades not to buy in the marketplace?

The recent commodity biography films examined in this chapter lack Vertov's anticapitalist utopianism and technical avant-gardism, although his love for the spectacle of mechanized production is recognizable in *Black Gold*'s scenes at the Illy coffee factory. Theirs, rather, is the ironic reflexivity of postconsumerism: Attempting to transform complicitous consumption into ethical consumerism, postconsumerism marks the moment when the self-consciousness about consumption and its external costs that shadows the entire history of capitalism becomes an ethos in itself. Here knowledge becomes a different kind of problem, with at least two manifestations.

The first is a conflation of knowledge and action, a "beautiful soul" version of complicitous consumption in which learning about a problem is confused with having done something about it, and reading for the planet is construed literally as a cognitive act with immediate effects in the world.[20] As Stacy Alaimo writes, "'awareness' is a comforting, mental, even ethereal state; it is magical thinking to protect us from harm" (2011, 19). The aesthetic satisfactions of watching a film are confused with the ethical satisfactions of changing the world; being the kind of person who watches such films is taken as a kind of moral distinction. The rerouting of consumption patterns that the films seek to effect is interrupted by the consumption of the film itself. The second manifestation of the problem of knowledge arises when consumers actually make changes in their behavior. As we saw in *Black Gold*, postconsumerism privileges the consumption of commodities that *have* biographies, whose stories of production are made legible. Such "knowledge" becomes the object of consumerist desire: the commodity's friendly face.

Postconsumerism offers solutions at the level of the imaginary while leaving structural inequalities, what Althusser called "real conditions of existence," largely unchanged, even if partially or fully revealed (2001, 1498). This is obviously true of the knowledge-mistaken-for-action manifestation of postconsumerism, perhaps less obvious but nonetheless true when consumers act upon what they know. There are several reasons why choosing a different product may have greater effects on the consumer's state of mind than on objective conditions of production. One problem is that commodities (and their corporate guardians) are not necessarily reliable narrators; many chickens labeled as such never see, let alone graze in, anything like the vast pastures evoked by "free range." A more complex set of problems inheres in postconsumerism's ambivalence about consumerism itself.

As I have shown, commodity biographies can effect a refetishization that risks inverting the conflation of knowledge and action. When stories about commodities become visible and value-added objects of desire, buyers of such products (and narratives) may forget they are consuming the commodities themselves. This version of postconsumerism elides the fact that it is still consumerism—an ethical predicament whose crudest approximation in caloric terms is the reluctant recognition that organic ice cream is just as fattening as industrial ice cream, and may even *be* industrial ice cream. This dynamic is particularly insidious in the case of "green consumerism" in which consumers take satisfaction in the reductions of carbon footprint or other environmental impacts effected by buying product X, without calculating the effect of buying product 0—that is, buying nothing. Again, it is not that the shift toward recycled, energy-efficient, or otherwise environmentally conscious products has no beneficial material effects on the disposition of nature; rather, postconsumerism risks overinflating these effects, which are outweighed by and confused for the consumer's affective state of self-satisfaction. Such confusions can lead consumers, in the name of conserving resources or otherwise mitigating ecological harm, to buy, and buy *more*. They also function as an atomizing withdrawal from the public/planetary demands of environmental citizenship: "The things-you-can-do-at-home-to-save-the-earth movement has become, in part, things-you-can-do-at-home-to-save-yourself" (Alaimo 2011, 92).[21]

Several challenges to the ideology of consumerism have emerged over the past two decades, driven by environmental or social justice concerns, bourgeois ennui (epitomized by discomfiture at post-9/11 exhortations to go shopping), and more or less involuntary recalibrations of consumer expectations and behavior in the wake of the 2007 collapse of the US housing market, the ensuing financial crisis, and the lopsided recovery. These challenges might reflect a desire to reorient public engagement in terms of acting upon collective values rather than individual desires and interests: *we* rather than *I*, citizenship rather than consumerism, democracy rather than the market as the arbiter of social life, in environmental philosopher Mark Sagoff's terms (1988). This polity could be extended beyond Sagoff's focus on the United States to include non-Americans or even nonhumans as "members of the community . . . as *one of us*" (8). Even before the emergence of an Anthropocene imaginary in the past decade, gestures toward human (and more-than-human) collectivity in the form of earth democracy or planetary citizenship have been articulated by thinkers including Peter Singer, Dipesh Chakrabarty, Deane Curtin, Michel Serres, Bruno Latour, Vandana Shiva, and Mary Louise Pratt. To the extent that postconsumerism intersects with these ideals of supranational and environmental citizenship, it consolidates and expands the geographic and ethical purview of consumerism understood as action on behalf of the collective—in Jean and John Comaroff's terms, consumption not merely as an individualist "index of self-worth," but "a material sensibility actively cultivated, for the common good" (2000, 294).[22]

Viewed more skeptically, the idea of the consumer-citizen conflates or collapses the rights and responsibilities of the citizen into a matter of consumer "choice" (or the ruse of choice).[23] In the United States, the legal corollary to consumerism's cooptation of citizenship is the 2010 *Citizens United v. Federal Elections Commission* Supreme Court decision, which cleared the way for corporate persons to become supercitizens whose influence on the democratic process is proportionate to their financial resources. Sagoff's assertion that "the deliberative rationality of democracy is just not like the interest-balancing rationality of markets" (1988, 97) may be true in abstraction, but it has been rendered nearly irrelevant in actually existing politics under neoliberalism and the derangements of Facebook feeds and "fake news."

In this view, the putative ethics of postconsumerism is not much more than consumerism repackaged and wrapped in the banner of ethics. Its promise of a more just capitalism might deliver just more capitalism. In its strongest form, postconsumerism disavows altogether the demands of environmental citizenship, green asceticism, or simple living: Not informed or mindful consumption but consumerism *an sich* is embraced as the solution to the injustices of globalization. Its variations are limited only by the market demographics and causes that can be brought into synergy. Consider, for example, (Product) Red, the marketing campaign spearheaded by rock star Bono, economist Jeffrey Sachs, and physician Paul Farmer, in which First World consumers buy high-end, celebrity-endorsed branded goods, gratified by the knowledge that a portion of the purchase price helps afflicted Africans through the Global Fund to Fight AIDS, Tuberculosis, and Malaria. At the 2006 (Product) Red launch at the World Economic Forum (complete with Hollywood-style red carpet), Bono barely suppressed a snicker while he read a litany about "doing good while looking good" (Richey 2007). Moral responsibility and conspicuous (rather than complicitous) consumption can apparently go hand in hand.

This version of postconsumerism's consumerism is particularly insidious in sidestepping questions about First World overconsumption and global inequality. Its valorization of affluence, aspiration, and social distinction through consumption depends upon and reinforces economic hierarchies, both locally and globally. Unlike *Black Gold*'s version of fair trade, (Product) Red's distant subalterns are construed as diseased supplicants rather than hale and hearty workers. It offers ethical cover to corporate-sponsored consumerism, rather than creating space for alternative models of production, or any awareness of production whatsoever. Rather than ask consumers to rethink their assumptions, it tells them to keep on doing what they are doing—with the added value of feeling good about it, in a branded, socially legible way. In this sense, postconsumerism's strongest form is also its weakest—only the latest version of capitalism seizing upon dissident impulses and turning them to its own ends.

The idea of consumption for the common good dates back at least to the abolitionist era. In the 1820s, the British East India Company sought competitive marketing advantage over sugar producers in the Western hemisphere by distributing sugar bowls with the inscription, "East India Sugar Not Made by Slaves" (Hollander 2003, 61).[24] A generation earlier, Olaudah Equiano had argued that making Africans into consumers of British goods would be more profitable than trading in their flesh. As with other slave narratives, his 1789 "Interesting Narrative," "Written by Himself," is a particularly charged instance of the erstwhile commodity telling its own story. In embracing Equiano's vision, European capitalism's shift from slave trade to "legitimate commerce" ushered in the era of high imperialism and the scramble for Africa, whose consequences of unfreedom remain legible in the postcolonial plight of Tanzania and Ethiopia documented in *Darwin's Nightmare* and *Black Gold*. Postconsumerism proffers an analogous faith that altruism and good intentions can mitigate the rapacity of capitalism, while displacing fundamental questions about sustainability and structural inequality that hover over every commodity circuit.

The next chapter takes up questions of consumption, production, and citizenship, as asked and answered "from below," by contemporary descendants of Africans whom Equiano hoped would become consumers of European goods. When Jonathan, the young painter in *Darwin's Nightmare*, declares himself a "citizen of the world," he echoes the appeals of young Africans for inclusion in "modern" life, as poignantly analyzed by James Ferguson in the case of two Guinean boys, Yaguine Koita and Fodé Tounkara, found frozen to death in 1999 in the landing gear of a plane in Brussels (2006, 155–56). The plane made at least three trips between Guinea and Belgium before the boys were discovered, along with a handwritten letter addressed to "Your Excellencies, members and officials of Europe." This petition appealed to Europe to mitigate suffering caused by war, disease, malnutrition, inadequate education, and so forth, by setting up "a great, effective organization for Africa so that it might make progress"; it urged that "you help us to study to become like you" (156). The ethical import of such appeals can be difficult to parse because they may sound like mere attempts to mimic the West or reprise what Europeans once branded as a civilizing mission. Ferguson asks, "how [are we] to deal with an object of alterity who refuses to be other? . . . What does one do with the cultural other who wants to 'become like you'?" (157). He argues convincingly that such appeals—acts of world-imagining from below—be understood as claims for social and political inclusion: "equal rights of membership in a spectacularly unequal global society" (174). What Ferguson argues about these boys' "failed crossing" from Africa to Europe at the turn of this century holds true for the hundreds of thousands of migrants who have braved the Mediterranean in the years since, some left to drift in boats stripped of their motors.

Still, such desires for inclusion can be too easily collapsed into an idiom of mimicry through consumption: We want to *buy* like you. After all, it was Marx who first asked us to imagine the commodity as "citizen" of a "whole world of commodities" (1977, 1:155). If humans become nothing more than producers, consumers, or even commodities, then commodities can become citizens, or *Citizens United*.[25]

What unites the variety of appeals, practices, and affective states that I have described as postconsumerism, and what distinguishes it from earlier forms of conscientized capitalism, can be understood by considering its analogous relationship to other "post-" discourses. Bono's snickers about "doing good while looking good" reveal some discomfort with, or self-consciousness about, the posture of irony that postconsumerism takes in relation to consumerism, even if that ironic stance can appear as earnestness, a sincere desire to do something other than business as usual. (Indeed, Bono epitomizes ironic earnestness.) That consumption has many modes and metabolisms will be evident to anyone who ponders the ironies in the label on a package of recycled toilet paper: "100% Recycled Paper, Minimum *80% Post-Consumer.*"[26] As with postmodernism, poststructuralism, or postcolonialism, the relationship between postconsumerism and its lexical and historical root is fraught. To say that consumerism (or modernism, structuralism, colonialism, or humanism) is under erasure is not to say that the slate has been wiped clean. Rather, the relation is one of disavowal, ironic distance, or ambivalent inheritance of what has come before. Perhaps even more than other "post-" discourses, postconsumerism retains its relationship to the earlier formation: It imagines itself as consumerism with a difference. New and improved.

CHAPTER 2

Hijacking the Imagination: How to Tell the Story of the Niger Delta

The promised lands of the 1960s no longer appear on
neoliberal maps of the future.

—MIKE DAVIS, *Planet of Slums*

Sweet Crude (2010), a documentary about movements for environmental justice in Nigeria, could be read as a commodity biography film. Its director, Sandy Cioffi, educates American consumers about environmental harm and political disenfranchisement caused by petroleum extraction in the Niger Delta, which can be described as Africa's largest wetland, one of the most polluted places on earth, or a historically important source of oil imports to the United States. (The film's title alludes to the desirable type of oil found in the Niger Delta: light, sweet crude is low in sulfur and generates a high yield of saleable products.) One scene in Cioffi's film features a thoughtful young activist-turned-militant describing why he joined the struggle. He speaks of his mother and her unattainable desires for things she's seen on TV: things "in America, what people regard as the civilized world." These desires might seem consonant with the consumerist idol worshiped on the cover of (and within) Ayi Kwei Armah's novel *The Beautyful Ones Are Not Yet Born*: a composite image of cars, large and small home appliances of convenience and entertainment, Coca-Cola and stiffer kinds of drink.[1] But the unattainable goods on TV, his mother's desires for which this man risks his life, are good roads: public goods and infrastructure, rather than what Armah dubs the "gleam" of consumer culture. In an eclipse of citizenship by consumerism different from that in Chapter 1, this woman has access to television but can only dream of a decent transportation network.

Longing for Infrastructure

Unattainable dreams and broken promises of infrastructure haunt many places in contemporary Africa, as was evident in the claims for inclusion as "citizens of the world" discussed in Chapter 1. In Kinshasa, Mike Davis notes in *Planet of Slums*, "basic public services" are popularly referred to as "memories" (2006, 155).[2] My thinking in this chapter unfolds in the shadow of James Ferguson's *Global Shadows: Africa in the Neoliberal World Order.* The ghosts of mid-twentieth-century promises of modernization that Ferguson examines are crucial for understanding Africa in the context of planetary environmental crisis. On one side, Ferguson sees African states withdrawing (territorially and ideologically) from the national project; on another, he finds Western intellectuals and neoliberal institutions abandoning developmentalist narratives. It is as if Africans are heard to say, we have never yet been modern, but at least we used to be on our way there.[3] Echoing the militant's mother's desire for good things accessible only on-screen, Ferguson writes that globalization "has brought an increasingly acute awareness of the semiotic and material goods of the global rich, even as economic pauperization and the loss of faith in the promises of development have made the chances of actually attaining such goods seem more remote than ever" (2006, 21). Unlike the late eighteenth-century moment when Olaudah Equiano envisioned an African consumer modernity, many of the excluded know what they are being excluded from. Acknowledging both the problematic assumptions that underwrote developmentalism and the disastrous policies undertaken in its name, Ferguson nonetheless insists that the *promise* of inclusion and equality was ethically and politically significant, as is its present abandonment.

Africans' desires for access to "economic and institutional conditions that they themselves regard as modern" (Ferguson 2006, 167) raise troubling questions—perhaps unanswerable, but in need of an answer—about the capacity of the planet, let alone politics, to realize such claims without a radical reorganization of the order of things. The teleology underwriting those forsaken narratives of development is *unsustainable*, in every sense. Desires for inclusion in modernity are not merely "consumerist" desires, but also desires for consumption and for the infrastructural prerogatives of citizenship. They complicate and implicate the predicament of complicitous consumption among the affluent, articulated in Chapter 1. They are something like preconsumerism, or pre-postconsumerism: a desire for the capacity to aspire, to adapt Arjun Appadurai's formulation (2004). The ethical force of Ferguson's analysis is to create a distinction between rightly discredited, self-serving Eurocentric progress narratives, on the one hand, and Africans' just desires for inclusion and a better life, on the other. Whether in the name of conservation, population control, or climate change mitigation, other people's desires for development have too often been held hostage to First World overconsumption—a pernicious Malthusianism with an inglorious history.[4]

An anecdote from the introduction to Ferguson's *Global Shadows* intimates how tricky these questions can be. Ferguson stages an epiphany about the ethical and political import of desires for development by recalling shifts in his assessment of Sesotho architecture during a 1983 fieldwork stint in Lesotho. Initially, he admired how the "old-style" Sesotho house he rented was warm in winter, cool in summer, and built inexpensively with local labor and materials. However, after talking with a Basotho man building a "European-style" house, Ferguson reconsidered his "appreciation" for the environmental suitability and sustainability of stone and thatch. Asking the young Ferguson what kind of house *his* father had, the man explained that a cement, steel-roofed house would be "modern," a virtue that apparently outweighed its considerable expense and discomfort. Can one recognize this man's desire as a "powerful claim to a chance for transformed conditions of life," as Ferguson urges, but still wonder about the losses and attendant consequences involved in such transformations (2006, 18–19)? When such desires are expressed as mimicry—"we want to be like you" (or your dad)—they might prompt consideration of which aspects of "modern" life are suitable for replication on a global scale, and which could be radically rethought.

The broken dreams to which Ferguson calls attention are particularly jarring in a site of resource extraction like the Niger Delta, where, as geographer Michael Watts writes, "one of the horrors . . . is that the ultra-modernity of oil sits cheek by jowl with the most unimaginable poverty. Around the massive Escravos oil installation with its barbed wire fences, its security forces, and its comfortable houses are nestled shacks, broken-down canoes, and children who will be lucky to reach adulthood" (Watts 2008, 44). In 2001, Watts noted that Shell—the largest and oldest of the multinationals operating in the Niger Delta—made $200 million in profits *annually* in Nigeria for forty years but had during that time invested

only $2 million *total* in local communities, building one road and award-
ing a hundred scholarships (2001, 198). Such statistics indicate why infrastructural longings for public goods and good roads remain unfulfilled;
neither corporate profits nor state revenues from oil extraction have ben-
efitted communities living amidst the drilling.

As with other commodity biography films, *Sweet Crude* uses its subjects'
consumption of media to invite reflexive solidarity between producers and
consumers, as well as with communities displaced and undermined by resource extraction. Likewise, it links consumption to citizenship: The predicament of complicitous consumption in the United States is juxtaposed
with Nigerians' thwarted aspirations for the infrastructural and political
prerogatives of postcolonial citizenship. Oil poses a particular challenge
for commodity biography, however, because it seems to have been always-
already defetishized. When "no blood for oil" becomes a bumper sticker,
the distant complaint of having received no roads for oil becomes difficult
to hear. Everyone knows that "dependence on foreign oil" in the United
States has profound costs, but those costs are tabulated mostly in the currency of American lives and treasure, whether military operations deemed
necessary to secure oil (sometimes dubbed "our" oil), price fluctuations at
the pump resulting from "instability" abroad, or, after 9/11, vulnerability
"over here" to blowback from oil-fueled despotism "over there." Against
such ethnocentric, provincial understandings of the world made by oil, this
chapter considers the Niger Delta as a site of both resource extraction and
world-imagining, where other costs and forms of violence are at stake.

Since Nigerian independence in 1960, the federal government has mo-
nopolized the monetary benefits of oil extraction while Niger Delta communities have borne the burdens.[5] These burdens include environmental
degradation, loss of farming and fishing livelihoods, and violence at the
hands of private security teams, the Nigerian military, and militant groups.[6]
The Nigerian state grants concessions to oil multinationals, with which it
operates in joint partnership. This legal/fiscal arrangement has also entailed cooperation in repression. A military dictatorship between 1966–79
and 1983–98, the Nigerian state has mobilized security forces (including
the ruthless "Joint Task Force") in the Niger Delta to protect oil installations and "smooth" their operations.[7] The contradictory outcomes of
underdevelopment—wealth for some, poverty for others—are concentrated
within this spectacular site. The literal and metaphorical substrate of wealth
in a hydrocarbon-fueled global economy, oil generates local degradation,
dispossession, and repression as it is unearthed and piped away for consumption elsewhere.

These dynamics find lyrical expression in Ogaga Ifowodo's long poem *The Oil Lamp* (2005), which opens in the Niger Delta in the "fourteenth month of the fuel crunch" (2). In this scene of local scarcity amidst inaccessible plenty, pipelines carry fuel "away/from rotting dugouts and thatched huts/ . . . to feed factories and the chain of ease/ . . . to make fortunes for faceless traders/in markets without stalls or hand-made goods" (4). This geography of resource extraction seems at first familiar: natural wealth expropriated to build what Frantz Fanon called "towers of opulence" in other lands (1968, 101). Yet at the site of extraction, one speaker in the poem compares his "shack in the swamp" with "oil staff estates" nearby; the contrast with the "carpet lawns, the quiet/order of the place, shamed me to the bone," he admits (Ifowodo 2005, 55). Just beyond the oil enclave, underdevelopment appears as *de*-development: development begun and turned backwards. Electricity—or *"eletiriki"*—is a "dream" that "burned bright/for forty years, powered by a plant, till the tree drilled its last barrel" (3). Now it's a "dimmed promise": the "electric Cyclops blinked, moved/to another well in another place/to guard a fresh promise of light" (3).

The Oil Lamp rearranges the plot of development. Infrastructural promises (with the intimation of a world-creating fiat: Let there be light) are grounded upon the noncyclical, nonrenewable flow and ebb of oil underfoot. When wells run dry, development is undone. This alternative plot of development can be traced through shifting significations of the eponymous "oil lamp." At the poem's beginning, it is a low-tech mode of domestic illumination made obsolete "by the flick of a switch" (2005, 3); at the end, it names the "red tongues" of "the gas-flaring stack whose awful mouth spits fire/without cease" (50); in between, an oil lamp is one possible cause of a conflagration at a leaking pipeline. The fat of human bodies consumed in that fire, "lighting up the sky" (8), are the oil lamp's most gruesome instantiation.

The book's first section, titled "Jese," depicts a devastating pipeline fire in October 1998 in the rural village of Jese (or Jesse) outside of the Delta State city of Warri, which claimed approximately one thousand lives. Some of the victims were gathered near a leaking pipe manifold when the oil ignited; during a local "fuel crunch," the opportunity to salvage petrol proved irresistible. The two-week-long fire still burning, the Niger Delta NGO Environmental Rights Action released a field report (Ola and Eighemhenrio 1998) that raised questions similar to those in Ifowodo's poem: what sparked the blaze? What factors—poverty, local fuel shortage, corporate neglect of infrastructure, corruption, the unaccountability of military rule—were its conditions of possibility? Relating several incompatible accounts of how the fire started, *The Oil Lamp* insists upon one decades-long narrative of underdevelopment as explanation: "This was how the damage was done" (Ifowodo 2005, 4). *Damage* denotes the conditions that created the fire, not the fire itself; this notion of damage echoes the multifaceted aspect of what Watts (1999, 2001) calls "petro-violence": the ecological, economic, social, and political modes of violence associated with oil extraction. Petro-violence, I argue, is a form of environmental harm whose subjects, objects, and instruments are multiple and multivalent, human and nonhuman.

In *The Oil Lamp*, Ifowodo contemplates how to tell the tale of Jese. In this chapter, I consider how to tell the story of the Niger Delta and the role of petro-violence in its narratives of development. "Nigerian thinking on the Niger Delta seems to start the story with 'secondly,'" argues Chimamanda Ngozi Adichie. She cites Palestinian Mourid Barghouti: "It is easy to blur the truth with a simple linguistic trick: start your story from secondly. Start your story with 'secondly' and the arrows of the red Indians are the original criminals and not the white man's guns" (2008, 102). Like Ifowodo, Adichie challenges the erasure of foundational acts of violence: How was the damage done? Where do narratives of injustice begin? How far upstream does one find the source? What itineraries of transnational imagining enable a Nigerian's citation of a Palestinian's invocation of the dispossession of Native Americans? To extend these questions to the concerns of this chapter, what narrative modes and cultural forms are adequate to the Niger Delta, its history and possible futures, and its links to other places, other deltas?

The Niger Delta flashes up in US media consciousness at moments of danger like the 2010 BP oil spill, when the corporate disaster in the Gulf of Mexico was measured against the environmental harm inflicted in the Niger Delta every day for half a century.[8] As with Hurricane Katrina five years earlier, the sinking of the *Deepwater Horizon* immersed Mississippi Delta communities, livelihoods, and ecosystems in a toxic mess, with the slowness of the oil's drift, rather than the speed of water's rise, the source of devastation. The (mostly) unspoken refrain was: *Things like this do not happen here.* Technological knowhow, governmental regulation, and an unexamined sense of American invulnerability turned out to be ineffective or illusory bulwarks against disaster of the sort that is business as usual in places like the Niger Delta. Thousands of citizens in the path of Hurricane Katrina found themselves—some suddenly, some once again—longing for infrastructure.

The BP spill created an opportunity to imagine between deltas, Niger and Mississippi. This moment of international visibility differed from that in November 1995, when writer-activist Ken Saro-Wiwa was hanged by the Nigerian military regime under General Sani Abacha. As Saro-Wiwa sought international support for the Ogoni struggle against what he dubbed the "slick alliance" of Shell Oil and the Nigerian state, one challenge he faced was "prejudicial failures of geographical imagining. In American intellectual and media terms, a region like Ogoniland is almost completely unimaginable," Rob Nixon wrote in 2005 (246). The BP spill offered a looking-glass view of American vulnerability to environmental harm and thereby breached this quarantine of the imagination. How to expand this imaginative conjuncture, when perceived differences between "us" and "them" begin to dissolve in the deltas' troubled waters? What if Nigeria, rather than the Middle East, became the face of "foreign oil" in the United States? How does the story of the Niger Delta become legible on the other side of what Ifowodo calls the "chain of ease"? Ifowodo's multivalent metaphor joins freedom with constraint: The chain of ease entails both the privilege of better living through petrochemistry and the systemic predicament of being tethered to the grid, unable to imagine alternatives to hydrocarbon-fueled modernity and its unsustainable costs, too often paid by others. It links consumers and producers, beneficiaries and victims, Apple stores and Foxconn factories (or e-waste dumps).

This chapter considers expansive, hospitable forms of world-imagining from the vantage of the Niger Delta.[9] In the BP spill, the chemical dispersants (and media bans) that kept oil slicks under the surface, out of sight, are but one instance of regimes of spectacle and visibility that enable the disregard of environmental harm. This disregard involves global structures of inequality, traffic lines of power, and myriad forms of violence (physical, ecological, economic, epistemological) that generally remain difficult to fathom, kept out of sight. The challenge, however, is not merely to make such relationships visible, but also legible: apprehensible and available to critical reflection and action.[10] One scopic paradox of the *Deepwater Horizon* blowout was that the unprecedented ability to watch on YouTube the uncontrolled flow of oil from the ocean depths did not equate with, and likely obstructed, a capacity to fathom the forms of harm being done. And in the Niger Delta, where riverine communities have been living for more than half a century in the shadow of petroleum extraction, evidence of environmental harm is all-too-visible in the eternal glow of gas flares and the unnatural sheen of polluted fields and creeks. What kind of imagining, then, can reach across vast geographical and experiential distances, and

through the spectacle of ecodisaster, in order to register meaningfully—
to make imaginable—other modes of petro-violence that encompass the
Nigerian state, multinational oil companies, and consumers at gas pumps
far away? And against such devastation, how do literary and cultural texts
about the Niger Delta participate in unimagining and reimagining regional, national, and planetary communities?

This chapter continues the discussion of citizens and consumers begun
in Chapter 1. In order to establish how the Niger Delta invokes and inter-
rupts plots of development, narratives of modernity, and models of citizenship, I turn to political theory and political ecology for their accounts
of relations among nature and nation, state and citizen, corporation and
body politic. Rather than look to social science for concepts to "apply" to
literary and visual texts, however, I assume a continuity, or at least overlapping terrain, between cultural production and political theory. This approach involves a twofold gesture: not only teasing out the conceptual
work done by poetry, prose fiction, photographs, and film, but also pursuing the most imaginatively suggestive—even magical—aspects of theories
of nation, state, and citizenship. The point is to draw out an eco/material
dimension within literary notions of cultural imagining, and a literary/
imaginative dimension in sociopolitical analysis: how can these disciplinary modes complement each other in the task of imagining environmental
community? Reading across genre and discipline, this chapter is alert to
how texts invite, and also stage within themselves, scenes of reading for
the planet, and how such readings are constrained by structural inequalities that shape the flow of oil, the disposition of nature, the movement of
the imagination, and the circulation of texts: in other words, the conjunc-
tures and disjunctures of petro-capitalism's and print capitalism's geographies of production and consumption.

Unimagining and Reimagining Community

The Nigerian example confirms and challenges some longstanding assumptions in literary studies about how cultural production fosters national
imagining. Because of the importance he placed on novels and newspa-
pers as platforms for imagining connections among distant strangers who
are also compatriots, Benedict Anderson's concept of the nation as "imagined
community" has been influential among literary critics. In Nigeria, the
first barrel of oil was exported from Port Harcourt two years before independence in 1960. 1958 was also a seminal moment in Nigeria's literary
exports, with the publication in London of Chinua Achebe's *Things Fall*

Apart. Nigeria's simultaneous entry into global print and petro-capitalisms on the eve of independence was coincidental, but the imbrication of oil and literature in national imagining and international circulation has continued for decades. The Nigerian novel boom followed the contours of the oil boom and bust: the number of new novels published each year increased steadily through the 1960s and 1970s, with explosive growth and wild fluctuations between 1979 and 1988. The crash of the global oil market and the Nigerian economy in the 1980s was followed by a significant decline in the number of Nigerian novels published domestically and abroad (Griswold 2000, 37–38). This overlap in the trajectories of petroleum and publishing reveals the extent to which national imagining has been fueled by petroleum from the beginning. However, because the Niger Delta has been politically marginal yet economically indispensable to the Nigerian national project, this process is better understood as an *unimagining* of national community.

Analyzing one of postcolonial Africa's most robust national literatures in terms of *unimagining* (rather than imagining) community helps to underscore and historicize contradictions in the nexus of petroleum and publishing.[11] These contradictions are at the heart of what I have called a political ecology of Nigerian literature—drawing on political ecology's concern with how "convergences of culture, power, and political economy" inform conflicts over "defining, controlling, and managing nature" and natural resources (Peluso and Watts 2001, 25)—in order to think anew about literary questions of form, intertextuality, and circulation.[12] A political ecology of literature is concerned not only with understanding literature *as if* it were a commodifiable resource like petroleum or palm oil, but also with material relationships between literary production and resource conflicts. Since Saro-Wiwa's execution, conflicts over oil have catalyzed what Watts calls an "unraveling—or unimagining" of national community (2008, 47). In both literary production and political theory, the sense of simultaneous experience and conviviality among strangers that Anderson sees the novel and newspaper as fostering are replaced by disjointed temporalities, contempt for all-too-familiar ethnic others, and disillusion with a shared national project: unimagining.

I use *unimagining* in two other ways, to name failures of the imagination that this book takes as a point of departure, rather than an end to thought. Notice that both Watts and Nixon, in remarks cited earlier, describe the Niger Delta as "unimaginable." As an adjective, *unimaginable* describes a state that cannot be described. But such passive descriptions, I argue, involve *acts* of unimagining: How do places like the Niger Delta *become* unimaginable? These imaginative failures and historical elisions tend to separate readers of world literature from those most threatened by environmental crisis. In this sense, *unimagining* is related to processes of underdevelopment that produce wealth for some, poverty for others. The material processes of "de-development" made legible in Ifowodo's *The Oil Lamp* have a cognitive counterpart in acts of unimagining. This third sense of unimagining (underimagining?) is a transitive process of unmaking both analogous to underdevelopment and produced with it: histories of immiseration are elided in imagining people as eternally poor and backward.[13]

This book seeks out imaginative modes that can grasp the elusive workings of unimagining: acts of un-unimagining, which, for the sake of simplicity and elegance, I will call *reimagining*. One activist in *Sweet Crude* insists cannily that before the oil companies arrived, "*We were not poor*," calling out habits of underimagining that understand poverty as a catalyst for development rather than a result of underdevelopment. Texts like *Sweet Crude* and *The Oil Lamp* invite a reimagining of these relations, as Niger Delta inhabitants link the devastation before them with the "chain of ease" at the pipeline's other end. However, they also foreground a difficulty in such gestures of world imagining, from above and below: the tendency of oil to capture the imagination. More precisely, the Niger Delta context reveals how oil holds the imagination captive, by kidnapping or hijacking it. Oil's spectacular aspects get in the way of understanding its ontology and political ecology, in regional, national, and planetary terms. This hijacking of the imagination is another mode of petro-violence.

Hijacking is not just a metaphor in a Niger Delta context, where the face of resistance to the slick alliance is not only Saro-Wiwa and his constitutional protest but the masked militant and his ransom demands for oil company personnel held hostage. Given the ways that oil hijacks the imagination, how can the story of the Niger Delta be told?

Up the Creeks: Frantz Fanon in the Niger Delta?

Curse of the Black Gold: Fifty Years of Oil in the Niger Delta (2008) is a coffee-table book that juxtaposes photographs by Ed Kashi with an introductory essay by Michael Watts and essays, poems, and interviews by writers, activists, and militants in the Niger Delta. My take on this book is inseparable from the scene where I first read it, a course on postcolonial theory I taught at the University of Michigan in 2009. Instead of subsuming this shared pedagogical experience into a univocal scholarly argument (a common practice when writing about texts we teach), I reflect upon scenes of my class reading the interplay of word and image in this book. How do the modes of planetary citizenship that *Curse of the Black Gold* fosters for its readers intersect with the modes of postcolonial citizenship (including violence-as-citizenship) it documents among its subjects?

Reading *Curse of the Black Gold* on a postcolonial theory syllabus provoked the question of how contemporary struggles for environmental justice can be understood in relation to mid-twentieth-century anticolonial struggles for national liberation. In other words, what would Frantz Fanon say about the Niger Delta? One might posit Kashi and Watts as latter-day Jean-Paul Sartres or Gillo Pontecorvos (of *The Battle of Algiers* fame), deploying their cultural capital to ensure that the story of petro-violence in the Niger Delta is told—stylishly, at that—to its unwitting beneficiaries and accomplices. *Curse of the Black Gold* invites readers to reimagine the unimaginable and their relationship to it.

Teaching *Curse of the Black Gold*, I searched for an adequate response to my students' visceral sense of complicity, despair, and anger at recognizing their implication in a global system that distributes environmental benefits and burdens unevenly. The book depicts the presence of Shell and other multinationals (including ExxonMobil, Chevron, Total, Elf, and Agip) woven into the fabric of everyday life. Kashi's photograph of the displaced community of Finima, living in the shadow of an ExxonMobil gas plant, offers a visual approximation of Ifowodo's shame-inducing contrast between "shacks in the swamp" and the built environment of oil extraction (see Figure 4). The roundness of the oil tanks (so massive they exceed the frame) is echoed in the child's toy, a metal ring perhaps salvaged from the materiel of petroleum extraction. The verticality of the gas flare stack in the background repeats in the post in the foreground, reminiscent of the kind of pole that might anchor telephone lines or electrical wires in a nearly forgotten dream of infrastructure. An apt caption for the photo might be Jamaica Kincaid's hypothesis, "perhaps every good thing that stands before us comes at a great cost to someone else" (1999, 152).

Gas flaring—burning off natural gas produced in drilling crude oil—is a harmful practice in the Niger Delta with local and planetary repercussions. Because it generates extreme heat, tremendous noise, acid rain, and numerous adverse effects on organisms and ecosystems, flaring is banned or tightly regulated in most places where oil is drilled, notable exceptions being Russia and North Dakota, where flaring is visible from space.[14] In the Niger Delta, "some children have never known a dark night though they have no electricity," observed environmentalist Nick Ashton-Jones after a 1993 visit (Rowell 1995, 21). This observation reflects multilayered

Figure 4. With the Mobil Exxon Gas plant looming in the background, the displaced people of Finima lead daily lives that move at a slow pace. Bonny Island, Nigeria, 2006. Ed Kashi/VII.

infrastructural neglect: one alternative to flaring natural gas would be to capture and use it for energy needs like electrification of local communities. Instead, in an act of improvisatory adaptation to spectacular petroviolence, women in several of Kashi's most striking photographs set trays of tapioca to bake in the heat of blazing flares; these images span the cover of Ifowodo's *The Oil Lamp*.

At a planetary scale, flaring contributes to global warming. In 1995, flaring in Nigeria was estimated to be the largest single source of greenhouse gas emissions in the world (World Bank 1995, 58). "Operation Climate Change" was a direct action campaign launched in December 1998 by the Ijaw Youth Movement in the Niger Delta; its Kaiama Declaration linked local struggles for "freedom, self-determination, and ecological justice" to the "the destructive effects of climate change principally from the burning of fossil fuel" (quoted in Ukeje 2001, 29). Although Nigeria's High Court ruled in 2005 that flaring violated constitutional rights to life and dignity, the practice has continued and was even inadvertently encouraged because subsequent law designated the financial penalty a "charge," rather than a "fine": to oil multinationals, flaring is not merely the cost of doing business; it's also been tax-deductible, a boost to the bottom line (Kazeem 2018).

This accounting trick epitomizes how the true costs of oil are externalized to faraway places and to the future. "The lure of oil is its cheapness,"
writes Nnimo Bassey in *Curse of the Black Gold*; "It is cheap partly because
oil's costs of extraction . . . are not reflected in the price at the pump. . . .
Poor people continue to subsidize the costs of crude oil through the losses
they suffer in environmental services, quality of life, and extreme environmental degradation" (2008, 90). The director of Environmental Rights
Action/Friends of the Earth in Benin City, Bassey insists upon factoring
in these forms of harm. Even when gasoline prices are high, these costs
remain illegible in price fluctuations that consumers have been trained to
interpret in terms of distant military conflicts or natural disasters that disrupt supply, rather than the business-as-usual costs of consumer demand.
Working against this incomplete defetishization, Bassey rejoins prices at
the pump to costs borne *every day* by "someone else": communities and ecosystems at sites of extraction. Making environmental harm legible as a
form of violence, Bassey reimagines these underimagined geographies of
production and consumption: He reads for the planet.

For my students, this counter-accounting of the cost of oil elicited
powerful reactions; they saw how their own lives were subsidized by the
suffering of others whom they will never meet. This response was partly
the familiar (and often unhelpful) precipitate of a postcolonial pedagogy:
a mostly white, middle-class, liberal guilt, perhaps the inverse of the subaltern shame described in Ifowodo's poem. Yet the location of our scene of
reading complicated this reflex response. My University of Michigan
students were reimagining the Niger Delta while also grappling with the
prospective death of Detroit, which also paid a steep price for the phantasmagoric cheapness of oil. As the Big Three automakers faced bank-
ruptcy in early 2009, the national debate on the federal bailout of Chrys-
ler and General Motors felt urgent in our classroom. Familiar binaries like
consumers vs. producers, First World vs. Third World, affluence vs. abjection, were destabilized for students with relatives or family friends who
had lost auto industry jobs. Even for those personally unaffected by job
losses, the specter of abandoned neighborhoods in Detroit, and shuttered
storefronts, crumbling infrastructure, and grim employment prospects
elsewhere in the state, pointed toward a different kind of petro-violence.
Students contemplated the geographically remote, too often invisible environmental and sociopolitical costs of a hydrocarbon economy and its unsustainable illusion of unlimited cheap energy. But they also confronted
the local and all-too-real pain of deindustrialization, a late phase in the
narrative of development that is equally difficult to perceive for those still

waiting for "modernity" (in Ferguson's sense) to get underway. Though with differences in kind and degree, here too infrastructure and the prerogatives of citizenship threaten to migrate to the realm of memory, so that everyone is remembering modernity's lost promise—whether from the late phase of a progress narrative run its course into rust and decline, or still awaiting an abandoned future that has never yet arrived.

Many of my postcolonial theory students confessed that they didn't get what Fanon was talking about in *The Wretched of the Earth*—they couldn't accept the necessity of revolutionary violence—until they encountered *Curse of the Black Gold*. The visual force of Kashi's photographs had much to do with these responses, but the experience of *looking* at images also sparked their *rereading* of texts. "Fanon's anger became my anger," one student wrote in response to the Niger Delta book (Braun 2009). This radicalization took me by surprise and posed challenges of its own. As they grappled with revolutionary violence and ecocide in the Niger Delta, some students began to imagine answering Fanon's call, nearly sixty years after his death. Yet I was horrified to recognize, fourteen years after the execution of Ken Saro-Wiwa, that the contemporary situation of the Niger Delta could be understood as an unforeseen consequence of Saro-Wiwa's campaign for environmental self-determination.

Saro-Wiwa had fought *for* more political autonomy, revenue-sharing, and community development for those living amidst the drilling, and *against* the petro-violence of the state and oil companies directed against local communities and ecosystems. In the Ogoni Bill of Rights (1990), Saro-Wiwa demanded "political control of Ogoni affairs by Ogoni people, the right to the control and use of a fair proportion of Ogoni economic resources for Ogoni development, adequate and direct representation . . . in all Nigerian national institutions . . . and the right to protect the Ogoni environment and ecology from further degradation" (Saro-Wiwa 1992, 95). After Saro-Wiwa's execution in 1995, oil companies gradually embraced a rhetoric of corporate social responsibility and community development. Both the companies and the federal government began to send a greater share of petro-naira to the region through community organizations, newly created states in the Nigerian federation, and new "Local Government Areas" organized around ethnicity.[15] With increased revenue sharing and enhanced avenues for political representation, these fiscal and political developments seemingly achieved some of Saro-Wiwa's objectives.

However, this decentralization of political authority and oil money did not result in a "livable Niger Delta, a just Nigeria," as Ogaga Ifowodo dreams in his dedication of *The Oil Lamp* (2005). Instead, corruption was localized, with Niger Delta ethnic minorities getting in on the game that had been the purview of Nigeria's ethnic majorities. The early 2000s also saw an explosion—a perverse "democratization" (Watts 2008, 46)—of violence. In the Niger Delta's traditionally gerontocratic societies, ethnic "youth" organizations (their membership ranging in age from late teens to early forties) evolved from their origins in sponsoring cultural practices like age group masquerading to become armed militias variously antagonistic toward or complicit with oil companies.[16] With the region awash in money and mired in poverty, violence was no longer top-down, the monopoly of the state and oil multinationals. Instead it became pervasive, capillary, interethnic and intra-ethnic, all against all—as if refurbishing for the petroleum economy Chinua Achebe's invocation in *Things Fall Apart* of an Igbo proverb from the palm economy that preceded petroleum: "If one finger brought oil it soiled the others" (1958, 89). This redistribution of corruption and corruption of redistribution are a far cry from the kind of polity that a Bill of Rights calls into being. To read the early twenty-first-century nightmare of the Niger Delta as the "success" of Saro-Wiwa's struggle may be perverse, but this trajectory points toward some unintended consequences of movements for environmental justice and national liberation, whether violent or nonviolent. Environmentalism, like environmental harm, can have unforeseen effects downstream, or in tidal creeks like those of the Niger Delta: multiple small streams where the current flows both ways but are difficult to see from afar. Some of the legal and fiscal developments in Nigeria since Saro-Wiwa may sound like progress, but in *Curse of the Black Gold* they look like apocalypse.

With the vivid photos and frank testimony of *Curse of the Black Gold* capturing their imaginations, my students felt the urgency of Fanon's message, but the geography of exploitation constellated around the Niger Delta is not the Manichean "world cut in two" that Fanon saw as the spur to anticolonial struggle ([1961] 1968, 37). The explosion of violence in the creeks is *not* the disciplined, revolutionary, nation-forging violence that Fanon theorized in *The Wretched of the Earth* as the only adequately dialectical response to colonial violence, I unexpectedly found myself arguing to my students.[17] They were responding to the visual and verbal rhetorics of *Curse of the Black Gold*, which evoke an almost anachronous sense of revolutionary heroism. Like oil, stylized violence hijacks the imagination. The book opens with Kashi's harrowing account of being detained by the Nigerian military while trying to make contact with the Movement for the Emancipation of the Niger Delta (MEND), a high-profile yet mysterious militant group that began armed operations against oil installations in 2006. Kashi's photographs of MEND militants are a riot of gorgeous local color, portraits of young fighters with guns. Watts worried that the book could be construed as a "promo for MEND," in a hoary tradition of Third World radicalism.[18] His essay evokes the mystique of revolutionary violence; about developments in the Niger Delta since Saro-Wiwa, Watts quips: "The pipe-smoking writer equipped with the power of the pen has now been replaced by the figure of the masked militant armed with the ubiquitous Kalashnikov, the typewriter of the illiterate" (2008, 37). *Curse of the Black Gold* updates in living color the revolutionary stylistics of *The Battle of Algiers*. The bespectacled intellectual Ben M'Hidi (a Fanonesque theorist of Algerian revolution) is replaced by the politicized thug Ali la Pointe; the quaint constitutionalism of Saro-Wiwa's Ogoni Bill of Rights is replaced by MEND's assaults on oil installations and kidnapping of Nigerian soldiers and oil company expatriates.

Yet the mystique of revolutionary heroism in *Curse of the Black Gold* is complicated in a statement attributed to a MEND spokesman that recurs throughout the book: "We are not communists or even revolutionaries. Just a bunch of extremely bitter men" (Watts 2008, 38).[19] This distinction between revolutionary politics and resigned nihilism is remarkable not least because the statement is effectively an antimanifesto: a first-person disavowal of insurgency and elision of radical politics articulated by the putative spokesman of a militant group. Another curious thing is the spokesman, one Jomo Gbomo, an elusive creature of the digital age. He began releasing communiqués in 2005 and exchanged emails with several journalists, but never met them face-to-face or on camera. In a chilling sequence that exposes the US mainstream media's reductive treatment of the Niger Delta after 9/11, Cioffi's *Sweet Crude* suggests that "Jomo Gbomo" tells the West what it wants to hear, rendering inaudible alternative MEND voices willing to face the camera without a mask, whether cloth or electronic.[20] Somehow Jomo Gbomo's disavowal of a radical political agenda made him an even more compelling figure for the Bush-era media fear machine: beware this "bunch of bitter men" with bombs. *Curse of the Black Gold* reproduces edgy emails between Jomo Gbomo and Ed Kashi, who comments, "Communiqués from Jomo continue to this day, albeit with a slightly slicker tone and voice. My assumption is that whoever Jomo is doesn't matter at this point. The struggle that MEND represents has grown beyond one person and will continue its fight until real change occurs in the Niger Delta" (Kashi 2008, 27). Kashi's observation about the mystery surrounding Jomo Gbomo brings to mind the hydralike, cellular structure of militant organizations anatomized by Colonel Mathieu in

The Battle of Algiers. Indeed, an anachronous Cold War anxiety haunts Jomo Gbomo's "bitter men" statement: Who bothers nowadays to deny being a communist?[21]

The communists/revolutionaries vs. bitter men statement is also remarkable because it expresses a controversy in Nigeria about the modes and motives of Niger Delta militancy: Is it an expression of "legitimate" politics and community activism, or self-interested criminality? Writing about generational conflicts in the Niger Delta, Ijaw youth leader Felix Tuodolo notes a "Janus faced" tendency: "One face points toward a thickening of civil society, the reform of stifling forms of customary rule, and the struggle for a new and true federalism. The other looks toward a world of disorder and violence" (2008, 115). Ledum Mitee, president of the Movement for the Survival of the Ogoni People (or MOSOP, the organization Saro-Wiwa founded and led until his death), also distinguishes between legitimate politics and criminality. Nonetheless, Mitee acknowledges that embracing violence can yield political recognition: "once you can carry a gun, you become the person that the government engages" (2008, 164).[22] Guns speak louder than pens, even if the conventional wisdom about Saro-Wiwa holds that it was his rhetorical capacity to mobilize Ogoni petition and constitutional protest, rather than the "trumped-up" charges of instigating murder, that necessitated his execution.

Jomo Gbomo's statement, then, is congruous with characterizations of Niger Delta militancy as entrepreneurial criminality rather than politics on behalf of a constituency: this account casts Ali la Pointe of *The Battle of Algiers* not as thug-turned-revolutionary but just a plain old thug.[23] Activists like Tuodolo and Mitee draw such distinctions to highlight their own organizations' political legitimacy, but Jomo Gbomo's antimanifesto was useful to the Nigerian state and the multinationals because it validates their claims about the conflict. (Some activists in *Sweet Crude* suggest that "Jomo Gbomo" is an agent of the Nigerian state or even the CIA.) Oil companies invoke the specter of criminality to explain away the environmental harm of oil extraction, which they attribute to sabotage and "bunkering" (unauthorized tapping of pipelines, for local use or sale on the black market) rather than what Mike Davis (1998) would call the "ordinary disaster"[24] of their own, largely unregulated, normal operations. The state has used the specter of criminality to justify repression. When Nigerian security forces razed the Ijaw village of Odi in November 1999 and massacred two thousand people, a spokesman explained, "government, by this act, has not violated any internationally acceptable human rights provisions as practiced elsewhere in the world. . . . How can it be said that a carefully planned and

cautiously executed exercise to rid the society of criminals is a violation of
human rights?" (quoted in Ukeje 2001, 33).[25] Jomo Gbomo's antimanifesto
converges with the state's dismissal of militancy as mere criminality; in effect, the government spokesman labeled the Odi villagers "a bunch of
bitter men." This ambiguous relationship between politics and criminality also manifests in literary genres: Helon Habila uses a noir suspense plot
in his novel *Oil on Water* (2010) to explore how the militant tactic of kidnapping oil company execs (work best left to the "professionals," one militant character says) is adapted by "amateurs" pursuing private, even
intimate, agendas.

In pondering what Fanon would say about the Niger Delta, what has
happened in the creeks since Saro-Wiwa's execution can be difficult to
parse. In his meditation on violence in *The Wretched of the Earth*, Fanon
distinguishes between disciplined, nation-forging anticolonial insurgency
and the various forms of self-destructive violence, endemic to the colonial
situation, that precede the emergence of a national liberation movement.
Both forms of violence are at work at the same time in the Niger Delta.
Even among groups with a clear political agenda that cannot be wished
away by the label of criminality, the turn to militancy tends not to forge a
unifying *national* consciousness, but to proliferate ethnonationalisms
instead.[26]

One problem in telling the story of the Niger Delta, therefore, is the
ambiguities regarding the narrative's characters, setting, and genre. Are
militants revolutionaries or criminals? Who or what is their antagonist?
If the geography of exploitation and emergence of militancy in the Niger
Delta do not accord precisely with a Fanonian narrative of national liberation against colonial occupation, what kind of narrative is it? The spectacle of petro-violence depicted in *Curse of the Black Gold* poses one set of
interpretive challenges for readers like my students, likely at a safe distance
from the Niger Delta, their imaginations captured—held captive even—
by juxtapositions of gorgeous color and abject harm verging on the apocalyptic. But the proliferation of violence and ethnic "oil minorities" poses
another set of challenges to conventional assumptions about nation, state,
and citizenship. Ledum Mitee's observation about the relationship between
violence and political recognition—that the state engages with those who
carry guns, even those "criminal" elements not acting out of "legitimate"
community interests—raises questions about the terrain of politics that
reframe the politics/criminality distinction. The paradoxical political legitimacy the state grants to men with guns suggests something about citizenship and the state, as constituted by petro-violence, in the postcolony.

The Niger Delta offers a disturbing answer to questions provoked by decolonization and neoliberal globalization: What is the state *for*? And what mode of citizenship is appropriate to it?

Subjects, Citizens, Criminals: What Is the State For?

The multiple referents of the "oil lamp" in Ifowodo's long poem—encompassing both rudimentary and capital-intensive modes of combustion—suggest an alternative plot of national development, in which petroleum extraction underwrites modern infrastructure only so long as oil keeps flowing from wellheads nearby. Similarly, the section of *The Oil Lamp* about the Odi massacre creates a historical palimpsest in which the 1999 razing of the village by Nigerian security forces echoes both the 1967–70 Biafran war in the wake of decolonization, as well as the 1897 Benin punitive expedition by the British during colonial conquest. The soldiers who come to destroy Odi in 1999 mistake the faded "combat kit" of "Sergeant Tobi, alias One Nigeria"—a veteran paralyzed while fighting to restore the Biafran secession—as belonging to soldiers whose recent death their massacre seeks to avenge (2005, 25–26). For the village elder Pa Piriye, a mere child when Benin was sacked to avenge the ambush of a British-led invading force, the attack on Odi stirs memories of having cursed the British, strange-looking foreigners "so evil they had no skin." "But who shall we curse now, who now is the enemy?" he asks (28). The "Odi" section of *The Oil Lamp* extends this palimpsestic dilation of history into the near future: a forgotten, undetonated "last grenade" explodes three years after the 1999 massacre, when a couple returns to rebuild their flattened home (30).

Ifowodo's poem shows how things that seem to belong to different historical moments overlap in the present. Modes of combustion coexist in the energy simultaneity of high-tech petroleum installations and low-tech palm oil lamps.[27] The same is true for the violence of colonization and decolonization, in the echoes and misrecognitions among punitive military reprisals spanning a century or more. This lyrical meditation on how petro-violence twists and reprises colonial and postcolonial history, thereby rerouting the plot of national development, offers a useful frame for rethinking received narratives of modernity, globalization, and governmentality that assume the inevitable transformation of subjects into citizens.

Consider how this recursive temporality helps explain the coexistence of multiple forms of violence by nonstate actors in the Niger Delta—both the seemingly "random" acts that precede Fanonian national consciousness and the organized ethnic movements that seek a bigger piece of the post-colonial national cake. MEND "is the violent child of the deliberate and long-running constriction of the public space in the Niger Delta in which ordinary citizens, now reduced to penurious subjects, can exercise their civil and political rights in the legitimate pursuit of material and social wellbeing. Behind the mask of the MEND militant is a political subject forced to pick up an AK-47 to restore his rights as a citizen," argues Ike Okonta (quoted in Kashi and Watts 2008, 209). Okonta's portrait of the aggrieved, resubjugated citizen behind the militant's mask implies a po-litical narrative of rupture and restoration. In some ways, this narrative hews to the plot of the classic Fanonian dialectic. The violence of colonial exploitation is met with revolutionary anticolonial violence; forged in this liberation struggle are not only the nation but also a new national culture, a new humanity, and, presumably, a public sphere where citizens can (in Okonta's words) "express their civil and political rights in legitimate pur-suit of material and social wellbeing" without resorting to (further) vio-lence. In *The Oil Lamp*, Pa Piriye recognizes a structural similarity between colonial conquest and postcolonial repression; the pathos of his question—"who now is the enemy?"—derives from the hope that the post-independence era would be something other than a repetition of the co-lonial past. Okonta's public sphere would not be *new* in the Fanonian sense of being forged during struggle, but instead a democratic ideal *re-stored* after having been betrayed after decolonization. The rupture of In-dependence and the "fact" (however spectral) of national sovereignty dictate that the militants' desire be framed as restoring citizenship in the wake of postcolonial loss rather than achieving it amid colonial lack: a re-turn to "One Nigeria."

Of course, the betrayal of dreams for decolonization also has a place within the dystopian narrative of the postcolony gone off the rails that Fanon anticipated in "The Pitfalls of National Consciousness." Fanon in-sists that independence means nothing without resource sovereignty: the right of a people to dispose of natural resources within its territory.[28] He warns against the betrayal of the national ideal by the comprador bour-geoisie, whose class interests align with the colonizer. A variant on this Fanonian national unimagining has played out in postcolonial Nigeria: pit-falls also lurk in the exploitation of the Niger Delta and its natural re-sources in the name of national development and the consequent prolif-eration of violence and ethnonational formations. Fanon's cartography of mid-twentieth-century decolonization and underdevelopment is a neces-sary but insufficient guide to current geographies of exploitation; the trajectories he imagined do not fully align with the historical shift from Cold War decolonization and modernization to contemporary globalization. But what if the ethnonational fracturing in the Niger Delta is situated at the other end of the plot of empire: not in terms of Fanon's meditations on the possible ends and afterlives of colonialism, but instead the invention and deployment of ethnicity in the consolidation of colonial rule—a process analyzed elsewhere in Africa by Mahmood Mamdani and the Comaroffs?[29]

Ethnic polities in the Niger Delta constitute themselves as they engage the oil multinationals whose concessions lie within their territories. Rather than a generic imperial logic of "divide and conquer," these engagements can be described as "recognize and coopt," as both the corporations and community leaders attempt to consolidate their positions.[30] Similar relations between commercial interests and local polities were crucial to the operation and expansion of European imperialism in West Africa (including the Niger Delta) in the nineteenth century: Chartered exploration and trading companies signed treaties with, and sometimes invented, local authorities in order to consolidate and promulgate their commercial operations. (One contemporary analogue of these nineteenth-century treaties is the "social license to operate" that entered oil company discourse after 1995.)[31] Then as now, argues William Reno, "foreign firms [became] important political actors, helping to shape factional struggles and consolidate the power of particular groups" (2004, 607–8). These relationships between company and community have repeatedly generated what I call *resource recognition*: a form of mutual recognition and subject constitution with political and not merely economic effects—a point to which I will return.

These echoes and imperfect analogies between the contemporary situation of the Niger Delta and the narrative of colonialism are important because the modes of governmentality at work in different moments help to make sense of the temporal assumptions that underwrite contemporary globalization. Rob Nixon writes of Shell's enormously profitable exploitation of the Niger Delta, which has brought little but immiseration for its inhabitants, that "the process seems more redolent of late nineteenth-century colonial buccaneering than it does of twenty-first century international economics. But if the idea of the nation-state continues to lose any vestige of popular appeal through a failure to deliver local benefits, and if rulers lack the will or the resources to command a national polity, the continent's poorest countries will continue to fall prey to a twenty-first century version of nineteenth-century concessionary economics, unhampered by regulations or redress" (2011, 119). Nixon deploys the shock of

anachronism to evoke outrage at Shell's profiteering (pirateering?), implying that such practices are not merely unseemly but also *untimely*, something we thought we had progressed beyond. (In *The Oil Lamp*, Ifowodo
makes a similar point about the historical palimpsest of Odi to indict the
failures of postcolonial rule.) These similarities between past(s) and present are better understood, I think, not as evidence of some anachronous
diversion from a steady trajectory of progress, but instead as a clue to
understanding what (de)colonization meant and how globalization works.
Instead of taking the promises of progress narratives at face value and
therefore understanding departures from those narratives as anachronous
regressions, these puzzling similarities between colonial and postcolonial
moments in time might lead us to question whose interests have been served
by those falsified progress narratives and their broken promises.

The conventional wisdom about contemporary neoliberal globalization
asserts that the nation-state is withering away and that we have arrived at
the denouement of a narrative in which the nation-state must fall to make
way for the continued rise of capitalism, its twin turned rival. (Notice the
historical irony at work when Engels's expectation that the state "withers
away" in the wake of proletarian revolution is repurposed to herald globalization as capitalism triumphant.) But places like the Niger Delta suggest an alternative understanding of globalization's political effects: "at
stake is the redefinition of the nation-state, rather than its decline"
(Coronil 2001, 81). While we were told that it was passé and withering
away, the nation-state was repurposed to meet capitalism's evolving demands for different forms of labor, new markets, and raw materials. Attention to the role of the nation-state, Fernando Coronil argued, can
elucidate "lines of continuity and change between modes of appropriating
nature under colonial and neocolonial regimes of domination" (68).[32] As
the international division of nature assumes new forms, the nation-state in
resource-rich regions is repurposed to facilitate resource extraction. The
nation-state remains indispensable, even if its key function is to disman-
tle its own regulatory regimes: this is perhaps the fundamental truth even
of the "nationalist" Trump era. The insistence upon the obsolescence of
the nation-state begins to sound like a disavowal that has abetted neoliberal globalization.

The question of what the state is for is entangled with another question: To whom do natural resources belong? Conflicts in the Niger Delta
can be read as a contest over the right to answer these questions. Activists
in *Curse of the Black Gold* and *Sweet Crude* who demand resource control

and self-determination hold fast to an ideal of the nation-state as a conceptual anchor of popular sovereignty, while they also protest the price that oil minorities have paid for "national development" under a series of military dictatorships. One consequence of the Biafran war, political theorist Charles Ukeje argued in 2001, was that Niger Delta activists tended to eschew secessionist rhetoric and instead assert ethnonationalist claims in the service of what Felix Tuodolo called a "new and true federalism";[33] federalism is also assumed in Saro-Wiwa's Ogoni Bill of Rights. Even as secessionist rhetoric has reemerged in the past decade, the commitment to the nation-state as anchor of sovereignty remains strong. Contrary to Nixon's claims about its dwindling popular appeal, a particular "idea of the nation-state" underwrites Okonta's narrative of the subjugated citizen's turn to militancy to reclaim the prerogatives of citizenship, or Felix Tuodolo's account of youth movements as a "thickening of civil society" (whose Janus-faced obverse is thuggish lawlessness), or Nnimo Bassey's conviction that "We must regain our sovereignty and ensure that our ballots decide who holds the rights of our government, who makes decisions, and how and when we want our resources extracted. . . . We say no more oil blocks until and unless it is with the express consent of the people" (2008, 91). Bassey echoes the landmark 1998 Kaiama Declaration of the Ijaw Youth Council: "we cease to recognize all undemocratic decrees that rob our people/communities of the right to ownership and control of our lives and resources, which were enacted without our participation and consent."

This language of citizens and subjects, civil society and the public sphere, links the emergence of militant insurgency in the Niger Delta to a failure of, and desire for, liberal democracy: Violence is posited as a path (back) to citizenship. The narrative of *Sweet Crude* is structured around a series of popular attempts at dialogue with multinationals and the state that are followed by betrayals, broken promises, and repression; the turn to violence by some activists is analogous to the reasoned turn to armed rebellion justified in the US Declaration of Independence. (My students' reconsideration of the necessity of Fanonian violence probably had as much to do with this discursive framing of violence as an expression of civic desire for liberal democracy—rather than for, say, *liberation*—as with Kashi's compelling photographs.) Bassey asserts that both political and "natural" (or resource) sovereignty derive from the populace: popular sovereignty should determine oil concessions. For these activists, the purpose of the state is to protect and adjudicate the rights of citizens and to represent the will of the people in disposing the natural resources within their territory.

These liberal democratic ideas of state sovereignty, no matter how quaint they may sound, are a fierce rejection of the Nigerian "petro-state," which epitomizes neoliberal globalization's repurposing of the state to facilitate resource extraction. The petro-state uses fiscal, political, and military mechanisms to capture and distribute oil revenues; in Watts' formulation, it is one element of an "oil complex" comprising federal and local government entities, oil companies, "traditional" forms of local rule, emergent youth movements, and the legislative framework that ostensibly governs interactions among these elements (2008, 44; 2004, 278). The purpose of the petro-state is to manage the spoils of oil, rather than to represent and effect the will of citizens.[34] Its very logic and raison d'être is the peculiar raison d'état dubbed "organized brigandage" by Saro-Wiwa: "There is no country. There is only organized brigandage. . . . Why is the international community supporting the massive fraud that is the Nigerian nation?" (1992, 91).

The concept of popular sovereignty forged during the European Enlightenment was, as Immanuel Wallerstein remarks, a "radical shift" that transformed the people into the citizenry, and subjects into citizens: "When the genie of the people as sovereign escaped from the bottle, it would never be put back inside. It became the common wisdom of the entire world-system" (2004, 51). The emergence of this "common wisdom" was irreversible; even the twenty-first-century authoritarian turn is premised on the putative will of the people. But the repurposing of the nation-state under contemporary globalization redefines citizenship downward. In Nigeria, the petro-state has been able to contain the genie of popular sovereignty by capturing oil rents paid by multinationals, instead of being solely dependent on the populace as a source of revenue through taxation.[35]

The petro-state offers a spectacular example of the nation-state repurposed for neoliberal globalization's international division of nature, accompanied by a diminution of the claims of citizenship: by underwriting the state, oil can undermine citizenship. This formation has two consequences for governmentality in the Niger Delta, where violence and ethnicity are important, if troubling, avenues of resource recognition. The first involves the tension between politics and criminality as frames for interpreting conflict in the Niger Delta. The conventional discursive technologies of the liberal public sphere have proved irrelevant, even fatally counterproductive, tools for achieving political recognition from the petro-state. Activists in *Sweet Crude* consider picking up arms after repeated attacks on unarmed citizens (including women) at nonviolent protests. Environmental lawyer Oronto Douglas observes,

The government turns a blind eye until the source of the rents and the royalties is threatened by youths and community people who are condemned as militants and terrorists. No genuine effort has been made to take seriously and engage with the voices of reason and peace, to talk to the purveyors of social justice and popular participation. Conversely, the face of government action looks like a rogues' gallery: those who have an insatiable appetite for cash and "carry go" seem to have the stamp of approval from individuals within corporate and governmental corridors. (Douglas 2008, 142)

Not only does this situation privilege violence as a path to resource recognition; in effect, the commitment of the petro-state to illegality renders moot the distinction between politics and criminality. Within this unimagining of the liberal democratic state, criminality among nonstate actors becomes a form of "citizenship," if citizenship is understood as engagement with the state and other citizens within the terms set by the state. Construed as playing by the rules of the game, even if the primary rule is to break all the rules, citizenship and governmentality in the upside-down world of the petro-state take curious forms indeed. This sense of politics as a nihilist game registers in terms of literary form and rhetorical structure in Helon Habila's novel *Oil on Water*. Military officers and militants not only speak in sound-bites that sound too much like what one might expect such characters to say; they also ventriloquize platitudes that they imagine their counterparts on the other side of the conflict would likely proclaim. Everyone knows everyone else's lines in this drama of the Niger Delta.

Within the oil complex, recognition through ethnicity and de facto rule by company generates "a form of consent by a form of force" that "undermines the very idea of the production of governable subjects" and spaces; instead, this mode of resource recognition generates "unrule" of "ungovernable spaces" (Watts 2004, 286, 293, 278). Read in terms of these facts on the ground rather than activists' expressed desires for liberal democracy, insurgent violence (and entrepreneurial criminality) in the Niger Delta are legible as a perverse *mode of citizenship* rather than as an exigent *path toward its restoration.*

The second consequence of oil money undermining popular sovereignty is that it gives the multinationals enormous leverage, and it exacerbates the pressure toward ethnicization as an avenue for political recognition and a share of petro-naira. "The companies have always thrived on a policy of divide and rule," Watts writes (2008, 46), an observation that invokes historical echoes with nineteenth-century treaties between charter companies and local "chiefs," whose authority was sometimes invented in the very act of treaty-making. The divide between state and nation in the postcolonial era has become as important as the divisions among ethnic formations; these two kinds of division allow the companies considerable room for maneuver within a fluid form of governmentality. Indeed, William Reno traces historical parallels with colonial charter companies in West Africa in order to make a broader argument about sovereignty in twenty-first-century extractivist economies. Challenging the assumptions that political disorder is inimical to foreign investment and that "states are universal features of global society," Reno outlines a symbiosis between corporations and weak (or failed) states (2004, 607).[36] In Nigeria, this symbiosis means that the companies "are only too happy to invoke national sovereignty when pressures are placed on them to improve their human rights or social responsibility records; and yet only too happy to operate—in Nigeria for the better part of two or three decades—in an environment in which they could get away with just about anything. In many communities, oil companies are perceived as, and function like, government" (Watts 2008, 46). Here seeing like a state is identical to getting away with anything; *sovereignty* means impunity and a lack of accountability to the people who are the presumptive constituents and source of sovereignty. The companies' protean ability to alternately defer to, ignore, conjure, coopt, or supplant the state enables the enduring power of the slick alliance.[37]

I avoid using the term "resource curse" to describe the Niger Delta because I share the view of social scientists who reject its determinism and narrow geographic focus. The "resource curse" argument holds that bad governance and violent conflict are the inevitable lot of states unlucky enough to be so well-endowed with desirable natural resources that they can base their entire economies on extraction—at least for a while, until things turn sour. This diagnosis sees the problem as the resource itself. It also assumes the absence of traditions of democratic accountability in the places, disproportionately in the Global South, seen as accursed; Norway is cited endlessly as the exception that proves the resource curse rule. Eliding the histories through which such states are drawn into global capitalism, the resource curse analysis construes an abundance of particular minerals or plants—rather than, say, Chiquita or the CIA—as a threat to democratic rule and social welfare. (Timothy Mitchell argues that the United States, and not just places like Saudi Arabia or Venezuela, should be understood as an "oil state"—not because of domestic production, but because of the singular indispensability of oil to US hegemony [2009, 400].)[38] From his vantage in the Niger Delta, Nnimo Bassey derides resource curse analyses for privileging "one set of local actors: the state/political elites, militia groups/warlords, and weak and inept bureaucracies. Very little attention is paid to the role of external and transnational actors and the lack of transparency that shrouds the extent of their involvement in these conflicts and violence" (2008, 91).

The one-size-fits-all "resource curse" label also ignores local and regional histories and misses the specific (and varied) terrains of politics in sites where it is applied. In Nigeria, it cannot capture the salience of violence or criminality as modes of political recognition, or the long history of trade in commodities like slaves, palm oil, and petroleum in successive resource frontiers that produced new ethnic polities and new modes of governmentality, political subjectivity, and citizenship.[39] In other words, it cannot grasp the diverse, dynamic micrologies of relationship entailed in resource recognition, even within the Niger Delta.[40] Like oil, the "resource curse" idea hijacks the imagination: it is appealing in First World analyses precisely because it lets consumers, their governments, and multinational corporations off the hook.

Chapter 1 examined the challenge to citizenship posed by US corporations that occupy the position of supercitizen; here, multinational corporations assume some functions of the state. In both cases, corporations claim the rights of citizens or the authority of states while evading the responsibilities entailed therein. Oronto Douglas recognizes the poison pill lurking within popular demands placed upon oil multinationals for community development or a share of the wealth: such demands formalize and normalize the multinationals' selective, opportunist assumption of functions of the state. He asks, "But must Shell, Chevron, Agip, ExxonMobil, TotalFinaElf be allowed—or expected—to provide the water we drink when we are thirsty, build the hospitals we attend when we are sick, fund the schools in which we instruct our youth? Must Big Oil act as our road builders? What . . . is the business of the governments that represent us?" (Douglas 2008, 142). Douglas asks what it means for dreams of infrastructure—desires for things like "good roads" in *Sweet Crude*, the "promise of electricity" in *The Oil Lamp*—to be outsourced to multinational corporations, with the force of the petro-state and the legitimating assumptions of the international state system behind them. The dependent clause in Douglas's sentence belies the relationships among petro-state, company, and citizenry in Nigeria; taken to a neoliberal petro-extreme, "the business of governments" is *not* to "represent us." In reality, if not in syntax, oil rents obviate the relations of mutual dependence and recognition between state and citizenry.

Divide and Rule: The Nation's Two Bodies

If sovereignty in the petro-state derives from petroleum rather than the polity, then the relationship between state and citizen cannot be understood without reference to a third term: nature. The nation is not one "body politic" but instead constituted by two bodies, one political and one natural. "As an oil nation," Fernando Coronil writes, "Venezuela was seen as having two bodies, a political body made up of its citizens and a natural body made up of its rich subsoil" (1997, 4). Arguing, in effect, for a shift from political economy to political ecology, Coronil develops this bodily metaphor by emphasizing the role of states in "configuring the metabolism between society and nature" (8). In Nigeria, oil figures as blood circulating through the national body, in sickness and in health.[41] During the 1960s and 1970s boom, oil (and, in transmuted form, money) pumped feverishly through the nation's veins, but after the 1980s crash, "oil was transformed from the lifeblood of the nation into the bad blood of corrupt government. . . . The immoral economy of petroleum . . . pumps bad money from beneath the ground, only to pollute and destroy the productive base of the eco-system" (Apter 2005, 251, 273).[42] What does it mean to imagine oil as the nation's lifeblood, when both are spilled so carelessly?

The oil spilled and blood shed in the Niger Delta materialize the antagonisms entailed in relations among state, citizens, and nature. In the oil complex, companies rival the state in a formal sense because they assume some of its functions—even as, in practice, they collude with Nigerian regimes in extraction and the repression deemed necessary for "smoothing" that endeavor. Rivalry also characterizes the relationships between the state and the nation's natural and political bodies: as suggested in the previous section, the purpose of the petro-state is not to nurture the nation's political body but to exploit its natural one. In Nigerian parlance, maintaining *resource control* trumps the rights of citizens. But more generally, states are produced out of a rivalry with the citizenry and other interests over the control of resources: "The process of mapping, bounding, containing and controlling nature and citizenry are what make a state a state. States come into *being* through these claims and the assertion of control over territory, resources, and people" (Neumann 2004, 202; see also Vandergeest and Peluso 1995). This statement of political ecology's fundamental logic requires elaboration to grasp the relations at work in the petro-state.

First, the production of internal sovereignty in relation to nature and citizenry has external implications beyond a state's position in the international state system. The petro-state not only "mediates the social relations by which oil is exploited" in Nigeria but also controls access to the global oil market (Watts 2001, 204, 208). Second, precisely because so much money (or, in Apter's phrase, "bad money") is at stake, the example of the Nigerian petro-state makes clear the force—indeed, the violence— necessary to achieve what might read as a bloodless process of "mapping, bounding, containing, and controlling nature and citizenry." The components over which the state asserts control—territory, resources, people—are not discrete members in a set, the necessary and sufficient conditions for a state, but instead potentially destabilizing to the state if they are not *made and kept* separate from one another. Coronil's conceptual distinction between the nation's political and natural bodies has literally been *enforced* in Nigeria in the past half-century or more with the sundering of polity from petroleum, another form of "divide and rule." The petro-state's claims upon territory or resources obstruct the people's claims by dismembering the nation's natural body from its political body (in the name of national interest) and invalidating peoples' direct claims to either natural endowments or territory. State violence provides an answer to that question regarding the disposition of nature, to whom do resources belong? Writing about Indonesia, Anna Tsing examines similar statist claims that nature and natural resources are wealth belonging to the nation as a whole, rather than to local biotic communities. Giving the lie to this familiar notion of the state as steward of national patrimony, such resources become "loot . . . free to those who could take them" (2005, 174). This version of resource sovereignty turns the "tragedy of the commons" on its head; whereas in Garrett Hardin's infamous 1968 argument, the only plausible bulwarks against "remorseless," unrestrained exploitation of "common" resources and lands are regulation and a private property regime (rather than moral suasion), here it is large-scale extractors who argue for collective ownership, freed from the claims (or restraints) of local, popular interests.[43]

In postcolonial Nigeria, the legislative framework for dismembering the nation's two bodies was forged under the first military regime. The 1969 Petroleum Act and the 1978 Land Use Act claimed mineral rights for the federal government and privileged oil-related uses of land over all others.[44] Here the right to dispose of natural resources as an aspect of postcolonial sovereignty entails a temperamental disposition toward oil

extraction as a mode of consolidating state power. In *The Oil Lamp*, Ifowodo dubs this legislative framework "theft by law" (2005, 37), a phrase
that expresses the upside-down world of criminality as governmentality.[45]
The third section of *The Oil Lamp*, "Ogoni," opens with a debate about
the rightful ownership of oil initiated by

> Major Kitemo, boss of the mob
>   chief pacifier
>   of the lower Niger's
> still primitive tribes. (Ifowodo 2005, 32)

Major Kitemo narrates the "Ogoni" section, and both he and his Ogoni
interlocutors cite territorial justifications in their respective federal and local claims to ownership of oil: oil is theirs "by its being on our land" (33).
Major Kitemo's "chief pacifier" epithet echoes Chinua Achebe's *Things Fall
Apart*; Kitemo occupies the pseudo-ethnographic position of Achebe's District Commissioner, an earnest student of native customs (or, in Kitemo's
case, local beliefs about oil and sovereignty) among the "primitive tribes
of the Lower Niger."[46] Like Achebe, Ifowodo uses a sudden shift in focalization to great effect: irony acts as a solvent that not only cuts through
the pieties surrounding the Ogoni issue after the martyrdom of Saro-
Wiwa, but also allows expropriative statist logic to undermine itself by
speaking in its own voice.

Despite their intellectual pretensions, neither Achebe's District Commissioner nor Ifowodo's Major hesitates to use force to get his way: Major
Kitemo discloses his more telling epithet, "Kill-Them-All."[47] Kitemo pa-
tiently explains to the Ogoni the logic of sovereignty:

> The powers
> That rule the country—your colony—
> That make you citizens
> Of a nation, known to law
> And safe from plunder,
> Decree the land and its wealth not yours. (Ifowodo 2005, 35)

Having invoked the authority of law and national sovereignty, Major
Kitemo (representative of a military dictatorship) loses his patience and becomes flabbergasted that an Ogoni woman and a young student ("a female
and a sapling") inquire further into the foundations of their legitimacy.
"*Who/or wetin make up dis Nigeria?*" the woman asks in pidgin with exceeding politeness; "in whose name, and by whose powers/ were the laws
you cite made?" the student excuses himself to ask (35, 36). Major Kitemo

recognizes that the first phase of his plan to pacify the Ogoni ("cure them of the lies") has failed; he moves on to sowing dissension and ultimately to repression, driving residents into the bush as he bombs their villages, so that even the "smartass quartet" who dared question the state's claim over the nation's natural body pleads for mercy (43). He turns to the tactic of state repression after his lesson in statist resource sovereignty fails. His cynical account of law and territoriality as the source of the state's claim to ownership of oil underground is unconvincing to those whose long history of living on the land as Ogoni, and their putative status as politically recognized Nigerian citizens ("known to law"), should keep them "safe from plunder" or murder by the petro-state. Ifowodo stages a clash between two modes of (un)imagining the relationship between the state and the nation's political and natural bodies.

A similar clash appears in Uwem Akpan's novella "Luxurious Hearses" (2008), in which a luxury bus becomes a mobile public sphere, a microcosm of the nation in a newly restored democracy in which passengers "tax" themselves, conduct elections, and debate who owns Nigeria's oil as well as its role in dictatorship and democracy. The passengers evince a canny understanding of how oil revenues underwrote the northern generals' power during military rule, how promises of oil leases smoothed their recent exit from power, and how now "dem *dey* use our oil money to establish Sharia" (Akpan 2008, 237). "Luxurious Hearses" fictionalizes the violence that followed the imposition of sharia law in several northern Nigerian states (particularly Kaduna) in 2000. Akpan's bus passengers are southerners and/or Christians, fleeing the north during a paroxysm of religious violence. Some of them had come to the north after their livelihoods in the Delta were ruined by oil-polluted rivers and fields. In an echo of the "who owns the oil?" scene in Ifowodo's "Ogoni," the southerners, particularly those hailing from Delta oil villages, scoff at police officers' claims to "federal government oil" (238). "I say, *na* our oil. . . . We *dey* democracy now," a feisty young mother named Monica retorts in the face of a police officer waving his gun while invoking the national interest (237). Monica's claim is not merely that of a citizen over the patrimony of the nation's natural body: "our oil" only fleetingly signifies the Nigerian people's oil, and is more vehemently claimed as "southern oil." What particularly enrages the passengers—waiting on the bus, seemingly interminably, while the driver scrounges precious fuel for the journey—is not the sight of *almajeris* (students in Koranic schools) in the fictionalized northern city of Khamfi "setting things and people afire," but the fact that they do so with jars of "free fuel . . . our fuel. . . . They're using southern fuel to burn our people and businesses!" (235–36). This vernacular analysis of regional resource tensions driving the "Sharia war" is countered by northern politicians' ingenious claims to ownership of oil, on hydrological, rather than statist, grounds: "the oil deposits in the delta were the result of years of sediments being carried from the north by the River Niger" (244). This claim appends the time of the nation to the deep geological time of sedimentation and fossilization, and it provides a reassuring answer to the question of "why Allah would have given the oil to the land of the infidels" (244).

This question is voiced by the novella's protagonist, Jibreel/Gabriel, a teenager whose safe passage on the southbound bus depends on keeping secret his Muslim identity, which is permanently inscribed on his body in the missing hand he lost to a sharia punishment for stealing. Anyone reading "Luxurious Hearses" would be convinced for at least a moment by Fredric Jameson's argument about reading Third World literature as national allegory, since Akpan is not shy about drawing links between Jibreel and his family history and that of his nation, both of which are "more complicated than what one tribe or religion could claim" (Akpan 2008, 210). He is the child of a northern Muslim woman and a Catholic man from a Delta village. I am particularly interested in how the Jamesonian national allegory intersects—and fatally collides—in "Luxurious Hearses" with Akpan's anatomy of Andersonian national imagining, in the form of news coverage of the riots playing intermittently on TVs in the bus.

Before analyzing Akpan's staging of nation-thinking, I want to join Coronil's idea of the nation's two bodies to the mode of literary analysis catalyzed by Benedict Anderson's privileging of the novel (and, slightly less interesting to literary critics, the newspaper) as technologies for imagining community. The notion that literature and other cultural production are deeply implicated in national imagining has become a critical commonplace. But in Coronil's account, the nation is not only a community or polity to be imagined, but also a biome or lifeworld to be inhabited: "national imaginings also depend on the very materiality of the nation as a life-sustaining habitat" (1997, 8). The nation's natural body is a material substrate that shapes the imagining of national community and the production of the state. This insistence upon the importance of the nation's natural body to the imagining of community by its political body offers a corrective in the Marxian vein of "men mak[ing] their own history": men and women imagine national community, but not, as Marx put it, "under circumstances chosen by themselves" ([1852] 1959, 320). The ecomateriality of those circumstances of imagining *matters*. To echo Fanon (and

Engels and Marx before him), consciousness of the nation's natural body is the only thing that will give the Andersonian imagined community a material-environmental-historical dimension.[48] As I have suggested, literature and oil—print-capitalism and petro-capitalism—are imbricated in underwriting the Nigerian national project: Oil has fueled imagining the nation and producing the state. The particular form the "metabolism between society and nature" takes in Nigerian national imagining is mutually determined by convergences of political, economic, and literary history as well as the singular physical qualities of oil. Far beyond the Niger Delta, oil fuels the imagining (and unimagining) of the nation itself.

Indeed, Akpan's implicit answer to "How to tell the story of the Niger Delta?" is to set the narrative far away—in a motor park of a northern Nigerian city (in "Luxurious Hearses"), or a murderous Lagos traffic jam (in "Baptizing the Gun").[49] Akpan stages Jibreel's transformation on the bus from northern Muslim to Nigerian citizen. At first, Jibreel's fiercely strict adherence to Islam has him rather comically torn between not looking at female passengers and not looking at the TVs, but gradually he yearns to be accepted within the ad hoc community of motley travelers; near his journey's end, "he envisioned the different peoples of his country connecting at a deep, primordial level" (Akpan 2008, 316). Jibreel initially imagines the south of the country as "more developed than the north, even if it was inhabited by infidels" (209), but these dreams of southern infrastructure are falsified by scenes from the south that he eventually dares to glimpse on TV (311). Akpan's narrator underscores this geographic parallel between north and south by suggesting the resemblance between violent scenes of turmoil in Khamfi and Abacha-era repression of Delta towns that dared ask "for their land to be developed after four decades of neglect and environmental degradation by government-multinational oil companies" (240). This parallelism is most obvious in breaking news TV bulletins that punctuate and catalyze the narrative, one titled "Religious Riots, Khamfi" and the other "Reprisal Violence in Onyera and Port Harcourt" (234, 316). Neither north nor south has a monopoly on violence, and luxurious buses full of corpses and refugees are headed north as well as south.[50]

Jibreel's trajectory from fierce partisan to tolerant citizen intersects and ultimately collides with the multiple versions of community fitfully imagined on a bus without fuel. During the interminable wait for the journey to begin, allegiances among the passengers shift rapidly and repeatedly; these shifts reveal fractures along obvious fault lines of Islam vs. Christianity, north vs. south, as well as ethnicity, language, gender, generation, education ("speak[ing] grammar"), more nuanced religious divides

(Catholic vs. Pentecostal, "foreign" religions of the book vs. indigenous spiritual practices), civilians vs. the authoritarian state, and divergent opinions about Nigeria's emergent democracy and its role in West Africa.[51] Regional differences in access to petroleum products and vulnerability to the costs of extraction are a more powerful obstacle to the ideal of Nigerian national unity than the sharia war that catalyzes the narrative. The "first sign of unity" amidst this fractious crowd (assembled on the bus because they all find themselves on the wrong side of religious conflict in the north) occurs when the TVs flicker on: "peacefulness and order reigned; almost everybody was looking in the same direction" (Akpan 2008, 232). "Beautiful foreign images" of consumer goods and global cultural icons "washed over" the passengers "like fresh air," but this peace is soon broken by breaking news from Khamfi and by policemen's insistence that the passengers watch local TV coverage rather than "foreign TV channels *dey* spoil de image of our country. Dese white stations *dey* make billions of dollars to sell your war and blood to de world" (233, 246).

Akpan's contemporary staging of a community imagined through commodified images joins the national politics of resource recognition to the global politics of cultural representation: the passenger-citizens are united both by their pacifying desire for inaccessible things shown on foreign TV stations and their sense that foreign channels, rather than national ones, tell the truth about what's happening in Nigeria: "When Abacha hanged Saro-Wiwa because of our oil, we saw it first on foreign TV!" (2008, 315).[52] Akpan's counterintuitive take on the global circulation of images must be read in terms of his own status as the author of an unlikely global bestseller, beloved by Oprah and the fiction editors of *The New Yorker*. The recent emergence and growing market significance of the global bestseller—that is, texts written by authors hailing from the Global South who find critical acclaim and wide readership through publication channels centered in New York, London, and Paris—demonstrate the wrongheadedness of David Damrosch's and Pascale Casanova's dismissal of "airport literature." While the global bestseller cannot fully represent the canons and questions posed by world literature, whether in its classic or newly fashionable versions, the outsized role such texts play in the transnational cultural imagining that is ostensibly the ambit of World Literature cannot be ignored.

Akpan is canny about the multivalent potential of TV images to mollify or ignite this volatile community. A TV interview with a southern Muslim of Hausa descent pleading for calm seems to bring peace "among the different religions of the bus," but immediately thereafter breaking news reports of fresh religious violence across the country stoke the south-bound passengers back to angry cursing of northerners and Muslims, a disheartening turn that leads to Jibreel's unmasking as a Muslim and swift execution by his fellow refugees. Jibreel's embrace of a capacious political and religious subjectivity coincides and collides with the passengers' ultimate inability to imagine a community as large and diverse as Nigeria. If, as I have argued, "Luxurious Hearses" flamboyantly stages a national allegory, the tension that drives the story is whether it is Jibreel or his fellow passengers who represent the nation. In a 150-page novella in which the bus community rarely agrees about anything, their lynching of Jibreel in less than a sentence is unimaginably shocking.[53]

National Unimagining and the Betrayal of Petro-Promise

The fractionated, combustible communities inside and outside the bus in "Luxurious Hearses" undertake a process of national *unimagining*. "Oil has unleashed a set of forces in Nigeria that have at once held Nigeria together and pulled it apart," writes Michael Watts, noting "a profound sense of the unraveling—the unimagining—of Nigeria as a nation. The patchwork quilt that is Nigeria is now deeply frayed, its stitching pulled apart at the seams by all manner of forces" (Watts 2008, 47). This unraveling of the national project is legible in a bitterly funny moment in "Luxurious Hearses" when Monica mocks a soldier returned from peacekeeping in Sierra Leone for *not* seizing his piece of the national cake: "Why you no steal? You no be good colonel at all, at all" she declares, as the entire bus, including the police, erupts in laughter. She heaps further scorn on the soldier's plan to retire as a farmer or fisherman in his ancestral delta village, whose fields and rivers are now ruined, she points out, by oil extraction (Akpan 2008, 284–85). Even as oil has fueled the imagining of national community and the production of the Nigerian state, underwriting its international visibility and viability, it also reveals "the state and the nation to be sham, decrepit, venal, and corrupt notions" (Watts 2001, 204, 208). If Nixon is correct that "region like Ogoniland is almost completely unimaginable" to Americans, perhaps it is because the Nigerian national community has been so violently *unimagined*.

Akpan's mobile public sphere—which for most of the narrative is actually stalled, out of gas—demonstrates how the cultural forms of the novel and TV news can be vehicles for *unimagining* national community. An honest look at Nigerian writing since the 1950s would find a multivalent role similar to that of oil in holding the nation together and pulling it apart;

even as the Nigerian novel offers a medium for imagining national community and establishing international visibility, it also lays bare the contradictions of Nigerian nationhood and the collisions between the state's image of itself and skeptical critiques. These disjunctures are evident not only in the thematic content of literature published since the disillusionments of the 1960s, but also in regional and class differences in literacy and readership, language, and genre, as well as the difficult state of Nigerian publishing and its fraught relationship to presses and readerships abroad. Even the remarkable twenty-first-century success of Nigerian writers living and publishing abroad compounds this sense of division, now between an Afropolitan elite (with a presumed audience outside Africa) and writers and readers on the continent.

To assert that Nigeria has been *unimagined* implies that it was imagined in the first place—that, as with the "promise of light" that falls victim to de-development in *The Oil Lamp*, there was once a coherent thing called Nigeria that has fallen apart. The north-south divide in "Luxurious Hearses" reflects the fact that, until 1914, Nigeria was not a single British colony but several protectorates and charter territories that were only consolidated into northern and southern protectorates in 1900. As with other African nation-states, this area was a multiethnic, multilinguistic territory of remarkable cultural diversity and with little longstanding cultural coherence, whose borders were inherited from lines drawn to suit the convenience of European imperial powers. The convergence of these multiple histories into a single colonial and postcolonial narrative intensifies the importance of oil as material substrate of national imagining and unimagining. With commercial oil deposits discovered and developed in Nigeria on the eve of Independence, oil was hailed by some as a medium for building a postcolonial nation. But the petro-promise associated with Independence was betrayed in that very moment.

In *Curse of the Black Gold*, political economist Ukoha Ukiwo recalls that petroleum appeared in the mid-1950s as "an angel of history . . . a mass commodity [that] presented itself as the Niger Delta's savior," much like palm oil (and slaves) had in centuries past (2008, 73). Ukiwo refers to the hope among Niger Delta ethnic minorities that oil would secure their economic development and political clout within an emergent political system favoring the Hausa, Yoruba, and Igbo majorities.[54] This was not to be, with oil rents never shared with oil-producing states in ratios that reflected the indispensability of the resource extracted from this region regarded as peripheral to Nigerian political and economic life. The relations of dependence and harm in the international division of nature also structure dynamics within Nigeria's borders that some have dubbed "internal colonialism."

For Nigeria as a whole, *unimagining* describes the shape of a national narrative of development fueled by petro-promise. Postcolonial Nigeria can be read as a story of de-development, a "catastrophic failure of secular nationalist development" that finds "most Nigerians poorer today than they were in the late colonial period" despite the billions of petro-naira that have flowed through the state's coffers (Watts 2008, 44). The implicit pathos in Watts's contrast between the colonial period and the present derives from developmentalist assumptions about how the story of a nation unfolds; petroleum, political independence, and/or their conjunction in the petro-state were to have been a path to development and "modernization." These assumptions are both temporal (time = progress) and political (the purpose of the nation's natural body is to develop its political body and the physical bodies of its citizens). Instead, the position of the Niger Delta in relation to Nigeria indicates the unevenness within the international division of nature, the contradictions of underdevelopment concentrated within a single site, and the enforced antagonism between the nation's natural and political bodies.

Narratives of progress promised and betrayed have a counterpart in tales of historical decline, told to set things right. In "The Novelist as Teacher" (1965), Chinua Achebe characterized his historico-political work in *Things Fall Apart* as a necessary attempt "to look back and try to find out where we went wrong, where the rain began to beat us" (1990, 43).[55] (This now-familiar proverb resonates with Ifowodo's inquiry into "how the damage was done.") In *Curse of the Black Gold*, Nnimo Bassey revives Achebe's formulation, but for him the moment "where we went wrong" in the Niger Delta was the mid-twentieth-century collusion between oil multinationals and the British Empire in its waning days.[56] Bassey looks back and finds that "the rain began to beat us" at the brink of Independence—described elsewhere as a moment of petro-promise—and also the very moment that *Things Fall Apart* launched its search for the onset of the punishing "rain" of earlier centuries. Four decades apart, Achebe and Bassey invite scenes of reading: They call for a communal reading of the past for clues about the cause of trouble in the present. But the ironic echo of Achebe's 1960s moment in Bassey's exhortation wrenches a linear narrative of national development into a recursive loop; the hopeful moment of Independence, a break from the colonial past, twists surreally (as in a Möbius strip) into the beginning of a postcolonial nightmare. To turn on its head Chimamanda Adichie's idea that stories of the Niger Delta always begin with "secondly," thereby eliding seminal acts of violence, these narratives of petro-promise and betrayal imagine national development as a false start that cannot even get to "secondly." For Akpan's weary passengers—citizens in a newly restored democracy at the turn of the millennium—the idea of a fresh start fueled by petro-promise registers only faintly and ironically as a target of derision.

Petro-Magic-Realism

When Ukoha Ukiwo describes the discovery of commercially valuable oil deposits in the Niger Delta as an "angel of history," he seems to have in mind an unexpected savior bringing prosperity, rather than a melancholic Benjaminian angel forced to look back on the accumulated wreckage of the past while the storm of history blows him helplessly into the future. Perhaps it is better to understand Ukiwo's viscous "angel of history" as a deus ex machina (or *oleum ex machina*): a miraculous agent, external to a narrative, whose arrival makes possible what is otherwise impossible within the narrative's own terms. That is to say, there is something almost antinarrative about oil, if narrative is understood as the working out of cause and effect and oil is understood to produce something out of nothing. Oil hijacks the imagination; it "harbors fetishistic qualities: it is the bearer of meanings, hopes, expectations of unimaginable powers" (Watts 2004, 280). In a passage that has itself captured the imagination of myriad critics, Ryszard Kapuściński writes about oil's false promises:

> Oil creates the illusion of a completely changed life, life without work,
> life for free. . . . The concept of oil expresses perfectly the eternal
> human dream of wealth achieved through lucky accident, through a
> kiss of fortune and not by sweat, anguish, hard work. In this sense oil
> is a fairy tale and, like every fairy tale, a bit of a lie. Oil fills us with
> such arrogance that we begin believing we can easily overcome such
> unyielding obstacles as time. (1992, 35)

All surplus! all the time! is the fantasy of oil. It is "a filthy, foul-smelling liquid that squirts up obligingly into the air and falls back to earth as a rustling shower of money" (34). Oil promises wealth without work, progress without the passage of time: the narrative mode appropriate to petro promise is not the developmentalist progress narrative of modernization, but the fairy tale of transformation at the wave of a magic wand, where every dream of infrastructure comes true.

For its role in imagining the nation and producing the state, oil is magic: *petro-magic*. "By condensing within itself the multiple powers dispersed throughout the nation's two bodies, the state appeared as a single agent endowed with the magical power to remake the nation" (Coronil 1997, 4).[57] At the height of Nigeria's oil boom in the late 1970s, a "'seeing-is-believing' ontology" emerged when "oil replaced labor as the basis of national development, producing a deficit of value and an excess of wealth, or a paradoxical profit as loss" (Apter 2005, 14, 201).[58] When oil is figured as the nation's blood, the state becomes a vampire that grows "by consuming this lifeblood of the people—sucking back the money that it pumped into circulation" and destroying "the real productive base of Nigeria, those agricultural resources that not even a state-sponsored green revolution could revive" (269). The alchemic relations among oil, blood, and money in Apter's account of Nigeria in the boom years reflect a broader tendency in cultural production across sites of oil extraction and consumption worldwide: a volatile metaphorical relay in which images of oil, water, blood, and money slide into one another. This transmutation at the level of figuration reflects poetic insight about how these substances are imbricated materially and politically in the "real world." Petro-magic is a version of petro-violence; its illusions of sweet surplus can mask the harm petroleum extraction does to humans and nonhuman nature, turning each into instruments of violence against the other.

The trajectories of imagining and unimagining in the texts examined in this chapter represent both the sweet lies and bitter truths of petro-magic. As with underdevelopment generally, or its variant of de-development in the Niger Delta, unimagining is a transitive process of unmaking. Its literary instantiations offer evidence not only of the imagination's failure, but also its fecundity. Indeed, *excess* may be the hallmark of the fossil-fueled imagination: in a scene in Ifowodo's *The Oil Lamp* inspired by an actual press conference, Major Kitemo boasts of his "excess of zeal," that he knows "two hundred and twenty-one ways to kill a man" (2005, 38). The actuarial specificity of the number 221 recalls Ifowodo's dedication of his book to "The thousand-and-one gone in the struggle," which itself evokes both the official death toll at the Jese pipeline fire as well as the book's epigraph from Salman Rushdie's *Midnight's Children*: "Numbers, too, have significance: . . . 1001, the number of night, of magic, of alternative realities—a number beloved of poets and detested by politicians." The excess of Kitemo's 221 methods of murder is countered by the 1,001 gone—the final digit standing in for those not included the official tally at

Jese, which enumerated only "charred remains, whole enough to count" (Ifowodo 2005, 14). Like Rushdie's *Midnight's Children* and *The Thousand and One Nights* before it, *The Oil Lamp* marshals the power of poets against politicians, so that storytelling becomes a strategy for warding off death.[59]

Ifowodo's invocation of Rushdie links *The Oil Lamp* to the literary mode of "alternative realities" known as magical realism, which Rushdie describes as "so dense a commingling of the improbable and the mundane!" (1982, 4). Yet, beyond the ethical force of pitting the literary imagination against forces of death and damage, *The Oil Lamp* does not immediately evince the fantastic excesses associated with magical realism. Pondering how to read *The Oil Lamp* as a magical realist text, I have come to focus on Ifowodo's depiction of nature within the unnatural landscape of oil extraction. In the "Jese" section, fields, creeks, and ponds are granted the power of speech to protest as the fire races through "a land marked by oil for double torment" (Ifowodo 2005, 12); trees vainly wave "green scarves for peace" at the onset of repression (20). Elsewhere, elements of the landscape are personified not as speaking for themselves but as instruments or even agents of petro-violence: the "tea-black water of the lake" explodes, seemingly of its own volition. The "air shrieked" and a tree in the "shuddering forest" is transformed from refuge to weapon as it "cleaved in two," crushing a mother and child as it falls (22). These personifications effect something like magical realism's natural(ized) supernaturalism, and they intimate the multivalence of the subjects, objects, and instruments of petro-violence.

The most striking "comminglings of the improbable and the mundane" in *The Oil Lamp* involve other transformations and juxtapositions. "Waterscape," the poem that serves as preamble to *The Oil Lamp*, depicts an "alternative reality" not of fantasy and imagination, but environmental history: a mangrove swamp prior to petro-modernity, with "ancestral lakes" home to eels, crab, mudskippers, and fish in such abundance that fishermen can enjoy more than one meal a day. This waterscape is also personified through metaphors of human culture and industry, its mangrove roots described as hands, tongues, and hair; the black water is "deeper than soot, / massive ink-well." The presence of humans in this preambular waterscape is radically different from that in the long poem proper. The "Jese" section contrasts now-spoiled rivers, erstwhile sources of life and livelihood, with "broken pipes, like the mouth of a river" which form "two brooks of kerosene and petrol" (Ifowodo 2005, 5). The abandoned, rusting "drilling tree" at a "drilled-dry well" mocks the trees of the forest (3, 5). These organic trees are of a piece with the drilling tree's technonature: trees of metal and trees of wood are all artifacts in a techno-ecosystem produced by and ever more vulnerable to human domination.[60] The fuel crunch effects a particular kind of disenchantment, forcing humans to disregard their "dread" of disturbing the "spirits that live in trees" (2). Even "green twigs" are threatened by the fuel crunch that "compelled choice between tree and human, /today and tomorrow" (2). Trees and humans are caught within the incommensurability between the time of nature and that of capitalist exigency.[61]

As its natural elements find counterparts in the machinery of oil extraction, the Niger Delta's singular landscape of petro-nature is juxtaposed with the totality of global capitalism: the "visible oil market where dealers/sold in kegs and bottles for naira" (Ifowodo 2005, 6) is contrasted with the distant electronic abstractions of "faceless traders/in markets without stalls or handmade goods" (4). Here magical realism's "commingling of the improbable and the mundane" reflects and produces incommensurability and disproportionality. The aggregate power of drilling trees, pipelines like rivers, brooks of hydrocarbons, and faceless, objectless markets over their "natural" counterparts makes them not of the same order, even if they coexist in the same place.

The force of technonature registers in *The Oil Lamp*'s recurrent image of rust. This electrochemical process is associated less with elemental nature (iron meets oxygen) than with industrial modernization having run its corrosive course, whose epitome is the American "Rust Belt" as index of the economic decline associated with deindustrialization. In *The Oil Lamp*, the de-development associated with resource extraction is legible in "rusted sinews of the [drilling] tree . . . a promise in rust-flakes" (Ifowodo 2005, 3). In the fuel crunch, trees of wood are too precious to be allowed to rot; for the "drilling tree" of metal, the phenomenon of rot—the cycle or end of its term of "life"—materializes not as falling leaves or branches but as flakes of rust.[62] Kapuściński's magical rustle of oil turned to money gives way to the rust of metal gone to ruin. Rust exposes the lies of petro-magic: all that is solid metal melts into flakes floating in sulfurous air. Corrosion of oil pipelines was the most immediate cause of "damage" at the Jese pipeline fire, for which Ifowodo seeks systemic causes: "A sickened earth rusted the pipes/and threw up the lie encased in hollow metal" (4). Such corrosion is accelerated in this techno-ecosystem by acid rain, a literal precipitate of gas flaring.

Ifowodo uses rust as a defamiliarizing image within the chronotope of petro-magic. Its visual dullness and association with industrial decline provide a necessary counterpoint to a more familiar image, the sickly iridescent sheen of oil as the emblem of modernity's Faustian bargain: these creeks must shimmer and die so that others may live, encircled within the "chain of ease." Major Kitemo's statist allegiances allow him to acknowledge "the devastation/that pours oil on rivers to float fish" in the Niger Delta while rejecting residents'

> ... claim for redress, that it should empty
> the coffers and deny the nation's engine
> its lubricant. Rust would follow; there'd be an end
> to motion and a nation to call our own. (Ifowodo 2005, 48)

For Kitemo and the nation-state he represents, oil as money is the lubricant and fuel that keep the machine of progress running; he must remain blind to the damage of underdevelopment, signified by the presence of the very rust he fears.

Rendering legible the lineaments (and lies) of petro-magic—the commingling of rot and rust, and the disproportionalities of a technonature produced by hydrocarbon capitalism—Ifowodo's *The Oil Lamp* gestures toward a literary mode I call *petro-magic-realism*, which combines magical transmogrifications and fantastic landscapes with the monstrous-but-mundane violence of oil exploration and extraction, the state violence that supports it, and the environmental degradation that it causes. Petro-magic-realism is a fantastic literary mode that makes legible the all-too-real effects of petro-magic—read here as a mode of violence that mystifies through the seductions of petro-promise. Petro-magic-realism, in other words, can reveal the secrets behind petro-magic's tricks.

A quintessential example of petro-magic-realism is Ben Okri's short story "What the Tapster Saw," which approximates *The Oil Lamp*'s disjunctures between trees and drilling trees, rivers and broken pipelines, in its superimposition of a landscape of petroleum extraction over the landscape of an earlier resource frontier and mode of combustion, that of palm oil.[63] Written in London in 1987 during the Nigerian oil bust, Okri's story offers a phantasmagoric glimpse into a degraded, privatized landscape where the "signboards of the world were getting bigger"; one signboard warns, "TRESPASSERS WILL BE PERSECUTED" (1988, 187, 185). The story's protagonist is one such trespasser, a palm-wine tapster whose work of extracting wine from palm trees in Delta Oil Company territory is jeopardized by petroleum extraction. Okri's tale of a tapster evokes the fantastic-modern world imagined in Amos Tutuola's novel, *The Palm-wine Drinkard* (1952), which itself draws upon a Yoruba narrative tradition in which the forest is a liminal space, peopled with transmogrifying creatures. Such creatures are encountered in Tutuola's novel when the eponymous drinkard, who "had no other work more than to drink palm-wine in my life," embarks upon a quest to Deads Town to bring back his deceased "expert palm-wine tapster who had no other work more than to tap palm-wine every day" (7). *The Palm-Wine Drinkard* offers a prescient, fantastical depiction of petromagic's disjuncture of work and wealth. Not unlike the actuarial specificity in *The Oil Lamp*, the drinkard's compulsion for outrageous numerical precision brings the "rationality" of capitalist accounting to the impossibilities and externalities of juju.[64]

In "What the Tapster Saw," the sun seems never to set or rise as the earth is bathed in the glow of gas flares, "roseate flames [that] burned everywhere without consuming anything" (Okri 1988, 189). Amidst this mysterious combustion without consumption, a talking snake glistens with the beautiful and deadly iridescence of oil spilled on water. In this landscape where boreholes crowd out palm trees, a palm wine tapster carries on plying his trade despite the ominous signboards;[65] when he falls from one of a "strange cluster of palm trees" (perhaps anticipating Ifowodo's drilling tree?), he spends seven days in a hallucinatory liminal state, persecuted by unseen assailants vaguely associated with oil company personnel trying unsuccessfully to "level the forest" with the help of "witchdoctors" and explosives "left over from the last war." The Delta Oil Company deploys the witchdoctors to "drive away the spirits from the forest" and to dry out its climate, while farmers living amidst unexploded bombs "as if the original war was over were blown up as they struggled with poverty" (Okri 1988, 186, 189, 188).

Juxtapositions of bombs and bullets, coups and executions, with herbalists and witchdoctors, talking animals and masquerades, in this fictional narrative about the collision of palm and petroleum, yield a petro-magic-realism that situates the magical and violent aspects of petro-modernity within an older fantastic tradition and an older extractive economy. Here the practice of "tapping" palm trees evokes both capital-intensive oil drilling and low-tech illicit "tapping" of pipelines snaking endlessly through fields and villages, in the practice known as "bunkering" oil for local use or black market exchange. Okri's tapster is not so much a direct descendant of Tutuola's character as a distant cousin within a broader genealogy the narrator acknowledges by referring to "mythical figures" including "the famous blacksmith" and the "notorious tortoise" (1988, 193). Direct allusion invokes not Tutuola but D. O. Fagunwa, whose story at the beginning of his seminal Yoruba novel *Ògbójú Ọdẹ nínú Igbó Irúnmalẹ̀* (1938; trans. Forest of a Thousand Daemons, 1968) about the hero's father shooting an antelope who turns out to be his wife is echoed in a fragmentary tale told with "curious irrelevance" at the opening of Okri's story (Fagunwa 1968, 12–13; Okri 1988, 183–84).[66]

Ben Okri is among the Anglophone African authors commonly mentioned in critical discussions of magical realism as a global literary phenomenon. Although Tutuola and Fagunwa are cited as precursors of West African magical realism, they are generally thought to lack sufficient cosmopolitan, ironic distance from the "traditional" or "indigenous" materials usually identified as the primary source of magic in magical realism.[67] But the role of petro-magic in political ecology suggests a different approach to the etiological question of who (or what) puts the magic in magical realism. That is to say, at stake in "magical realism" are the distinct realms of reality, representation, and reception that are too often conflated with one another—a confusion that becomes urgent in the context of magical realist texts' circulation in world literary space as commodity exports of the Global South in high demand in the northern hemisphere.

The distinction between the first two realms—reality and representation, or ontology and aesthetics—manifests in the tension between two seminal statements in the theorization of magical realism as a literary mode. For Alejo Carpentier, *"lo real maravilloso Americano"*—the American marvelous real—is a state of being shaped by the complex history and distinctive landscape of the Americas. Carpentier undertakes an accounting of this marvelous reality (compatible with petro-magic's promise of miraculous wealth) when he declares that there must be something marvelously real about the new world that causes Europeans to lose themselves in search of El Dorado: "a certain myth of El Dorado reflects a reality, a myth which is still fed by deposits of gold and precious stones." This insight construes the marvelous real as a different kind of resource curse that strikes European minds but also, in turn, afflicts colonized lands and bodies. By contrast, Franz Roh's 1925 discussion of postexpressionist European painting, where he coined the term *"der magischer Realismus"*—magical realism—describes an aesthetic strategy, a mode of representation.[68]

This divide between reality and representation is straddled by Harry Garuba in his influential 2003 essay "Explorations in Animist Materialism," which opens by citing a statue memorializing the god Sango in front of the Nigerian Electric Power Authority as an example of the presence of Yoruba cosmology in contemporary Nigerian public life. For Garuba, the label *magical realism* names one narrow (and inadequate) subset of literary strategies within a broader matrix of practices, beliefs, logics, "social imaginar[ies]," and "avenues for knowing our way around our world and our society" (2003, 283–84) that he describes variously as "animist culture" and an "animist worldview." Central to Garuba's conceptually ambitious argument is the notion that animist thought, contrary to Weberian narratives of modernization as disenchantment, opens itself to "the continual re-enchantment of the world" (284). Garuba's "animist materialism" and "animist unconscious" invoke Raymond Williams and Fredric Jameson to posit animism as a structuring set of political, economic, social, and cultural practices in Nigeria and elsewhere in Africa, thereby also reenchanting what Garuba sees (perhaps overstating the case) as the overly secularizing, matter-deadening thrust of Marxism. The materialism that Garuba renovates with animist spirit is thus the "old," Marxian one, rather than the newfangled one of the recent material turn. But as Nigerian ecocritic Cajetan Iheka observes, Garuba's analysis anticipates this reckoning with the agency of inanimate objects and other nonhumans: "the 'relational epistemology' promoted by indigenous cultures, once dismissed as evidence of primitive thinking, is becoming fashionable in mainstream criticism" (2018, 59–60).

Indeed, the question that gnaws at me while reading Garuba is the same which gnaws at me reading Jane Bennett: what's the difference—or, *is there* a difference—between animism (or vibrant matter) and the literary imagination? Where does a deeply imaginative, *enchanting* investment in metaphor and personification slide into an *enchanted* orientation toward matter that contemplates the political and ethical claims of its agency and personhood? (I return to these questions in Chapter 3.)[69] Garuba posits as continuous the "scripts that our societies—and our artists—enact" (2003, 266); because the "physical world of phenomena is spiritualized" and the "*materialization* of ideas . . . [is] a normal practice" within animist worldviews, they can be said to "authorize" animist literary techniques and narrative strategies that lend "the abstract or metaphorical a material representation" (284, 273). Although modeled on it, Garuba's animist unconscious seems to function without the torsions and displacements between social contradiction and literary form at work in Jameson's political unconscious. The continuity between animist subjectivity and literary representation undoes the oxymoron implicit in "animist realism" or "magical realism" when the real is understood to be suffused with spirit.

Garuba's analysis is helpful for its account of animism as a cultural logic—one perhaps predisposed to the promises of petro-magic. The blurring of distinctions among narrator, author, and writer in the work of Amos Tutuola comes to mind as an extreme (and problematic) example of how animist "codes" can shape multiple registers of experience. It is less helpful in understanding either petro-magic as a global phenomenon, or the antagonism I perceive between petro-magic and petro-magic-realism. Petro-modernity effects its own "continual re-enchantment of the world," promising wealth without work and machinic work without physical labor, but this enchantment paradoxically tends to operate without recourse— and often in explicit opposition—to animist traditions of thought. Indeed, a kind of petro-magical enchantment and disenchantment are at work in the failure to reckon with the indispensability and astonishing transformative powers of fossil fuels for those who inhabit energy abundance; this disenchantment works through disregard of the time, organic matter, and energetic potential compacted, through the near-magic of fossilization, within oil, gas, and coal.

One of my aims in joining political ecology's analysis of petro-magic with the literary mode of magical realism is to consider how reality and representation converge, but also collide: I coined *petro-magic-realism* to show how writers like Okri and Ifowodo imagine the pressures of a particular political ecology within a particular literary idiom. Drawing attention to petro-magic's devastating material effects and unimaginable disproportionalities, their texts invoke literary precursors like Fagunwa, Tutuola, and Rushdie. Theirs is a mode of national reimagining that encompasses petro-magic's castles in the air and its shacks in the swamp. Petro-magic offers the illusion of wealth without work; petro-magic-realism pierces such illusions, evoking a recognizably devastated, and recognizably fantastic, landscape. (As with the slippages in magical realism, here the geographic and aesthetic senses of *landscape* converge.) Petro-magic-realism reveals the rust-inducing acid rain that follows the "rustling shower of money." Ifowodo and Okri are angels of history, surveying the wreckage of petroleum's progress from the treetops, the vantage of the fabled palm-wine tapster.

These questions of mimesis are complicated by pressures of reception: the politics of reading within the global literary circuits that World Literature takes as its purview. *Magical realism* has become as much a reading practice or marketing shorthand as a descriptor of realities or representational strategies existing *out there* in the world or in literary texts.[70] I intend the rubric *petro-magic-realism* to complicate and historicize the empty globalism of the label (or even "brand") *magical realism*, in which *magical* denotes anything unfamiliar to a European or American reader. Magical realism can function as a literary equivalent of the resource curse hypothesis; it allows distant readers to erect a comforting *cordon sanitaire* of "difference" and "distance" in narratives that might be read otherwise as tracing more complex geographies and complicities.

In his landmark essay "Magical Realism as Postcolonial Discourse," Stephen Slemon acknowledges that magical realism "threatens to become a monumentalizing category" by offering a "single locus upon which the massive problem of *difference* in literary expression can be managed into recognizable meaning in one swift pass," thereby "justifying an ignorance of the local histories behind specific textual practices" (1995, 409, 422). Magical realism is often invoked when ethnographic interpretation proves inadequate for making sense of a text. Perhaps such a broad, reductive approach to the fine-grained textures of local particularity explains Neil Bissoondath's dismissal of "What the Tapster Saw" in an otherwise admiring *New York Times* review of Okri's 1988 collection, *Stars of the New Curfew*; he finds, in the story which he declares "devoid of social observation," that the "fantastical strides beyond the wondrous into the chaotic" (Bissoondath 1989). One wonders whether Bissoondath would have found the story more sensical after the execution of Saro-Wiwa made international headlines in 1995.[71] In this mode of reading magical realism—radically opposed to Garuba's animist materialism—the local literary genealogies that inform Okri's story (including the Yoruba folktales that Fagunwa textualizes) become a different kind of "curious irrelevance," or irrelevant curiosity.

The problem with the magic in magical realism is broader than the sanctioned ignorance of metropolitan readers of world literature, however. The relationship between realism and magic tends to be read as a binary opposition between the West and the rest, between a singular (but European) modernity and multifarious worldviews variously described as premodern, prescientific, pre-Enlightenment, non-Western, traditional, indigenous—or, in more recent, more subtly patronizing formulations, alternatively modern. In his metacritique of magical realism, Michael Valdez Moses notes that "if the paternity of the magical realist novel is everywhere the same" (in the European realist novel), then "in each locale where the magical realist novel is born, its mother appears to be different, distinct, and as it were, native to the region" (2001, 115, 110). This analogy casts magical realism and its many mothers as the product of cross-cultural, imperialist polygamy. The cumulative effect of such strangely binary readings of magical realism—one term always the same, the other always different—is to consolidate the West as a single entity confronting innumerable local traditions.

This reification of the West undermines claims for magical realism's subversive, antihegemonic, or decolonizing thrust. The playful definition of magical realism offered by Lois Parkinson Zamora and Wendy Faris, as a "return on capitalism's hegemonic investment in its colonies . . . now achieving a compensatory extension of its market worldwide," is perhaps more telling than they intend (1995, 2). Read in terms of reception and the reduction of difference, magical realism moves smoothly through circuits of culture, power, and profit established by colonialism, rather than obstructing or rerouting them. Such magical realist habits of reading (some of which congeal in the production and circulation of texts) reduce elements of the fantastic or excessive into a reified, unexamined "cultural difference," rather than registering the critical acts of reimagining at work in petro-magic-realism's exposure of petro-magic's tricks.

The politics of reading world literature intersect with the question of how to tell the story of the Niger Delta. The relationships among reality, representation, and reception in magical realism have ideological and temporal implications for narratives of modernization. Ifowodo's juxtaposition of incommensurable local and global markets, and Okri's tale of the palm wine tapster's nightmarish experience in Delta Oil Company territory, stage the conflict between established and emergent modes of production (and, I would add, modes of combustion and resource extraction) that Fredric Jameson posits as constitutive of magical realism (1986, 311). In these landscapes of petro-nature, the texts reimagine decidedly modern realities by drawing upon fantastic idioms with venerable literary histories that include both local narrative traditions and world literature. These texts insist that petro-magic is no vestige of precapitalism, nor a simple clash between tradition and modernity, or between local content and foreign form.[72] Petro-magic's enchantment (and eventual disenchantment) is that of a petro-modernity at once intensely local and shaped by global capitalism, congruent with the "world-ecology" described by environmental historian Jason Moore (2003). The ecological ravages of petro-modernity effect a forcible disenchantment by "driv[ing] away spirits from the forest" (Okri 1988, 189), but petro-magic effects its own modern enchantments, creating and obscuring its own reality. Petro-magic-realism stages the illusions of petro-magic only to puncture them, revealing the phantasmagoric effects of petro-violence. The extravagant modernity of petro-magic-realism obstructs the consumption of magical realist texts as nostalgic encounters with an exotic yet vanishing world. It rejects the quarantine of the imagination that underwrites the resource curse diagnosis. The bespectacled turtle that serves as the tapster's Virgilian guide in Okri's story takes his place alongside endangered sea turtles burned alive in the Gulf of Mexico in 2010: this improbable image epitomizes the horrific land- and waterscapes created by the BP spill.[73]

As Moses observes, the production and consumption of magical realist texts by "those *who would like to believe* in the marvelous" but who do not actually believe involves a tacit assumption that a disenchanted "modern world . . . is the only one with a historical future" (2001, 106). Garuba finds the same assumption about modernization as telos "in the rhetoric of African politicians and philosopher-activists" who inherited "colonial narratives of progress"; deviation from that narrative generates a discourse of "failure, crisis, and collapse" (2003, 280). Viewing history as a narrative of progress into a future perfect of secular modernization makes the dialectical and contradictory effects of underdevelopment and unimagining difficult to grasp, particularly in extractive economies that generate wealth and poverty simultaneously. This assumption of linear progress allows Ifowodo's Major Kitemo to invoke the fearful prospect of rust as a reason for continued exploitation of the Niger Delta without seeing the damage rust has already done. It allows Michael Watts to describe the juxtaposition of "ultramodern," capital-intensive oil installations with extreme poverty as a "horror." The shocking economic contrast is meant to imply historical anachronism. It motivates and complicates James Ferguson's attempt to disentangle the ethical weight of contemporary Africans' dreams of a better life from European-authored progress narratives that are increasingly discredited as ideological cover for colonizing projects.

This assumption might also explain why some of my students were disturbed by what they perceived as exoticism in *Curse of the Black Gold*, which describes some Niger Delta militants arming themselves with magical amulets to become invisible or invulnerable to bullets. Half a semester's introduction to postcolonial theory had made the students wary of Orientalist representations of Third World subjects but unaware of local traditions of masquerading and spiritual warfare at work in Niger Delta militancy.[74] The students were not fully cognizant of the distorting force of hegemonic assumptions that "magic" (or supernatural belief outside the Judeo-Christian tradition) has no place in a documentary text or in the "real world."[75] When read with a critical awareness of such assumptions, petro-magic-realism can uncover both the lies of petro-magic and the temporal contradictions of underdevelopment. It can implicate metropolitan consumers of magical realist texts and petroleum products not in modernization's inevitable disenchantment of vestigial tradition, but in petro-modernity's phantasmagoric ravagements of societies and lifeworlds. In this sense, petro-magic is the future.

Blood Oil: Metonymy, Metaphor, Reading Across

This chapter has constellated texts, genres, and media that grapple with how to tell the story of the Niger Delta. Habila's *Oil on Water* evinces world-weariness in this regard: how to tell *yet another* Niger Delta story? His answer in this noir page-turner is less earnestly pious, more canny about the pitfalls of international circulation, than other texts discussed here.[76] Habila's knowingness about his position within a global culture industry hovers over his novel like the restless ghosts his journalist-protagonist, Rufus, imagines at an abandoned oil village, or like the "dense, inscrutable mist" curtaining the delta's ever-changing waters that will elicit Conradian associations for some readers.[77] As he travels in search of the missing wife of a British oil executive, Rufus hears two wrenching tales of villages confronting the arrival of oil companies: one framed as expulsion from paradise, the other a fraudulent fairytale promise of escaping poverty. In these generically distinct narratives, the infernal glow of gas flaring stacks seduces local communities longing for infrastructure: for one community, it is a satanic temptation, "its flame long and coiled like a snake, whispering, winking, hissing" (Habila 2010, 42); for another, it is a wondrous "fire that burns day and night . . . the Fire of Pentecost"—at least until it poisons the village (152–53). For each story of temptation and ruin, Rufus insists, there are many more.

One Niger Delta story comes to stand in for another. When he begins telling the story of an oil fire that raged through his hometown of Junction, Rufus must correct the British oil exec who interjects, "Yes, I have heard of that, isn't that a place called Jesse?" to which Rufus responds, "That is a different place. There are countless villages going up in smoke daily" (Habila 2010, 103). Junction, Jesse; Ogoni, Ijaw; militant, criminal: these local variations on a regional theme are what make stories of the Niger Delta so powerful and so problematic. Their slippages reveal the deliquescent line between metonymy and metaphor, reading across one thing to another thing—a dynamic epitomized by the figure of Saro-Wiwa himself.

Chimamanda Adichie argues that the challenge of the Niger Delta is how not to start the story from "secondly"; an additional challenge, I think, is how not to start and end the story with Saro-Wiwa. As told in the United States, the Niger Delta story is dominated by two protagonists: Shell Oil and Ken Saro-Wiwa, names forever linked by spectacular petro-violence in a morality tale of exploitation and resistance so appealing (and horrific) that it hijacks the imagination. But to reduce the story to a man vs. company conflict risks several forms of forgetting. It risks forgetting that Saro-Wiwa was not alone at the gallows: the now-familiar refrain is that "Ken Saro-Wiwa and eight others" were hanged in November 1995. Of the Ogoni Nine, all but Saro-Wiwa were largely consigned to anonymity; nearly erased from distant discourse on the Niger Delta are the names of Baribor Bera, Saturday Dobee, Nordu Eawo, Daniel Gbokoo, Barinem Kiobel, John Kpuinen, Paul Levura, and Felix Nuate. (Ledum Mitee was arrested with them but narrowly escaped execution.) It risks forgetting that the corporate entity now called Royal Dutch Shell is not the only company operating in the region. As noted earlier, Nnimo Bassey warns that resource curse analyses indict "local actors" while ignoring "external and transnational actors"; a necessary corollary is that overemphasizing a single external actor is equally problematic, if it elides the varied relations between the multiple multinationals and the ethnically diverse communities where their concessions operate. Finally, a refusal to forget Saro-Wiwa risks missing the contemporary situation of the Niger Delta, whose petro-political terrain has been dialectically shaped—but not determined—by his struggle of more than two decades ago. The continuing vilification of Shell for its complicity in the death of Saro-Wiwa and his comrades might obscure the historical evolution and quotidian workings of the oil complex: the more systemic, less spectacular, aspects of resource extraction that shape how corporations interact with the state, pursuing their own advantage by selectively assuming and disavowing its conventional functions.

A Niger Delta story reduced to a Saro-Wiwa vs. Shell plot is a dead metonym, an act of unimagining in which the larger context (the eight others, and other others) disappears from view. The problem of making Saro-Wiwa stand for something else exists at multiple geographic scales, with multiple forms and valences of erasure. Postcolonial ecocritics Graham Huggan and Helen Tiffin worry about Saro-Wiwa's "metonymic function as a global spokesperson for social and environmental issues . . . that can easily lead to moralistic generalizations about endemic political corruption in Africa, or the nefarious role of transnational companies in robbing local people of their livelihoods, or the heroic part played by freedom fighters and resistance movements prepared to take on the assembled might of global commerce and the state" (2010, 41). At the national scale, Andrew Apter argues that by the time of Saro-Wiwa's execution in 1995, Nigerians recognized in the Ogoni struggle against "the predations of the military-petroleum complex" a movement that "came to represent the contradictions of oil capitalism" as a nationwide problem: "state vampirism" extracted wealth and welfare from the Nigerian polity as a whole. "Ken

Saro-Wiwa's demand for Ogoni autonomy escalated into a struggle for universal citizenship," Apter writes (2005, 261, 259, 269).

Neither Huggan and Tiffin's anxiety about a global metonymic reading of Saro-Wiwa, nor Apter's assertion of a national one, seems quite right. It's unclear whether the former critics are more concerned about the "global" or the "spokesperson," the generalizing or the moralizing, the geographic scale or the ethico-political attitude.[78] Huggan and Tiffin seem almost to dismiss the possibility of critical/political interventions sufficiently mindful of the discursive trap of painting Africa in such broad strokes. Heroic resistance and arguments about corruption and corporate neocolonialism in places like the Niger Delta are urgently necessary—and can be made with micrological specificity, rhetorical facility, and political nuance. As several critics argue, Saro-Wiwa's singular contribution was to synthesize environmental justice, indigenous rights, and human rights discourses in order to make the Ogoni struggle legible internationally.[79] To insist upon a local and literal frame for reading the Ogoni struggle, where it stands only for itself, would miss Saro-Wiwa's own commitment to imagining across spatial scales and between discourses—a fundamentally metaphorical mode of thinking, in the etymological sense of *bearing across*.

Nevertheless, the issue of generalization does reveal something important about forms of erasure latent within the cultural work of making things legible, when someone or something is made to stand (or substitute) metaphorically for other things or to gesture metonymically toward related things. These figurations can generalize when they seem to specify or localize—the equivalent of mistaking *a* world for *the* world. Saro-Wiwa as martyr erases the eight others, I have noted; Saro-Wiwa as "global spokeperson" disregards the specificity of his struggle, Huggan and Tiffin worry. Something is lost in metaphor's too hurried transit from tenor to vehicle, or metonymy's gesture from near to there (or synecdoche's proffering of part for whole). Drawing too strong a line between metaphor and metonymy is tricky because at stake in the Niger Delta is precisely this tension between metaphoric distance/difference and metonymic contiguity/relation. In positing a Nigerian embrace of the Ogoni struggle, Apter argues, in effect, that Saro-Wiwa catalyzed recognition of the nation as bounded, contiguous whole within which metonymic thinking could operate. The spectacular plight of the Niger Delta became a metonym for less spectacular harms enacted upon the entire nation. But who gets to chart the geography of metonymic contiguity, or the boundaries across which metaphoric thinking travels? Whose interest is the "national interest"?

What new lines of imaginative (and material) traffic would be necessary for the emergence of

> ... a livable
> Niger Delta,
> a just Nigeria

as Ifowodo dreams in his dedication of *The Oil Lamp*?

Abstracting the Ogoni (and other Delta minorities) into a figure for the nation's plight erases forms of physical and ecological harm that are spatially specific and differentiated. Coronil's idea of the nation's two bodies is a multilayered metaphor yoking the human body to the materiality of natural resources and the idea of national community: In this metaphoric metabolism, oil becomes the nation's lifeblood. But this rhetorical commingling of oil and blood looks different from the subnational vantage of the Niger Delta. "Remember your petroleum which is being pumped out daily from your veins, and then fight for your freedom," was the cry Isaac Boro used to mobilize his fellow Ijaw in the short-lived Niger Delta Republic of 1966, which preceded the Biafran secession of 1967–70 (quoted in Watts 2008, 37). Assuming a regional/ethnic congruity and contiguity among physical, natural and political bodies, Boro emphasizes the violence of the state's appropriation of the (ethno)nation's natural body. Pumping petroleum from Ijaw people's veins into Nigeria's circulatory system wrenches this metonymic contiguity into metaphoric division. Pledging, in effect, to *shed our blood for the oil (figured as blood) being extracted from us*, Boro does something more than assert a regional, ethnonational priority over the claims of the nation-state. He makes it possible to understand metonymic relation in terms of "fatal contiguities" of environmental injustice, the physiological "embeddedness" within toxic landscapes, where "contiguity kills" (Hsu 2011, 151–52). Boro described petroleum pumped from ethnonational "veins," but the flow of this corporeal image can be reversed to apprehend the hydrocarbons that seep into soil and water and are absorbed into human and piscine bloodstreams when pipelines bisect communities like central arteries.[80] This commingling of oil and blood is literal, not figurative; the transits and translations of metaphor (the Latin *translatio* an echo of the Greek *metaphorein, carrying across*) can miss actual flows of matter across and through organisms, what Stacy Alaimo calls "trans-corporeality."[81] "The human body is never a rigidly enclosed, protected entity," Alaimo argues, but rather materially "intermeshed with the more-than-human world" (2011, 28, 2). Here the implicit rallying cry against unjust exchange is toxicological rather than geopolitical: not *no blood for oil*, but *no oil for blood*.

Metaphor and metonymy figure an imagination on the move—the obverse of the quarantines of the imagination examined throughout this book, in which what happens "over there" seems unconnected to where one stands "over here." The respective pitfalls of these two modes can be distinguished in terms of speed: with metaphor and metonymy, things can get lost in moving too fast from one term or scale to another, whereas quarantines of the imagination involve stopping short at a seeming frontier of difference. Reimagining entails reading across those geographic and experiential divides, working against the foreclosures of unimagining: the impossible necessity of *reading for the planet*. But the slippages between metaphor and metonymy also demonstrate that the *acrossness* in reading across is not given but contingent, shaped by the position of the interpreter and working at multiple scales. Parts do not always neatly resolve into wholes, and the line between metaphoric leaps and metonymic relays can dissolve when the ground of figuration turns out to be larger than it first appears, part of a whole that enfolds and implicates the interpreter.

A similar shift of ground and scale is at work in James Ferguson's observation about the postcolonial nation-state. Mid-twentieth-century decolonization occurred at the same postwar moment that control over macroeconomics moved beyond the nation-state to international institutions. Consequently, narratives of liberation focused around independence, self-determination, and development at the scale of the nation-state can become a "trap" because "the wider system of economic relations that is constitutive of many of these [putatively national] 'problems' is kept from view" (Ferguson 2006, 12, 50, 65; see also 23). In *The Wretched of the Earth*, Fanon refuses this trap: "We are not blinded by the moral reparation of national independence; nor are we fed by it. . . . The spectacular flight of capital is one of the most constant phenomena of decolonization" (1968, 102–3). Narrow focus on the scale of the nation-state without attention to the workings of global capitalism across borders can be another quarantine of the imagination, another alibi for inequality.

At stake in the Niger Delta are several modes of citizenship and world imagining. Reading for the planet in this context means drawing links between hospitable imaginings of world or planetary citizenship, on the one hand, and struggles within Nigeria to reframe the meaning of postcolonial citizenship and (re)claim democratic sovereignty, on the other. Photographs in *Curse of the Black Gold* in which the subject's gaze meets the implied gaze of the viewer can break through quarantines of the imagina-

Figure 5. Residents of Aker Camp, a slum of Port Harcourt, Nigeria, pick through the remains of their lives after the neighborhood was attacked by members of the Nigerian military. Ed Kashi/VII.

tion by inviting viewers to reimagine webs of connection beyond the borders of the nation-state—those, say, that link the Niger Delta to Detroit. The eyes of Kashi's subjects meet those of viewers, piercing the photograph's frame and plane and linking the site of its production to the site of its consumption. They invite a reflexivity about what it means to look upon such beautiful images of harm that is largely missing from the "ruins porn" that proliferated during Detroit's early twenty-first century nadir.[82] The reflexivity of Kashi's Niger Delta images is most acute in a photograph of the owner of a Port Harcourt bar destroyed by the Nigerian military (see Figure 5). She stands amid the ruins, a stack of photographs from better days in her hands, her slanted gaze in barely-more-than profile view asking the viewer *something*, although precisely what is undecidable. Perhaps, "What are *you* looking at?" Or maybe, "Can you believe this?" As with the reflexive scenes of film and TV spectatorship in Chapter 1, this photograph facilitates a transfer of viewers' awareness of their complicitous consumption of oil to an awareness of their consumption of image and text. Whether the bar owner is inviting solidarity with viewers or resisting their scopic attention, her gaze implicates them as it reaches across from her site of viewing photos to theirs.

There are many imaginative pathways for thinking from near to there, and each one has its pitfalls. "Blood Oil" was the term coined by the United States Institute for Peace in a 2009 Special Report on the Niger Delta, which drew upon postconsumerist awareness about conflict minerals sparked by the 2006 Leonardo DiCaprio blockbuster *Blood Diamond*.[83] (Helon Habila's *Oil on Water* also originated when he was commissioned to write a script for a film envisioned by its producers as a *Blood Diamond* about the Niger Delta.) The account of "blood oil" in the Institute for Peace report is nothing like Isaac Boro's image of petroleum pumped from Ijaw veins, nor the toxic transcorporeality of petrochemicals absorbed into bloodstreams. Here "blood oil" names not the structuring petro-violence that has underwritten the Nigerian "slick alliance" of state and corporation for decades, but instead the more recent trade in bunkered or "stolen oil" by local residents, militant groups, and rogue officials that "fuels insurgency" and "poses an immense challenge to the Nigerian state" (1). The problem with blood oil, according to this report, is that it undermines the Nigerian economy and keeps the oil industry from pumping at full capacity, which means less supply and higher prices for American consumers.[84]

Framed this way, blood oil is an arresting image. It hijacks the imagination. Beginning the story from "secondly," it renders illegible longer histories and constitutive structures of violence. Blood oil invites the cultivation of postconsumerist awareness, but it leaves unimagined the costs borne daily by denizens of the Niger Delta, many of whom understand quite differently the provenance and referent of "stolen oil." Although divided by history, ethnicity, microregion, and struggle tactics, both Isaac Boro and Ken Saro-Wiwa regarded as stolen the oil extracted "legitimately" by multinationals in alliance with the state. In the Niger Delta, *blood oil* signifies oil "paid for with our blood," in Ledum Mitee's formulation: "When I travel outside Nigeria people often ask me how far away Ogoni is. I tell them it's as far as the nearest Shell service station. . . . The petrol in the tank of your car has been paid for with our blood" (quoted in Daminabo and Frank 2015, 46). In this defamiliarizing elastic geography, the seemingly remote becomes all too proximate. Oil, blood, money, and water substitute for one another in exchanges and transmutations that exceed even the ratios in Marx's phantasmagoric account of the commodity.

Once upon a time, in 1995, Shell was a less-than-innocent bystander as Ken Saro-Wiwa and eight others were executed. At that time, one could take some postconsumerist satisfaction in passing by the Shell station and filling up elsewhere, as Ledum Mitee urged readers of the postcolonial studies journal *Interventions* in 1999: "The United States imports 60 per cent of Nigerian oil. With freedom, each of you has the choice not to purchase particular oil company products, for example, those of Shell, and with democracy, you have the power to influence your governments" (438). "Freedom" here denotes consumer choice: Mitee addresses readers as consumers first, citizens second. The idea of boycotting Shell now feels quaint—just as boycotting BP in 2010 seemed beside the point.[85] The problem with petroleum is bigger than any one bad actor.

The challenges facing consumer-citizens on either side of the chain of ease are more intractable than the mere "choice" of whether to fill up at BP, Shell, Exxon, or some less objectionable alternative, as the "Citizens and Consumers" part of this book has sought to demonstrate. The challenges include an increasing awareness of costs of oil not factored into the price at the pump, and the ubiquity of petroleum as the literal and metaphorical substrate of hydrocarbon modernity. The uneven predicament of complicit consumption for some, and unrealized desires for consumption and the prerogatives of citizenship for others, presents an impasse that can seem all but inescapable. Consumer "choice" is increasingly recognized as ruse, while citizenship, conceived as the democratic capacity to influence one's government, has been downsized or displaced out of reach.[86] How to imagine beyond the disaster du jour, beyond petroleum (to borrow BP's erstwhile slogan), and create the conditions for meaningful choice?

Reading for the planet shuttles between the micrologically specific and the world-historical, across both space and time. The Niger Delta is but one of many instances of petro-violence around the globe. This chapter's inventory of different versions of the Niger Delta story offers a necessary counterpart to new grand narratives of scholars like Timothy Mitchell and Dipesh Chakrabarty, whose provocative reperiodizations link the emergence of mass democratic movements, organized labor, Enlightenment, and the Anthropocene to energy transitions from wood to coal to oil. Historian G. Ugo Nwokeji reads across time when he recalls that the task of the eighteenth-century abolitionist movement was to transform slave labor from perceived necessity to moral scourge; "a time may come," he writes, "when oil will be viewed in a manner not unlike eighteenth-century slavery, the greenhouse gases emitted from hydrocarbons perhaps akin to slave-produced sugar, and free labor as a parable for renewable energy" (2008, 65). One can reject this analogy between "hydrocarbon exploitation" and the slave trade as thinking too far or too fast between one thing and another, but even the act of articulating a demur brings the worldwide lineaments of petroleum into sharper relief, makes the facts of the slick alliance harder to forget, and holds out the possibility of an alternative.

PART II

Resource Logics and Risk Logics

CHAPTER 3

From Waste Lands to Wasted Lives: Enclosure as Aesthetic Regime and Property Regime

*If the common aspects of life in nature are not cultivated by
imaginative rather than instrumental reason, nature will cease
to be an object of vital interest and eventually render us homeless.*

—GEOFFREY H. HARTMAN, *The Fateful Question of Culture*

*Perhaps there are few questions in which the general feeling has
undergone a greater change than the estimation in which trees and
forests are held in India. In former days . . . forest, jungle, malaria,
and fever were regarded as almost synonymous and convertible
terms. . . . Those who had been most prejudiced against the trees
were compelled to admit the great increase in sickness which had
followed their destruction. . . . Since we have taken the trouble to
ascertain their real character, we have come to regard the trees as
friends instead of enemies; and whereas we used to look upon
the backwoodsman with admiration, as a modern Hercules
cleansing the Augean jungle with his lively axe, we are now
plaintive in our entreaty, "Woodman, spare that tree."*

—N. A. DALZELL, "The Influence of Trees on Climate" (1869)

Waste isn't what it used to be.

In a metabolic or industrial sense, there's something beguilingly literal about this statement. Waste is excreta, byproduct, remnant: the unlovely remainder of processes of transformation, manufacture, or consumption. Waste is what used to be food, fuel, raw materials, or other once useful things at the end of their wonted, wanted life.

Industrial wastelands, wasted lives: As with toxic waste or mountains of refuse, remnants of ruin are too much with us. In the form of greenhouse gas emissions, waste products of hydrocarbon modernity fill the earth's atmosphere, with CO_2 having crossed the critical threshold of 400 parts per million. On the earth's surface, "human waste" is Zygmunt Bauman's horrific pun for disposable populations of "wasted humans," reserve armies of surplus labor unlikely to be called up (2003, 13). "Our planet is full," Bauman declares. Late modernity brought the closing of a global frontier in which the "deepest meaning of colonization" was a kind of (human) waste management. Lands beyond Europe offered "natural destinations for the export of 'redundant humans,'" "dumping sites for the human waste of modernization" (4–6). Now the planet is full; there's nowhere left to go.

But in the beginning, waste was something else entirely. "In the beginning," John Locke wrote in "Of Property" (1690), "all the world was America" (1988, 2:49). For Locke, *waste* meant unenclosed, unimproved land awaiting the infusion of human labor. For land to be left in that state of nature would be profligate (i.e., wasteful), contravening the intentions of the Creator who gifted the earth to "men in common" to labor upon and make productive (2:26). This version of waste is, in the formulation of New Zealand *pakeha* poet Charles Brash, "uncolonized nothing" (quoted in Newton 1999, 90): a void that demands to become *something*. Waste lands were the original raw material of capitalism and colonialism awaiting transformation into arable, cultivated, revenue-producing land. Yet the products of that transformation are also known as waste, of the sort with which we in the twenty-first century are familiar. Thus, waste isn't what it used to be—in either the material or conceptual sense.[1] This chapter closes the circle between these versions (or moments) of waste: between the earth as empty frontier and a polluted planet that is overfull; between waste as the beckoning origin of development and as troublesome end product.

Waste begets waste. Waste is a performative concept and a productive category: One form of waste generates others. By disregarding any value besides economic productivity, waste lands are transformed into wasted lands and wasted lives—lands and lives *laid waste*. (As in Ann Laura Stoler's transitive account of *ruin* as ruination [2008], *waste* is not only a noun but also a verb that names the infliction of harm: *wasting, laying waste*.) The engines of this transformation are enclosure and "improvement," urbanization and industrialization, and, more recently, deindustrialization, financialization, and neoliberal privatization. Bringing "waste" land into capitalist production means excluding people from their livelihoods and rendering them surplus, their previous lifeways and very presence often criminalized. Whereas Locke thinks back to the "first peopling of the great common of the world" (2:35), Sir Thomas More's *Utopia* (1516) depicts enclosure as a tumultuous "unpeopling": Because of the "increase in pasture" to graze them, sheep "may be said to devour men and unpeople not only villages, but towns" (quoted in Dawson 2010, 8). What God peoples, enclosure unpeoples.

This chapter thinks between material processes and cultural logics of waste: between the commons and common sense, between land and landscape, and between private property and rhetorical propriety in describing the natural world, as in debates about the pathetic fallacy. Cultural logics inflect what is taken as "real" or "natural" in the disposition of nature. Unpeopling involves both literal removals of people from land and the cognitive erasure and disregard described in previous chapters as *unimagining*. "Acts of enclosure always take place on cultural terrain," Ashley Dawson writes; "culturally specific assumptions are portrayed as universal and logical, setting up a series of binary relations between reason and unreason, science and superstition, modernity and the archaic which work ineluctably to legitimate acts of enclosure" (2010, 14–15). I share Dawson's sense of the importance of cultural logics in acts of enclosure, but I want to complicate these putatively binary relations by examining moments of representation and reflection when incompatible visions of land and nature collide. Are trees enemies or friends? So wondered nineteenth-century British colonial forester N. A. Dalzell as India's lands and forests underwent one of the most significant enclosures in history, and the "text" of a tree was read in radically different ways.

The British colonization of India figures prominently in Karl Marx's account of primitive accumulation, the process of alienating people from their means of production and subsistence, thereby pushing them into wage labor. Along with "the conquest and plunder of India," Marx mentions "the discovery of gold and silver in America" and "the conversion of Africa into a preserve for the commercial hunting of blackskins" as "the chief moments of primitive accumulation" (1977, 1:915). Primitive accumulation is not merely a catalyzing moment at the "dawn . . . of capitalist production" (1:915), but an ongoing process of "accumulation by dispossession," as David Harvey (2003) and others have argued. From this perspective, the history of capitalism appears as successive "waves of enclosure and the production of vast floating populations of landless and often illegal people" (Dawson 2010, 8–9). Later waves of enclosure include the multiple scrambles for Africa—whether late nineteenth-century high imperialism, or twenty-first-century land grabs in which countries and corporations capture arable land in Africa (and elsewhere in the Global South) as a hedge on their own food security. These "new enclosures" have claimed for capitalist accumulation different kinds of "commons," such as the genome and other forms of intellectual property, civil society, the airwaves and the Internet, even big data. At a planetary scale, the emergent understanding of anthropogenic global warming retrospectively reveals the de facto expropriation of the earth's atmosphere and oceans as sinks for the waste products of industrial agriculture and fossil-fueled modernity. The industrialized world has thereby enclosed the future of the rest of the world by using up these sinks' capacity to absorb waste within the parameters that have sustained life on Earth as humans have known it. As with the 1884–85 Conference of Berlin, which aimed to impose order upon a European scramble for Africa already underway, contemporary efforts to create a market for carbon offsets would formalize an expropriation of the atmospheric commons by the Global North that has been underway for centuries. The effects of these enclosures are cumulative and unevenly distributed; the most disruptive effects of climate change will be borne by "the same subsistence farmers who have been subjected to the most intense waves of [land] enclosure in the global South during the neoliberal era" (Dawson 2010, 22).

In India, successive waves of enclosure intersect with global warming in several ways—and not merely in the twenty-first century, when the fate of the planet may hinge on whether India pursues a development path fueled by coal or solar power and other renewables. These waves of enclosure are neither inexorable nor linear. Rather, they oscillate among various approaches to land policy and practice (laissez-faire private property vs. state conservation; prioritizing agriculture vs. forests; tolerance, cooptation, or exclusion of local subsistence users). They vary across the subcontinent and between the scales of local or centralized control, whether by the Mughal Empire, the British East India Company Board of Directors, the India Office, or the independent nation-state. Rather than a binary opposition between civilized improvement and barbarous waste, multiple cultural logics shape this history, often unpredictably and contradictorily. These contradictions emerge in my reading of Bengali writer-activist Mahasweta Devi's short story "Dhowli," the literary text anchoring our examination here of the global history of waste and wasting, which begins (if we follow Locke) as a planetary America and might be said to end (if we follow Mahasweta) at the margins of a forest in rural Bihar.

Written and set in the late 1970s, "Dhowli" offers a seemingly anachronous account of the cognitive dissonance of climate change, as I elaborate at the end of this chapter. The slow violence and dilated temporality of global warming do not merely disrupt chronology, causality, and what it means to be out of time, however. How far back must one go to trace the "prehistory" of the Anthropocene? Nineteenth-century observers in India, including colonial medical officers ("surgeons"), botanists, and forestry officials, linked deforestation to decreased rainfall, soil erosion, drought, and famine; they also speculated about broader chemical changes in the earth's atmosphere. These personnel of empire witnessed the effects of imperialism's "improvement" as the transformation of forested, uncultivated waste into wasted lands, thereby helping to lay the groundwork for contemporary climate science, if not necessarily for climate justice movements. Such moments of cognitive dissonance are crucial to the contradictory cultural logics of waste.

Before turning to "Dhowli," however, let us return to Locke's beginning, when all the world was waste. Locke's apologia for private property unfolds as an insidious argument-by-encroachment: first a slow drift, then a sudden claim and consolidation of facts on the ground. You grant him the inch of his initial premise that eating food amounts to appropriation by quite literally incorporating it—making it "part of" oneself (2:26)—only to find that he's taken the mile (or the planet!) of concluding that humankind, through its use of money, has universally assented to economic inequality: "it is plain that men have agreed to disproportionate and unequal possession of the earth" (2:50). For Locke, money is hardly the root of all evil; rather, it is the conceptual hinge and temporal hedge that resolves the contradiction of waste.

Locke explains that land "left wholly to nature, that hath no improvement of pasturage, tillage, or planting, is called, as indeed as it is, *waste*; and we shall find the benefit of it amount to little more than nothing" (2:42; emphasis added). Through their labor upon this waste, men improve and earn title to the land. Rather than mere economic self-interest, such enclosure-by-improvement is a "moral duty," political theorist Onur Ulas Ince explains, because "*rescuing* land from waste . . . consummates" the purpose of God's gift of the earth (2018, 49). The only moral limit to this process Locke recognizes is, somewhat paradoxically, another form of waste. One may (must?) enclose as much land as one can use the produce from "before it spoils." For Locke, a laborer's ownership of land in excess of "the bounds of just property" has to do not with "the largeness of his possession, but the perishing of any thing uselessly in it" (2:30, 2:46). What solves this problem is money—"a little piece of yellow metal, which would keep without wasting or decay" (2:37)—which cheats the time of nature by enabling accumulation without spoilage, the industrious improvement of waste land without the sin of wasted produce. It resolves the contradiction between "*letting waste* and *making waste*" (Ince 2018, 52).

For Locke in the 1680s, much of the world was still America. The European "discovery" of America reset the clock on an overcrowded Europe, returning the world to that moment of limitless promise, as Locke repeats endlessly, "in the beginning." (His version of waste and Bauman's are not unrelated; for Locke, the world only *seems* full; see 2:36.)[2] With a new continent beckoning, Locke is unconcerned about destruction through *laying waste*; the problem with overproduction is the spoilage of overabundant produce, not the despoliation of overworked land nor the dispossession of those living lightly upon it. His is a world without scarcity, without limits to growth. Quite the contrary: The enclosure of land, as a subtraction from God's gift of the earth in common, "does as good as take nothing at all" (2:33). In Locke's magical arithmetic of enclosure and accumulation, subtraction transmogrifies into addition: "he who appropriates land to himself by his labour, does not lessen, but increase the common stock of mankind"; an industrious proprietor who *takes* ten acres from a hundred lying in common "may truly be said to *give* ninety acres to mankind" through the yield of his land (2:37; emphasis added). "Of Property" teems with exuberant ratios of surplus, in which "the wild woods and uncultivated waste" of America serve as the revelatory second term: one acre of "inclosed and cultivated land" yields as much as ten, or even 100, acres "lying waste in common" (2:37). The *indigenes* of America were blessed with abundant natural riches, yet they "have not one hundredth part of the conveniencies we enjoy, and a king of a large and fruitful territory there feeds, lodges, and is clad worse than a day labourer in England" (2:41). (That day laborer, don't forget, was likely cast off the land in an earlier wave of enclosure.) By positing such miraculous increase as a gift to the "common stock of mankind" rather than solely a boon to the proprietor, Locke can argue for the moral virtue of accumulation and dispossession. For Locke, the privatization of the commons (and the colonization of America) is the "precondition for universal prosperity . . . while persistence in holding things in common . . . appears as virtual theft from the prospective wealth of mankind" (Ince 2018, 54).

One could say that to allow such theft would be a tragedy of the commons: the tragedy of preventing the commons—whose value Locke estimates at "little more than nothing"—from becoming common stock. The shift from *commons* to *common stock* is fundamental to Locke's account of property. Both belong to humankind as a whole: the first as God's paradoxically worthless gift, the second as potentially limitless capital. By positing as a "tragedy of the commons" Locke's fearful prospect of unimproved lands lying waste, never to realize their potential, I mean to distinguish Locke's moment of waste from our own. The more familiar "tragedy of the commons" was articulated by ecologist Garrett Hardin in 1968, amidst Cold War anxieties about overpopulation and emerging concerns about natural limits to economic growth. Invoking Alfred North

Whitehead's literary definition of tragic drama as a "remorseless working of things," Hardin rued the tragedy of an unmanaged commons *laid waste* by unrestrained exploitation (1244).[3]

At first glance, the worlds that Locke and Hardin survey seem antithetical: for Locke, too much land, too few people; for Hardin, ruined commons, scarce resources, and overpopulation fears. Hardin uses *waste* in the late-modern sense of pollution or gluttony, not as an early modern near-synonym for commons. Yet Hardin is Locke's ideological heir. They share a blind faith in private property as a form of "reason" that construes the commons as the opposite of common sense. (For Hardin, God is irrelevant and altruism is for fools.) They are separated by several generations— by centuries of enclosure, improvement, and empire for which Locke provided legitimation. Although Hardin does not recognize it, the land he surveys is the product of processes Locke helped inaugurate.[4] As Rob Nixon writes, both early nineteenth-century enclosure and mid-twentieth-century concerns about resource capture and new enclosures underwrite Hardin's parable in which the pastoralist "still roams the Third World as an embodiment of profligacy awaiting market rationalization" (2012, 596). Hardin is astonishingly blind to the historical processes that brought the world to the condition he laments; why else would he offer a thought-experiment about an early nineteenth-century "plainsman" who eats only the tongue of a bison and blithely throws away the rest, when in fact bison were for Native Americans a versatile mobile commons that didn't collapse in a "tragedy" of overexploitation but was targeted for eradication by an expanding and enclosing United States, to be replaced by fenced pastures and fields? Tobacco and sugar, cornerstone crops of plantation slavery, play a similarly vexed role in Locke's argument about the possessive individual's appropriation of land through labor.

The tone and horizon of expectation in Locke's "Of Property" is not tragedy but optimism about the limitless wealth to be made from waste: a comedy of the commons. Ince identifies this stance as a "progressive and acquisitive gaze that perceives the world as a reservoir of potential value to be extracted and accumulated" (2018, 54). For Locke, waste isn't what it *will be*. This expectant gaze underwrites the cultural logic of waste: Its vision is narrowly focused on the economic, yet also prodigiously unrestrained in *imagining* a future latent within, but quite distinct from, facts on the ground. We might call it the moment a teleology is born. The "improving eye" is Mary Louise Pratt's term for this stance, in which a spatial prospect—a European explorer surveying the landscape—implies the temporal prospect of a "Euro-colonial future": "resources to be developed, surpluses to be traded, towns to be built" (1992, 61). In this narrative convention, inventory joins with proleptic imagination to take stock of improvement that will have happened in a future perfect. A seminal instance of this convention appears in the narrative of the first voyage of Christopher Columbus. An entry for November 12, 1492, reports the presence, along the newly named Rio de Mares, of gold, jewels, spices, cotton, aloe, and mastic to be traded and pliant souls to be converted; it imagines further still, transforming the landscape: "The mouth of this river forms the best harbour I have yet seen; being wide, deep and free from shoals, with a fine situation for a town and fortifications where ships may lie close along the shore, the land high, with a good air and fine streams of water" (1998, 124–25). What distinguishes Locke from Columbus or the explorers Pratt analyzes is the planetary scale of his prospect: His concern is not with this river or that valley but with the earth itself and the project of improvement that, as Ince writes, "strives to put an end to the waste of the world" (2018, 53).

This chapter inflects that phrase, "the waste of the world," in ways beyond what Locke could allow himself to imagine in his world-imagining, untangling relationships among the multiple senses of waste articulated earlier—beckoning land, troublesome by-product, surplus lives: waste as thing and deed, noun and verb, the waste of the world laid waste. These aspects of waste coalesce around *resource logics*, by which I mean ideologies and habits of mind through which humans understand nature as something other than themselves, disposed for their use (as a "resource"), and subject to their control. In resource logics, nature has always-already entered economics, as "natural resources": stuff-waiting-to-be-sold-and-used, along the lines of what Heidegger called *das Bestand*, the standing-reserve. But as with the proleptic temporality of Pratt's improving eye, in which river mouths will-have-become ports, this chapter understands resource logics as sites of prodigious imagining, even as they are naturalized into tacit common sense.

Seeing the Forest and the Trees in Colonial India

The contradictions within these cultural logics are everywhere apparent with regard to waste and wooded lands in India—before, during, and after the British Raj. "Every period in Indian history had its own 'forest line,'" writes environmental historian Mahesh Rangarajan, emphasizing the "fluidity of the border between forests and cultivation" (1996, 11; Menon 2004). As hinted in the epigraph, when the British personnel of empire looked at trees and forests in India, they saw different things. At the end of the eighteenth century, a moment of sustained naval conflict with France, some saw a source of timber and masts for shipbuilding to replace the woodlots of the newly independent United States of America (themselves an alternative to the exhausted forests of Britain and Ireland); this is just one way that Indian forests have long been global.[5] This strategic variant of resource logic—with the British navy figured as the "wooden walls" of empire—took a new form in the 1860s, in the demand for railroad ties (or "sleepers") as tracks were laid across the subcontinent to consolidate colonial control. Beyond timber's uses for imperial transport, some perceived forests in India as an impediment to British rule, whether as a refuge for bandits or rebels (as they were in Ireland), an unhealthful reservoir for miasmatic disease (Dalzell's "Augean jungle"), or, most significantly, an uneconomic use of land that could be cleared for agriculture to produce both revenue for the colonial state and food as a bulwark against famine. Some who looked at woods saw only waste; however, the strategic imperatives of ship- and railroad-building also spurred efforts to conserve and manage forest resources, rather than allowing unrestrained timber extraction and/or land-clearing for agricultural enclosure. During these swings of the land policy pendulum between two variants on resource logic (state conservation and laissez-faire emphasis on revenue-producing private property), only rarely and in times of resistance were forests perceived by the British from the perspective of local subsistence users, as an indispensable source of livelihood.

The emergence of Company rule spurred a geographical transformation of which the 1793 Permanent Settlement of Bengal was only the beginning, as the East India Company's coastal trade enterprise evolved into a nascent colonial state. This "survey and settlement" aimed to document and regularize systems of land tenure and taxation. (In later decades, the ambition of this knowledge project extended even to transport animals kept by nomadic pastoralists, whose "camels, ponies, horses, mules—were to be enumerated, registered and branded" to facilitate military conscription by the state [Bhattacharya 1998, 83].) A primary consideration within this cadastral endeavor was maximizing revenue for the Company—a priority invoked by its central Court of Directors in response to local presidencies' competing concerns, such as shipbuilding in Bombay. Uncultivated lands appeared as Lockean waste; casting an improving eye over its expanding territories, the Company forged policies that aimed to transform imagined futures into infrastructural and revenue realities (Whitehead 2012). EIC regulations held that the infrastructural imperative of building roads, canals, and railways trumped private property rights (Kasturi 2008). By the early 1850s, the Company had claimed trusteeship over all uncultivated waste lands; from 1856 onward, even after the 1858 shift to Crown rule, there was a push to sell off these lands and bring them under cultivation and taxation—the only way British citizens could acquire land in mid-nineteenth-century India (Singh 2012). Yet it was from these waste lands that forest reserves were carved out; the Forest Acts of 1865 and 1878 and other subsequent regulations asserted state control over all uncultivated and forest land, and even over valuable hardwood species like teak, sal, deodar, and shisham (Indian rosewood) growing on private lands (Rangarajan 1996, 62).

This capture of Indian forests seemed to realize the argument Dr. Thomas Preston made in 1791 to a Suffolk commons committee, that "Countries yet barbarous" were "the right and only proper Nurseries" for hardwoods like oak (quoted in Albion 1926, 119). Preston welcomed the decimation of England's "great Plenty of oak" as the salutary effect of agricultural expansion. He offered a progress report of sorts on the Lockean project of waste reclamation: "the Scarcity of Timber ought never to be regretted, for it is a certain proof of National Improvement." Preston scorned the practical unreason, resource illogic, and temporal "mischief" of maintaining oak groves in England while importing wheat and oats: "where is the Owner who will sow a Crop of 100 Years?" (119).[6] As R. G. Albion explains in *Forests and Sea Power*, oak and corn demanded rich soils, and the eighteenth-century enclosure movement elevated the fortunes of corn over the "crooked oaks growing in the hedgerows thrown down to unite the little fields" (118). As with money for Locke, imperial expansion seems to cheat the time of nature: with India as a hardwood "nursery," England could have its teak and eat corn too.

For the British, however, India was no America. Rather than beckoning waste land utterly unencumbered by social compacts, the British perceived India as an extant empire and ancient civilization: not tabula rasa but historical palimpsest. The EIC's work of "survey and settlement" was deeply concerned with understanding the precedent and claiming the authority of the Mughal Empire, so that—as Ranajit Guha shows in his magisterial genealogy of the 1793 Permanent Settlement, *A Rule of Property for Bengal*—notions of "Oriental despotism" were invoked favorably by British policymakers to legitimate state control over land and revenue. In these debates, as Vinay Gidwani (1992, 2008) has shown, "waste" became something more than an ecological or revenue category; it took on a normative dimension as a marker of social, cultural, and moral difference that provided justification for colonial rule.

In *Orientalism*, Edward W. Said identified the 1798 Napoleonic campaign in Egypt as a seminal moment for the Orientalist power/knowledge project. As Aamir Mufti observes, however, the mid- to late eighteenth-century shift from trade to rule in what became British India spurred a "need for systematic knowledge of Indian society"; this efflorescence of Indology was an early instance of Orientalist knowledge production that Mufti identifies as a seminal moment and condition of possibility for world literature (2016, 103). The inquiries of figures like Alexander Dow and Philip Francis into Mughal systems of land tenure (which Guha analyzes in *A Rule of Property*) can be understood as imbricated with the multilingual literary inquiries of the Orientalist Sir William Jones, as part of an *epistemological* survey and settlement.[7] Jones's enthusiasm about the vast riches of Indian writing in Persian, Arabic, and Sanskrit provoked a notorious retort from Thomas Babington Macaulay, who scoffed in his 1835 Minute on Indian Education that "a single shelf of a good European library was worth the whole native literature of India and Arabia" (1969, 45). Note the symmetry with Locke's ratios of English productivity and American profligacy in this assertion of civilizational superiority: Macaulay surveys the landscape of Indian knowledge production and finds only waste, of a sort holding little promise for the future.[8]

With regard to India's forests, Mughal precedent and precolonial practice were seen by several colonial officials and observers, including Francis Wrede, Nathaniel Wallich, W. H. Sleeman (theorist of "thuggee"), and Alexander Gibson, as legitimating state control and providing a model of sound management through royal *shikargarhs* (protected hunting groves) and other forest reserves (Grove 1996, 396–496 passim). One perennial question in the historical vagaries and regional variants of land policy concerned the relationships among state, landowner, and peasant or other subsistence users, in terms of revenue, rights, and responsibilities. Most urgently, with regard to the socioecological displacements associated with enclosure, did local subsistence users have the right to hunt, collect forest produce, and graze livestock, either on private land or government-controlled forest reserves?

Environmental historians disagree about the state of the commons before and during the British Raj. Countering Madhav Gadgil and Ramachandra Guha's (1993) rather idyllic account of a precolonial managed commons, Grove cites instances of local users in the nineteenth century who enjoyed more access than before; he insists that concerns about de-forestation, timber shortage, commodification, village removal (cf. Sir Thomas More's "unpeopling"), and the exclusion of commons-use from forest areas also swirled around Mughal-era enclosures (1996, 386–87, 459). Acknowledging such precolonial precedents of forest management and control, Rangarajan nonetheless emphasizes that British policy in India was unprecedented in the scale of its ambition to impose "an absolute notion of landed property" and to "regulate the production patterns and settle-ment patterns of groups on the fringes of settled arable cultivation" (1996, 8, 16). In the late nineteenth century, the Forest Department designated vast territories (regardless of tree cover) as reserved forest, "not so much for the purposes of forestry, as for the alienation of property rights in land" (Rangarajan 1996, 74).

Such historiographical debate delineates contradictions within the cul-tural logics of waste in India. Enclosure and "unpeopling" are not an in-exorable, linear process that began only in the (European) colonial era; the British positioned themselves not only as Lockean civilizing improvers, but also as (enlightened) heirs to empires and Oriental despots past. Debates over colonial Indian forest policy were informed by the war on waste in Britain and Ireland, when "the woods became a managed and controlled landscape rather than untamed forest" and trees became something like crops, as Dr. Preston of Suffolk vividly intimated (Rangarajan 1996, 16). Nonetheless, Orientalist notions of ruin and faded glory may have informed British understandings of Indian jungles not as primeval waste awaiting improvement, but as formerly cultivated land "lapsed into a state of nature," the "result of the abandonment of agriculture" (17).[9] This dynamic had ur-gent policy implications: in a 1772 essay urging permanent settlement of Bengal, the physiocrat Henry Pattullo lamented that the prevailing prac-tice of short-term leases obstructed the spirit of improvement, "laying many of the cultivated lands so soon waste and desolate" (20).[10] Transfor-mation of menacing jungles into revenue-producing cultivated land on a permanent basis would therefore be waste *reclamation*.

Waste and Want: Commons Confusions

Regardless of the histories that informed or were thought to inform set-tlement policy, one persistent contradiction involved the confusing and pernicious overlap between waste and commons as frameworks for think-ing about land, particularly woodlands. In debates preceding the Forest Act of 1927, J. W. Nicholson, Indian Forest Service Provincial Research

Officer in Bihar and Orissa, advocated total exclusion of local users, in terms that anticipate Hardin's tragedy of the commons: "forests require protection from man. It is a common failing in human nature that whenever any product is found in abundance its use is abused without thought for the future. . . . The great Indian epics tell of the mighty forests which used to exist in the Gangetic plain. . . . Left to himself, the villager takes no care of his forests" (1926, 5–6).[11] Such assertions posited tight state control over forests as a necessary bulwark against villagers' inevitable depredations. But after centuries of settlement and various state approaches to forest management, villagers had hardly been left to themselves; rather than "human nature" leading inexorably to overexploitation, the historical pressures of enclosure can be understood to exacerbate demands upon a dwindling commons. As with Hardin's bizarre example of Native Americans' "wasteful" use of bison, local subsistence users were often blamed for overexploitation caused by commercial or strategic extraction. During the 1857–58 Sepoy Rebellion, jungles were described by Mandla garrison commander H. F. Waddington as "the worst enemy" of the British because of the refuge they provided rebels; a few years later, the demands of railway expansion, spurred partly by the Rebellion, shifted the colonial calculus about the value of wooded lands, and "officials began to blame tribals for excessive felling of timber trees" (Rangarajan 1996, 98). This example demonstrates how the colonial appropriation of waste land (bringing uncultivated lands within a property regime predicated on extracting revenue) was a dialectical and blind relation, transforming "waste" lands into *wasted* lands, leaving them barren and overworked, and placing the blame for such wasting on indigenous peoples and other local users dependent on them for survival. Rather than a tragedy of the commons à la Hardin, this remorseless dynamic is better understood as a "tragedy of the private" (Bartolovich 2010, 44).[12]

One place where these tensions surface is the stinging 1886 report of Alexander Anderson, a Forest Settlement Officer in the hill district of Kullu, currently in Himachal Pradesh. As an employee of the Revenue Department (bureaucratic rival to the Forest Department), Anderson recognized that forest access enabled small cultivators to grow crops to pay taxes, as well as the broader importance of forests as a commons necessary to subsistence. About the Forest Department's tendency to extinguish forest access rights in the name of conservation, Anderson wrote forcefully, "The people are dependent on these rights for their very existence, and the extinction of the rights would be the most unjustifiable *expropriation*. . . . Difficulties arise when the waste to be reserved is just what the people require for the supply of their daily wants" (quoted in Singh 2012, 5–7; emphasis added). This reframing of *waste* as *daily want* makes imaginable an alternative logic (or "rule") of property, in which claims to a relationship to land would find justification in the baseline of community subsistence, rather than solely imperial prerogative or the accumulation of wealth through the production of surplus and "improving" labor. (A century later, an assessment of forest policy "from the point of view of the forest dwellers" would declare: "We cannot distinguish between those who destroy trees legally and those who destroy them without the support of the law. The history of the last two hundred years . . . [proves] that the guardians of the forest law are not able to protect that which had been protected by the forest-dwellers for centuries" [Dasgupta 1986, 96].) To be clear, Anderson's guiding interest was fixing property rights to generate colonial revenue, but his antipathy toward the Forest Department allows us to glimpse a vast gulf in perception: Where the colonial state sees forest/waste in need of improvement or protection (in either case, for the sake of revenue), local communities see a sustaining commons.[13]

This perspectival gulf reveals the error of observers like Locke and Preston, who looked upon waste and woodlands and saw only "mischief": an economic void standing in the way of a prosperous future. Locke estimated the "benefit" of uncultivated land at "little more than nothing" (and even less than nothing, given its effective theft from potential improvement), but this accounting reckons only economic value, only in the short term, only in the direct proceeds of settled agriculture or industry. It reads as waste what functions as commons, missing the vital importance of such land in sustaining reproduction and other forms of production. And it misses the ecological roles such lands play in maintaining the health of soils and waterways, flora and fauna. In the short term, there may seem to be an inverse correlation between the economic and ecological value of land designated "waste." However, the misrecognition or disregard of the ecological function of such "waste" lands leads to lands laid waste, which can in turn depress economic production. In the words of Bombay forest official Alexander Gibson, the "improvident" felling of trees, bushes, shoots, and saplings leaves the poor scrambling because firewood, "formerly so abundant," has become "one of the chief items of expense . . . a deprivation severely felt." This practice also yields wasted lands, "leaving nothing but the bare laterite hills which will remain for ever afterwards utterly sterile and useless" (quoted in Stebbing [1922] 2010, 1:120–21). In the long term, neither the temporal hedge of money nor the spatial fix of colonialism can cheat the time of nature and the wasting of waste lands.

The terminological confusion between commons and waste in India persisted throughout the twentieth century and into the present. The end of British imperialism did not bring an end to enclosure and exclusion; the developmentalist imperatives of a postcolonial nation-state foster an improving eye, which assumes that land designated *waste* is uneconomic and disregards its function as a sustaining commons for millions (Singh 2012; Ghotge 2011). Since independence in 1947, new waves of enclosure have targeted uncultivated land for agricultural or industrial development in the name of poverty alleviation and the "national interest"; these include the desperate effort to boost agricultural yields after the 1943 famine, the redistribution of agricultural land in postindependence land reform, "social forestry" and other poverty-alleviation programs of the 1970s and 80s, and contemporary neoliberal State Economic Zones (Kasturi 2008).[14] Too often, efforts to make "better" use of land perceived as waste have not recognized the extant social or ecological function of fallows or grazing lands. Something about a waste not only wants to be put to use but also obscures the ways it is already—or *still*—being used.

In a 1986 study published in the Indian left journal *Economic and Political Weekly*, sociologist N. S. Jodha documented how the commons had shrunk and degraded since independence, in part because of privatization measures ostensibly aimed at helping the poor, from which they tended not to benefit. Despite this diminution, Jodha found that "common property resources" (CPRs)—defined as "resources accessible to the whole community of a village and to which no individual has exclusive property rights," which include "village pastures, community forests, waste lands, common threshing grounds, waste dumping places, watershed drainages, village ponds, tanks, rivers/rivulets, and riverbeds" (1169) as well as canals and irrigation channels—were the major source of sustenance and livelihood for a significant proportion of the rural poor. Between 84 and 100 percent of landless laborers and small farmers relied on CPRs for food, fuel, fodder, and fiber (1172). Access to such resources was found to reduce income inequality and to serve as a "cushion" in times of crisis (1171). Nonetheless, Jodha observed, researchers and policymakers fail to apprehend the indispensability of CPRs to the rural poor because "they are often available as a matter of routine" (1169). The ordinariness (or commonness) of reliance on the commons obscures its crucial role.

At this late date in the wasting of the world, perhaps the most dangerous aspect of new enclosures is the assumption that the commons is a thing of the pre-capitalist past: that enclosure is complete. As George Caffentzis remarks, reliance on the commons is how the millions of people around the world said to live on a few dollars a day are able to survive (2010, 24). Even in an era of rapacious enclosures, in guises old and new, the commons is a hidden subsidy, the margin of survival on the margins of society. This is what the improving eye cannot see.

Living on the Margin: Mahasweta Devi on Forests

The precarious yet persistent reliance on a dwindling commons is a predicament to which Mahasweta Devi drew incisive attention for more than four decades. Beginning in the 1970s, she documented the plight of some of India's most marginalized citizens in West Bengal and Bihar: low-caste and indigenous communities caught between oppressive social dynamics and dependence upon scarce or degraded resources like agricultural land, forests, water, and salt. Her fiction shares the documentary impulse of her activist journalism on behalf of communities she visited and lived among, offering an unflinching depiction of what it means to be on the losing side of material and cultural conflicts over the disposition of nature: conflicts, that is, over how its benefits and burdens are distributed, and the frameworks through which it is understood and valued.[15] Again and again, her characters, many drawn from people she met, are reduced to bare life on scorched earth.

Many of Mahasweta Devi's narratives depict the desperation of Indian forest dwellers and others dependent upon waste and wooded lands for their livelihood and survival. "The Hunt" depicts forests and fauna degraded by commercial logging, while "Strange Children" narrates problems associated with mining. In "Salt," local communities are excluded from state-controlled reserve forests and vulnerable to elephants protected there. Forests in "Draupadi" are sites of refuge for Naxalite guerrillas and state-militarized zones where boulders turn out to be soldiers. Her novella *Pterodactyl, Puran Sahay, and Pirtha* situates drought-induced famine and pesticide-contaminated water as acute crises within a broader structural predicament jeopardizing the survival of an *adivasi* community in central India, which, she intimates, stands in for tribal India as a whole.[16]

Published in Bengali in 1979, Mahasweta Devi's short story "Dhowli" takes a different approach to the experience of enclosure and exclusion. Unusually for her fiction of this period, problems of deforestation or limited access to forests are nowhere to be seen in "Dhowli," whose eponymous protagonist is a low-caste widow who is forced from her village after being seduced and impregnated by the son of a Brahmin landlord, whose family refuses to support her. Compared with the spectacle of environmental crisis staged in a narrative like *Pterodactyl* (written shortly after the 1984 gas disaster in Bhopal, discussed in Chapter 4), "Dhowli" can be read as a run-of-the-mill tale of caste oppression in rural India, without much overt environmental concern.

What interests me about this story is its rhetorically complex account of life on the margins and its attention to the logics of waste and enclosure that shape Dhowli's plight. Mahasweta's concern in "Dhowli" is not with documenting the "facts" of deforestation or bonded labor,[17] but with probing the imaginative and affective terrain of Dhowli's experience, narrated through free indirect discourse. Dhowli repeatedly misreads her relationship to the forest, and the story's focalization through her means that readers are implicated in the notions of common sense, propriety, and scandal whose naturalization the narrative excavates.[18]

Dhowli is a young Dusad widow from Tahad, a remote village in southeastern Bihar. (This area, home to many *adivasi* communities, was incorporated as the new state of Jharkhand in 2000, the result of agitation against the underdevelopment gap between the region's rich mineral and forest resources and its crushing poverty.) After being widowed, Dhowli leaves her husband's family and returns to her mother, who lost the lease to her own husband's land when he died. Without access to land, the two widows survive by tending the goats and sweeping the courtyard of their former Brahmin landlords, the Misras. Dhowli returned to her mother to escape the sexual advances of her late husband's brother, but she becomes the object of dangerous desire—now of Misrilal, young son of the Misra family. Dhowli avoids the Misra house and arranges to tend their goats in the forest, but Misrilal finds and seduces her there. He claims to be in love with her and promises to defy his family and break caste taboos by marrying her, leaving the village together, and opening up a shop in Patna, Bihar's bustling capital. Their forest trysts become regular, and Dhowli becomes pregnant; Misrilal reveals their love to his family but fails to stand up to their defense of caste protocols. To punish Dhowli, the Misras attempt to "kill [her], but not directly," by starving her. When she "figures out the means of survival" and "defeats [their] revenge" by turning to prostitution, they force her from the village (Devi 1990a, 192, 202).

Part of the brilliance of "Dhowli" is that the forest becomes a dangerous space precisely because of the restoration and refuge—subsistence, sexual, psychic, imaginative—it seems to offer. Far from being a site of conflict or deprivation, the forest functions as a commons keeping Dhowli and her mother alive: they graze their goats and collect roots and tubers there when nearly every other source of sustenance is blocked. It is such an uncontested site that, unusually for Mahasweta's fiction, we are not told who owns or manages it. It is the closest thing Dhowli has to a room of her own, a place of peace and solitude where she can "be alone . . . with time to think one's own thoughts. . . . The forest felt so peaceful that the constant discomfort and fear she had after hearing the Misra boy speak so strangely to her was slowly going away. She was at peace again" (Devi 1990a, 190).

The forest offers Dhowli the "marginal independence" movingly described by Raymond Williams in *The Country and the City* (1973, 101). In the chapter "Enclosures, Commons and Communities," Williams reflects upon the economic, temporal, and psychic "breathing-space" found in the margins, lands dubbed "marginal" either because they abut areas of cultivation and settlement or because their soil is unsuited to commercial agriculture. "Such marginal possibilities are important not only for their produce," Williams writes, "but for their direct and immediate satisfactions and for the felt reality of an area of control of one's own immediate labour. . . . When the pressure of a system is great and is increasing, it matters to find a breathing-space, a fortunate distance, from the immediate and visible controls" (102–3, 107). For Williams, the spatial, economic, affective, and temporal aspects of these marginal possibilities are inextricably related; there "a man has time and spirit to observe, to think and to read . . . against all the apparent odds" (100). Life on the margins can entail a life of the mind. This marginal independence is among the things laid waste by enclosure (101, 107).

Dhowli finds such a breathing space in the forest, a space of emancipatory exception from grinding exploitation and social norms. Some of the thoughts she thinks there (before Misrilal finds her) are about escaping the backbreaking labor, hunger, and maternal responsibilities looming as her inevitable future. The narrator tells us, "Dhowli had no desire for that kind of life, the only kind of life for a Dusad girl" (Devi 1990a, 190). The forest allows Dhowli to imagine an alternative life the narrator deems impossible; in Williams's terms, the pressure of the system is too great. Equally strong, however, is the lure of a folkloric tradition figuring the forest as a protective space of alternative possibility: "In the solitude of the forest, the Misra boy was dauntless, telling her of his plans, and his words seemed to mingle with all the myths associated with the old forest, taking on an enchanted and dreamlike quality" (192). Dhowli is seduced as much by this cultural inscription of the forest—the enchanted home of fairies, or the romantic refuge of illicit lovers—as by Misrilal's scandalous promises. What Williams describes as breathing space becomes for Dhowli a space of danger when the forest allows her to imagine an impossible life beyond sexual vulnerability and domestic drudgery, and its "fantastic associations" lead her to succumb to Misrilal's erotic advances. This sexual transgression, a seemingly "natural" act in the forest's marginal space of exception, results in a situation even more dire than the conventional plight of remarriage to a Dusad man that she sought to escape.

Yet, at the level of narrative form, the story keeps open some literary analogue of that breathing space in its attention to Dhowli's contemplation of her own misreading of the forest. After Misrilal abandons her, Dhowli reflects:

> In that same forest, beside that stream, a Brahman youth once called a Dusad girl his little bird, his one and only bride-for-ever. Didn't they once lie on the carpet of fallen red flowers and become one body and soul? . . . It is hard to believe that these things ever happened. They now seem like made up stories. All that seems real is the baby sleeping in her lap and the constant worry about food. (Devi 1990a, 198)

Reversing Dalzell's terms, the forest that seemed to be Dhowli's friend turns out to be her enemy. The cultural inscription of the forest is subjected to a kind of ideology critique, in which not merely these forest fictions, but also the facts of Dhowli's own experience in the forest, "seem like made up stories." Furthermore, she does not perceive her situation as having mistaken *this* forest for the forest of myth. Rather, *this* forest, "that same forest," is where people she knows have seen fairies or met illicit lovers: "These were true events—they happened—and yet sound like mythical stories. Their love was true too, and yet it feels so unreal now!" (198). In this crisis of truth, Dhowli becomes estranged even from the reality of her own experience.

I see this moment as paradigmatic, both in "Dhowli" and in the cultural logic of waste. As I will show, the story's narrative structure features a series of moments where marginal possibilities are first richly imagined, then suddenly foreclosed—always by acts of enclosure and wasting, and sometimes violently. This foreclosure occurs at the level of plot—people doing things to other people, even if "not directly" (as with the Misras)—but it registers in the narrative as a rereading or double vision in which two incompatible understandings collide. By staging the improving eye and its discontents, these moments in the narrative represent the workings of dispossession in the realms of ontology and aesthetics—and, in less fancy terms, in what passes for social and economic common sense. Dhowli's crisis of truth, in other words, involves larger questions about the "nature of nature" (Buell 1995, 187) and things as they actually are.

1: ROMANCE OR RESOURCE?

"Dhowli" represents forests as overdetermined spaces of material and cultural production: sites of contemplation, imagination, inscription, and interpretation, but also subsistence, intensive resource extraction, and exploitation. Dhowli's reading of the forest (and the story's focalization through her) initially obscures attention to the commercial logging underway. As with the hungry baby in her lap, the timber-felling team working for a forest contractor in cahoots with the Misras only registers in the narrative—"seems real"—once Dhowli has been abandoned and begins to abandon her illusions. (It is unclear whether the Misras *own* this woodland, a narrative ambiguity that points to the longstanding problem of illegal logging on private and state-controlled land.) Even when she registers their presence, Dhowli perceives the timber workers' threat as sexual rather than ecological. Aware of her predicament, they wait to see if she will "end up opening her door at night when the pebbles strike"—a euphemism for informal, coerced sex work (Devi 1990a, 198). The timber workers bring to the narrative a counterintuitive temporal horizon: not wasting, deforestation, and resource exhaustion, but instead a scandalous *sustainability*: They "did not mind the wait" to see whether the Misras would relent and provide for Dhowli, because "the contract for cutting logs and splitting lumber was to continue for a while, and she was worth waiting for" (195–96). Here the improving eye is a leering eye.

This narrative shift exposes a rift between Dhowli's romantic reading of the forest and that of a resource logic—between "the tree of the poet" and "the stick of timber of the wood-cutter," as Ralph Waldo Emerson wrote in his essay "Nature," to which I will return (1836, 6). "Dhowli" probes further into this double vision, to show how this variant of the improving eye incorporates Dhowli within its survey of land and its prospects. Misrilal's elder brother Kundan counts Dhowli as part of his vast, beautiful "empire": "so much farm land and orchards, so many illegitimate children and so many fertile untouchable women, so huge a moneylending business" (Devi 1990a, 203). Women like Dhowli are like fields to be ploughed and sown; if they make trouble, they can be eliminated like parasites.[19] (Dhowli considers ingesting pesticide but vows not to die "before seeing that betrayer once more face to face, eye to eye" [187].) When she ignores the resource logic underwriting timber extraction, Dhowli also misses how she is always-already factored in as a resource.

This inventory of Kundan's empire resituates the seeming scandal of Dhowli's pregnancy within the context of gendered caste exploitation and notions of "untouchability"—a variant of resource logic with the status of common sense in the story's world. This cultural logic of wasting and "unpeopling" takes a different form and idiom than in Locke, Preston, and Columbus, yet bears important similarities with it. As readers might expect, Dhowli's pregnancy provokes a crisis in the village. A relationship between a Dusad woman and a Brahmin man disrupts the Hindu ritual ecology of regulated commensality and conviviality that generates either caste purity or pollution.[20] Yet as Kundan's inventory suggests, the Misra men have not "left untouched" (Devi 1990a, 187) any of the untouchable young women of the village. What *is* marked as scandalous is that Misrilal courts Dhowli (rather than forcing himself on her) and wants to marry her. Both the Misras and Dhowli's Dusad community are appalled. Had she been raped, the Dusads would support her (so the narrator says); had Misrilal not confused a sexual outlet with a prospective bride, his family would support her and her child as they had in previous cases. In this counterintuitive logic (which is a resource logic), the illegitimate children of Brahmin men and low-caste women enjoy a certain legitimacy so long as their fathers do not hatch crazy notions of marrying their mothers. Dhowli's pregnancy and the crisis it provokes point not only to an ideological fiction of intercaste "untouchability," but also to social precedents and everyday practices regulating the exploitation of low-caste women. Ideology and practice converge in the statements, "The fault is always the woman's" and "all the blame goes to Dhowli." These consonant, commonsense judgments are pronounced by Misrilal's mother and "village society," respectively; they are also internalized by Dhowli, who "never even thought of protesting" (193). While the narrative implicates almost everyone in the village, the woman pays the price.

2: PROPRIETOR OR PROSTITUTE?

Dhowli's plight and her response to it are logical consequences of the Misras' exploitation; her scandalous exception reveals the deeper scandal of the ordinary in which low-caste women are another resource to be disposed by the Misras. She defeats the Misras' revenge by opening her door to the timber workers, but as with the crisis jeopardizing her survival, her solution subverts expectations within the narrative and for the reader. When the Misras refuse to provide land, food, money, or work for Dhowli and her baby, nobody is surprised that she resorts to prostitution; what nobody expected is that she would embrace this role without shame. Both the village herbalist and her first customer suggest it would be better to become the exclusive consort of a wealthy client, but Dhowli eschews that "respectable" arrangement and accepts whoever can pay. Although at first self-consciously ignorant of what is "involved in preparing for the customer of one's body," she quickly becomes a no-nonsense proprietor, refusing to sell on credit and making sure to "pay [her client] back, with her body, to the very last penny" (Devi 1990a, 202). Once the forest (and the Misras) turn on her, Dhowli carves out a second space of "marginal possibility" that perversely embraces (and exposes) the logic of primitive accumulation, as is evident in the mercantile language above. She stops seeing her comely body as her enemy (189) and recognizes it as a means of production from which—unlike land or forest—she cannot be alienated. Dhowli's entrepreneurialism resonates with Williams's account of the margins as offering "direct and immediate satisfactions . . . the felt reality of an area of control of one's own immediate labour" (1973, 102–3). She seeks to reclaim herself and her body from the Misras' enclosure: low-caste women within their empire are not merely marginalized by being cast off the land but themselves turned into productive territory, analogous to land.

Dhowli intuits the fundamentally (if perversely) ecological logic of capitalism, as described by Fernando Coronil, in which "people may 'count more' or 'less' than natural resources only in terms of a perspective that equates them; the value of people can be compared to the value of things only because both are reduced to capital. The definition of people as capital means that they are to be treated as capital—taken into account insofar as they contribute to the expansion of wealth, and marginalized if they do not" (2001, 77). This unpeopling is the furthest implication of a logic that reduces humans and nonhuman nature to resources. Resource logics "discount" social relations and norms (Medovoi 2010, 141) so that, in moments of crisis when they are pushed to the brink, the poor may have no recourse to the ethical and political grounds upon which even to *claim* the right to survival: no recourse to common ground.[21] Dhowli seems to accept this logic even as she attempts to turn it to her own ends by becoming her own proprietor. In accord with Coronil's analysis of the gendered aspects of this rapacious accumulation, Dhowli's turn to prostitution as "a strategy of individual survival reveals a link between the naturalization of market rationality and the perverse commodification of human beings through the transformation of what are generally considered 'natural' functions or private activities into a marketed form of labor power" (2001, 75). In "Dhowli," sex work functions simultaneously as a rationalized equivalent to the privatization of nature, and a means of survival: a canny alternative to the logic of enclosure and wasting.

Mahasweta Devi depicts the vibrancy of this marginal possibility in terms of Dhowli's physical and emotional well-being: Once she opens the door at night, Dhowli sleeps well and can feed her mother and child. "She never knew it would be so easy to sell one's body, without any emotion, for corn and millet and salt," the narrator tells us, noting that Dhowli regrets only her previous stupidity in resisting the pressure to prostitute herself (Devi 1990a, 202). This space of possibility is no less precarious than the forest, however. The sight of a glowing and carefully groomed Dhowli, wearing a colorful sari inappropriate for a widow yet similar to those he once bought her, enrages Misrilal when he returns and recognizes what she has become, if not his role in her transformation. His anger at this sight is the narrative catalyst that breaks the impasse between Dhowli and the Misras and leads to her expulsion from the village. Misrilal seizes the prerogatives of "a man and a Brahman" that his hardhearted brother and the spurned, defiant Dhowli both accuse him of being too weak to claim (204). The narrative exposes a multilayered scandal: In her castigation of Misrilal's smitten behavior, Dhowli invokes as normative the patriarchal, caste, and class privileges and objectifying resource logics that the narrative would have readers recognize as the broader scandal of the Misras' "empire."

3: Incorporation or Dispossession?

Dhowli's expulsion closes down the space of survival and flourishing she found in servicing the timber workers, but even when she is forced to leave Tahad, Dhowli views her situation in terms of marginal possibility. As she departs for Ranchi to register as a prostitute, her mother laments that Dhowli should have stayed with her brother-in-law instead of returning, widowed, to Tahad. Dhowli thinks to herself, however, that had she remained in the household she married into so young that she cannot remember her own wedding, she would have been

> a whore individually, only in her private life. Now she is going to be a
> whore by occupation. She is going to be one of many whores, a
> member of a part of society. Isn't the society more powerful than the
> individual? Those who run the society, the very powerful—by making
> her a public whore—have made her a part of the society. Her mother is
> not going to understand this. (Devi 1990a, 205)

Dhowli understands herself as agent rather than victim. Her dawning recognition of a gendered class consciousness reframes exclusion as social incorporation: those who are made marginal to society are therefore "part of the society." Dhowli perceives that the possibility of solidarity with the "many whores" effects a kind of repeopling, against the Misras' attempt to erase her.

This powerful, world-altering moment of recognition is significant within the narrative structure of possibilities repeatedly opened and fore-closed in "Dhowli," as well as the imagining across scales examined in this book. Although not as explicit as the demand for inclusion and world citizenship articulated by Jonathan in *Darwin's Nightmare*, Dhowli's reframing and rescaling of her experience is a world-imagining from below that transmutes the predicament of having been rendered surplus into a claim for social inclusion. In "Dhowli," this moment is the third (and final) time the narrator depicts Dhowli reflecting upon a space of marginal possibility—here hoping she will find in the city an autonomous life not dissimilar to what she imagined in the forest. Dhowli's powerful—if unvoiced—critique reflects a subaltern woman's recognition of her place within structural injustice and the possibilities for negotiating it. This narrative strategy is common in Mahasweta's fiction. Her subaltern characters perceive glimmers of systemic exploitation, but the full implications of their insights—what lies beneath the "superficial truth" (Devi 1981, 38)—are often voiced only for the reader. Dhowli's epiphany about the social aspect of her plight echoes a moment in "Douloti the Bountiful" (1995) when the bonded laborer (*kamiya*) Bono Nagesia remarks that before he left his village, "I didn't know how large our kamiya society was. . . . That's why I no longer feel alone. Oh, the society of kamiyas is so large" (72, 75). Bono's epiphany emerges from his travels throughout India to document the outlawed practice of bonded labor. Like Dhowli, Bono is empowered by recognizing his experience as structural and by situating it at a broader scale, even as his evidence-gathering project confirms, without hope of remedy, that bonded labor is "all over India" (93). Dhowli grasps her position even before she leaves Tahad for the city; unlike Bono, however, she has no way to articulate this knowledge (save through the narrative's free indirect discourse), which brings her position closer to that of Bono's niece Douloti, who suffers fourteen years of bonded prostitution yet cannot even formulate the terms of protest.

A similar half-epiphany occurs in Mahasweta's story "Salt" (1981), which, like "Dhowli," probes how marginalized people dependent on the commons pay the cost for what passes as common sense. The story stages the politics of knowledge through its narrative form, using both dialogue and free indirect discourse to posit the relationship between knowledge and ignorance as a function of class and geographic scale. In "Salt," *adivasi* villagers sneak into a government-protected Reserve Forest to steal salt the Forest Department provides for elephants. They are driven to this dangerous and seemingly illogical act, described as "unimagined" and "unprecedented" (21, 33), when Uttamchand, the Hindu moneylender and shopkeeper in the village, refuses to sell them salt, to exact revenge for their exercising their rights after the 1976 abolition of bonded labor. "I'll kill them slowly. I won't give them salt," he vows (24), choosing a slow violence strategy of indirect murder resembling the Misras' in "Dhowli."

"Salt" features an extended conversation between a concerned youth in a nearby town and a newly arrived health worker, who offers a long monologue on the physiological effects of salt deprivation in the human diet. This scientific soliloquy, so textbook-dry it actually contains bullet points, functions as exposition and critique; it offers readers a precise understanding of the physical consequences of Uttamchand's revenge, but it also makes clear the futility (or illegibility) of such knowledge, heard by the town youth as an "avalanche of incomprehensible words" (Devi 1981, 27). For his part, the health worker cannot wrap his head around how meager the usual diet of the *adivasi* community is, let alone their current crisis: It defies common sense that anyone would steal salt, "one of the cheapest commodities in India" (25). The town youth recognizes that "to make this powdered and polyester wrapped dandy understand the problem . . . was like fighting with shadows, doomed to failure." The dialogue stages this epistemological impasse (or double vision) simply and poignantly:

> "How do I make an ignorant fellow understand!"
> "So what the hell are you an expert for?" (25)

Not privy to this conversation, the salt-starved *adivasis* interpret their stiff limbs and labored breathing as the anger of the gods. Dispossessed even of the history of their exclusion, they "don't even know that there was a time when the land belonged to them" (22). The incommensurability of these perspectives is only one aspect of their predicament. "What's the use of our knowing?" they ask, aware of how little recourse they have against Uttamchand (23).

The climax of "Salt" traces overlapping forms of (il)logic, knowledge, ignorance, and disbelief when the elephant exacts his own revenge against the villagers who stole his salt, and he is declared rogue and shot. In a virtuoso fugue of dramatic ironies, the narrator strategically claims and withholds access to the mental states of various characters (including the elephant), to emphasize the general befuddlement about why anybody would risk their lives to steal salt: the story is as much about who knew or thought what about the action as about the action itself. The narrator sardonically relates the general conclusion drawn from these strange events, that the *adivasis* "cannot at all be trusted": "how difficult it is to preserve wild animals from human rapine" (Devi 1981, 37). This sly critique of enclosure and exclusion undertaken in the name of environmentalism (here, wildlife conservation) complements Mahasweta's attention to indirect forms of violence undertaken through nature and control over natural resources, as in the revenge strategies of Uttamchand and the Misras. This violence against people, waged through nature, is the corollary of resource logics that equate humans and nonhuman nature as resources for capital. When it acquires the status of common sense, such violence becomes naturalized, normative, and thus largely invisible.

The orchestration of points of view in "Salt" leads to the half-epiphany of a "Village Elder," who reflects upon the dead elephant and the village youths it killed. His thoughts progressing slowly, the elder traces culpability for these deaths to "the law and the system under whose protection Uttamchand could with impunity refuse to sell salt," but all he can say aloud to the privileged babus gathered around is "This was not right" (Devi 1981, 38). In the story's final paragraph, the villagers retreat silently to "their familiar world," "the world in which there was no disbelief, no easy explanation for the death of Purti and his friends, or of the objective truth of their existence" (38). The prevailing common sense about cheap salt and vulnerable elephants evicts the *adivasis* from their own knowledge; they are excluded from what passes for reason and common sense. This epistemological gap between worlds finds vivid expression earlier in "Salt," when the narrator observes, "The teashop of [the town] was not a million miles from [the *adivasi* village], yet they were in two different stars of this universe . . . the dark space between them, stretching across millions of miles" (27–28). Zooming out to the cosmic scale, this image crystallizes the sort of relation and claim about the shape of the world at work elsewhere in this book—for example, in the gulf between tourists and natives in the commodity biography *Life and Debt*—in which people occupy the same geographic location yet might as well inhabit different worlds, different corners of a vast universe.

Similar narrative strategies are at work in the conclusion of "Dhowli." As Dhowli boards the bus to leave Tahad, neither the bus driver nor the timber contractor can bear to look at her. The contractor's shame derives, presumably, from having been the first man to whom Dhowli opened her door. For her part, Dhowli eschews a last look back at her mother and son, for fear that she will also glimpse "the brass trident atop the temple of the Misras" symbolizing their cosmological rectitude and patriarchal dominance (Devi 1990a, 205). This complex scene of spectatorship, interweaving acts of looking and not looking upon a scene of injustice, echoes the orchestration of knowledge and ignorance in "Salt," as well as scenes of reflexive spectatorship analyzed in previous chapters (in commodity biography films or Ed Kashi's Niger Delta photos) that implicate readers and viewers in the politics of looking.

Like "Salt," "Dhowli" concludes with a dizzying shift in scale, to devastating effect:

> The bus sped up. The distance between Ranchi and Dhowli is shrinking, the sun is rising. Just like every morning, the sky is blue and the trees are green. She had not known that there would be no change in nature's daily routine. Tears are falling from her eyes with the pain of this blow. Shouldn't it all have changed from today? A-a-a-ll of it? The day Dhowli became a whore? Or has even nature accepted the Dhowlis becoming whores, this nature that the Misras did not create? These tree-sky-earth—have they been sold to the Misras too? (Devi n.d.)[22]

These questions undermine Dhowli's empowering epiphany about being a "part of society." None of the human characters can look upon this scene of injustice; only nature looks on unmoved. Nature (*prakriti*)—a new term in the narrative—functions as a limit to Dhowli's resolve: its indifference is an unexpected "blow." Not only is Dhowli's sense of marginal possibility decisively foreclosed, but at the story's end, the conflict between "the Dhowlis" and "the Misras" also expands to the scale of the worldwide. The waste of the world has, perhaps, been sold to the global Misras, laying waste the Dhowlis. A story that begins at the end of the road in a remote village, "cut off from the outside world" during the monsoon (185),[23] concludes by positing the enclosure of tree-sky-earth and dispossession at a planetary scale. This moment offers a historical bookend to Locke's exuberance, in a trajectory that begins with his "all the world was America" and ends with a question: Has all the world been sold?

A Trick of the Eye: Property, Poetry, and the "Nature of Nature"

"Dhowli" ends paradoxically, with a momentous conclusion where nothing happens. Everything appears the same as before, the trees green "just like every morning." Even the shattering possibility of the earth's enclosure is phrased as an unanswered question, one explanation for nature's

indifference to Dhowli's plight. Yet here Mahasweta lays bare the deepest
implications of resource logics, their dispossessions effected as much
through the cultural imaginaries shaping Dhowli's experience as through
the murderous actions of the Misra family. In both explanations for nature's indifference—that nature has become resigned to "the Dhowlis becoming whores," or been bought by the Misras—Dhowli is always-already
doomed; her attempts at marginal independence appear in retrospect as
a series of category mistakes about "the nature of nature" and her place in
the world.

The "nature of nature" is a phrase borrowed from ecocritic Lawrence
Buell's discussion of the literary personification of nature that was a central concern for British Romantic and Victorian poets (1995, 187)—a moment in literary history coincident with the British colonial enclosure of
India examined above. At stake in "the nature of nature" is its "objective
reality" (ibid.), against which literary representations can ostensibly be
measured as faithful or fanciful, realist or romantic. Thus, Buell writes,
"personification is a swerve away from realism" (188). But what, precisely,
are the facts of nature taken to be? To return to Emerson's distinction between the "timber of the wood-cutter" and "the tree of the poet," how
closely do these versions of nature hew to "things as they *are*" (Ruskin 1888,
III.ii.vii)—or as they are taken to be in any given historical configuration?
In the Anglo-American literary-critical tradition, such questions constellate around what John Ruskin dubbed the pathetic fallacy, the poet's projection (or, in William Wordsworth's valorizing account, "bestowal"
[quoted in Miles 1965, 6]) of emotion or other human qualities onto elements of landscape. In her 1942 study of the pathetic fallacy in nineteenth-
and twentieth-century British and American poetry, Josephine Miles
articulates the broader implications of such debates.[24] At stake is not merely
a poet's choice of rhetorical device, but larger phenomenological and ontological questions: "a way of seeing the world," a "plan of the world," a "theory of objects" (1, 17). What assumptions about the natural world underwrite
literary conventions for thinking between humans and nonhuman nature? How are such assumptions naturalized, and in what historical circumstances are these conventions regarding the disposition of nature
destabilized, subverted, or subject to critique?

This section considers the relationship between Ruskin's pathetic fallacy and histories of enclosure, within the British Isles and the beyond of
nineteenth-century imperial expansion—one historical circumstance
where the "nature of nature" was being contested. In our own moment,
too, the facts of nature are under revision—both empirically, with unpre-

cedented anthropogenic changes in the Earth system; and conceptually, with the rise of new materialisms, object-oriented ontology, and speculative realism. There is something strangely timely about Miles's observation that the pathetic fallacy entails a "theory of objects"—an insight with theoretical (rather than only historically specific) import. Ruskin valorized poets able to "feel strongly, think strongly, and see truly," but that aesthetic ideal assumes that seeing has no history, that nature is "there" to be seen and rendered faithfully. But Ruskin knew better—as explained at the end of this section. The facts of nature are subject to the sedimented cultural common sense examined throughout this chapter. A resource logic would likely perceive no difference between the woodcutter's stick and objective reality, which is part of the tragedy of private property. Economics and poetry are not taken as parallel modes of construing the "facts" of an autonomous nature; instead, one passes for fact, the other relegated to fancy. On the other hand, the cultural inscriptions of forests and waste analyzed in this chapter make plain that literary genres and aesthetic modes—no less than property regimes—are implicated in contests over the disposition of nature. As Carolyn Lesjak insists, "the status of the real is an interpretive problem rather than a given" (2013, 254). Beyond poetry and economics, neither woodcutter nor poet would necessarily grasp the facts of nature that EIC surgeons and foresters began to discern in the nineteenth century: that trees play indispensable roles in soil health, hydrology, and climate at multiple scales.

Oscillating Landscapes

We tend to understand the pathetic fallacy as a particular disposition toward the literary personification of nature, but this account claims an agency for literature that may belong to nature. In other words, the concept of personification assumes that nature is not already a person, whether in the legal sense of an entity with rights before the law (see Christopher Stone's 1974 essay *Should Trees Have Standing?*), or in the intersubjective sense of an entity imbued with emotions or sentience. One upshot of the European Enlightenment was an impoverished view of nature—if not exactly dead, then certainly dull and dumb—that was, somewhat paradoxically, amenable both to instrumentalization through resource logics and to the revivifying tonic of Romanticism, what Wordsworth called the "imagining eye" (quoted in Miles 1965, 60). The recent posthuman turn is a redistribution of agency—and personhood—whose account of vital matter resituates humans somewhere other than at the center of a more-than-human world. Literary criticism has yet to reckon fully with what this more-than-human nature means for our understanding of what personification is and does: What counts as realism (or descriptive restraint) or a "swerve away" from it would shift if nature has a new nature. In addition to the new natures proliferating around us, Enlightenment views of nature (not to mention the pathetic fallacy as an aesthetic convention consolidated in their wake) demand to be historicized and provincialized, rather than taken as given or neutral. This task is particularly urgent in postcolonial and other transnational studies like World Literature, where what is often at stake is the collision of multiple ontologies and understandings of the relationship between humans and nonhuman nature.[25]

In "Imperial Landscape," W. J. T. Mitchell posits landscape aesthetics—"a field that goes well beyond the history of painting to include poetry, fiction, travel literature, and landscape gardening"—as an important cultural site for mediating between "the Human and the non-Human" (2002, 6). In Mitchell's analysis, landscape becomes legible as "not only a natural scene, and not just a representation of a natural scene, but a *natural* representation of a natural scene, a trace or icon of nature *in* nature itself, as if nature were imprinting and encoding its essential structures on our perceptual apparatus" (15). The operative word here is *naturalization*, a subtle and insidious operation not entirely distinct from personification: it generates a common sense that seemingly lets the facts of nature speak for themselves. (Think of Hayden White's classic account of narrativity as "discourse that feigns to make the world speak itself and speak itself *as a story*" [1980, 7].) I find useful Mitchell's suggestive, open-ended hypothesis: "landscape, understood as concept or representational practice" is "something like the 'dreamwork' of imperialism, unfolding its own movement in time and space . . . and folding back on itself to disclose both utopian fantasies of the perfected imperial prospect and fractured images of unresolved ambivalence and unsuppressed resistance" (2002, 9–10). Unlike *Orientalism*, which traces a historical nexus of knowledge and power that Said dates to Napoleon's Egyptian campaign (undertaken partly to undermine the British in India), Mitchell's account of landscape as imperial dreamwork is not concerned only with modern European imperialism. Citing examples from China, Japan, and classical Rome, Mitchell argues that the emergence of landscape aesthetics, as a putatively "new" and more "natural" way of looking at nature, might be a defining feature of imperialism writ large (6–9). This impulse to "free" landscape from aesthetic convention tends to emerge with the impulse to bring territory within an imperial property regime of tribute or taxation. As I will elaborate, Ruskin's brief against the pathetic fallacy is a signal instance of imperial naturalization.

These expanded and flexible notions of personification and naturalization, landscape and imperial expansion, can help make sense of the end of "Dhowli" and its implications for cultural logics of waste. The immediate questions I seek to answer are why Dhowli is so wounded by nature's indifference, and what kind of thing she assumes nature to be. My broader questions are about the discursive and material processes through which nature is disposed as property on the one hand, and poetry on the other, and whether those processes are understood as related or distinct. Emerson's distinction between woodcutter and poet grounds a more complex comparison between proprietor and poet, or land and landscape:

> The charming landscape which I saw this morning, is indubitably made up of some twenty or thirty farms. Miller owns this field, Locke that, and Manning the woodland beyond. But none of them owns the landscape. There is a *property in the horizon* which no man has but he whose eye can integrate all the parts, that is, the poet. This is the best part of these men's farms, yet to this their warranty-deeds give no title. (1836, 6; emphasis added)

Mitchell reads this passage from Emerson's "Nature" to emphasize how landscape is construed as the antithesis of land, an aesthetic "ideal estate" as opposed to "real estate" (2002, 15). This antithesis, we might say, offers a prospect without prospects: a view that cannot be reduced to economic value. What is most fascinating about Emerson's vignette is that, far from positing resource logic and poetry as incommensurable (as his timber vs. tree distinction implies), they are two property regimes; the poet, no less than the proprietor, stakes a claim to "property in the horizon," through the scopic labor of "integrating all the parts." Emerson identifies a sort of aesthetic air rights, distinct from—but described in terms homologous with—property in land: Both are enclosed through labor. Leave Locke to improving his land; through his integrating eye, Emerson owns the landscape, its "best part."

Consider the tricks of the eye at work here: this passage oscillates between incompatible images of forest and farm, while the act of looking is valorized as a form of skilled labor at once aesthetic and appropriative. (As Williams writes in a not unrelated context, "This is an alteration of landscape, by an alteration of seeing" [1973, 87].) Positing the superiority of poetic "property in the horizon" over mere landownership, Emerson nonetheless draws upon the logic of improvement and enclosure. (Notice that Emerson's essay is nearly contemporaneous with Macaulay's 1835 Minute on Education that found no value in Oriental learning—a signal instance of disavowal that masks the twinned role of Orientalism in literary/cultural and capital accumulation.) Does Emerson's entrepreneurial metaphor for poetic landscape undermine the logic of landed property, or entrench it? Does this visual oscillation function as a lenticular image that flickers and shifts depending on the angle from which it's viewed, or does it resolve into 3-D stereoscopy, where right eye of poetry lends the illusion of depth to the left eye's focus on economy—akin to the naturalization in the landscape that Mitchell posits as the dreamwork of empire?[26]

These questions adopt a structure of oscillation, which I understand as a trace of the ontological and ideological instability in the nature of nature. This structure of oscillation appears at multiple levels in "Dhowli": in the rereadings and double visions that accompany the repeated foreclosures of marginal possibility, in the broader cultural inscriptions of forest and waste, and in the two horns of the planetary dilemma that closes the story. Does nature condone the plight of the Dhowlis, or does it belong to the Misras? The question of what nature *is* is inseparable from the question of how Dhowli sees, and her survival is staked upon the relationship between "things as they *are*" (in Ruskin's phrase) and how she perceives them to be.

Nature Personified, Humans Objectified

What is remarkable at the conclusion of "Dhowli" is that nature appears unchanged; the scene's pathos derives from the disjuncture between nature and the social, or beauty and justice. This moment differs from one earlier in the story, when Misrilal fails to return as promised, and the forest—which Dhowli has perceived as a site of refuge and possibility—takes on a menacing aspect: "The woods looked horrible to her, the trees looked like ghoulish guards, and even the rocks seemed to be watching her" (Devi 1990a, 194). Misrilal has betrayed her; even the forest appears sinister. By contrast, at the story's end, the sky and the trees are neither sinister nor sympathetic; their ordinary beauty (their *naturalness*) is the mark of their indifference to Dhowli's plight. In nature everything appears the same, while for Dhowli everything has changed. Taken together, these two moments might amount to a contradictory double vision, two irreconcilable views. But I understand them to be of a piece; what distinguishes them is not the appearance of nature but Dhowli's position in relation to land and landscape.

This is another way of saying that the critical norms and ontological assumptions of the pathetic fallacy can only take us so far in making sense of "Dhowli." In "Of the Pathetic Fallacy," Ruskin valorizes poets who love nature enough to be moved by it, but still maintain the proper mental "command" and "government" that prevents them from erroneously imbuing nature with emotion or sentience (1888, 3:164, 169). In a moment of overwhelming emotion, Dhowli *wants* to find her plight reflected in nature, yet does not; this pathetic disjuncture leads her to contemplate the possible truth (Ruskin's lodestar) of nature's acceptance of injustice or its expropriation by the powerful. But I don't think we are supposed to dismiss Dhowli's pained perception of an indifferent nature as impropriety, an unfortunate cognitive error, or a pathological symptom of overwrought emotion. Even the forest contractor is ashamed at what is happening to her.

An alternative path into this interpretive problem is to consider the temple of the Misras, the human-constructed element of the landscape that Dhowli so fears her gaze alighting upon that she will not risk a last look back at her mother and child. In this moment, the temple with its trident performs a function not unlike that which Williams identifies in the great English country houses, which were situated, he argues, not for their pleasing prospects viewed from within, but "for the other effect, from the outside looking in: a visible stamping of power, of displayed wealth and command: a social disproportion which was meant to impress and over-awe" (1973, 106). The Misras' temple is an emblem of class and caste domination; the Misras occupy a position somewhat akin to landed gentry, but they are also privileged heirs to a Hindu sacred geography. To extend the improbable analogy a little further, perhaps Dhowli will not look upon the Misras' *mandir* because her mistake all along has been to view the forest as if from its hegemonic vantage. She misrecognizes her own marginal position in the version of land and landscape indexed by the temple, in which people like her have long been unpeopled or naturalized—in effect, *reduced* to land and landscape.

Mahasweta invites us to view Dhowli's plight in terms of layered histories of conquest and waves of enclosure in India, dating back to the misty horizon where myth meets history. The cadastral endeavor of British colonial settlement charts another map for a territory already inscribed within a sacred geography legible in tridents atop temples. Dhowli's initial retreat to the forest, to escape Misrilal's advances, "think [her] own thoughts," and imagine a life other than "the same routine of backbreaking work, with kids in your lap, kids following you around" (190), might position her—albeit ironically—in terms of the third of four ideal stages of male Brahmin life. Leaving behind the domestic responsibilities of the householder, the *vānaprastha* leads a quiet life of meditation in the forest. But note how this Brahmin ideal of contemplative forest dwelling is contingent upon the transformation of wild, untamed land into peaceful forest, partly through the pacification or eradication of its previous inhabitants, human and nonhuman. Indeed, this process works at a discursive level by transforming human forest-dwellers into nonhumans.

An important transformation in the early environmental history of the Indian subcontinent was the eastward expansion of settled agriculture and pastoralism across the Indus-Gangetic alluvial plains, which resulted in the clearance of primary forest cover and the assimilation and/or retreat of extant *adivasi* communities into forested hill zones. As an early instance of agricultural expansion involving the transformation of "waste" land and the dispossession of previous inhabitants, this socioenvironmental conflict between settled agriculturalists and forest dwellers (who subsisted on hunting, foraging, and shifting cultivation) is legible in the narrative conflicts that drive the Indian epic tradition. (Recall that in *The Forests from Within*, his 1926 brief for the exclusion of local users, Forest Service Officer J. W. Nicholson eulogized "the mighty forests which used to exist in the Gangetic plain," as recorded in the "great Indian epics.") Drawing on anthropologist Iravati Karve's historical reading of the *Mahabharata*, Gadgil and Guha associate the rise of Brahminism with fire sacrifice rituals that had the mundane effect of consuming wood and clearing forests for agriculture and grazing (1993, 71–90; see also Dove 1992, 236–37). As described in the *Mahabharata*, Brahmins can be understood as "pioneers" in this forest conquest; when their meditations and sacrifices are molested by animals, demons, or human inhabitants of the untamed, menacing woods, the Brahmins are defended by *kshatriya* warriors charged with clearing the forest of demons (79). In one particularly violent episode in the *Mahabharata*, the warrior Arjuna and his ally Krishna encounter a Brahmin ascetic in the Khandava forest who reveals himself to be the fire god, Agni, and implores them to burn the forest for his food. Karve describes how Krishna and Arjuna ignited the forest and "guarded all sides so tightly that the creatures fleeing from the blaze found not a single chink to escape through. . . . Having consumed the flesh and fat of every last creature in the forest, Agni went away satisfied" (1969, 138). Beyond this literal unpeopling of the forest, some of the demons disturbing the Brahmins have been read as *adiva-*

sis defending their territory and lifeworld, thereby joining epic clashes among gods and demons to a history of intrahuman conflict.[27]

In her study of post-Enlightenment European travel narratives, Pratt observes a generic division between natural history and ethnography that "separates landscape from people, accounts of inhabitants from accounts of their habitats" (1992, 61). This is one way "the European improving eye produces subsistence habitats as 'empty' landscapes, meaningful only in terms of a capitalist future" at the same time that it erases how "these same spaces are lived as intensely humanized, saturated with local history and meaning, where plants, creatures, and geographical formations have names, uses, symbolic functions, histories, places in indigenous knowledge formations" (61). Call it the Disney effect: *The Lion King* offers up a lively African continent largely devoid of humans. This peculiar mode of primitive accumulation occurs in the realm of discourse; through such *emptied* landscapes, imperial regimes of representation separate human communities from their means of subsistence at the level of the imaginary, and thereby help "free up" both for capital.[28] Something similar is at work in the epics' transmutation of *adivasis* into demons or nonhuman animals that must be eradicated to pacify the forest. But this discursive evacuation of the landscape has the additional effect of displacing alternative dispositions of nature to the realm of distant, mythic history, outside the human fold.

"Nature changes its aspect according to the aspects of those who people it," writes Edward Dimock about the representation of forests in Valmiki's *Ramayana*, the other key text in the Indian epic tradition (1974, 64). He explains, "'forest' means any tract of land that is not under active cultivation; it may indeed be a forest, but it may also be wilderness in general . . . the stark bleak wasteland of sheer mountain drops, impenetrable rain forest, and barren desert" (64). This vivid account equates *forest* with varied forms of waste and wilderness (i.e., land outside agricultural production), emphasizing a normative *social* distinction rather than a topographical or ecological description. We might say, then, that the nature of nature is bound up with that of its inhabitants and their modes of habitation. In English, the current use of *forest* to designate wooded land survives an obsolete meaning: land *outside* the walls of settlement, waste or wild; *forest* and *foreign* share the same French/Latin root. A similar tension is at work in Sanskrit, in which *vana* and *aranya* (generally translated as forest) denote land under tree cover, but also waste and wild land beyond the agricultural complex of village and field: "uninhabited except possibly by wild animals, demons, and barbarians" (Zimmermann 1987, 37).

Although his analysis may be overly infused with the binary tendencies of French structuralism, Francis Zimmermann identifies a fundamental divide between "brahminic India, the flat country . . . [and] barbarian India, the mountains-forest-marshes" (1987, 55), which centers on the Sanskrit word *jāṅgala*. Zimmerman argues that this term in his classical sources designated, in its broad sense, a place dry and salubrious enough to be suitable for agriculture and settlement (comprising village, field, and forest), and in its narrower sense, either waste land and forest margins not yet brought under cultivation, or the secondary growth of thickets and savannah where cultivation has been abandoned. In Sanskrit, *jāṅgala* is the setting for the "drama . . . between land clearance and land abandonment" (41) in the eastward spread of the Indus Valley civilization. Thus *A Code of Gentoo Laws*—the Orientalist Nathaniel Brassey Halhed's translation (by way of Persian) of a Hindu legal code for the East India Company—decrees that "Land waste for five years [or more] . . . is called *Jungle*" (1781, 168). However, *jāṅgala* is a misleading cognate with "jungle," which entered English in the late eighteenth century by way of Hindi and Marathi *jangal*. This vernacularization is associated with a shift in meaning: from dry, healthful lands to wet and luxuriant—that is, malarial—forest growth, and from land not yet or no longer cultivated to wild land beyond the pale of civilization (Zimmerman 1987, ix, 17–19). This shift, argues anthropologist Michael Dove, reflects not etymological confusion, but an environmental history of changing land use patterns since ancient times, resulting from increased population density and intensive cultivation: "The jangala has disappeared, and its place has been taken by the jangal." Moreover, it involves a reversal in polarity: "Whereas jangala encompassed ancient civilization, contemporary civilization excludes jangal" (1992, 238, 240).

In tracing this cultural logic of waste, one of Zimmermann's challenges is extricating from a Sanskrit corpus of medical, legal, political, and religious texts the relationship between a system of brahminical norms and revealed knowledge, on the one hand, and empirical description and environmental history, on the other. Zimmermann goes so far as to assert that in this textual tradition, the imperceptible cosmological qualities and essences (*rasa*) of plants, animals, and landscapes *determine* its adherents' perception and understanding of the facts: "for a Hindu, what these texts say represents reality" (1987, 4). One need not accept this strong claim to recognize an entanglement between modes of rule and understandings of nature akin to the dynamic Mitchell analyzes, and which Dove describes as a dialectical transformation in both material relations between humans and nonhuman nature and the categories through which that relation is understood. The significance of the *Ramayana* within Indian culture implies a hinge between poetry and property that may be inherent to the epic genre itself: the *Ramayana* traces Rama's journey into the wilderness and back as staking a civilizational claim upon the subcontinent, and its conventionally recognized author, Valmiki, is valorized as the founder of a literary tradition: *adi kavi* (first poet). Himself a forest hermit, Valmiki would figure prominently in the notion of India as *aranya sanskriti* (a forest culture), an ecological and cultural ethic of contemplation, renewal, and harmony at odds with a Western industrial model of maldevelopment.[29] Yet this identification of Indian civilization with the forest erases the history of conflict and conquest legible in the epics' accounts of encounters in the "forest" (broadly defined). It elides the perceived threat that forest liminality poses to cultivation, in every sense of the term. As Dove writes, "the ancient barbarians were pushed *out* of the jangala . . . but the contemporary equivalent . . . are pushed *into* the jangal," even as "civilized society" has removed itself from nature (1992, 240). Within the cultural traditions underwritten by the epics, forests can signify both civilization and its discontents.

"Dhowli" recasts this conflict and contradiction regarding the place of forests in Indian cultural imaginaries. The forest's mythic associations lead Dhowli to embrace the hegemonic version of this narrative of conquest while forgetting her own overdetermined, marginal position within it. Her embrace of the forest as a peaceful site of contemplation and relief from domestic drudgery lays claim to a cultural role from which her age (and gender and caste) disqualify her. For Dhowli, nature changes its aspect when she recognizes that Misrilal will not make good on his promises to disregard caste norms; in a terrifying modulation, suddenly the "woods looked horrible to her." A temporal layering is at work here: Dhowli's incorporation into the Misras' "beautiful empire" in postcolonial India is superimposed over older waves of settlement, dispossession, and erasure.

This layered history reframes the possible explanations for nature's indifference at the end of "Dhowli," by suggesting that the Misras have long had nature on their side, no matter how one understands the nature of nature. When the narrator asks whether "even nature has accepted the Dhowlis becoming whores," I think we are invited to compare this moment with those in the *Ramayana* and *Mahabharata* when faithful wives are publicly accused of sexual impropriety or whoredom: gods, nature, or both respond to such false charges with outraged horror. This intertextual connection is explicit in Mahasweta's "Draupadi," which restages Draupadi's public shaming and rescue by Krishna in the *Mahabharata*. Similarly, in

"Douloti the Bountiful," Douloti's plight echoes Sita's trial by fire in the *Ramayana* tradition. When Sita is forced to prove her fidelity by stepping into a fire, the god of fire brings her out unharmed, saying that her purity burned even him. Gods and nature serve as the ultimate warrant for justice when these chaste women are shamefully abused and accused. Dhowli is a poor, twentieth-century Dusad widow and prostitute, not a twice-born epic heroine like Sita or Draupadi; yet even in this disenchanted, modern world, it is scandalous, this unflinchingly realist narrative suggests, that nature acts (or fails to act) as it does.[30] Dhowli's pain at nature's indifference is legible in these terms: we might say that she reels at nature's failure to *intervene*, rather than merely at the lack of concord between its ordinary appearance and her extraordinary plight.[31] One way of reading the questions that close the narrative is that they transport us from the last vestiges of an epic chronotope (where nature is aligned with justice) to a worldview in which private property relations obviate any affective or ethical correspondence between nature and humans by subjecting both to a resource logic that instrumentalizes them in the service of capital. The momentum of these final questions carries us beyond Dhowli's pained recognition of nature's indifference to the more scandalous possibility of its expropriation by the powerful. The lack of correspondence between nature's appearance and Dhowli's emotional state suggests that even if nature is understood to cast judgment on human social dynamics, its authority would be mooted by human ownership of nature. In this logic, nature disposed as property would lack (or lose) the standing to have emotions or cognition.[32]

Laid bare in this moment are two sides of cultural logics of waste: The personification of nature is bound up with the objectification of humans at work in resource logics. In both cases, at stake are the nature of nature and the ethical grounds upon which marginalized communities might claim the right to survival. Resource logics objectify humans and nonhuman nature by reducing them to nothing but economic value (or waste); personification attributes to natural objects what are generally regarded as human qualities. Legible in "Dhowli" are multiple traces of such logics, superimposed upon each other. Dhowli's pain at nature's indifference resonates with Anglo-American debates about the pathetic fallacy, which are contemporary with the colonial land policies that shape Dhowli's fate, yet the conditions and sacred geographies that underwrite her plight precede and exceed those debates in ways that are crucial to making sense of the narrative. This is another way of saying that neither postcolonial studies (defined narrowly in terms of modern European empires and their after-maths) nor World Literature alone provides an adequate framework of leg-ibility for this text. We might say that Dhowli is "between habitations," as John Newton writes about the clash between Maori and *pakeha* understand-ings of land and landscape in New Zealand (1999, 94). Newton uses "be-tween habitations" to describe the colonial collision of different (but sometimes mutually reinforcing) understandings of the nature of nature and ways of living in the world, but the phrase also evokes (to my ear) the threat of vagrancy for those cast off the land in histories of settlement and enclosure.

This relay between personifying nature and objectifying humans is, I argue, an instance of the naturalization Mitchell observes in imperial land-scapes: imaginative and poetic renderings of landscape draw upon and reinforce the dehumanizing common sense that underwrites a property re-gime. I offer this hypothesis in the spirit of Mitchell's capacious notion of landscape as the "'dreamwork' of empire." Rather than asserting a single correlation, whether direct or inverse, between imperialism and the pa-thetic fallacy,[33] I suggest that while landed property and rhetorical propri-ety are not easily separated, they intermingle in myriad and contradictory ways. In "Of the Pathetic Fallacy," there is more than a whiff of civiliza-tional superiority in Ruskin's distinctions between "great" and "smaller" men's abilities to "command" their feelings and avoid succumbing to "ig-noble" irrationality in the face of great emotion (1888, 3:164, 169). This valorization of sovereignty over lesser impulses implies that poets who in-dulge in the pathetic fallacy might be understood, in effect, to have gone native. In the context of nineteenth-century European imperial expansion, claims for the agency or emotional capacity of nonhuman entities could serve as a mark of either overwrought poetic emotion or the animist, "primitive" mind. Indeed, colonial discourse on primitive animism and fe-tishism in Africa and elsewhere draws civilizational differences between different understandings of the nature of nature: in rocks and trees and things, natives were thought to find the kind of personhood that in Eu-rope was banished to the realm of the literary.[34] Some colonial observers were not without sympathy for this tendency, given the unruly landscapes and wild natures they encountered. In *The Lower Niger and Its Tribes* (1906), Arthur Glyn Leonard explained the "naturism" practiced in the Niger Delta in terms of the region's ecology: "there is not in existence on the whole surface of the globe a more fitting environment for the centre of natural religion than this pestiferous and malarial region" (138).

HISTORIES OF SEEING

It is hardly sufficient, however, to situate the pathetic fallacy against the backdrop of European imperialism and to consider how it invited comparisons between lesser poets and primitive others, each ostensibly susceptible to prodigious imaginings at odds with "things as they *are*." The inverse of such untamed imagining and fecund (or febrile) landscapes was a horrifying emptiness that registered as "uncolonized nothing," in Charles Brash's phrase—a void of meaning analogous to the void of economic value Locke perceived in uncultivated land. Both voids seem to cry out for colonization; something in a waste wants to be put to use or infused with meaning. A startling instance of this tendency appears in Ruskin's "The Lamp of Memory," in *The Seven Lamps of Architecture* (1849).

Ruskin opens the chapter by describing a remembered scene "marked by more than ordinary fulness of joy or clearness of teaching"—a springtime sunset in the Jura Mountains, north of the "savage" Alps (1849, 162). The mountains are at a human (rather than sublime) scale, the flowers blooming, a lone hawk gliding over the cliffs and river below. Ruskin's description repeatedly swerves into the terrain whose hazards he would chart in "Of the Pathetic Fallacy," yet his account of "rude and changeful" rivers, spring flowers "coming forth in clusters crowded for very love," and the general "tenderness" of the scene is not necessarily evidence of *excessive* emotion, but perhaps in "majestic concord" with it (162). Ruskin concludes his description thus: "It would be difficult to conceive a scene less dependent upon any other interest than that of its own secluded and serious beauty" (163).

In an astonishing thought-experiment, Ruskin then transplants this scene out of Europe:

> but the writer well remembers the sudden blankness and chill which were cast upon it when he endeavored, in order more strictly to arrive at the sources of its impressiveness, to imagine it, for a moment, a scene in some aboriginal forest of the New Continent. The flowers in an instant lost their light, the river its music; the hills became oppressively desolate; a heaviness in the boughs of the darkened forest showed how much of their former power had been dependent upon a life which was not theirs, how much of the glory of the imperishable, or continually renewed, creation is reflected from things more precious in their memories than it, in its renewing. Those ever springing flowers and ever flowing streams had been dyed by the deep colors of human endurance, valor, and virtue; and the crests of the

sable hills that rose against the evening sky received a deeper worship, because their far shadows fell eastward over the iron wall of Joux and the foursquare keep of Granson. (163–64)

This passage effects a trick of the eye; as in a lenticular image, all light and warmth flicker out of this Swiss scene when Ruskin teleports it to "the New Continent"—by which he probably meant the Americas (as in Alexander von Humboldt's thirty-volume travelogue, completed in 1834). The seeming autonomous beauty of the scene turns out to have been impressed upon it by (Ruskin's awareness of) a history of human habitation, of a particular sort: "endurance, valor, and virtue." As lands beyond the pale, untouched by such enlivening shadows, New Continents paled in comparison with European nature. Ruskin performs the inverse of an improving eye: even in a natural scene seemingly set apart from human habitation, still shining upon it is the lamp of memory, whose light Ruskin can perceive only by discovering (in his imagination) its absence in a land without history. It's an emptying of a landscape that did not appear as peopled to begin with; this discursive evacuation also withholds from New Continents the possibility of human meaningfulness predating the arrival of Europeans.

This passage reveals a divide implicit in the question of what happens (or should happen) when the poetic imagination encounters nature and transforms land into landscape: at issue is not merely the nature of nature but the extent of imperial expansion and the state of "progress" from exploration to enclosure and settlement. Outside the realm of settled property, the waste of the world becomes a limit-case for legislating rhetorical propriety and poetic engagement with the nature of nature. It was, after all, William Cowper's "Verses Supposed to be Written by Alexander Selkirk, During his Solitary Abode in the Island of Juan Fernandez" that elicited William Wordsworth's briefs against excessive emotion encrusted in stale poetic convention. Selkirk was the early eighteenth-century castaway whose narrative inspired *Robinson Crusoe* and thereby launched the realist novel. In his 1802 appendix to *Lyrical Ballads*, Wordsworth argues again for a "poetic diction" drawn from the "real language of men" (1974, 160). He laments Cowper's description of the island where Selkirk was stranded—

But the sound of the churchgoing bell
These valleys and rocks never heard,
Ne'er sigh'd at the sound of a knell,
Or smiled when a Sabbath appeared.

—as "an instance of the language of passion wrested from its proper use . . . vicious poetic diction" (163–64). Note the inverse similarity with Ruskin's teleported scene: for Wordsworth, Cowper's impropriety derives from a faulty distinction between smiling, sighing "rocks in civilized countries" (Buell 2001, 188) and the impassive "valleys and rocks" of Selkirk's desert island. In these examples, it's Wordsworth who pleads against overwrought emotion and for natural language (what Mitchell calls "*naturalization*, a freeing of nature from the bonds of convention" (2002, 12)), and Ruskin who valorizes, in its hypothetical absence in an imagined colonial periphery, the humanized aspect of "rocks in civilized countries" inscribed upon the landscape. In both cases, an argument about poetry—whether for or against the "naturalization" that Mitchell finds in landscape aesthetics— is premised upon the polarities of imperial geography.

The two versions of the Jura scene troubled Ruskin throughout his career. He conducted an ongoing conversation with himself (and Wordsworth) in layers of footnotes and cross-references that trace the history of his own seeing. First, annotating the passage in "The Lamp of Memory," he qualified his imagined loss of the flowers' light and the river's music (1849, 204n15), by acknowledging it to be an instance of the erroneous belief he analyzed in the second volume of *Modern Painters*, "that in uninhabited countries the vegetation has no grace, the rock no dignity, the cloud no colour" (1888, 2:32). (This was also Cowper's mistake, as Wordsworth pointed out half a century earlier.) From the vantage of advancing years in 1883, Ruskin annotated the passage in *Modern Painters* and reaffirmed the soundness of his original insight in *The Lamp of Memory* about nature uninscribed by human feeling: "As I have grown older, the aspects of nature conducive to human life have become hourly more dear to me; and I had rather now see a brown harvest field than the brightest Aurora Borealis" (1888, 2:241n42). The world as shaped by imperialism put pressure on the aesthetic norms articulated in "Of the Pathetic Fallacy" and continued to trouble him as the century wore on. Thus, despite Ruskin's late insistence that "the beginning of all my political economy" was the conviction that "beautiful things are useful to men because they are beautiful, and for the sake of their beauty only; and not to sell, or pawn—or, in any other way, turn into money" (1888, 2:x), such grubby matters as modes of habitation, property regimes, and imperial expansion literally laid the ground for beauty (or its absence) as he saw, remembered, and made sense of it.

Ruskin suddenly finds himself between habitations—the self-induced homelessness of imagining himself out of a humanized landscape. His oscillation between the Jura and the New Continent performs in miniature the shuttling between centers and peripheries that Mitchell identifies in imperialism,

> which conceives itself . . . as an expansion of landscape understood as an inevitable, progressive development in history, an expansion of "culture" and "civilization" into a "natural" space in a progress that is itself narrated as "natural" . . . And this movement is not confined to the external, foreign fields toward which empire directs itself; it is typically accompanied by a renewed interest in the re-presentation of the home landscape, the "nature" of the imperial center. (2002, 17)

This contrapuntal relation helps us recognize the British settlement of land and forest rights in India and the Romantic and Victorian debates about poetic propriety with regard to nature as not merely contemporaneous but instead two aspects of a larger imperial landscape project. Widening the historical lens to recognize the multiple, successive waves of conquest and colonization over millennia in India resituates Dhowli's predicament of straddling multiple modes of being on (and being cast off) the land.

Owning Up

When Mitchell writes, "Like money, landscape is good for nothing as use-value, while serving as a theoretically limited symbol of value at some other level" (2002, 14), one can recognize two processes of abstraction at work in the disposition of nature, transforming waste land from lifeworld into private property. First, the abstraction of money, which for Locke cheated the time of nature, resolved the contradiction of waste, and paved the way for limitless accumulation; and second, the abstraction of landscape aesthetics, Emerson's "property in the horizon." At stake in any instance of enclosure are how these economic and aesthetic abstractions shape one another (how nature becomes both property and poetry), and how that relationship is understood and imagined, even if (as is often the case) as incommensurable or diametrically opposed. In showing how the personification of nature is shadowed by the objectification of humans, I make a claim about one possible relationship between these abstractions. So does Pratt, when she observes that the European improving eye offers "visions of 'improvement' whose value is often expressed as aesthetic" rather than economic; this aesthetic of improvement "naturalizes a transformative project embodied in the Europeans" (1992, 61). Together with Locke's apologia for the Christian morality of improvement, this stance aligns a colonial mode of habitation with the beautiful and the good. Forest policy in British India was shaped by fiscal and strategic considerations, but also by aesthetic notions of what forests should look like (Rangarajan 1996, 66). What registers as beautiful assumes the naturalness of imperial expansion. Williams goes so far as to remark that conventional histories of English landscape insinuate that "the eighteenth-century landlord, through the agency of his hired landscapers, and with poets and painters in support, invented natural beauty," in the same way that colonial explorers purportedly "'discovered' . . . other men's countries" (1973, 120). Thus the narrator's sardonic observation in "Dhowli" about Kundan Misra's "beautiful empire" of so much land and so many women. This alignment of natural beauty and economic value suggests that perhaps the sky is blue, the trees green like any other day at the end of "Dhowli" not despite their having been sold to the Misras, but because of it.

The tricks of the eye examined in this chapter are moments when histories of contestation over the "facts" of nature flicker into visibility; one becomes aware, even if briefly, of naturalization as a process, along the lines of what Neil Smith called the production of nature (2008). Making sense of such moments requires a reading practice that remains between habitations. Consider the strange passage in *The Country and the City* where Williams exhorts the reader to be something other than a tourist on the country estate circuit, "guidebook in hand": "Look at what those fields, those streams, those woods even today produce. Think it through as labour and see how long and systematic the exploitation and seizure must have been, to rear that many houses, on that scale. . . . How much robbery and fraud there must have been, for so long, to produce that degree of disparity, that barbarous disproportion of scale" (1973, 105). The gap in scale readers are asked to extrapolate is that between the monstrous accumulation that built the great estates and the "ordinary scale of human achievement" in small farms tended by a single family over generations (105); it is an invitation to read between conflicting modes of habitation. Looking for labor, as Williams exhorts, one finds that such wealth doesn't add up unless understood in terms of a history of dispossession reaching far beyond the English countryside. Is it the case, the narrator asks at the end of "Dhowli," that "these tree-sky-earth," "this nature that the Misras did not create," are now owned by them?

But who always wants to see such horror lurking behind the picturesque? Aesthetic regimes—particularly those coded as appreciation of "natural beauty"—can help manufacture consent for property regimes. This is what Mitchell has in mind when he urges that while "no one 'owns' this landscape in the sense of having clear, unquestionable title to it . . . everyone 'owns' (or ought to own) this landscape in the sense that everyone must *acknowledge* or 'own up' to some responsibility for it, some complicity in it" (2002, 29). This idea of "owning up" to complicity in the social relations underwriting land and landscape democratizes and radicalizes Emerson's "property in the horizon" that comes from looking upon someone else's land. Can the poetic bestowal of feeling and sentience upon natural objects that Ruskin worried over in "Of the Pathetic Fallacy" be understood as a way of not owning up to the transformation of land relations in Britain and its colonies?

This notion of complicity can be extended in an environmental direction to reframe debates over the nature of nature. Although Ruskin ultimately remained committed to a humanized (European) landscape, an exhortation to depict "things as they *are*" could be a salutary invitation not merely to visual fidelity and close empirical observation, but also to a non-anthropocentric parsimony that acknowledges the autonomy and vitality of the nonhuman world: a pre-posthuman effort to meet nature on its own terms rather than "bestowing" qualities (emotion, sentience, meaning) upon it.[35] Read against the grain, Emerson's "property in the horizon" could spur us to own up to acquisitive, enclosing impulses that lurk within the scopic or emotional labor of looking upon landscape, particularly with a personifying eye. In this context, a stance that warned against committing what Ruskin dubbed the pathetic fallacy would seek not to impose or police a divide between human vitality and dead nature, but to recognize the alterity of nature: something other than a mirror of, or handmaiden to, human feeling. As the name for a category of literary tropes, *personification* may not be a sharp enough tool for making sense of newly urgent questions about the nature of nature raised by the new materialist turn. Personification does not necessarily tell us anything about the underlying ontological question of "nature's personhood," the recognition of which, for Buell, is necessary to an environmental "ethics of care" (2001, 217–18).

"Dhowli" demonstrates the difficulty of owning up to landscape in this overdetermined way. The scene where nobody can bear to look at Dhowli as she boards the bus stages a general refusal to acknowledge responsibility for her plight; she, in turn, refuses to look upon the trident, emblem of the Misras' domination. The social relations and cultural logics that shape her relationship to the forest mean that it is difficult to understand nature's indifference in this moment in terms of the non-anthropocentric parsimony and ethical recognition of nature's autonomy described earlier. By closing with the terrifying prospect of earth, sky, and trees in thrall to the Misras, the story opens up a gap between nature and culture only to close it again with the idea of nature reified as private property. Perhaps nature no longer serves as the warrant for justice; its indifference, however, derives not from its autonomy but instead its subordination as the instrument of a greater injustice. Personification and objectification are two sides of cultural logics of enclosure. Shifting the scale from the unwanted spectacle and local scandal of Dhowli's expulsion to a broader conflict between "the Dhowlis" and "the Misras," the story invites a "spatial dialectic," in Lesjak's phrase, that can "hold together the visceral, affective, and local textures of experience and the global, virtual, derivative-driven flows of capital" (2013, 264).

Coda: In the Beginning (of the Anthropocene)

The recent explosion of Anthropocene discourse in the humanities and social sciences asks us to read for the planet in new ways. Making sense of the effects of greenhouse gas emissions and other human actions on the Earth system demands a recalibration of past, present, and future, as well as jarring shifts in temporal and spatial scale. To Williams's exhortation to look for labor over several generations of capital accumulation, we can add the imperative to look for energy regimes and modes of combustion over several centuries of carbon accumulation in the atmosphere and oceans. The Anthropocene demands new forms of "owning up" to complicity for actions whose consequences were initially not well understood and are not easily framed around notions of ethical choice. Built environments and ways of life predicated on cheap and easy access to fossil fuels have sedimented around them forms of common sense and ideas of aesthetic value that are now shaken by strengthening storms and rising seas. The prospect of the earth shifting into geophysical conditions outside the parameters that have fostered human life serves as a rebuke to Locke's moralizing optimism about the wealth to be made from waste, without limits to growth. An Anthropocene perspective reveals that neither money nor migration can ultimately cheat the time of nature. Environmental justice movements are rightly positing the development of the industrialized world (which Locke would view as a gift of increase to the "common stock of mankind") as a theft of their future. Here the waste of the world—in a latter-day, petromodern sense—rewrites what we thought we knew about the nature of nature.

In other words, the Anthropocene is the quintessential trick of the eye: When the causes and consequences of modernity turn out to be different from what we thought, this planetary epiphany generates an uncanny double vision oscillating between "things as they *are*" (or had seemed) and glimpses of a spatiotemporal dialectic that demands rethinking of how those things came to be and what those formerly unapprehended and unimagined processes mean for things to come. To inhabit the present in this way is to think between habitations and temporal horizons. For this reason, I read the end of "Dhowli" as an expression of an Anthropocene structure of feeling avant la lettre. Reading "Dhowli" as a model for the current planetary predicament may seem improbable, since it was written more than four decades ago about a fictionalized Indian village nearly cut off from the rest of the world: The road ends at Tahad, and Dhowli's carbon footprint can't amount to much. In arguing that "Dhowli" may offer timely insight into a global crisis that is vividly imagined, undeniably in process, yet not fully realized, I have in mind not the story's referential and mimetic aspects, but the temporal and social implications of its narrative structure.

"Dhowli" begins with a generalized sense of expectation (everyone wonders whether Misrilal will return to support Dhowli's unborn baby) and ends with provocative questions about a nature that is at once unchanged and imbricated in a system of exploitation at a planetary scale. Pursuing its suggestion of a broader conflict between "the Dhowlis" and "the Misras," I cannot now read the end of Mahasweta's story without thinking about the narrative implications of global warming, which defamiliarizes setting, dilates the relationships between cause and effect, and introduces strange new protagonists. The damage is already done, and it continues; the full effects are displaced into the future yet become ever more evident in the present. And the Dhowlis will suffer more than, and because of, the Misras. It is an anticipatory haunting by a future devastation that appears each day a bit less distant, a prophetic memory that points toward the costs of the status quo and what has passed for common sense: what nature accepts, in the story's terms, "as a matter of course." This structure of feeling is one of distance from the most devastating aspects of environmental crisis: distance, in other words, from the front lines of the politics of survival. This distance is geographic and economic, since the costs of development in the affluent North will be paid all over again by the poor in the underdeveloped South. It is also temporal and cognitive. At this distance, many drive around like nothing's up, water still comes out of the tap, the lights still are on—at least usually, most of the time. The trees seem as green as ever; the sky, blue as in other days. This predicament, I suggest, evinces a contest between cultural logics: a tension between imagined, imminent catastrophe and seeming normality, at least if one doesn't look around too carefully or worry over what things cost. Whereas Dhowli looks in vain for her plight to be reflected in nature and the narrative raises the bleaker possibility of nature's expropriation, the discrepancy between understanding what is happening to the planet and appreciating a beautiful "seasonal" day can evoke any number of responses: cognitive dissonance, melancholy, angry skepticism ("what global warming?" is the refrain when temperatures drop).

This tension could also be understood as the obverse of the situation at the end of "Dhowli." Nature *is* responding to the monstrosity of what has been done, and it is humans (or some powerful subset) who remain, for all practical purposes, scandalously unmoved. The shock of the story's conclusion derives partly from the fact that Dhowli's disastrous embrace of forest fictions obscures "things as they *are*," or what is "actually" happening there: readers see neither the act nor the effects of the ongoing logging of the forest. Crisis is what goes wrong "when things go right," Eric Cazdyn remarks in showing how crisis and its overcoming are built into the metabolism of many systems, including capitalism (2007, 647). This notion of built-in crisis echoes the scandalous sustainability of the timber workers' vigil at Dhowli's door: "their contract was to continue for a while, and she was worth waiting for." This counterintuitive logic of the self-sustaining (yet unsustainable) status quo is evident in oil company advertising campaigns proclaiming their green bona fides and future relevance, or in post-consumerist marketing strategies that shepherd the environmentally concerned and financially comfortable toward "green" consumerism.

Even on its own terms, there is something scandalous about sustainability, a reconstructed form of the logic of improvement. Sustainability discourse, in Lee Medovoi's account, presents itself as an alternative to the waste of natural and human resources, promising an "invaluable, longer term revenue stream" (2010, 138). What remains obscured in this calculus of waste reclamation is that the resource logics of sustainability "*require* the exploitation of nature and humanity. . . . 'Sustainability' indexes nature and humanity's depletion only to convert them back into 'capital,' the very force that depleted them in the first place" (138). There is a similar sleight of hand in the phenomenon Caffentzis (2010) observes in the World Bank's seeming *volte-face* in the early 1990s, when it embraced community resource management and commons thinking after having provided ideological and financial support for the worldwide waves of privatization dubbed the "new enclosures." Caffentzis labels this shift "Neoliberalism's 'Plan B'": using "the tools of the commons to 'save' Neoliberalism from itself" (25) and keep the ravaged world safe for capitalism. In an ironic echo of Williams's account of the margins as saving grace, Caffentzis argues that tolerating some margin of the commons amidst the march of privatization not only keeps social protest and environmental degradation from "destabilizing . . . the general exploitation of a territory or population"; it also contains and reroutes those social energies to "transform neoliberalism into common sense" (28–29, 39). This "pro-capitalist commons" erects some limits on enclosure to ensure the continuing viability of capitalist accumulation. On the other hand, the very things the logic of improvement once promised as ends—civilization, civil society, the state, the commonwealth as a social compact to protect citizens and their property—appear now as an intolerable commons, an unproductive waste in need of privatization and resource-stripping. "There is no such thing as society," Margaret Thatcher declared in 1980—a quintessential example of the "'discount' on the value of human social relations" neoliberalism extracts for the sake of profitmaking (Medovoi 2010, 141). This rapacious metabolism of crisis and overcoming closes the circle on the dynamic with which this chapter began. The waste products of capitalism beckon as new frontiers for accumulation.

Perhaps only anticipatory glimpses of neoliberalism and the Anthropocene are legible in "Dhowli," published in 1979 on the brink of the Thatcher-Reagan revolution and the consequent market-driven Washington consensus, as well as NASA astrophysicist James Hansen's development of computer-modeling techniques to demonstrate human effects on the earth's climate. Anachronism, however, is arguably the crux of Anthropocene reading, since greenhouse gases, radioactive waste, and persistent organic pollutants scramble temporality: These substances persist in the environment over long timespans, and their effects (as well as understandings of those effects) erupt into the present unpredictably, nonlinearly.[36] A reading practice that perceives anticipation and retrospection as entangled and understands time as out of joint with itself will find insights about inhabiting the Anthropocene in unlikely places (and times), unfazed by what Graeme Macdonald calls the "chronological backflips" of seeking guidance for a post-oil future in fiction that predates the age of automobility (2017, 165). At this moment of paradigm shift resulting from a geological epochal shift, a temporal double vision characterizes the Anthropocene, which designates both the geophysical changes at work on the planet as well as the emergent conceptual frameworks for making sense of those changes and their implications across all realms of discourse: the *self-conscious* Anthropocene.

There are other ways of situating "Dhowli" in relation to anxieties about climate and the costs of enclosure. To speak of "global environmental crisis" assumes that a global environment is a self-evident thing; as Anna Tsing observes, however, "scale is not just a neutral frame for viewing the world; scale must be brought into being: proposed, practiced, and evaded, as well as taken for granted" (2005, 58). Forest policy debates in nineteenth-century India are one instance where the idea of nature at a planetary scale was brought into being, in EIC scientists' mounting concerns that deforestation resulted in decreased precipitation. They linked "desiccation" to such interrelated ills as drought and desertification; erosion, topsoil loss, and flooding; famine; and the accumulation of carbon dioxide in the atmosphere. These observations joined those made by their counterparts in an emergent global scientific network, or "invisible college" (Rajan 2006, 21–36, 66). Changes observed locally were increasingly understood to have effects at a larger scale and analogues elsewhere in the world: "deforestation could no longer be treated as a purely local problem amenable to local solutions" (Grove 1996, 439; see 435–8). In an 1839 report on Oudh, EIC surgeon Donald Butter lamented "the slow, but certain process by which India, like all other semitropical countries (such as central Spain, Southern Italy, and the Western territory of the United States), has its green plains—no longer capable of entangling and detaining water in the meshes of a herbaceous covering—ploughed into barren ravines" (9). Drawing on studies by Joseph Priestley, Alexander von Humboldt, and Jean-Baptiste Boussingault, as well as previous observations of EIC officials stationed on Mauritius, St. Helena, and Ascension, these personnel of empire built the case for desiccation theories and thereby documented the deleterious environmental effects of local and European capitalism in colonial settings (Rajan 2006, 65–66). Since the mid-eighteenth century, island habitats served as de facto laboratories where environmental changes catalyzed by colonial presence—most notably, the extinction of species— were readily perceptible. In "On the General and Gradual Desiccation of the Earth and Atmosphere," a paper presented to the British Association for the Advancement of Science, J. Spotswood Wilson hypothesized that the environment was changing at a *global* scale, as a result of imperial expansion and enclosure; he concluded that associated changes in the earth's atmosphere could result in the extinction of the *human* species itself (1859, 156). This work paved the way for modern climate science.

This is not to say that these nineteenth-century observers understood the effects of humans on the Earth system in the same way scientists do now. Wilson understood *that* carbon from burning coal catalyzed changes in the atmosphere but not precisely *how* (1859, 156). Nonetheless, these observations and conclusions can historicize present day climate fears—as well as their troubling implications for politics and cultural common sense. Entangled with these meteorological observations were notions of "atmospheric virtue" whose moralizing determinism about causal links between climate and human character is now difficult to take seriously (Grove 1996, 14, 401–2, 408, 416, 478). Although British policymakers in India had always been suspicious of swidden or shifting cultivation, desiccation theories offered a new opportunity to blame local users outside settled property regimes not only for destroying the forest, thereby reducing revenue and rainfall, but also for their "lawless and vagabond habits" (Cleghorn et al. 1860, 51). Small-scale users marginalized by a private property regime were blamed for the environmental effects of that regime—just as the "limits to growth" discourse emerging when Hardin published "The Tragedy of the Commons" emphasized Third World overpopulation rather than First World overconsumption. This differential calculus about modes of habitation continues to shape current dilemmas about how to reconcile the imperatives of decarbonizing the economy and alleviating poverty in the underdeveloped world.

In whatever century, it can be difficult to tease apart cultural bias from scientific insight in parsing the policy implications of climate change concerns. An early statement of the precautionary principle appears in an 1849 report by Madras surgeon Edward Balfour: acknowledging that the precise mechanisms through which trees promote soil, hydrological, and atmospheric health were not yet fully understood, he nonetheless urged that the observed effects of deforestation demanded immediate action (14–15, 4). This stance resonates with historian Paul Edwards' powerful argument (2010) that knowledge about the climate, though incomplete, nonetheless provides an adequate basis for action:

> Do we really need to know more than we know now about how much the Earth will warm? *Can* we know more? . . . Our climate knowledge is provisional and imperfect. Yet it is real, and it is strong, because it is supported by a global infrastructure . . . built on old, robust observing systems and refined predictive models. . . . The climate's past and its future shimmer before us, but neither one is a mirage. This is the best knowledge we are going to get. We had better get busy putting it to work. (438–39)

EIC scientists and their counterparts around the world were among those who built those "observing systems," the foundation on which contemporary climate knowledge rests. While their ethnocentric concerns about atmospheric virtue and "vagabond habits" may raise questions about the robustness of this foundation, they also confirm Edwards's broader call for an approach to science and technology studies that historicizes science without delegitimizing its capacity to provide insight on urgent matters like global warming.

These personnel of empire articulated a forceful critique of the environmental and social harms of European imperialism. They are perhaps precursors of figures like Donna Haraway, Naomi Klein, Andreas Malm, Jason Moore, Rob Nixon, Françoise Vergès, and Slavoj Žižek, who insist that capitalism and colonialism must be seen as primary drivers of the Anthropocene. However, in terms of the immediate policy outcomes of the EIC scientists' critique of colonialism, a more apt analogue may be the World Bank's partial embrace of commons thinking to navigate a crisis of capitalism. Forest conservation measures undertaken in response to desiccationist concerns were, in effect, the Company's Plan B—a minor corrective to ensure the "sustainability" of the broader enterprise (see Rajan 2006, 68–75). The Bombay Forest Department was created after Alexander Gibson circumvented local officials of the Bombay Presidency in 1846 and sent a report on deforestation to the Company's Board of Directors in London; in this moment, "a new economic balance was struck between the short-term priority of land revenue and much longer-term priorities relating to sustainability in patterns of resource use and to social stability" (Grove 1996, 436). The anthropogenic climate change observed by the Company's medical staff "threatened the whole of the colonial enterprise and the future of company rule in India," since decreases in agricultural productivity risked not only famine and social unrest, but also a reduction in revenues (439). Although bitter debates continued in the final years of Company rule about whether private property owners, local presidency officials, or the central administration were the best stewards of land, these arguments of the 1850s assumed that the British were in India to stay. Acknowledging the need to factor in the time of nature alongside short-term profit was about saving the Company from itself, keeping India safe for imperial modes of accumulation, and ensuring profit over the long term. Episodes of drought and famine spurred conservation efforts, resulting in a series of expansions of state control over land that "almost always took place at the expense of traditional rights and customs over forests and grazing" (468); those rights had often meant the margin of survival for local users. In other words, the dawning recognition of enclosure's effects tended to consolidate—not challenge—modes of habitation premised on enclosure. Rather than a "this changes everything" moment, as Naomi Klein (2014) argues about confronting climate change and global capitalism together, nineteenth-century climate anxieties in India led to expansions of state control to ensure the continued viability of colonial capitalism.

The force of the desiccationists' arguments derived partly from their comparative method that situated India in relation to phenomena observed elsewhere. This spatial dialectic has a counterpart in the stratigraphic procedures and criteria necessary to designate a geological period in the earth's history. Stratigraphers look for a marker (or "signature") of change legible in rock or ice at one particular location, a Global Stratotype Section and Point (GSSP), which is correlated with "auxiliary stratotypes," additional markers elsewhere that indicate "widespread changes to the Earth system occurring at that time" (Lewis and Maslin 2015, 172). In other words, the periodization of geological history hinges upon correlating a primary marker of change at one location with other signatures in other locations. These shifts in spatial scale involve a particular kind of reading for the planet, reading from the "here" of a GSSP to the "theres" of auxiliary stratotypes, as signatures of the history of Earth as a whole. In debates about the formal designation of the Anthropocene epoch, some observers are more attuned than others to how this sifting of stratigraphic evidence will reverberate into the future, with implications far beyond geology.

In a controversial article in *Nature*, ecologist Simon Lewis and climatologist Mark Maslin emphasize the relationship between dating the Anthropocene and consecrating a particular causal narrative for it: "The event or date chosen as the inception of the Anthropocene will affect the stories people construct about the ongoing development of human societies" (2015, 178). Outlining several alternatives (including the emergence of agriculture, the Industrial Revolution, and the detonation of nuclear weapons), Lewis and Maslin propose a narrative and date they call the "Orbis hypothesis" of an Anthropocene onset in 1610, when a century of European colonization of the Americas becomes stratigraphically legible. Lewis and Maslin identify in the "mixing [and homogenization] of previously separate biotas" in the Old and New Worlds (i.e., the Columbian exchange) a "swift, ongoing, radical reorganization of life on Earth without geological precedent" (174). The GSSP they identify, however, is a signature of death rather than life. Ice core samples from Antarctica point to a 7–10 ppm dip in atmospheric CO_2 at the beginning of the seventeenth century, which they argue is the result of the decimation of the human population of the Americas, estimated to have dropped from between 54 and 61 million to 6 million in the century after Columbus' landing, as a result of disease, war, famine, and enslavement. This colonial genocide resulted in a near halt to agriculture and the use of fire, which facilitated carbon uptake in an estimated 50 million hectares of regenerated forest and grassland (175). Lewis and Maslin make an argument compelling to humanists and social scientists, if not to geoscientists, that European annexation of the Americas is the seminal event that provided access to resources and markets that enabled the Industrial Revolution and the widespread use of fossil fuels. Their "Orbis" hypothesis borrows the Latin word for *world*, to acknowledge the emergence of the modern capitalist world-system. The onset of European colonialism in the sixteenth century was the catalyst for the subsequent changes that others (including Crutzen and Steffen [2000], who initiated the current debate about the Anthropocene) argue should define the new geological epoch.

If nothing else, Lewis and Maslin's Orbis hypothesis for the Anthropocene offers a new way of understanding the waste of the world contemplated by Locke in the 1680s. When Locke surveyed the American continent with his improving eye, he saw so much uncultivated land and so few people that it was, he admitted, almost not worth the enclosing. Nonetheless, he urged industrious men to infuse it with their (or their slaves') labor and transform it into productive property to increase the common stock of mankind. But Locke was hardly the first European improver to survey the Americas. What he perceived as empty waste land awaiting improvement, remaining nearly as it was when given by the Creator, was in fact wasted land, largely emptied of its human inhabitants. In the beginning of this Anthropocene, all the world was America.

CHAPTER 4

How Far Is Bhopal? Inconvenient Forums and Corporate Comparison

The plant's safety systems did not fail; they were not designed to be
capable of handling a reaction of this magnitude.

—TOMM F. SPRICK, Union Carbide Information Center

It is precisely the nature of modern mass murder that is it not visibly
direct like individual murder, but takes on a corporate character,
where every participant has limited liability. The total effect,
however, is a thousand times more pernicious than that of the
individual entrepreneur of violence. If the world is destroyed, it will
be a white-collar crime, done in a businesslike way, by large numbers
of individuals involved in a chain of actions, each one having a touch
of innocence.

—HOWARD ZINN, "Dow Shalt Not Kill"

At that time, we thought whoever died, died at once, and whoever
lived, lived whole.

—"MR. BINH," South Vietnamese Special Forces soldier

A little more than a year after a 7.0 magnitude earthquake struck Haiti in
2010, Dow Chemical released *One World: One Water* (2011), a documentary touting the efforts of a globe-spanning team of Dow scientists and
technicians to provide clean, safe drinking water to Haiti after the earthquake. As a foray into visual culture, *One Water* overlapped with Dow's
award-winning "Human Element" campaign, which featured close-up portraits of ordinary people from around the world by *National Geographic*
photographer Steve McCurry. "Including the Human Element on the Periodic Table of the Elements changed the way Dow looked at the world
and the way the world looked at Dow," explained John Claxton, the campaign's creative director (Grbic 2010). *One World: One Water* also invites
viewers to change how they look at Dow by featuring "Dow people whose
shared sense of responsibility for humanity merges with their knowledge
and expertise to bring hope where it is needed most." The film concludes

with its principals reflecting on the meaning of "one world": cooperation, peace, "we're all in this together." The voiceover's final words posit safe drinking water as an issue of not merely "sustenance" or even "hope," but "humanity's quest for justice."

"One World/powered by the Human Element" was part of a rebranding campaign led by Andrew Liveris, who became Dow Chemical's CEO in 2006. In one sense, Dow *is* the world: a United Nations of applied chemistry, with operations in over 160 countries. Liveris took the helm of what had recently become the world's second-largest chemical company, after the acquisition of Union Carbide as a wholly owned subsidiary was completed in 2001. The early 2000s were rocky years for Dow, as the twentieth anniversary of the 1984 gas leak at the Union Carbide pesticide plant in Bhopal, India, provoked urgent questions about what liability (or other responsibility) Dow bore for what is commonly described as the world's worst industrial disaster.

In the night and early morning of December 2 and 3, 1984, forty tons of deadly methyl isocyanate (MIC) and other gases were accidentally released from the Union Carbide factory that manufactured the pesticide marketed as Sevin. Carried on the wind, the gas emitted after a "runaway reaction" in the MIC storage tank killed at least three thousand people immediately (and up to twenty thousand in the years since) and left at least 300,000 injured or persistently "gas-affected," including fetal abnormalities passed to subsequent generations.[1] The victims of the 1984 gas leak still await justice; they were never properly treated, rehabilitated, or compensated. Furthermore, residents of neighborhoods surrounding the factory continue to suffer less widely known toxic exposures. The groundwater near the factory site was contaminated by wastewater improperly managed during the plant's operation and by stockpiles of chemicals left at the site after the accident.[2] By describing potable water as part of "humanity's quest for justice," *One Water* strikes a cruelly ironic note and might therefore be dismissed as a brazen instance of corporate greenwashing (Lappé 2011).

This chapter investigates what Bhopal and Dow—and the multinational corporation more broadly—mean for world-imagining, whether from corporate boardrooms, clinics tending to gas-affected survivors, or the many spaces in between. What is the shape of the world that corporations imagine, and how do those imaginings shape the world we inhabit? In what ways are all people "Dow people"? What does it mean to say that "we all live in Bhopal," as one American observer did in 1985? To pursue these questions, I want to take seriously (rather than dismiss out of hand) the cheery globalism of Dow's self-positioning as responsible corporate citizen—not because I am convinced that Dow is a force for good in the world, but because its planetary imaginary cannot be so easily disavowed.

Compare the spatial and social imaginary of "One World" with the remarks of another embattled Dow CEO, Carl Gerstacker, at a 1972 White House conference on "The Industrial World Ahead." Gerstacker's statement (particularly its first sentence, italicized here) is often cited by critics of neoliberal globalization as the epitome of an imperious corporate worldview:

> *I have long dreamed of buying an island owned by no nation and of establishing the World Headquarters of the Dow Company on the truly neutral ground of such an island, beholden to no nation or society.* If we were located on such truly neutral ground we could then really operate in the United States as U.S. citizens, in Japan as Japanese citizens and in Brazil as Brazilians, rather than being governed in prime by the laws of the United States. It has been suggested to me that the first thing to do after acquiring my island would be to attack the United States and to lose very quickly; after that there would be no problem obtaining foreign aid to develop the island. We could even pay any natives handsomely to move elsewhere.[3] (100)

Gerstacker's 1960–1976 tenure as CEO at the Midland, Michigan, headquarters spanned the Vietnam era, during which Dow Chemical was a major, sometimes exclusive, military supplier of napalm and the herbicides Agent Orange and Agent White. This relationship sparked nationwide controversy, college campus protests against Dow recruiters, and Saran Wrap boycotts in the late 1960s, as concern about US tactics in Vietnam coalesced into a broader antiwar movement. Gerstacker's desire for "truly neutral ground" (as strangely uncorporate as *One Water*'s invocation of "humanity's quest for justice") may be informed by fact that he defended Dow's napalm business as the "duty" of "simple good citizenship" (quoted in Brandt 1997, 353)—a justification that hewed too closely to the just-following-orders defense discredited at Nuremberg.[4] The historical analogy with Nazi Germany gained enough traction in public discourse that Dow's president, H. H. Doan, had to rebut it in a 1967 *Wall Street Journal* editorial. In 1970, Nobel laureate and Harvard biologist George Wald cited Nuremberg in arguing that Dow was responsible for war crimes and crimes against humanity: "If a soldier must accept individual responsibility for his part in a war crime in spite of being ordered to commit it, how much more heavy the responsibility of an industrial concern, for whom an order represents only an opportunity for profit?" With an island to call its own—perhaps Gerstacker imagined as the Vietnam War raged on—Dow could better navigate these entanglements of citizenship.

Gerstacker's dream is rife with contradictions. The phrase "anational company" never caught on; for Gerstacker, the difference between *multinational* and *anational* is that the latter would become "companies without any nationality, belonging to all nationalities" (1972, 99). An anational company would be "beholden to no nation" because it would hold multiple citizenships, one in each country where it operates. "Being governed in prime by the laws of the United States" was undesirable for Dow's global operations at a moment when the American environmental movement was winning real victories: 1970 saw the first Earth Day, the creation of the Environmental Protection Agency, and major amendments to the 1963 Clean Air Act, followed by the passage of the Clean Water Act in 1972. The localized specificity of being a Brazilian in Brazil, and so forth throughout the world, seems more intensely *multinational* than the dream of inhabiting an island of one's own.

Even if his anational island utopia was more like a globe-spanning multinational archipelago, Gerstacker's dream of not being "beholden . . . to society" strikes a different chord than the intimate globalism of Dow's "Human Element" and *One Water* campaigns, whose planetary imaginary dispenses with the nation-state altogether.[5] *Leave us alone to do our work, people*, one can almost hear Gerstacker plead. Architecture critic Reinhold Martin finds a similar dynamic in comparing the midcentury monumentality of Union Carbide's Manhattan headquarters (a fifty-three-story skyscraper completed in 1960) with its late 1970s relocation to a single-story building in Danbury, Connecticut, which was designed to be "visible only from the air": Union Carbide's global expansion engendered a "tendency toward invisibility" (2010, 129–32). It would be wrong to assume that Gerstacker's dream was about nothing more than what he called "the profit motive," a bottom-line candor better suited to closed-door meetings than PR campaigns. He concluded his remarks by proclaiming, "The anational company may be the major hope in the world today for economic cooperation among the peoples, for prosperity among the nations, for peace in our world" (Gerstacker 1972, 103). Even in its current imperfect form, the multinational corporation is "the new melting pot," more likely to produce "citizens of the world" than the United Nations (99). Gerstacker's is a "One World" vision in a more impersonal key (i.e., lacking the human element), attainable if companies like Dow have the autonomy of island-worlds.

These beneficent world-images of global capitalism contrast starkly with the terrifying scenario examined in Chapter 3 of "the Dhowlis" confronting "the Misras" with the world and nature on their side. This image in Mahasweta Devi's short story is powerful because of the extreme spatial dilation it effects, from a village in rural Bihar to the expropriation of nature itself. But notice how Dow's world-imaginings also rely on an elastic geography, finding a telescoped image of the world in one face or place, or in an island home for a corporate citizen of many countries. The tensions within Gerstacker's statement may be the source of its utopian appeal; Dow could be every place and no place at once. More practically, these images offer clues about how corporate globalization works now: interpellating individuals into its planetary imaginary, while navigating facts on the ground in widely varying situations, among and within the nearly two hundred countries of the world. These localizations are fundamental to what globalization is and does. Both Union Carbide and Dow have sought to avoid being held to account for Bhopal through this sort of localization.

In terms of the cultural logics of waste examined in Chapter 3, Bhopal is a notorious example of lands and lives laid waste by industrial development, the toxic omega of waste rather than the beckoning alpha of undeveloped waste land awaiting improvement. Instead of the nature of nature, this chapter delves into the constituency of humanity and the personhood of the corporation. (*Personhood* is a legal and philosophical category; *human* is not synonymous with *person*.) More salient here than the calculations of resource logic—which equate nature and humans for their utility as inputs to capital accumulation—is the actuarial logic of risk, weighing the potential casualties of possible disasters against the costs of prevention and the profits to be made. In the wake of unprecedented industrial disasters in Bhopal and Chernobyl, German sociologist Ulrich Beck articulated an influential analysis of "risk society," in whose sinister logic the "people or groups who are (or are made into) 'risk persons' or 'risk groups' count as nonpersons whose basic rights are threatened. Risk divides, excludes, and stigmatizes" (2009, 16). Both resource logic and risk logic can effect a kind of unpeopling, but only within a logic of risk could the safety systems of a factory that harmed hundreds of thousands of people be said not to have failed, as a Union Carbide spokesman explains in the epigraph opening this chapter.

Resource logic and risk logic are forms of world-imagining. Resource logic is centripetal, the appropriative dynamic by which capital draws the world to itself in its disposition of nature; risk logic is centrifugal, displacing the costs of risk elsewhere, beyond the pale of responsibility. (For Zygmunt Bauman, Europe's colonial-era use of "*global* solutions to *locally* produced overpopulation problems" gives way to a worldwide late-modern predicament of having to seek *"local* solutions to *globally* produced problems" [2003, 6].) Juxtaposing his apocalyptic vision with that of T. S. Eliot, we might say that Howard Zinn, railing against Dow in 1967, imagined that the world may end not with a bang but a white-collar whimper, everyone enshrouded by a limited-liability "touch of innocence." This chapter is less concerned with enclosure than *exposure,* in its various and related senses. Most obviously in the case of Bhopal, physiological exposure to toxic substances and financial exposure to economic losses. But also *exposure* in its visual senses: the exposure to light through which the medium of photography operates, and the experiential sense of familiarity, knowledge, and awareness, which takes acute form in the journalistic notion of *exposé*—bringing misdeeds into public view.

These senses of exposure are all at work in Indra Sinha's *Animal's People,* a novel set in a fictionalized Bhopal nearly two decades after what the novel calls "that night." Sinha's raucous and irreverent novel, shortlisted for the Man Booker Prize and awarded the 2008 Commonwealth Writers Prize, upends the conventional wisdom in which journalistic exposure is an indispensable tool in environmental justice struggles. When communities are exposed to toxic harm, so the logic goes, the exposé can force corporate polluters to acknowledge something other than risk to their bottom line. Consider, for example, Sheila Jasanoff's assertion that *Animal's People* "may have done more to revive international interest in Bhopal, and thus to touch the conscience of the world, than decades of medical or legal action" (2008, 692). This claim by a scholar of science and technology studies may be true in the narrow sense of renewing awareness about Bhopal. However, Jasanoff misses the novel's skepticism about the efficacy and ethics of "touching the conscience of the world" and its intimation that the exposure *of* harm can effect further exposure *to* harm—what Alexandra Schultheis Moore calls "overexposure" (2015, 113). *Animal's People* asks readers to contemplate whether and how their reception of the book differs from something like the gauzy globalism of Dow's *One Water.*

In *Animal's People,* Bhopal becomes legible as a scene of reading. This chapter compares the modes of distant reading implicit in a novel like *Animal's People* with those of corporations like Dow and Union Carbide. In decades of litigation to determine civil liability and criminal culpability for the disaster, one contested issue has been *where* the scene of reading Bhopal should be located—a charged instance of globalization working through localization. Seeking to dismiss cases brought in American courts, lawyers for Union Carbide and Dow repeatedly argued that the United States is not the proper forum for litigation. They invoked the legal principle of *forum non conveniens*—"inconvenient forum"—which "allows a court to refuse a plaintiff's action within its jurisdiction when the court determines that a case is better brought in another forum, due, for example, to reasons of language or the location of defendants or evidence" (Open Society 2005, 16). (*Forum non conveniens* was also invoked by Royal Dutch/Shell in a successful motion to dismiss a suit brought by Ken Wiwa; the dismissal was reversed on appeal in 2000.) In 1986, US District Court Judge John F. Keenan granted Union Carbide's motion to dismiss a consolidated civil suit of 145 cases involving 200,000 plaintiffs. Accepting the company's invocation of *forum non conveniens*, Keenan determined that the Indian court system offered an "adequate alternative forum" for litigation, and the civil suit was shifted there.[6] The principle of *forum non conveniens* was cited in the 2012 dismissal of a suit to force Dow to clean up the factory site.

The legal questions of language and location at stake in *forum non conveniens* resonate with more literary questions; they give particular urgency to reading for the planet. Translated from legal argument to literary interpretation, *forum non conveniens* elicits questions about narrative jurisdiction: the spaces where narratives circulate, and the comparisons that make them meaningful.[7] What does it mean for narratives of environmental injustice to circulate "inconveniently"? What forum would be "adequate" for such narratives? What kind of forum, whether convenient or inconvenient, does contemporary world literature offer?

Animal's People is well suited to such questions because of its reflexivity and metafictional explicitness about the transnational "forum" comprising its narration and anticipated reception by the imagined, distant reader it calls "Eyes." Sinha's novel figures reading as looking: Its optic technology allows readers to see beyond their field of vision, a mode of exposure with effects not always welcome or beneficial. After examining in the next section the legal principle of *forum non conveniens*, the topography of the multinational corporation, and their implications for comparative literary study, I consider in subsequent sections the novel's rhetorical address to a distant reader, its staging of collisions among languages and linguistic registers, and its intertextual invocations of literary genres and texts, in order to probe its skepticism about meaningful communication in such a forum. How and what do distant readers see? How does the world they imagine compare with the ones offered by corporations like Dow Chemical and Union Carbide? How far is Bhopal?

Convenience and Comparison

When lawyers for Union Carbide invoked the doctrine of *forum non conveniens* in 1985, they argued that Americans could not understand or imagine life in Bhopal, normal or otherwise:

> The relevant public interest factors . . . the properiety [*sic*] of deciding foreign controversies where they arose, the reluctance of American courts to apply foreign law and the realistic uncertainty that they can apply it correctly and fairly—also mandate an Indian forum. Indeed, the practical impossibility for American courts and juries, imbued with US cultural values, living standards and expectations, to determine damages for people living in the slums or "hutments" surrounding the UCIL plant in Bhopal, India, by itself confirms that the Indian forum is overwhelmingly the most appropriate. Such abject poverty and the vastly different values, standards and expectations which accompany it are commonplace in India and the third world. They are incomprehensible to Americans living in the United States.[8] (Kelley Drye & Warren [1985] 1986, 30)

The lawyers argued successfully against the possibility of distant reading: American courts and juries couldn't make the comparisons between near and there that would allow them to understand Bhopal and determine appropriate compensation to the victims.

This argument against distant reading demands careful examination. Its insistence on localization runs counter to "we're all in this together" visions of globalization as "one world." Instead, Union Carbide's lawyers shielded the company from liability by asserting the "practical impossibility" of distant reading and the mutual illegibility of different "values, standards, and expectations." Their claim regarding the "incomprehensibility" of life "in India and the third world" puts the force of law behind the dynamics of unimagining and challenges of legibility examined throughout this book. In this legal context, *comprehending* is tied to *quantifying* damages. The lawyers are not so much worried that Americans are *unable* to understand or sympathetically imagine Third World living conditions—that their imaginations would *fail* in the face of these conditions—as fearful that they would understand them *incorrectly* and *unfairly* (according to American values and expectations): that is, too sympathetically. The lawyers maintain that a lack of exposure to everyday realities in the Third World could lead an American jury to be overgenerous; an Indian court, for whom the fact and face of "abject poverty" would be "commonplace," would be more correct, fair, and parsimonious in deciding liability. The motion to dismiss is a pointed instance of unimagining, in the transitive sense of making a situation unimaginable: Union Carbide used claims of incomprehensibility to prevent overly sympathetic imaginings from determining its financial exposure to liability for toxic exposure in Bhopal. The sanctioned ignorance of Americans about life in the Third World was invoked to provide legal cover for corporate criminality.

A literary critic might be tempted to dismiss this darker reading of the lawyers' *forum non conveniens* argument as inferior to literary imagining, if the literary is understood to be predicated upon, rather than suspicious of, generous imagining.[9] But I want to keep alive the multiple meanings of incomprehensibility and the stakes and motives behind such claims. The history of Bhopal litigation is full of what Indian legal scholar Upendra Baxi calls "extraordinary inversions" (1986b, 1): profound ironies that demand attentiveness to gaps between words and meaning, and between parties' arguments and their interests. Most striking among these is what Judge Keenan dubbed a "paradox" in his 1986 dismissal. To allow the case to proceed in an American court would be, Keenan declared,

> yet another example of imperialism, another situation in which an established sovereign inflicted its rules, its standards, its values on a developing nation. . . . To deprive the Indian judiciary of this opportunity to stand tall before the world and to pass judgment on behalf of its own people would be to revive a history of subservience and subjugation from which India has emerged. India and its people can and must vindicate their claims before the independent and legitimate judiciary created there since the Independence of 1947. (1986, 25–26)[10]

Mindful of Union Carbide's argument about differences in "values, standards, and expectations" in the United States and the Third World, Keenan posits cross-cultural imagining as an act of neoimperialism. (These legal arguments from the mid-1980s resonate strangely with academic discourse of that moment: expressing concern about disparate value systems, Union Carbide's lawyers sound like good cultural relativists during the rise of multiculturalism; the same year Ngũgĩ wa Thiong'o published *Decolonising the Mind* [1986], Keenan took a stand against cultural imperialism by asserting that the Indian legal mind had been, and must remain, decolonized.) The "paradox" Keenan identifies in ruling against the plaintiff's bid for a US trial is that the plaintiff was the Indian government itself.[11] Keenan's concern for India's postcolonial sovereignty contravenes the Government of India's remarkable argument, supported with analysis commissioned from American legal scholar Marc Galanter, that its legal system could not handle a case of this magnitude and complexity ("Affidavit" [1985] 1986).[12] This is a stunning example of colonial cringe (the inverse posture of "standing tall"), in the strategic interest of securing a judgment against Union Carbide.

Another reason to consider multiple valences of (in)comprehensibility is that the legal principle of *forum non conveniens* is so suggestive for literary inquiry. The issues of language, location, and life experience at stake in *forum non conveniens* overlap in significant and surprising ways with questions of translation and circulation that are the purview of World Literature, the newly globalized friendly face of comparative literary studies. Keenan noted the linguistic difficulties of a trial in the United States, since much of the documentary evidence and the testimony of many witnesses would not be in English: "fewer translation problems would face an Indian court than an American court" (1986, 18).[13] Before the disaster, however, the fact that safety manuals, logs, and equipment at the Bhopal factory were monolingual—printed in English—was a matter of concern only to workers and trade unions (Hanna, Morehouse, and Sarangi 2005, 33). (In a trivial but telling analogy, Dow's *One Water* features a comical moment when a Spanish technician who travels to Haiti to install Dow's ultrafiltration system discovers that the instructions are in Chinese.) The stakes of translation and living across and between multiple languages are immense with regard to Bhopal—a fact reflected in the multilinguistic texture of *Animal's People*, a novel written (mostly) in English but narrated by a protagonist who is speaking (mostly) Hindi. As elaborated later in this chapter, the linguistic relations in *Animal's People* and the history of Bhopal litigation and activism demonstrate the cosmopolitan provincialism and political inadequacy of a world (and a World Literature) that favors English as a language of convenience without regard for its role in histories of conquest, thus impeding the circulation of alternative narratives.

The primary question involved in *forum non conveniens*—is there an alternative forum that is adequate to provide a remedy?—could prompt literary critics to consider whether and how literature functions as an "alternative forum" to the law. Joseph Slaughter makes an argument along these lines in *Human Rights, Inc.*, which sees the bildungsroman facilitating the cultural imagining of a "human rights international" in advance of an effective and consensual international legal regime (2007, 317).[14] Literature might offer a supplement to the law because its expansive notions of jurisdiction, protocols of interpretation, and systems of precedent are suppler, unconstrained by legal niceties. But what are the implications—and

limitations—of this analogy with the law? If a novel is an "alternative forum" (as Jasanoff's assessment of *Animal's People* implies), how would that
forum be "adequate"—and to what? What remedy can a novel provide?
Certainly not jail time for Union Carbide CEO Warren Anderson (who
died in a Florida nursing home in 2014) or his corporate successors, nor
monetary compensation for decades of harm.[15] These questions, framed
in terms of *forum non conveniens*, can help us think concretely between law
and literature as forums for narrative. Perhaps the literary imagination
traffics in an alternative currency, something like what Rob Nixon calls
the "compensatory realm of symbolic activism" (2011, 265); perhaps it facilitates the work of justice in other realms, including the legal one. Yet
this tantalizing analogy between literature and the law demands both cir-
cumspection and a rather dogged directness (or a literalness about the
metaphoric). It demands humility about what literature as an "alternative
forum" can do and attention to the *how* of that doing.

Before turning to close formal analysis of this "how" in *Animal's People*,
we should consider the importance of comparison in legal and environmental contexts. Comparison across geographic sites is a premise shared
by environmental racism and struggles for environmental justice. As with
gas flaring in the Niger Delta, comparison is at work when a corporation
does *over there* what it would or could not do *here*. This is the benefit of
being the citizen of many nations, in Gerstacker's dream of localized globalization. Environmental inequities are produced by inequalities of race,
class, and other axes of social and political difference that shape varied regulatory and enforcement regimes.

In their 1985 *forum non conveniens* motion, Union Carbide's lawyers argued against comparing the United States and Indian (or Third World)
contexts: values appropriate to one context would lead Americans to make
faulty judgments about the other. This contention evokes an earlier, obsolete meaning of *convenient:* proportional, congruous, and in accord (as
opposed to current usage, in which *convenient* means expedient or com-
modious). As with *comparison*, *convenience* in this etymological sense entails bringing things together. In effect, the lawyers' argument holds that
American judgments about the Indian context would be inconvenient: in-
congruous, incommensurate, or disproportional. Judge Keenan also confronted the comparative principle inherent to *forum non conveniens*: While
the doctrine "is designed in part to help courts avoid conducting complex
exercises in comparative law," some minimal comparative exercise remains
necessary to demonstrate that the alternative forum can provide some remedy rather than none at all (1986, 6).[16]

Lawyers and activists on both sides have compared the Union Carbide India Limited factory in Bhopal with the Union Carbide Corporation factory in Institute, West Virginia, in terms of plant design, construction, operations, maintenance, and safety provisions. To the extent that the Indian plant compared unfavorably with the one in the United States, the Union Carbide Corporation (UCC) sought strenuously to differentiate itself from Union Carbide India Limited (UCIL), a subsidiary in which it held a 50.9 percent controlling share in 1984.[17] Dismissing the consolidated civil suit in 1986, Judge Keenan accepted Union Carbide's description of the Bhopal incident as an Indian problem at an Indian company's Indian factory with Indian employees and Indian victims that was best adjudicated by Indian courts.[18] This dismissal "ensured an outcome which would localize a catastrophe brought about by global actors," Baxi argues (1986b, 9)—echoing Nnimo Bassey's critique of how resource curse analyses of the Niger Delta ignore transnational actors. This is an extreme example of neoliberal globalization's strategy of localizing risk, which I understand as a spatial corollary of the truism that neoliberalism socializes risk and privatizes profit. This localizing effort to distinguish the American parent company from the Indian subsidiary (and thereby quarantine responsibility and avoid liability) only intensified when Dow acquired Union Carbide in 2001.

Localization can also be a strategy for apprehending and interrupting how globalization works, turning its faraway abstractions into sensuous concretions and breaking through quarantines of the imagination. An amicus brief submitted by religious and public interest organizations against Union Carbide's *forum non conveniens* motion noted, "On the morning of August 11, 1985, the perceived distance between Bhopal and the United States was dramatically shortened when a release of toxic material . . . into the air from Union Carbide's Institute plant hospitalized 134 residents of that [West Virginia] town" ("Brief Amicus Curiae" [1985] 1986, 287). In this cartographic imaginary, space becomes elastic. How far is Bhopal? Only as far as the nearest Union Carbide operation, just as the Niger Delta is (in Ledum Mitee's formulation) only as far as the nearest Shell station.

These elastic maps of risk and complicity chart distance and proximity in terms of the multinational corporation, rather than the nation-state. They enable new vectors of affiliation, community, solidarity, and responsibility, while also raising new questions about fault lines papered over (and reinscribed) by one-worldist imaginaries and assumptions of First World invulnerability. After the Bhopal disaster, UCC officials tried to reassure Americans that "it can't happen here."[19] But it already had. Only after Bhopal did residents of Middleport, New York learn that MIC was involved in a November 1984 chemical spill at a nearby UCC plant (Fortun 2001, 76–77). A half century earlier, the Union Carbide and Carbon Corporation was responsible for the worst industrial disaster in the United States: the knowing exposure of two thousand workers to silica dust when a contractor for its subsidiary, the New Kanawha Power Company, excavated the Hawk's Nest hydroelectric tunnel near Gauley Bridge, West Virginia, in 1930–31. In what US Representative Glenn Griswold condemned as "grave and inhuman disregard of . . . the health, lives, and future of the employe[e]s," ("Silicosis Deaths" 1936), the largely African American migrant workforce was (unlike management) neither provided with protective gear nor allowed to use exposure-reducing procedures as they tunneled through rock composed almost entirely of silica. The death toll from acute silicosis is not known because so many stricken laborers were chased out of town.

Griswold's subcommittee hearings on this horrific episode in the history of Union Carbide are incorporated into Muriel Rukeyser's poem sequence *The Book of the Dead* (1938), whose speaker goes down from Manhattan to West Virginia to confront what sort of country she lives in: "These roads will take you into your own country" (2005, 73). Like *Animal's People*, Rukeyser's poem innovates formal strategies to stage an encounter between a second-person distant witness and victims of Carbicide (death by Union Carbide). Rukeyser assays the documentary capacity of poetry by invoking visual technologies including maps and x-rays (the "landscape mirrored in these men" [106]), filmic montage and the "camera eye" (78). (Note the echo of Dziga Vertov, discussed in Chapter 1.) Observing the will-to-mastery of both hydroelectric and corporate power—the thermodynamic conservation of energy juxtaposed with legal strategies of corporate immortality—the speaker closes by positing a countervailing power of documentary as prosthesis: "Carry abroad the urgent need . . . / . . . to extend the voice" (110). Yet most of these technologies demand glass and/or electricity, thereby materially implicating the documentary within the atrocity it seeks to expose, and potentially subjecting its subjects to malign forms of exposure. These strategies, and this self-reflexive critique, find their counterparts in *Animal's People*, as I discuss in the next section.

The scale of encounter in *The Book of the Dead* is national rather than transnational, confronting internal race and class divides. Nonetheless, there are similarities in the communities most severely affected, with hostility toward migrant laborers compounding the effects of toxic substances.

In Bhopal, some victims were twice displaced by the Green Revolution: peasants cast off their land came to the city seeking work, only to become slum dwellers in the *bastis* near the factory (Everest 1986, 64). As with the African American workforce at Gauley Bridge, many poor Muslim migrants in Bhopal retreated back to the countryside in the wake of disaster.

Corporate malfeasance, industrial accidents, and toxic chemicals know no borders. This shared vulnerability to corporate power and poisonous substances engenders tricky imaginative terrain, given the "unevenly universal" predicament of vulnerability to environmental harm (Nixon 2011, 65). Nixon's formulation captures the necessity and difficulty of comparison. On the one hand, Union Carbide insisted that comparison between Bhopal and the United States was impossible or unnecessary. On the other hand, such comparison can be too easy, *inconvenient* in the sense of disproportionate: claiming the solidarity of a shared predicament of inhabiting a risky world (One World?), without recognizing the stratifications that expose some more than others. This is the central tension of this chapter.

Corporate cartographies also pose challenges for international law, which views the world through the lens of the nation-state. "International law currently says little, and does less, about human rights violations associated with [multinational] corporate activity," argues international law scholar Patrick Macklem (2005, 281). At the 2002 United Nations World Summit on Sustainable Development (or Earth Summit), Greenpeace International articulated "Bhopal Principles on Corporate Accountability," calling for international and domestic legal regimes adequate to protect the world—both people and planet—from border-crossing corporate harm. These principles outline an expansive notion of multinational enterprise liability spanning a corporation's various entities (including parent companies and local subsidiaries), across space ("beyond national jurisdictions") and time ("cradle to grave responsibility for manufactured products") (Hanna, Morehouse, and Sarangi 2005, 271–73). Invoking the 1992 Rio Declaration on Environment and Development, the Bhopal Principles aimed to create legal mechanisms for ensuring corporate accountability, but industry lobbyists nixed a legally binding multilateral treaty at the 2002 summit (Clapp 2010, 166). The Bhopal Principles remain just that, shaping corporate behavior through voluntary social responsibility initiatives rather than as a global norm with the force of law behind it.

The shape of the world charted by the liability-limiting structure of the multinational corporation poses legal difficulties that remain unresolved. It also offers (or demands) new approaches to literary study. Dow's public relations and Union Carbide's legal strategy offer important, if troubling, rubrics for reading for the planet from a site like Bhopal; corporate discourse can be juxtaposed with literary discourse as modes of world-imagining. More fundamentally, in terms of the discipline's organizing categories, what if the transnational footprint of a corporation, rather than the boundaries between nation-states and national literatures, were the axis for literary comparison? As suggested in my juxtaposition of *The Book of the Dead* and *Animal's People* as literary responses to Carbicide, that methodology could read across geographic sites linked by corporate histories of harm, as a counterpart and counterforce to the multinational archipelago dreamt by Gerstacker. What might the world according to Dow Chemical mean for world literature?

I offer these questions as a provocation, at a moment when transnational and environmental approaches to literary studies are ascendant, yet corporate histories of harm remain all but uncharted, mere random dots waiting to be assembled into a pattern.[20] The nation is increasingly regarded as an inadequate analytic framework; political geography charted in terms of the nation-state obscures how power, money, and matter flow across the planet. Nonetheless, a concomitant reckoning with the role of the multinational corporation in this reshaping of the world and these vectors of command and circulation has not occurred in literary studies. An undifferentiated globe cannot perform the organizing role played by nations (and their empires) during the heyday of national literatures, even if "World Literature" and "Global Anglophone" have unseated other rubrics in departmental hiring and professional organizations like the Modern Language Association.

I return to this provocation in this chapter's final section, which makes an initial foray toward this comparative methodology by tracing a thread in *Animal's People* linking Bhopal to Vietnam. A complete literary history constellated around the history of Dow Chemical, including its subsidiaries, acquisitions, and spun-off units, is beyond my competence and the scope of this chapter; it would require a collaborative, accretive effort to read texts in multiple languages from Australia, Canada, India, New Zealand, the United States, Vietnam, and many elsewheres (more than 160 countries). This endeavor could yield another kind of alternative forum, writ large: The transnational literary space charted by this reading practice would refuse quarantines imposed by legal structures of incorporation designed to distinguish among corporate entities or between "natural" persons and corporate persons, thereby to limit (or "veil") liability.

Although no literary methodology can breach a legal quarantine against corporate accountability, using the multinational corporation as an axis for literary comparison could breach quarantines of the imagination; this reading practice could render legible the webs of risk and harm linking sites around the world, thereby charting alternative maps of solidarity and responsibility. It might make legible how multinational corporations (including publishing companies) inflect local, regional, national, and transnational imaginaries and imaginations. (Consider the world as delivered by Amazon, which leapfrogged from literature to world domination.) This version of reading for the planet would be inconvenient, in the best sense, to multinational corporations that rely upon limited liability, invisibility, and amnesia to isolate individual disasters and obstruct a collective response. It would entail a new planetary materialism, attentive to myriad forms of traffic, transit, and trespass at scales ranging from the far-flung (and willfully complex) structures of multinational corporations to the permeable membranes of plant and animal cells. It would offer a variant of Anthropocene reading attuned to these new dispositions of nature: not only the redistribution of life forms across the planet and the changes in the earth's oceans and atmosphere caused by greenhouse gases, but also the anthropogenic rearrangement of molecules *within* and across life forms in the past century. (Here localization and externalization manifest as organisms' *internalization* of harmful substances.) Assembling an account of world literature according to corporations like Dow would help to chart transnational imaginaries of transcorporeal harm.

Middle Vision: Reading, Looking, Sympathetic Imagining

Animal's People is set around 2003, nearly twenty years after the catastrophic release of a cloud of toxic gas from a factory in the fictional city of Khaufpur, whose geography and history mirror those of Bhopal.[21] The survivors' endless wait for slow justice is punctuated by visits from an endless parade of foreign journalists and others drawn to Khaufpur by their curiosity and desire to help. The survivors' leader is Zafar, a charismatic middle-class activist who has "given up everything in his life for the poor" (22). Zafar's authority and tactics are challenged by the arrival of Elli, a young American doctor who opens a free clinic for survivors. Elli's clinic elicits suspicion because, in the novel as in real life, medical care and information (particularly about effects of and proper treatment for MIC exposure) became entangled with liability issues, beginning on "that night."[22] Narrative suspense in *Animal's People* derives partly from the mystery behind Elli's arrival and her possible connections to what the novel calls "the Kampani." Fearing that Elli is, say, collecting clinical data to support the Kampani's contention that only a few Khaufpuris still suffer health effects from "that night," Zafar deputes Animal, the novel's narrator and protagonist, to keep an eye on Elli. Animal is an orphaned survivor born just days before the disaster. His name derives from his misshapen body; his once-straight spine gradually folded upon itself so that he must move about on all fours. Determining who Elli is and what her presence means for Khaufpur—and for himself in particular—is the focus of Animal's narrative, set against the gas leak's long aftermath and the collective struggle for justice.

The novel's narrative structure and direct address to a reader evince a remarkable self-consciousness about its circulation within an uneven global cultural landscape. The novel comprises the transcripts of twenty-three cassette tapes on which Animal records his narrative. He received the recording equipment and other gifts from an Australian journalist who wanted to publish his life story; a canny survivor, Animal accepted these gifts without intending to follow through. The journalist advised Animal to imagine his audience as one sympathetic individual; when he is finally inspired to tell his story, Animal addresses that imagined person: "You are reading my words, you are that person. I've no name for you so I will call you Eyes. My job is to talk, yours is to listen. So now listen" (13–14). "Eyes" is Animal's name for this sympathetic, curious, if poorly informed metropolitan reader/listener.

This appellation, "Eyes," construes reading as looking; it implicates distant readers as spectators, a relation the novel treats with fierce ambivalence. Animal acts as Zafar's "eyes" in the community, a role interpreted rather broadly when he peeps into Elli's room as much to see her naked as to discern her motives. This illicit surveillance of the American doctor is an ironic reversal of Khaufpur being reduced to a spectacle of wretchedness: Animal resents the prying eyes and condescending fascination of "all you folk from Amrika and Vilayat, jarnaliss, filmwallass, photographass, anthrapologiss" who "look at us with that so-soft expression, speak to us with that so-pious tone in your voice" (184–85).[23] Viewed from Bhopal, the problem is not invisibility, as readers might expect; rather, it is hypervisibility, overexposure, being always the object of a gaze, or nothing but a spectacle. Animal recognizes the grotesquerie and violence implicit in the Australian journalist's self-description of his role as visual prosthesis:

"thousands of other people . . . looking through his eyes." Animal recoils at this "awful idea. Your eyes full of eyes. Thousands staring at me through the holes in your head. Their curiosity feels like acid on my skin" (7). His question, "These cuntish eyes, what do they know of our lives?" (8), expresses exasperated vulgarity, but it's also incisive in positing outsiders' curiosity as analogous to the imperious, illicit desire of the "thousand-eyed" Hindu god Indra. Indra's "thousand-eyed" epithet refers to the punishment he incurred for seducing a beautiful woman by disguising himself as her husband. In earthier versions of this episode in the *Ramayana* tradition, the angry, cuckolded husband cursed Indra that his body should be marked by a thousand vaginas—a punishment commuted when the genitalia were transformed into eyes.[24] In Indra Sinha's novel, Animal challenges the equation between seeing and knowing entailed in the work of exposing injustice. His weariness and wariness at being looked at reveals how the curious humanitarian gaze can feel like acid; like the improving eye in Mahasweta Devi's "Dhowli," the gaze of sympathy can seem like leering.

When Animal begins his narration, a similarly frightful image of being surrounded by hungry eyes recurs:

> Whichever way I look eyes are showing up. . . . I don't want them to
> see me. . . . As the words pop out of my mouth they rise up in the dark,
> the eyes in a flash are onto them, the words start out kind of misty,
> like breath on a cold day, as they lift they change colours and shapes,
> they become pictures of things and of people. What I say becomes a
> picture and the eyes settle on it like flies. (12–13)

This vivid description of words transmediated from breath and sound to mist and image offers an alternative account of the mechanical process of recording, transcription, translation, and reception that readers are told resulted in *Animal's People*; the novel is preceded by a *Robinson Crusoe*–style editor's note describing the cassette tapes and the process of transforming them into a book. The pestilent image of eyes-as-flies echoes Animal's description of journalists as "vultures"—scavengers "come to suck our stories from us, so strangers in far off countries can marvel there's so much pain in the world" (5). These stories are consumed and produced in an asymmetrical cultural landscape: the curiosity of the world "turned us Khaufpuris into storytellers, but always of the same story. Ous raat, cette nuit, that night, always that fucking night" (5).[25] Animal reserves particular scorn for distant editors who set the terms of the journalists' work: "how can foreigners at the world's other end, who've never set foot in Khaufpur, decide what's to be said about this place?" (9). He resents the abjection the story-seekers and story-shapers expect him to perform, as well as the fact that, despite Khaufpuris' endless recitations, among the "many books [that] have been written about this place, not one has changed anything for the better" (3). This strangely static economy of hypervisibility and compulsory narration packages pain for consumption elsewhere but fails to bring change for the sufferers: Khaufpuris are neither invisible nor unseen, but they may as well be.

If such narratives are supposed to offer an "alternative forum" to litigation, Animal deems them no more adequate than the courts to provide a remedy for decades of harm. For him, the global circulation of Bhopal narratives is shaped as much by power and pity as by language and location: he sings jauntily, *"if you dare to pity me / I'll shit in your shoe and piss in your tea"* (172). He is equally suspicious of the sympathy of outsiders as were Union Carbide's lawyers in their *forum non conveniens* motion; whereas the lawyers feared a too generous judgment against their client, Animal finds that the circulation of Khaufpur stories has not changed anything for Khaufpuris. In neither legal nor literary forums for Bhopal narratives has strangers' marveling at the surplus of pain resulted in the Kampani having to pay.[26] Another echo of the lawyers' claims of incomprehensibility is the novel's concern with the mutual ignorance of Khaufpuris and outsiders. "We know zilch about their lives, they know nothing of ours, that's the problem," says Zafar about Americans (66). Union Carbide's lawyers cited unbridgeable differences in values (which they feared jurors might paper over with overgenerous monetary damages) as a reason to change the venue and change the subject; the novel ostensibly raises the problem of mutual ignorance in order to address it, here and now, within its alternative forum. Read this way, *Animal's People* aims to make the incomprehensible comprehensible: to imagine the unimaginable.

Yet Animal intends his narration not as an alternative forum to the law, but as an alternative to previous alternatives (i.e., as a third-order "alternative forum") that were also inadequate. "Eyes" is best understood as the locus of Animal's desire for a different relationship between Khaufpur and the world; "Eyes" is the site of Animal's hope that distant reading can be a mode of looking other than voyeurism or caustic curiosity. (And hope is marked in the novel as a dangerous thing—"a crutch for weaklings," in Animal's brawny-chested, four-footed estimation; "Let go of hope and keep fighting, it's the lesson of Khaufpur," Zafar agrees [75].) "Eyes" names and summons into being the lone sympathetic reader amidst the scavenging strangers: "In this crowd of eyes," Animal says, "I am trying to recognize yours. I've been waiting for you to appear" (13). Relating his story, Animal makes himself the visual prosthesis that the Australian journalist described, but Eyes—as opposed to the crowd of eyes—represents the possibility of transforming vicarious vision from predatory spectatorship to sympathetic sight. This individualization of the distant sympathetic reader is a narratological corollary to the focus of humanitarian narratives on the suffering of a single protagonist rather than nameless thousands or millions.[27] These globalizing gestures work through localization.

Animal's anxious hope is palpable in a long description of the abandoned factory, condensed here to emphasize Animal's address to Eyes: "Eyes, I wish you could come with me into the factory. . . . Listen, how quiet it's. . . . Eyes, imagine you're in the factory with me. . . . Eyes, are you with me still? . . . That herb scent, it's ajwain, you catch it drifting in gusts. . . . Here we can climb up. . . . Eyes, you see a black pipe climbing into the sky, I see Siva dark and naked, smeared with ashes from funeral pyres" (30–32).[28] Animal adapts the journalist's visual prosthesis; "staring . . . through the holes in [another's] head" is replaced by seeing with or alongside another. Sympathetic imagining is figured as spatial proximity and sociality. The reader accompanies the narrator; this companionable perception extends beyond vision to all the senses. The counterfactual contiguity enabled by the forum of fiction serves to narrow, without closing entirely, the gap of incomprehensibility cited by Union Carbide's lawyers. Where Eyes sees a black pipe, Animal sees a dancing god. Narrative offers a space of possibility for reimagining rather than unimagining.

The rules of Animal's narrative gambit mean that Eyes never talks back to confirm or challenge Animal's suppositions: "Eyes" names a structure or act of reception that is anticipated (or imagined with wary hope) rather than narrated. Elli functions as an additional surrogate for the distant reader, but her scopic relations with Animal complicate his hopes for sympathetic imagining. She is an American in Khaufpur, yet spatial proximity is not sufficient to dissolve the divide of incomprehensibility. In a pivotal scene, Elli inspects the slum near the factory and laments its improvised chaos and lack of sanitation: "Seriously . . . this whole district looks like it was flung up by an earthquake." Animal overhears this judgment while spying on Elli; seeing his life through her eyes inflicts a defamiliarizing violence that echoes his perception of distant readers' curiosity as unwelcome exposure, "like acid on my skin":

something weird and painful happens in my head. Up to that moment
this was Paradise Alley . . . a place I'd known all my life. When Elli
says *earthquake* suddenly I'm seeing it as she does. Paradise Alley is a
wreckage of baked earth, mounds and piles of planks on which hang
gunny sacks, plastic sheets, dried palm leaves. Like drunks with arms
round each others' necks, the houses of the Nutcracker lurch along
this lane which, now that I look, isn't really even a road, just a long gap
left by chance between the dwellings. Everywhere's covered in shit and
plastic. Truly I see how poor and disgusting are our lives. (106)

In this sudden reversal of perception, Paradise Alley is revealed to be a hell
of "shit and plastic." This vignette dramatizes the lawyers' incomprehensibility scenario, staging a clash between "vastly different values, standards
and expectations" held by Americans and those living in "abject poverty"
in "slums or 'hutments' surrounding the UCIL plant in Bhopal." Elli's
brisk, confident interpretation of the situation is the one the lawyers fear
most. Her comprehension does not fail in the face of abjection; rather, she
understands exactly what needs to be done (infrastructure, public health
education, community organizing) and breezily dismisses the objections
of her guide, a "government doctress," who responds from the other side
of the values divide: "these people, they don't know any better . . . from
where is the money to come?" (105).

   This exchange hews closely to the Union Carbide lawyers' scenario, but
Animal's response complicates it in surprising ways. He describes the encounter from the position of the prospective object of intervention, not that
of the Kampani trying to avoid footing the bill. But the earthshaking violence of mental upheaval comes from his *acceptance* of Elli's perception and
judgment. Her perspective—deemed by the lawyers *inconvenient* in the obsolete sense of disproportionate to Third World poverty—is privileged by
Animal as truth: "Truly I see how poor and disgusting are our lives." In
this moment, Animal's shame discredits the lawyers' cultural relativist posture: "Difference is not to be equated with deficiency," Indian lawyer
N. A. Palkhivala insisted in an affidavit for Union Carbide attesting to the
adequacy of India's legal system ([1985] 1986, 223). In the contest of values
imagined in the lawyers' scenario, Animal's response reveals that some perspectives are more powerful than others.

   In terms of the dynamics of spectatorship, suspicion, and sympathetic
imagining described here, it is significant that Animal sees himself through
Elli's eyes (in a sociological sense) and yet remains unseen by her as he overhears a judgment not meant for his ears. In *Regarding the Pain of Others*,
Susan Sontag describes a polarized global politics of spectatorship, where

the fault line of power manifests as a divide between seeing and being seen: she identifies the "dubious privilege of being spectators, or declining to be spectators, of other people's pain," in a world where "the other, even when not an enemy, is regarded only as someone to be seen, not someone (like us) who also sees" (2003, 110–11, 72). To see without being seen is the privileged position of spectatorship in this scenario.[29] This Manichean economy of suffering and sympathy has also been analyzed with reference to evolutionary biology; in *The Experience of Landscape* (1974), Jay Appleton links the scopic relation between predator and prey to the aesthetic relationship between prospect and refuge in the picturesque. Both arguments link power to perspective; a shift in scopic relations therefore might shift the contours of a world divided between those who see and those who are seen, exposed to view. What if the seers and the seen traded places and reversed the scope, or imagined themselves seeing and being seen? As argued in previous chapters, moments of scopic reflexivity are pivotal in commodity biography film and Ed Kashi's photographs of the Niger Delta: Depictions of characters viewing images and/or returning the viewer's gaze unsettle the privileged position of spectatorship as unseen seeing.

In effect, Animal holds up an unbecoming mirror to the privileged spectator, whether immediate and proximate or mediated through the visual prosthesis of photographic image or narrative: all those ravenous eyes. His narration to Eyes is warily hopeful not least because it redefines otherness, in Sontag's terms: Animal is "someone (like us) who also sees" and invites us to see along with him. In his tour of the factory for Eyes, Animal sees rather than being seen; he is subject rather than object, narrator rather than character. Yet the scene where he spies on Elli and sees his life through her eyes suggests that reversing the scope is not necessarily sufficient to shift asymmetries of power and privilege. It is uncertain that the force of Animal saying to the eyes, "I see you seeing me" is as powerful as that of seeing himself being seen by Elli. The fact that he is spying on her (the privileged, even predatory position of unseen seeing), yet accepts her judgment as truth, points to another character/position in this drama of spectatorship: a more complex person behind the mask of alterity construed as "someone to be seen." Animal occupies what I understand as a middle position, a middle vision (along the lines of the grammatical middle voice). This position entails a bracketed, not-quite agency of seeing the seers, seeing oneself being seen by them, yet being unable to challenge their hegemonic worldview—and even internalizing it. Rearranging scopic relations is not enough to change the world as Sontag maps it, because scopic asymmetries derive from and stand in for more fundamental inequalities. The "imaginary proximity" proffered by images of suffering, Sontag writes, is a deceptive "proximity without risk," "one more mystification of our real relations to power" (2003, 102, 111) in which seeing is not necessarily knowing and certainly not "owning up" to complicity, in W. J. T. Mitchell's sense. This insight has important implications for the novel as a technology of world-imagining; its elastic geographies are world-altering of inner landscapes (as in the "earthquake" in Animal's head), yet treacherously immaterial. As Mitchell writes of Appleton's habitat theory of the picturesque, "the frame is always there as the guarantee that it is only a picture . . . and the observer is safe in another place—outside the frame" (2002, 16).

Nonetheless, the position of middle vision can begin to demystify these scopic relations, not least by naming them. Sanctioned ignorance is a luxury the poor cannot afford; sometimes they can see through structures that position them as "only to be seen." "At least they will know we know," said one "witness" about Abderrahmane Sissako's 2007 film *Bamako*, in which the World Bank and IMF are put on "trial" in the courtyard of housing block in Mali's capital, and local witnesses line up to give testimony (Tattersall 2007). Sissako turned his father's housing compound in Bamako (and the film) into an alternative forum, a fictional trial with real witnesses stating their grievances against the international financial system. In *Animal's People*, the oscillation between Animal's and Elli's perspectives has similar potential to rewire the relay between seeing and knowing, not least because it is entangled with Animal's reason for finally telling his story, which does begin to reroute conventional traffic lines of spectatorship.

At the beginning of the novel, Animal mentions an enigmatic epistemological problem as the impetus for his narration: "I've a choice to make, let's say it's between heaven and hell, my problem is knowing which is which" (11). Only at the end does Animal reveal the horns of his dilemma. He is deliberating whether to accept Elli's offer to travel to the United States for surgery to correct his spine: "I will tell this story, I thought, and that way I'll find out what the end should be" (365). The sudden transfiguration of Paradise Alley into a hell of shit and plastic is but one moment in the novel's mapping of multiple geographies of heaven and hell, both cosmic and mundane. Animal's fate rests upon whether he continues to adopt Elli's vision as his own; daring to embrace her hope to see him walk upright again would require accepting her view of Paradise Alley as hell.

The more radical effect of Animal's revelation is to revise the rhetorical scenario of his narration: Animal tells his story to discover his own desire, not to implore the sympathy or solidarity of the world. (His immediate motive is to find out what he knows, not "so they will know" he knows.) Animal remains the hero of his story rather than the supplicating would-be object of humanitarian intervention, even the inadequate sort that equates reading a novel with having "done something." He, not Eyes, is the primary audience of his story; if this Khaufpur story, unlike all the others, will change something, it is because it will help him know what to do. Taking *Robinson Crusoe* as his lodestar, Ian Watt argued in *The Rise of the Novel* that the mimetic procedures of the realist novel offer readers "a full and authentic report of human experience" not unlike what the "rules of evidence" demand for "another group of specialists in epistemology, the jury in a court of law" (1957, 32, 31). Following the convention identified by Watt, Animal's narration is a process of discovery and deliberation not unlike the legal trial, but Animal reveals himself to be both witness and jury. This revelation effects a change in venue that parallels the one resulting from Judge Keenan's decision to grant Union Carbide's *forum non conveniens* motion: The question in this case will be decided by Animal, not by Eyes.[30]

The characteristic stance of formal realism inaugurated by Defoe is an imposture of veracity: Defoe disavows his own fiction-making in the prefatory note that declares *Robinson Crusoe* (like *Animal's People*) to be a found object. Crusoe's aim in keeping his journal is not identical to Defoe's in writing his novel; it is Defoe's readers (rather than Crusoe's) whom Watt sees as analogous to a jury. *Animal's People* internalizes Watt's analogy by making the narrator, not the reader, the primary deliberating figure. Nonetheless, Eyes is a remainder that points not only to the difference between Animal's motives and Sinha's (i.e., what effects can a narrative have on its narrator, as opposed to its listener/reader?), but also to the inadequacy of the juridical model to account for Animal's story. Animal claims the right to decide his own fate, yet the forum of his narration is transnational,[31] staked on this gesture of seeing his predicament through other Eyes. In Animal's narration, world-imagining from below intersects with distant reading. To understand himself, Animal attempts to make himself comprehensible to a distant other.

This idea veers uncomfortably close to the banal one-worldist pieties with which this chapter began, but it also resonates with the trajectory of Bhopal activism as the convergence of toxic and geographic exposure. The gas leak and its aftermath "forced many in the affected communities, particularly women, to learn about and face the dynamics in the outside world that brought Union Carbide to their doorsteps" (Hanna, Morehouse, and Sarangi 2005, 210). In 1996, journalist Suketu Mehta printed in the *Village Voice* excerpts from a letter written by gas widow Sajiba Bano, addressed to "those Carbide people": "Big people like you have snatched the peace and happiness of us poor people. . . . Like a living, walking corpse you have left us." Mehta writes that Bano "wants to eliminate distance, the food chain of activists, journalists, lawyers, and governments between her and the people in Danbury [Connecticut]," Union Carbide's headquarters (Hanna, Morehouse, and Sarangi 2005, 115). This desire to bridge distance parallels Animal's address to Eyes. These appeals mark a process of self-discovery staked upon an elastic geography: imagining the transnationality of one's local condition and the gaze of a distant other, and circulating a narrative of that process within a transnational circuit that cuts across class divides. To know the shape of the world is perhaps to begin to change it.

This transnationalism from below echoes the gestures of Jonathan in *Darwin's Nightmare* as a self-declared "citizen of the world," the "failed crossing" of the Guinean boys Yaguine Koita and Fodé Tounkara, found frozen to death with their petition for inclusion in a "modern world society," *The Oil Lamp*'s drawing of lines between "shacks in the swamp" and the "chain of ease," and Dhowli recognizing herself as a part of society, just one of the Dhowlis locked in struggle with the Misras. These moments of world-imagining from below refuse global capitalism's localizing pressures and quarantines of the imagination. They evince a subaltern planetarity: grittier than the high-minded cosmopolitanism of the Apollonian view from above, which Animal defamiliarizes as the gaze of a thousand cuntish eyes. Rather, it is Animal's bent-over, crotch-level view, writ large: "Whole nother world it's, below the waist" (2). In this counterintuitive planetary subjectivity, the subaltern imagines herself as a transnational subject, while "big people" like Judge Keenan fail to understand what stakes beyond India the Bhopal case might have, such as how regulating the behavior of multinational corporations might be in the public interest of Americans as well as Indians.[32] Rather, Keenan took an insistently localized view of the catastrophe and its remedy. These instances of world-imagining from below reveal such blinkered, quarantined vision to be a function of privilege and power, one way that "big people" see the world. Those exposed to risk, at the receiving end of such power, can less afford not to understand how it works. Not only is seeing (understood as the privileged spectatorial position) not necessarily knowing; it can entail its own forms of blindness.

Animal's ambivalent gesture to Eyes ("If you want my story, you'll have to put up with how I tell it" [2]) externalizes (or globalizes) his perspective on the slum. The description of Paradise Alley as hell exudes a whiff of the familiar—a conventionality linking it to accounts of Third World cities like Mike Davis' *Planet of Slums*;[33] to mid-twentieth-century African novels by Ekwensi, Abrahams, Paton, La Guma, Armah, or Mwangi; and to a longer tradition, ranging from Blake's "dark satanic mills" through Dickens and Engels, that portrayed urban squalor as demonic and dehumanized. Identifying the conventions of this tradition in nineteenth-century English writing on the city, Raymond Williams emphasizes the shift from an external to internal perspective: from bourgeois distant horror of the abject to a humanized sense of habitation: "what it is like to live in hell . . . what it is like to get used to it, grow up in it, see it as home" (quoted in Lazarus 2011, 63). In *Animal's People*, Elli's disgust defamiliarizes Animal's view of Paradise Alley as home. To extend Williams's analysis into the present, does Animal's acknowledgment of Elli's external, "global" perspective indicate a broader perspectival shift, a reflexivity that says, "I know what this looks like to you"? *Animal's People* takes the reflexive gestures examined elsewhere in this book to their logical conclusion, not only featuring characters that function as surrogates for a distant reader (e.g., Elli, the clueless dandy in Mahasweta Devi's "Salt," or the British hostage Isabel Floode in Habila's *Oil on Water*), but also internalizing the act of reception in the structure named by Eyes.

This reflexive world-imagining from below is a counterforce to both the one-worldism and the insular impulses of the multinational corporation as a vector of globalization. Yet it demands a further critical turn, at least in the case of a novel like *Animal's People*. Sinha's novel stages a hybrid internal/external view of Paradise Alley that is not incompatible with a global culture industry whose stock in trade is exoticism's blend of the foreign and the familiar, as Graham Huggan (2001) and Sarah Brouillette (2007) argue with regard to postcolonial literature. Animal is a narrative prosthesis for Indra Sinha, a writer of middle-class origins, educated in India and England, who, like Salman Rushdie, worked as an advertising copywriter in London before fiction writing became his day job. *Animal's People* is published by Simon & Schuster, part of the CBS corporation since 2006, "with publishing and distribution capabilities in the United States, Canada, the United Kingdom, Australia and India" that "can distribute its titles in physical and digital editions in more than 200 countries and territories around the world" (Simon & Schuster 2018). The Man Booker Prize, for which the novel was shortlisted in 2007, implicates *Animal's People* within the corporate histories of Booker-McConnell Ltd., a firm with colonialist roots in Guyana, and the Man Group, an investment management company.[34] With regard to this chapter's consideration of the shape of the world imagined by multinational corporations, *Animal's People* is both a product of that imagining and critical of it: wrought by the metropolitan literary agents and editors whom Animal curses; a corporate commodity that decries the power of the Kampani; a bestselling book from a "Big Five" US/UK publisher that challenges the infrastructural inequalities shaping the circulation of Bhopal stories. We might say (borrowing terms from Chapter 3) that in corporate publishing, poetry and property are the same thing. Or, perhaps there should be another floor—for book publishers— in the skyscraper Zafar imagines in a dream vision of the Kampani head- quarters, an image of vertical integration that includes a paramilitary force; Kampani directors consorting with global elites; and accountants, lawyers, doctors, engineers, chemists, and public relations consultants. In *Against World Literature*, Emily Apter (2013) associates the recent rise of World Lit- erature in the academy with similar mercantile impulses. The next sec- tion of this chapter surveys the unevenness of this cultural landscape in terms of language and translatability: What does it mean to read and write the world (and World Literature) in English?

उस रात, *Ous Raat, Cette Nuit, That Night: Inconvenient Translation*

Animal's ambivalent hope to be understood by Eyes manifests in the novel's engagement with multilingualism and translation: *Animal's People* is as much about language as about Bhopal. The published novel is ostensibly the product of recording, transcribing, and translating Animal's spoken Hindi into written English. Sinha's authorship thus comprises Animal's narration and the fictional Editor's translation; what Sinha writes conveys a sense of having been translated. Animal's narration is punctuated by mo- ments of interlinguistic complexity and knots of meaning that dispel the illusion of transparent immediacy; it is jarring when Animal marks infre- quent moments where characters actually speak English. Interspersed with the novel's "English" is a lot of language that is variously not-English. This multilingualism draws on, yet exceeds, the conventions of the postcolo- nial Anglophone novel. Animal often uses the now familiar strategy of fol- lowing non-English phrases with an in-text translational gloss; at the end of the book appears a glossary. Another familiar aspect of the text's multi- lingualism are scenes of subversive translation, where characters with a bridge language "translate," according to their own desire and agenda, con- versations between characters who do not share a language; readers are privy to the liberties these translators take.

What distinguishes *Animal's People* from the multilingual strategies of other Anglophone novels is how pervasively this mediation between languages shapes the novel. Its cheeky glossary defines only Hindi words and "Khaufpuri" dialectical variants, even though French also has significant presence in the novel. Animal provides in-text glosses of Hindi and French (although somewhat less for French); "Eyes, if you don't know francais," is how he prefaces a gloss of French early in the novel (56). Animal picked up much of his French from his foster mother, a French nun he calls Ma Franci; his impressive repertoire of French curses (among the numerous non-English words he does not gloss) came from a French journalist. Trilingual reduplication of words and phrases in French, Hindi/ Urdu, and English is among Animal's stylistic tics: Elli is "très baisable, wah, what a sexy!" (66). (These phrases aren't synonyms, and they derive from different registers of their respective languages; "wah" is the appropriate response to Urdu poetic eloquence.) Another distinctive aspect of Animal's narration and its translation is the frequent use of Hindi syntax, particularly in placing the verb, or subject-verb, at the end of the sentence: "Brave you're" are Animal's first words to Elli (71). Thus, traces of the Editor's "translation" of Animal's speech remain even in sentences whose words are all in English. One unfortunate effect of this style is that readers unfamiliar with Hindi might parse it as Animal's idiosyncrasy (he sounds somewhat like Yoda in *Star Wars*) rather than as the precipitate of interlinguistic encounter.[35]

This exuberant multilingualism defamiliarizes English for Anglophone readers—a linguistic equivalent of seeing oneself seeing, being seen, or seen to be seeing. Animal glosses words that don't seem to need it, implying that English—ostensibly the lingua franca of contemporary globalization—is defined as much by its local variations as by its worldwide reach: "Eyes, you want to know what is an auto, it's a scooter rickshaw with three wheels, except the way Khaufpuris drive they spend more time on two" (50). (Animal's misprision of Eyes' lexicon makes this unexpectedly necessary gloss nearly tautological; *scooter rickshaw* doesn't necessarily clear things up for those who haven't seen one.) Animal largely avoids using speaking styles as a mode of characterization, with one remarkable exception: When he takes Elli on a tour of poor neighborhoods around the factory, an old woman's complaint about her daughter's toxic breast milk makes him want to burst out laughing at "these village types, their outlandish accents and rustic way of talking." The woman's archaic speech is rendered at length in sixteenth-century English diction and orthography; "The infant yeaxeth incessantly," the granny concludes.[36] Elli doesn't know the unspecified Hindi word the novel translates as *yeaxeth*; for readers equally in the dark, the baby hiccups, offering a somatic gloss (108).

Additional aspects of the novel's defamiliarization of English derive from transliterations between Hindi's Devanagari script and the Roman alphabet. Words of English origin that are common usage in Hindi appear (semi)phonetically or as hybrid compounds: "jarnaliss, filmwallass, photographass, anthrapologiss" (185), mashin, Amrika, Ostrali, and, of course, Inglis.[37] Other phonetic terms, unexplained by gloss or glossary, are idiosyncratic: *Sanjo*, author of the small black book that warped Ma Franci's worldview and left her obsessed with the "Apokalis" (her name for "that night") must be Saint-Jean (i.e., Saint John the Divine), author of *Revelation*'s apocalyptic narrative. From Ian Fleming, Animal borrows *Namispond Jamispond* as a calling card to describe his work of spying on people; that his grasp and pronunciation of English are far from fluent is evident in his self-identification as "Jamispond, jeera-jeera-seven," which to Hindi speakers sounds not like Bond's 007 but rather *"cumin-cumin-seven"* (194).

Animal is fascinated by transliteration partly because he learns to read Hindi (and then English) during the events he narrates. He describes the moment he learns to translate the shapes क, ल, ज, and ह into the sounds *ka, la, ja,* and *ha*. These Devanagari characters (the equivalent of Roman ABCs) are printed in the text, as is Animal's name in Hindi: "जानवर, Jaanvar, meaning Animal." He adds an etymological explanation: "Jaan means 'life.' Jaanvar means 'one who lives'" (35). The presence on the page of graphemes from Devanagari decenters the Roman alphabet as one script among many;[38] Animal's deciphering of them also offers readers a basic Hindi lesson.

Animal's energetic interest in intersections among languages and scripts makes him a "translator par excellence in Khaufpur's cosmopolitan world," Pablo Mukherjee remarks (2010, 161). As a pseudonym for Bhopal, *Khaufpur* is an apt multilingual pun: in Hindi, it means "city of fear"; in Hindi-informed English, it sounds like "city of coughs." Animal isn't wrong when he says he has a "gift for tongues," "not just an ear but an eye for meanings" (35). But the delight of the richly multilingual texture of *Animal's People* derives partly from things he doesn't get quite right: what gets lost (and added) in translation and transliteration. For example, Animal wrongly assumes that any word written in Roman script that isn't French (which he knows) must be English. Thus he categorizes as "Inglis" the Vietnamese words inscribed on the Zippo lighter that the Australian journalist leaves for him, as well as the Latin motto inscribed on the arch of Khaufpur's Pir Gate: "PROCUL HINC ABESTE PROFANI." (For readers without Latin, Khaufpur's notorious beggar Abdul Saliq provides a gloss as he stands beneath Pir Gate and cries, *"Keep away, you faithless gits!"* [118].) Another

224   *Resource Logics and Risk Logics*

suggestive error is Animal's description of "Thighs-of-fate, it's an Inglis name, I do not know what the Hindi might be" (112). *Thighs-of-fate* isn't an English name but a phonetic approximation of sodium thiosulphate, the Greco-Latinate scientific term for a cyanide antidote administered with some success to Bhopali gas victims in the immediate aftermath of the gas leak. Within weeks of the disaster, the use of sodium thiosulphate was effectively banned by the Indian government (at Union Carbide's request) because its observed efficacy in detoxification implied that the gas contained cyanide (Rajagopal 1987, 136–38). In other words, government and Kampani acted scandalously in trying to avoid panic or scandal, probably sealing the fate of many victims. Yet "thighs-of-fate" could also describe Elli, clad in her much-remarked-upon skintight jeans, promising Animal the possibility of walking again.

This example indicates the kinds of things gained in Animal's not-quite-right movement among languages, and here we begin to see what the novel's multilingualism has to do with Bhopal. Animal identifies a gap between *reading* and *knowing* in his citation of a Coca-Cola sign, in both English and Hindi/Devanagari: "I can't read the sign but I know what it says," even if he doesn't know what Coke tastes like (18, 35). (Animal approximates for readers this experience of knowing-followed-by-reading when he explains the Devanagari characters क (ka) and ल (la) in the same paragraph where he cites the sign in Hindi: कोका कोला. Readers without Hindi can begin to decipher it too.) When he learns to read, it is the first of the "signs in the street [that] gradually came to life" (35). The Coca-Cola sign is a Rosetta Stone partly because it is an icon for a global consumer capitalism that is almost universally legible, even to the illiterate and those who can't afford to buy.[39] This unequally distributed power over signs and meaning, Animal tells the Australian journalist, makes words like *"rights, law, justice* . . . sound the same in my mouth as in yours but they don't mean the same" (3). Speaking from the other side of the interpretive divide identified by Union Carbide's lawyers, Animal's understanding of how power and inequality shape language and meaning allows him to read between the lines of Khaufpur's homegrown literary genres: anti-Kampani demonstration signs and graffiti spanning the concrete walls enclosing the factory grounds. Animal translates "high-sounding shit like JUSTICE FOR KHAUFPUR" into low-sounding, expletive-filled expressions of what the authors mean but cannot say (177).[40]

Animal is a subaltern translation theorist; his reflexivity raises questions about the capacity for comprehension between people who do not speak the same language, and between people who think they do. (A similar dynamic appears in the aporetic conversation between the village youth and the town dandy in Mahasweta Devi's "Salt.") Analogous questions have shaped Bhopal litigation, under the doctrine of *forum non conveniens* and its concern with difficulties of language and location. Judge Keenan argued in his 1986 dismissal that while English is understood in Indian courts, Hindi is not understood in US courts; therefore, "fewer translation problems would face an Indian court than an American court" in sorting through the relevant documents (18). The same dynamic applies to witnesses, "since English is widely spoken in India" (19). This judgment oversimplifies India's language landscape, overlooking asymmetrical stratifications created by empire and reinforced by contemporary globalization, where, to mimic Animal's insight, "law, rights, and justice" don't even sound the same.[41] The most significant aspect of Elli's character is that, unlike most foreigners in Khaufpur, she speaks good Hindi. Nonetheless, Animal concludes, "Despite living among us and speaking our language, she knows next to nothing about us Khaufpuris" (292). This speaking-without-knowing is the inverse of Animal's knowing-without-reading; it is akin to the seeing-without-knowing that is the caustic humanitarian gaze. Elli acknowledges this gulf of incomprehension. In a moment of frustration while visiting a *basti* near the factory, she shouts (presumably in Hindi) "HEY, ANIMAL'S PEOPLE! I DON'T FUCKING UNDERSTAND YOU!"—an exclamation gleefully parroted by the neighborhood kids who throng around a foreigner (183). It is an instance of inelastic imagining—imagining across difference stretched beyond the breaking point. In this moment, the "incomprehensibility" cited by Union Carbide's lawyers as an obstacle to litigating Bhopal in US courts persists even for Americans who take the trouble to learn Hindi because they want to help survivors.

However, *Animal's People* takes incomprehensibility as a productive challenge rather than a barrier to the circulation of Bhopal narratives. In the novel, the gas leak catalyzes different linguistic transformations for different characters. Elli learns Hindi out of disgust at the Kampani's refusal to take legal responsibility for Khaufpur; Ma Franci survives "that night" unscathed except that "her mind was wiped clean of Hindi, and of Inglis too." Despite the fact that she can no longer understand them, Ma Franci stays in Khaufpur out of a conviction that "her place was with its suffering people" (37). Ma Franci demonstrates an uncanny capacity, similar to Animal's, for understanding beyond linguistic comprehension: she chats contentedly with "Huriya Bi, Ma's best friend in Khaufpur she's, not a word of each other's speech do they understand" (104). Their understanding-without-understanding is supple enough that Huriya Bi orchestrates Ma

Franci's clever escape from the priest who comes to take her back to France. Yet Ma Franci's postdisaster inability to understand any language but French is also an absolutist monolingualism, antithetical to Animal's gift for tongues. She cannot even recognize that people speaking "in Hindi or Inglis, or come to that in Urdu, Tamil, Oriya, or any other tongue used in Khaufpur . . . were speaking . . . a language, she thought they were just making stupid grunts and sounds" (37). After the gas leak, Ma Franci privileges French as "la langue humaine" (142); everyone else utters bestial nonsense. And she believes that "the Apokalis"—her name for "that night"—"took away their speech," instead of recognizing that it left her with only one tongue. Animal wonders "how anyone can get it so totally wrong" (100).

Sinha is spoofing French linguistic chauvinism, which hears every tongue but French (and a certain kind of French) as just a bit barbaric, if not quite bestial. Scholars of World Literature might find in Ma Franci's attachment to *la langue humaine* an ungenerous caricature of literary critic Pascale Casanova, for whom the capital of the world republic of letters can only be Paris. Casanova posits translation into French as the mark of prestige and literary arrival for writers from what she calls less "well endowed" regions and languages (2004, 177). I describe the multilinguistic texture of *Animal's People* in detail not only because of its implications for the capacity of distant readers, consumers, citizens, and prospective jurors to comprehend the putative "incomprehensibility" of Bhopal, but also because this novel undertakes the work of reading between languages and locations that the discipline of comparative literature takes as its purview. What is the shape of the world that World Literature imagines?

Animal's People is born translated. Its narrative premise maintains that what readers read is a translation (and transcription) of Animal's spoken Hindi. It gleefully flaunts the traces of that transit (a process that never actually happened, except perhaps in Sinha's mind).[42] I use "born translated" pointedly, at odds with what Rebecca Walkowitz intends in her discussion of "comparison literature," a subset of contemporary novels "written by migrants and for an international audience, that exist from the beginning in several places" (2009, 573). For Walkowitz, such novels are "written for translation," anticipating their near-instant circulation among the world's "metropolitan centers" (569, 568). Because authors like J. M. Coetzee and Kazuo Ishiguro know their work will be translated almost simultaneously with its original publication, they (ostensibly) eschew the stylistic idiosyncrasies and language play that give translators nightmares: "Born-translated novels are designed to travel, so they tend to veer away from the modernist emphasis on linguistic experimentation" (570).[43] To be born-translated in this sense is to be unmarked by the tangles of linguistic complexity found in *Animal's People*.

I have argued that *Animal's People* is of interest to World Literature scholars because it thematizes the processes of comparison and transnational circulation Walkowitz examines with "comparison literature," which, like Sinha's novel, "anticipates its own future as a work of world literature" (2009, 569). But linguistic play (of the sort that characterizes *Animal's People*) is what Walkowitz dismisses in making a strange, strong claim: far from ignoring questions of language, texts that are born-translated (in her sense) "confront readers with the history and politics of language, and *they do this better* than many so-called untranslatable novels that emphasize vernacular culture and idiomatic expression. . . . Novels that treat multilingualism through narrative events, characterization, and structure *are more likely* than novels that treat multilingualism through idiom to retain in translation an engagement with local histories of language" (571; emphasis added). In one way, this claim is commonsensical: What is untranslatable or lost in translation is, presumably, simply untranslated or lost. A novel's diegetic announcement of interest in multilingualism and language play may be more easily, conveniently, and legibly rendered in translation than actual sentence-level interlinguistic encounters and language play. But what structures of power and privilege underwrite this seeming common sense?

This vision of world literary space perceives little beyond well-established "migrant" writers who write for readers in metropolitan centers: The only thing distinguishing Walkowitz's born-translated comparison literature from cosmopolitan literature is that this version of cosmopolitanism not only professes to be interested in local color and regional particularity but also claims to be *better* at conveying them than less-mobile natives or narratives. It is no surprise that "comparison literature tends to be written in English . . . because English has become the most-read, most-translated language in the world" (2009, 571). In the name of championing novels that need no champion, Walkowitz would have us accept that the homoglossic, ostensibly unaccented Anglophone novel and its translated siblings are best suited to trace both the ascendancy of globalized English and the myriad local histories of what it has overcome.[44] These are not innocent claims at a moment when departments of comparative literature and foreign languages in the US struggle to justify their existence, confronting not only the usual humanities-skeptical administrators and budget allocators (whether legislative or familial), but also a mode of World Literature that works through exclusive inclusion: claiming to encompass the world while relegating the rest to the back of beyond. Walkowitz deems "better" what the global literary marketplace has judged "fittest." This vision of world literature is congruent with, and perhaps even the epitome of, the cultural logic of neoliberal globalization: texts that offer little resistance to translation are perfect analogues for a world that offers no resistance to the market.[45]

These claims are also not innocent in the era of the multinational corporation, when (as at Union Carbide's Bhopal factory) safety materials were written in English and not necessarily legible to workers who needed them most. Here Judge Keenan's ruminations on language and translation are surprisingly circumspect, even if they ignore the transnational *politics* of language dissemination and stratification. Keenan recognizes that the English language, in its ostensibly unaccented use in a metropolitan forum (like the US court system) characterized by default monolingualism, is hardly an adequate medium for representing the complexity of a multilingual situation.

Thickets of linguistic particularity in a novel like *Animal's People* are *inconvenient* to the task of translation. (Even so, translations of *Animal's People* into Chinese, Czech, Danish, Dutch, French, German, Hungarian, Italian, Japanese, Polish, Romanian, and Spanish appeared within a year or two of its publication in English—one of Walkowitz's definitions of "born-translated.") Its ambivalence about language and understanding— the impossible necessity of communication across language(s)—registers in two moments of seeming untranslatability in the novel's long climax. The first is when Animal's young friend Aliya succumbs to illness from drinking poisoned water in the neighborhoods around the factory. Animal implores Elli to do something; he pleads with her in French to spare Aliya's family, but he also remarks, "Eyes, I won't translate, there's not a language in this world can describe what's in my soul" (326). Here translation is a second-order problem to the inadequacy of language itself to convey—to bear across from mind to mouth—the anguish of Bhopal.

Untranslatability functions differently in another scene, when an old woman named Gargi challenges one of the Kampani's American lawyers: "Mr. Lawyer, we lived in the shadow of your factory, you told us you were making medicine for the fields. You were making poisons to kill insects, but you killed us instead. I would like to ask, was there ever much difference, to you?" (306). Gargi's question asks the lawyer to show the math behind the Kampani's risk calculations. Her plaint speaks volumes about environmental racism as a differential exposure to risk and a form of unpeopling that casts some communities on the other side of the species divide between humans and nonhuman animals. Nixon cites this passage as evidence that "some afflicted communities are afforded more visibility— and more access to remediation—than others" (2011, 64). But it is important to note the specific, poignant way this dynamic holds true within the novel's diegesis, where Gargi's question remains, in effect, unheard. The Kampani lawyer cannot understand what Gargi says; the journalist whom the lawyer asks to translate can say only, "I don't know how to translate it." The lawyer pulls a Rs.500 note (about $12.50 in 2007) from his wallet in response to Gargi's demand for "just and proper compensation from the Kampani," which the journalist glosses as "she's asking for money" (306–7). Nixon's point about environmental racism and pesticides "as both indiscriminate and discriminatory" (2011, 63) would be even more powerful by recognizing that Gargi *remains* invisible to the Kampani lawyer even after confronting him—a fact made legible in the incommensurable calculus of Sinha's exchange rate, which converts her dignified demand for just compensation into his throwing a bill at a beggar. This example points toward the subtle work of environmental imagining that, paradoxically, can be occluded by reading thematically—for the nature bits—as opposed to teasing out matters of form, texture, register, and rhetorical situation. It is the danger of reading a literary text as if it were born translated in another sense: "written for translation" into the language of one's (eco)critical concerns. Gargi says powerfully and plainly what postcolonial ecocritics want and need to say in the lesser language of academic prose, but the most telling aspect of this scene is that the lawyer still cannot hear her.

This scene of refused and reductive translation is written in a plain, unmarked style Walkowitz might deem "written for translation." The encounter between Gargi and the lawyer handles questions of comparison and linguistic complexity through plot rather than style. But the scene also demonstrates how claims of untranslatability can serve as alibis for power and the status quo. The encounter between Gargi and the lawyer is one instance where the history of Bhopal litigation enters the novel's diegesis; the workings of the legal forum are represented (and represented as inadequate) within the novel's alternative literary forum. Like the scene where Elli judges Paradise Alley, this scene dramatizes a gulf of incomprehension. It makes explicit the Union Carbide lawyers' implicit link between incomprehensibility and the quantification of damages; here, as with Animal's suspicion of stories told about Khaufpur, the calculus favors the Kampani. Still, what remains incomprehensible to the lawyer is communicated to the reader: Animal's narration registers and renders Gargi's speech, thus offering an "alternative forum" to the historical realm of activism and litigation indexed in this scene—particularly if readers hear what, and the fact that, the Kampani lawyer cannot. Staging a scene of unimagining, *Animal's People* gestures toward reimagining the relationship between Bhopal and the world. I do not mean to assert moral equivalence between Union Carbide's *forum non conveniens* motion and the putative inconvenience of literature not "written for translation"; I am not suggesting that literary critics are responsible for the kind of harm for which the lawyers aimed to shield Union Carbide's liability. However, both arguments about untranslatability work to make a world more convenient to global capitalism (or its cultural wing); the specious localism of such claims is no less dangerous than a faux one-worldist universality in facilitating neoliberal globalization. In literary and legal contexts alike, appeals to linguistic expediency and professed concerns with untranslatability shape the circulation of narratives in ways that entrench the power of the already powerful.

Where I'm Reading From: Comparative Apocalypse and Incendiary Intertextuality

Animal's People is not only insistently multilingual; it is also wildly allusive, drawing on numerous literary texts and traditions. Multilingualism and intertextuality intertwine in quotations of poems and songs in languages including French, Hindi/Urdu, Persian, and Bhojpuri: The novel dwells between literary habitations. Its central tensions, as I will demonstrate, are expressed in an implicit contest among literary forms and genres: The question of what kind of novel *Animal's People* is can be answered by considering the kinds of texts it invokes. Readers will construe that answer differently, depending on the intertexts that resonate most for them. In terms of intertextuality, Animal is more *bricoleur* than translator: drawing from here and there, but not always explaining what he is doing. Thinking about how *Animal's People* performs—or elides—the work of comparative literature by reading across literary traditions, one becomes aware of many possible eyes inhabiting the structure named "Eyes," and the angles from which they read Animal's narration. It is unclear who the ideal reader of *Animal's People* might be, which raises new questions about distant reading, incomprehensibility, and the novel's interpretive forum. This section teases out the intertextuality of *Animal's People* in some detail, because it is another realm where questions of circulation and audience raised by World Literature intersect with demands for environmental justice.

One moment where questions of language, literature, and the possibilities of sympathetic imagining converge in the novel occurs during Ashura, which marks the martyrdom of Imam Hussein, grandson of the Prophet Muhammad. "Everyone in Khaufpur knows the story of Imam Hussein," Animal says, noting resonances between Hussein's lonely defiance of the tyrant Yazid at the Battle of Karbala and the Khaufpuris' struggle against the Kampani. He explains how ritual mourning on this ninth night of Muharram takes the form of marsiyas, which are

> chants and laments for Imam Hussein. . . . Some are in Hindi, others in Arabic and Persian, but whichever language they are in you catch the same meaning, at least I do. It's like every good thing in the world is dying and the people of the world, they see but do not care. . . . For me, who am neither Muslim, nor Hindu, nor Isayi, this is a music that could comfort Isa miyañ dying on the cross or go with Sri Rama into exile from Ayodhya. It's all one to me, what I like is the defiance. (215)

For Animal, marsiyas need no translation; their elegiac lament speaks across language and religious tradition, from Jesus on the cross to Rama in the forest exile recounted in the *Ramayana*. Marsiyas, in Animal's account at least, hew toward the novel's more optimistic (or less suspicious) view of sympathetic imagining or solidarity across barriers of difference or incomprehensibility.

Marsiya chants (rendered in English) structure the scene during Ashura where Elli confronts the gulf separating her from the experience of "that night." "Then Eyes, it comes into my head with perfect certainty what she is thinking," Animal relates. His free indirect narration of Elli's thoughts alternates with italicized lines from a marsiya:

> What must it have been like, that inferno? *O who will speak now for the orphans?* She has heard so many stories of that night, so many accounts of that vast slaughter of innocents. *Who now will speak for the poor?* What must have been the terror of waking in the dead of that night, blinded by acrid gas *who will protect these wretched ones* running out into the night gulping fumes that tore and burned your insides *where now will they find refuge* causing you to drown on dry land because your lungs have wept themselves full of fluid. *Ya Hussein! Ya Hussein! Ya Hussein!* (219)

Here "you" refers not to Eyes (as elsewhere in the novel) but to Elli projecting herself sympathetically into the horror of that night, even as Animal projects himself into her thoughts. Driven by the marsiya's lament, the passage builds to a climax as Elli confronts "the horror, also the failure of her imagination" to overcome divides of space, time, and privilege.[46] Just

as Animal can "catch the same meaning" in a marsiya regardless of its original language, the passage describes vividly what Elli is "unable to imagine" (219), including the novel's only account of Animal's experience on that
night, when his dying mother wrapped her newborn in a shawl and left him
in a doorway, hoping he would be found. As with Gargi confronting the
lawyer, this passage depicts unimagining and reimagining simultaneously:
It marks the failure of Elli's imagination but overcomes that failure, although in whose imagination (prior to the reader's) this reimagining takes
place is left ambiguous. The passage creates the illusion that the reader
hears through Elli's ears and sees through her mind's eye; the concrete viv-
idness of the scene, bolstered by the marsiya's lament for orphaned
children and murdered bridegrooms, is nonetheless Animal's projection of
"what she is thinking."[47] Instead of being aversive or painful, as with the
Australian journalist's visual prosthesis, here seeing through another's
eyes—or imagining oneself being imagined—is ecstatic and revelatory:
Marsiyas become a different kind of prosthesis, through which the artifice of communally chanted poetic language builds a heightened sense of
"reality" that aids in reimagining the unimaginable.

The marsiya scene also helps make sense of the novel's long climax,
when the remembered horror of "that night" returns as the apocalyptic tumult of "this night" (329). Protests roil Khaufpur at the possibility of a
settlement with the Kampani; Zafar seems to succumb to his hunger strike
against the settlement; the factory burns, again spewing toxic fumes; Animal swallows a handful of datura pills and wanders in a fantastic forest wilderness that may or may not be Paradise. In other words, Ma Franci's
long-awaited Apokalis arrives; as Animal says of marsiyas, "It's like every
good thing in the world is dying." What's remarkable about this apocalyptic climax is its juxtaposition of imagery from Muslim, Christian, and
Hindu sacred texts, which gives concretion and imaginative force to the
dilemma motivating Animal's narration—the choice between heaven and
hell, and knowing which is which. "Tonight is this night the night of Qayamat which Ma calls Apokalis, a word in which is Kali's name, who's also
called Ma. Yes, Ma is Kali Ma, why did I never think of this? Garlanded
with bones she'll stalk the streets of Khaufpur crying the end of the world":
Animal figures the mad Catholic nun as the Hindu goddess of death and
destruction on the rampage on Qayamat, the Muslim day of judgment
(333). Whereas Animal hears the defiant lament of marsiyas speaking beyond their Islamic context to Christian and Hindu scenes of heroic suffering, his account of "this night" braids the traditions together. The
apocalyptic Christian imagery in Ma Franci's ravings about horsemen and

the return of Isa and Sanjo (Jesus and Saint-Jean) helps construe Zafar's hunger strike as martyrdom and resurrection: He returns from the presumed-dead.[48]

Animal also believes that the datura pills he swallows in despair on "this night" have killed him; Animal too is narratively "resurrected" when he learns that he swallowed poison but did not die. What turns out to be Animal's weeklong delirium—rather than his death and arrival in Paradise, as he initially believes—is fascinating in terms of the novel's interweaving of sacred traditions. There are more textual details in the account of Animal's poisoning that construe him as a Siva (Shiva) figure than there are hints of Zafar as Christlike; however, the figuration of Animal as Siva remains implicit rather than explained, which is relevant to questions of circulation, comprehensibility and the reader(s) imagined by *Animal's People*. The Shaivite imagery is so dense as to be almost heavy-handed, but so unmarked in the narration that, say, Eyes (or Elli) would be unlikely to assemble the scattered allusions into an allegorical gesture. This lack of explicitness is strange, not only because Animal often glosses such things for his distant audience, but more pointedly because the story of the god Siva swallowing poison so that it does not destroy the universe is so obviously pertinent to a Bhopal-inspired eco-apocalypse, more than the Christian overtones of Zafar as resurrected martyr. In a famous episode that appears in many Hindu sacred texts, Siva is enlisted to swallow a poison so deadly that its toxic fumes have begun to threaten all creation; this bowl of poison emerged when gods and demons churned the cosmic ocean to obtain *amrit*, the nectar of immortal life. Siva holds the poison in his throat—thus his epithet, *nilakantha*, or blue-throated. Animal mentions that his friend Nisha's father, Somraj, has a "music room which he keeps sacred to goddess Saraswati and blue-throated god Siva" (123), but readers have to know *why* Siva's throat is blue (which Animal doesn't say) to understand the pathos of this detail. Somraj, the former *Aawaaz-e-Khaufpur* (Urdu for "voice of Khaufpur"), lost his famed singing voice "that night," when gas seared this throat.

The churning of the cosmic ocean so disrupts the meteorological order of the universe that it sparks forest fires, which the god Indra brings rain to quench. In the novel, too, the relief of the denouement has an objective correlative in cooling rain that marks the end of Nautapa (the nine days of searing heat before the monsoon arrives) during which the climax unfolds. Just as Ma Franci's ravings about the Apokalis make a different kind of sense if readers recognize Sanjo as the visionary author of the Book of Revelation, Animal's toxic delirium reads as intertextual and allegorical, rather than the idiosyncratic product of a feverish and solipsistic imagination, if the details of his forest wandering constellate around an image of Siva, three-eyed destroyer and creator of the universe, garlanded in cobras; Siva is the denizen of Mount Meru for whom the datura is a sacred plant. In one manifestation, he is the universe itself, without birth or origin: *svayambhu*, or self-existent. "A ball of fire is rising between my eyes," Animal says; "a cobra slides up out of my throat," "a datura is growing my gut," "in my throat's a new fire of thirst," "out of my head slides the universe" (347, 344). During his hallucination Animal declares, "If this self of mine doesn't belong in this world, I'll be my own world, I'll be a world complete in myself. My back shall be ice-capped mountains, my arse Mount Meru, my eyes shall be the sun and moon" (350).

I am less certain what the allegorical thrust of Animal as Siva *means* than that it is *there*. Certainly there is an irreverent joke in reading Animal's obsessive sexual frustration in terms of Siva's dual sexuality: Siva is both celibate and a desirous partner to his wife, Parvati. As Animal never tires of saying, he is blessed (and cursed) with an enormous penis that, read as a Siva allegory, might evoke a lingam. More generally, like Siva, Animal is destroyer and creator both: during his toxic delirium, he sparks the fire at the factory that threatens to engulf Khaufpur again in deadly fumes, yet his narration is the breath that creates the literary universe contained within *Animal's People*. In terms of the novel's climactic eco-apocalypse, it is difficult to see how Animal's swallowing the datura compares, except unfavorably and ironically, with blue-throated Siva's saving the universe from world-destroying poison. Far from sacrificing himself to save the world, Animal only has the datura pills because he has been surreptitiously giving them to Zafar to suppress his libido; Animal swallows the whole vial when Zafar's fiancée Nisha rebuffs Animal's marriage proposal in the wake of Zafar's seeming death. In other words, Animal poisons himself at the climax of the novel's individualist plot regarding his own fate—whether he will have the surgery Elli offers, a question for him connected to whether he will win Nisha away from Zafar. He believes that walking upright is the key to getting the girl, any girl.

The allegorical echoes between Siva and Animal as swallowers of poison—one saving the world, the other unable to find love or get laid— underscore how the individualist plot of *Animal's People* strains against the collective plot involving the struggle between Khaufpuri survivors and the Kampani. This collective plot traces the progress of litigation to compel American executives of the Kampani to appear in the dock in Khaufpur or face the seizure of its Indian assets, the prospect of a settlement between

Kampani and government with a deal to drop the charges, as well as activism surrounding these proceedings, involving mass demonstrations, symbolic waving of brooms to sweep the Kampani out of India, disruptions of closed-door Kampani meetings, and hunger strikes. (In other words, the collective plot distills decades of activism in Bhopal.) The novel's long climax, which I have described as apocalyptic, could also be described as revolutionary; the power of the people is unleashed against the state's Chief Minister, the Kampani's American lawyers, and the factory itself.

In the collective plot, a patchwork of texts from multiple traditions constructs a revolutionary sublime that complements the apocalyptic tenor described earlier. Throughout the novel, Zafar theorizes and mobilizes the "power of nothing": because "people who have nothing have nothing to lose, we will never give up, out of nothing comes a power that's impossible to resist" (111). The Kampani, on the other hand, has "everything on its side" (54).[49] In this contest between nothing and everything (congruent with a world divided between the Dhowlis and the Misras in "Dhowli"), Zafar clings to "the invincible, undefeatable power of zero. Against that que dale, zilch, nil, rien de tout, the Kampani's everything stands no chance" (229–30).[50] Animal's tic of linguistic reduplication here compounds the power of nothing.

Zafar's impossible arithmetic—a revolutionary sublime in which nothing is greater than everything—draws upon several kinds of inspired language. When Zafar asserts, "*Jahaañ jaan hai, jahaan hai*. While we have life, we have the world," Animal is so moved by the beauty of Zafar's words that he sheds his wonted cynicism and responds with the "wah! wah!" that signals appreciation of Urdu poetic eloquence (284). In its echoes among *jahaañ*, *jaan*, and *jahaan*, Zafar's line adds homophonic complexity to the proverbial Hindi/Urdu phrase "*jaan hai to jahaan hai*" (If there's life, then there's the world). Zafar's pithy algorithm ramifies his theory about nothing's power: even for those who have been unpeopled and reduced to nothing—to a life so bare it is seemingly not worth living—that remainder of life (*jaan*) remains the world (*jahaan*). Although Animal doesn't spell it out, this equation of *jaan* with *jahaan* construes his chosen name, Animal—in Hindi, *jaanvar*: one who has *jaan*—as powerful indeed. Zafar's bon mot not only recodes the resource and risk calculations that define certain populations as "surplus"; it also erases distinctions between humans and nonhumans in its valorization of all *jaanvar*, all beings who have life. (The ambiguous possessive in "Animal's people" tropes on the species divide: One thing conventionally distinguishing humans from nonhuman animals is that the former can possess the latter, but not the other way round.) The contest between the power of the Kampani and the power of nothing involves a biopolitical contest between poison and *jaan*.

Zafar's power of nothing draws its revolutionary spirit and world-historical force from several other intertexts. The first is a protest song Animal says "is always sung at our Khaufpuri demos" and "brings tears to Zafar's eyes" (264). "The whole world shakes, when the people march": The verses Animal cites here come from a Bhojpuri poem written in the 1970s (and revived in 2000 by the band Indian Ocean) by revolutionary Hindi poet Gorakh Pandey:

> *janata ké chalé paltaniya, hillélé jhakjor duniya*
> *the people's platoons are on the march*
> *the earth trembles, mountains quake,*
> *the motion ripples rivers and lakes*
> *huge waves rush across the ocean*
> *the whole world shakes, when the people march.* (264)

Images of platoons marching and earth trembling are woven throughout the novel's climax to indicate radical energies set loose, with their effects manifest in nonhuman nature, by mass anger at the purported death of Zafar and the latest obstacle to justice. The world-shaking power of the multitude resounds in the novel's final lines, "We are the people of the Apokalis. Tomorrow there will be more of us" (366). This pledge or portent—at once soul-stirring and ominous—projects Zafar's sublime arithmetic into the future: Tomorrow the power of nothing will be greater still; there will be more people on the march, with even less to lose. These lines also echo the conclusion of Leon Trotsky's pamphlet *The War and the International*:

> The revolutionary epoch will create new forms of organization out of the inexhaustible resources of proletarian Socialism, new forms that will be equal to the greatness of the new tasks. To this work we will apply ourselves at once, amid the mad roaring of the machineguns, the crashing of cathedrals, and the patriotic howling of the capitalist jackals. We will keep our clear minds amid this hellish death music, our undimmed vision. We feel ourselves to be the only creative force of the future. Already there are many of us, more than it may seem. Tomorrow there will be more of us than today. And the day after tomorrow, millions will rise up under our banner, millions who even now, sixty seven years after the *Communist Manifesto*, have nothing to lose but their chains. ([1914] 1996, III.XI)[51]

Trotsky's revolutionary internationalism anticipates the planetary scope of the Khaufpuri struggle against corporate purveyors of poison. In a globalizing dream-vision that could be juxtaposed with the conclusion of "Dhowli" and Gerstacker's island utopia, Zafar soars above the earth, looking down at a skyscraper from which "the Kampani controls its factories all over the world" (229). He warns that Khaufpur isn't "the only poisoned city." Mexico City, Hanoi, Manila, Halabja, Minamata, Seveso, Sao Paolo, Toulouse: "each one . . . has its own Zafar" (296). Against the Kampani's global reach, the poisoning of the earth sparks resistance movements (and literature) of world-historical, planetary significance: a global archipelago of local struggles.

Nearly overcome by his delirious vision of the Kampani's vast power, Zafar "sees the land of India spread out beneath him with all its forests and fields and hears his own voice crying *agar firdaus bar roo-e zameen ast, hameen ast-o hameen ast-o hameen ast* and he remembers that he is not helpless, that he possesses the invincible, undefeatable power of zero" (229). Here Zafar's impossible arithmetic, where nothing is greater than everything, is underwritten by another unlikely intertext, a couplet attributed to the thirteenth-century Persian and Hindustani Sufi poet Amir Khusro: "If there is any paradise on earth, it is this, it is this, it is this." In India, the referents of "this . . . this . . . this" are multiple: the Persian couplet is inscribed on the walls of the Diwan-i-Khas at the Lal Qila (Red Fort) in Delhi built by the seventeenth-century Mughal emperor Shah Jahan. *This*, "paradise on earth," is often taken to be Kashmir, a judgment ascribed to the previous emperor, Jahangir. For Zafar, however, *this* refers not to glories of the Mughal Empire but to his people, Animal's people, the kingdom of the poor.

The couplet is crucial in the novel because it links the apocalyptic and revolutionary threads together. To assert that *this* is paradise on earth (particularly when *this* refers to Khaufpur's Paradise Alley, or the poisoned city writ large) is a transcendent rejection of transcendence that resonates with revolutionary Marxism's transposition of Judeo-Christian millennialism to secular time and space. The couplet anchors the novel's multiple mappings of heaven and hell in realms both cosmic and mundane—as well as Animal's dilemma of knowing which is which. In this moral geography, Paradise Alley runs through the kingdom of the poor, while hell is the home of overweening power: Jehannum (Islam's hell) is the nickname for the gleaming white hotel on a hill over a lake in Khaufpur, where American lawyers for the Kampani stay.[52] The novel's apocalyptic/revolutionary thrust builds to a climax partly by weaving together Muslim, Christian, and Hindu imagery (where a Christlike Zafar and Shaivite Animal are re-united in a post-Apokalistic Paradise), as well as these intertexts that theorize the power of nothing as a planetary force of people who possess not much more than life itself. This composite poetic expression of the collective plot is so powerful that the text's world shakes, drawing readers toward Trotsky's new dawn: "Already there are many of us, more than it may seem." Maybe you're one? Join us.[53]

The novel's long climax is generated as much by this constellation of texts as by its plot: this intertextuality is a volatile mix, whose components might combine differently for each reader. One peculiar thing about *Animal's People* is how its explosive climax deflates and dissolves into something other than Zafar's nothing: the world, once again, stands still. Whereas the dilemma that catalyzes Animal's narration is knowing heaven from hell—whether to have corrective surgery (and thus whether to be guided by self-interest or the interest of the community)—Sinha's dilemma is how to calibrate the collective plot with the individualist one: how to tell the story of Khaufpur (distilling decades of Bhopal activism) and elicit a revolutionary sublime without ignoring the historical fact of justice yet undone. As Animal says when he completes his narration, "Everything the same, yet everything changed" (364). Climactic scenes of heroic mass action and surreal eco-apocalypse give way to a startlingly domesticated, mundane resolution; this modulation, too, emerges through subtle gestures to literary precursors. Animal reveals that that he has saved up more than ten thousand rupees working for Zafar; rather than a mere streetwise urchin, he is a man in possession of a (relative) fortune. As students of the novel form know, this can mean only one thing: "*It is a truth virtually acknowledged, that a single man in possession of good fortune, must be in want of a wife*" (36). So Animal reads in a book borrowed from Zafar while Nisha teaches him English. This reference to the famous opening of Jane Austen's *Pride and Prejudice* appears early in *Animal's People*, but its significance becomes legible only on the last page, when Animal reveals his accumulated savings and his decision about his dilemma: He will use the money to redeem from prostitution a fellow orphaned survivor to be his life-companion, rather than travel to the United States for the operation.

Animal's implicit account of himself as a man "in possession of [a] good fortune" (Austen includes the indefinite article, which denotes wealth rather than luck) has several contradictory potential effects. *Animal's People* deflates the apocalyptic collective plot by containing its explosive energies within a conservative narrative form: instead of a cosmic day of judgment for the Kampani (which has yet to arrive for Union Carbide/Dow), the novel's apocalyptic arc gives way to Animal's individual trajectory, where he chooses the mundane domesticities behind Door #3. This invocation of the bourgeois European novel's marriage plot reroutes the novelistic possibilities of Animal's conscientization and his attempt to discern heaven from hell, Paradise Alley from a hell of shit and plastic. In class terms, Animal's "good fortune" catalyzes marriage to a woman of his station (a fellow orphan and prostitute) rather than educated, middle-class women like Nisha or Elli. The fact that Animal borrows the book from Zafar is an interesting twist: The selfless activist moved to tears by revolutionary songs and Sufi poetry is also an Austen fan?

Still, this unexpectedly conventional ending is radical in its own way, given the novel's self-consciousness about its circulation in the uneven landscape of world literature. The parody of Austen confirms that Animal is not merely the focalizer but also the hero of his tale, not a mere subaltern sidekick to the more conventionally worldly, serious Zafar. Animal is Don Quixote, not Sancho Panza; Rama, not Lakshman.[54] Animal's decision to remain as he is in the kingdom of the poor, rather than go to the United States to walk upright, does not merely endorse the bourgeois marriage plot for a protagonist who does not seem bourgeois; it also forcefully rejects the contemporary globalization plot that depicts the "salvation" of a Third World protagonist through rescue/redemption by a benevolent American character and/or arrival in the United States. This narrative form appears in numerous global bestsellers like *The Kite Runner* and *Reading Lolita in Tehran*, and child soldier/refugee narratives like *A Long Way Gone* and *Beasts of No Nation*. This plot structure rewrites the white man's burden for the twenty-first century; it also accounts for things like Oprah's South African schoolgirls and international adoptions by Madonna and Angelina Jolie. Even if not quite earthshaking, it is nonetheless groundbreaking that "paradise on earth" has several possible locations in *Animal's People*, none of them in America.

To read *Animal's People* in terms of its literary affiliations is to understand Animal both as a Siva figure to Zafar's Christ (or Hussein, pitted against the tyrant Kampani?) and as an unlikely Austenian bachelor to Zafar's Trotsky. These multiple allusive strands give shape to the constitutive tensions running through what sometimes seems a chaotic jumble (particularly as the novel's long, druggy climax drags on), but they also indicate the complexity of Animal's (and *Animal's People*'s) gestures to a distant (or proximate) reader. It may seem perverse to trace Animal's (or Sinha's) literary sources while Khaufpur burns; perhaps this discussion ranges far afield from properly "ecocritical" concerns.[55] I would argue, however, that the fuel for the fire of the novel's climax (and the contest between its individual and collective plots) is its intertextuality. Whether it elicits revolutionary solidarity with the kingdom of the poor or liberal sympathy for Animal, the novel's affective, rhetorical, and environmental appeal derives from stirring language and familiar plot structures borrowed from a dizzying range of sources.

These tensions give motive force to the work Jasanoff sees *Animal's People* having done to return Bhopal to international awareness. Its intertextuality and narrative structure are central to the how of that doing. "*I am Animal fierce and free / in all the world is none like me,*" Animal sings defiantly on the novel's last page, renouncing the desire to become once again "an upright human . . . one of millions" instead of remaining "the one and only Animal" (366). In terms of the possible outcomes of sympathetic imagining associated with *forum non conveniens*, Animal's narration makes him both *comprehensible* and *incomparable*. The literary vehicles through which Animal arrives at the decision to embrace his incomparable singularity are incompatible and discordant (i.e., inconvenient). They run in opposite directions. They pit the conventionality of the individualist marriage plot against a final statement of collective solidarity and the revolutionary sublime: "We are the people of the Apokalis. Tomorrow there will be more of us" (366). These tensions—between individual and collective, singularity and solidarity—are entangled with another kind of comparison: the one readers are invited to make between Animal (and/or Khaufpur) and their own toxicological predicament. Who are the people of the Apokalis? Who are Animal's people? What is the shape of the world that *Animal's People* invites readers to imagine? Not unlike Mahasweta Devi's "Dhowli," *Animal's People* drives toward a narrative crux about nature and the world entire; Sinha's novel goes a step further by asking readers to reflect upon their place in that world. Do readers close the book feeling sympathy (from a safe distance) for the incomparable Animal and his kingdom of the poor, or an empathetic sense of their own vulnerability to the deadly, Apokalistic mix of Kampani poison and power?

The novel invites both readings, which might collide or converge—as in Nixon's "unevenly universal" vulnerability to environmental harm. We read in *Animal's People*, "everyone on this earth has in their body a share of the Kampani's poisons" (236).[56] This universal "share"-holding in the Kampani translates voluntary financial risk into involuntary toxic risk and capitalist modes of corporate investment into passive, (trans)corporeal ones. Socioeconomic inequality and global class stratification give way to an unequal contest pitting bodies and biomes against corporate-chemical agents. This was the lesson drawn in 1985 by George Bradford (a pseud-onym for David Watson): "We All Live in Bhopal," he argued in the anar-chist quarterly, *The Fifth Estate*. Bradford cited Bhopal as an example of US corporations dumping toxic technology in the Third World, but his main concern was to catalogue industrial disasters, ubiquitous chemicals and everyday incremental poisoning in the United States and Europe as slow violence avant la lettre, or a latter-day *Silent Spring*: "The poisons are vented in the air and water, dumped in rivers, ponds, and streams, fed to the animals to go to market (mad cows in a mad world), sprayed on lawns and roadways, sprayed on food crops, every day, everywhere. The result may not be as dramatic as Bhopal (which then almost comes to serve as a diversion, a deterrence machine to take our minds off the pervasive reality which Bhopal truly represents), but it is deadly" (Bradford [1985] 2005, 285).

Bradford portrays the waste of the world in a latter-day sense: chronic, pervasive exposure to toxic chemicals is punctuated across space by the acute hazards of waste dumps or petrochemical industrial zones ("cancer alleys"), and punctuated across time by disasters like Bhopal. Whereas Union Carbide's lawyers fomented self-serving doubts that Americans could meaningfully cross experiential divides separating them from Bhopal, Bradford perceived a universal vulnerability to poisonous substances and corporate power. In this view, Americans should be able to comprehend or imagine what it was like for Bhopalis to be poisoned by a corporation, because—whether chronically, acutely, or both—they already have been. Sites like Bhopal invite a recognition of the universal inscription of syn-thetic chemicals on living things and life worlds, an inscription that can change the functioning of DNA and RNA, turning the body against it-self. This mode of globalization is experienced at the most intimate scale.

Such expansive gestures of solidarity through shared vulnerability are preferable to Union Carbide's localizing attempt to quarantine to India the cause, significance, and remedy of the catastrophe in Bhopal. Capturing the attention of the world has been a tactic of activism since 1984. "Bhopal will now come alive in every corner of the world," survivors were singing in 1985 (Hanna, Morehouse, and Sarangi 2005, 211). In her acceptance speech for the Goldman Environmental Prize in 2004, Rashida Bee, a Bhopal survivor and activist, described the Union Carbide disaster as only "the most visible example" of a broader "corporate crime against humanity" that creates "slow and silent Bhopals all over the world" (Hanna, More-house, and Sarangi 2005, 117), echoing George Wald's 1970 indictment of Dow's role in Vietnam.

Figure 6. Hindi graffito in Bhopal: "*Gas peedit jo naari hai / phool nahiin, chingaari hai*" (A gas-affected woman is not a flower; she's a flame). Joe Muddy.

As we saw in Chapter 2 with regard to Ken Saro-Wiwa's role as national symbol or "global spokesperson," gestures of planetary solidarity—particularly when extended from outside Bhopal—risk discounting the specificity and extremity of Rashida Bee's suffering and her struggle. Rashida Bee and her fellow organizer Champa Devi Shukla used the Goldman Prize to found the Chingari Trust, which provides rehabilitative services and support to children suffering effects from groundwater contamination and their parents' and grandparents' 1984 MIC exposure. *Chingari* is Hindi for "spark," which echoes a rousing chant popularized by Bee and Shukla's Bhopal Gas Peedit Mahila Stationery Karamchari Sangh (Bhopal Gas-Affected Women Stationery-Workers' Union), a rhyming couplet in Hindi that translates as *gas-affected women are flames, not flowers*. (The consonance between *flame* and *flower* in English stands in for the rhyme in Hindi between *naari* and *chingaari*: woman and spark/flame; see Figure 6.) Animal's allusion to this chant in *Animal's People* (312) could be misread as simply a feminist rejection of women's belittling as delicate ornaments. In her acceptance speech, Bee localizes the flower/flame distinction by denouncing corporate/state developmentalism cast in the idiom of Hindu religious devotion: "We are not flowers to be offered at the altar of profit and power. We are dancing flames committed to conquering darkness" (Hanna, Morehouse, and Sarangi 2005, 117).

The tension between specificity and solidarity is evident in Ulrich Beck's account of modern industrial society as a "universalization of hazards," which echoes the novel's contest between poison and *jaan*: "A community among Earth, plant, animal and human being, . . . a *solidarity of living things*, that affects everyone and everything equally in the threat" (1992, 74). Elsewhere in his influential analysis of risk society, Beck is more circumspect about whether everyone is equally vulnerable in risk's disposition of nature: "the *same* pollutants can have quite *different* meanings for *different* people," he acknowledges (26), and "there is a systematic 'attraction' between extreme poverty and extreme risk" (41). This "attraction" between poverty and risk finds geographic expression at a global scale, in terms that echo James Ferguson's analysis of how underdevelopment shadows modernity: the Third World is "already confronted with the *side effects* of global industrialization while still awaiting the arrival of modernization" (Beck 2009, 186).[57] Nevertheless, risk tends to "boomerang" back to the developed world: "risks of modernization sooner or later also strike those who profit from them . . . *perpetrator* and *victim* sooner or later become *identical*" (1992, 23, 38).

This strong claim makes sense only if toxic exposure and financial exposure are both read as risk: ignoring differences in kind and degree, this logic equates the immiseration endured by Bhopal survivors with the balance-sheet losses of Union Carbide and Dow. (As if in demur, Animal marvels that "in the same world there are people like the [Kampani's] lawyers and creatures like me" [263].) A corrective to such flattening appears in Reinhold Martin's discussion of calculation, counting, and choice with regard to Bhopal. Martin emphasizes the radical inequality at work when "deaths that are counted abstractly (as calculated risk) while remaining uncounted in actuality . . . are incorporated as a variable in the spreadsheets of global capital" (2010, 141, 143). In terms that echo Zafar's marshaling the power of nothing against the Kampani's everything, Martin argues that such calculations produce a new form of subjectivity, "a techno-economic figure composed of numbers inside and out" (142). The actuarial subjects simultaneously produced and unpeopled by corporate calculation are "subject to its threats *without a choice*" (145; emphasis added). Risk cannot be an equalizer when the power to count (in every sense) is so unevenly distributed.

This is the needle I see *Animal's People* attempting to thread: How to elicit planetary solidarity yet calibrate it with an awareness of uneven vulnerability? How to refuse the "false opposition between the bare life of the victim . . . and the liberal subject" (Moore 2015, 5)? If we want to imagine the earth as a greater Bhopal, then it is imperative to recognize that some people live much closer to the Kampani's factories than others—with better health care, access to information, remediation, representation, and so forth. Combined with the spectacular harm and structural inequalities at stake, the instability between sympathy and solidarity as responses to *Animal's People* might account for the suspicion pervading the novel.[58] When Elli insists to Animal that they are equals— friends who shouldn't pay each other for favors like him giving her a tour of the slum—Animal retorts powerfully, "Elli, this equality leaves me broke" (176). This pithy statement names an invidious form of inequality that results from not recognizing the fact of inequality. Like the "proximity without risk" Sontag warns against in consuming images of distant suffering, this superficial equality is the result of sanctioned ignorance that persists within the humanitarian gaze and other well-meaning gestures of global understanding and sympathetic imagining. To say "we all live in Bhopal" can effect a displacement: a gentrification of the imagination. One possible effect of the novel's anticlimax, with its collapse of apocalyptic revolution into a proto-bourgeois marriage plot (in which readers learn that Animal isn't, in fact, broke), is that both the privileged sympathy of liberal fellow-feeling, and the intoxication of too-easy radical solidarity, may come to feel inadequate. Perhaps we need a middle position of distant reading, a corollary to the middle position of spectatorship Animal occupies while he watches Elli looking at Paradise Alley. As Edward Said suggested in *Culture and Imperialism*, if "interpreting Jane Austen depends on *who* does the interpreting, *when* it is done, and no less important, from *where* it is done" (1993, 93), then Jane Austen might point the way toward a more nuanced interpretation of transnational race and class divides—and their inflections in environmental risk.

One World: World Literature, Brought to You by Dow

Our consideration here of the narrative structure, multilingualism, and literary intertextuality of *Animal's People* has brought the disciplinary concerns of comparative literature to bear on the question— still urgent after more than thirty years of activism and litigation—of what it means to interpret and imagine situations like Bhopal from afar. This final section speculates about what Bhopal could mean for literary studies, thinking the discipline anew by taking the multinational corporation rather than the

nation-state as an axis for literary comparison. With such a method, literary critics might supplement the work of activists in charting new maps of
empire: not the familiar image of the world colored in European imperialism's rainbow hues, but the largely unapprehended territories bound and
unbound by the far-flung operations of multinational corporations. Reading for the planet here means constellating literary texts around transnational histories and geographies of corporate harm; this mode of comparison
can calibrate toxic solidarity with a recognition of stratified vulnerability.
Perhaps we don't all live in Bhopal, but we do all live in a world interfused
by Dow.

This section offers only a preliminary sketch of this method, by pursuing threads of connection between Bhopal and Vietnam woven through
Animal's People: These are sites of spectacular harm merged into a single
corporate history by Dow Chemical's acquisition of Union Carbide in 2001.
In the novel, Zafar and his circle are suspicious of Elli's possible connections to "the Kampani"; the revelation that Elli was married to a Kampani
lawyer correlates the failure of her marriage with her decision to help the
Kampani's victims in Khaufpur. But the job "Doctress Elli" left behind
was at a Veterans Affairs hospital in Pennsylvania; among the books in her
office, a newly literate Animal observes, is *Veterans and Agent Orange* (137).
In addition to napalm B, Dow Chemical supplied the US military with the
herbicides Agent Orange and Agent White during the Vietnam War.[59] To
the extent that the "Kampani" can be equated with Union Carbide/Dow,
these details indicate that Elli was helping the Kampani's victims long before she arrives in Khaufpur. Another Bhopal/Vietnam link in the novel
is the Zippo lighter the Australian journalist gives to Animal—the same
lighter with which Animal ignites the factory. The Zippo has "a picture of
a cannon on it, plus some writing," whose "Inglis letters" Animal assumes
are the journalist's name: "PHUOC TUY" (10). Phuoc Tuy is the South Vietnam province where Australian and New Zealand military forces were
based from 1966 to 1972, and one of two provinces where the CIA's experimental spraying of herbicides begun in 1961 escalated in 1965–66 into
chemically assisted warfare on a massive scale (Murphy 1993). Between
1966 and 1968, no less than 202,910 gallons of Agent Orange were sprayed
over Phuoc Tuy, in addition to 156,750 gallons of Agent White and 2,700
gallons of Agent Blue.[60]

These objects—Elli's book and the Vietnam souvenir lighter—link the
Kampani's operation in India to Dow Chemical's role in Operation Ranch
Hand (initially known as Operation Hades), in which the US military
sprayed millions of gallons of toxic chemicals in Vietnam, for purposes of

"food denial" to starve enemy agents and "defoliation" to increase visibility. (Here *visibility* means exposing enemies to military surveillance and
attack.) The Australian journalist's Zippo from Phuoc Tuy suggests either
that he is a Vietnam vet (possibly exposed to Agent Orange), or that his
beat is the trail of Dow's disasters. The Australian gives the Zippo to Animal after having it inscribed with Animal's name in Hindi: reading "PHUOC
TUY" on one side, "जानवर" on the other, the lighter admits Animal to a
brotherhood and sisterhood of veterans whose bodies become the terrain
of an unending battle against Dow's poisons. The Zippo from Phuoc Tuy
marks Australia and New Zealand as important sites in the geography of
Agent Orange.

However, Zippo lighters weren't just engraved as souvenirs during the
Vietnam War; they were also weapons. Viewers of a controversial 1965
CBS News report saw GIs using their Zippos to ignite thatched roofs of
civilian huts; these search-and-destroy missions became known in GI parlance as "Zippo missions" or "Zippo raids" (Buchanan 2007, 12).[61] The
questions about US military policy and practice raised by this disturbing
image are echoed in *Animal's People*, when Animal recognizes that he must
have used his Zippo to set the factory on fire during his datura delirium.
The Zippo links Animal to complex histories of harm as both victim and
perpetrator, at multiple scales of proximity that complicate the notion that
overcoming distance (through sympathetic imagining) is an ethical form
of movement. In Vietnam, death and destruction rained from the sky but
also nestled intimately in a pocket next to a pack of cigarettes, and many
GIs carried home toxic compounds in their cells.[62]

Just as Zippos gave a consumer brand name to this intimate mode of
counterinsurgency in Vietnam, Dow Chemical became the corporate face
of what was promoted as better warfare through chemistry (to adapt the
slogan of DuPont, which also manufactured components of Agent Orange,
and which merged with Dow in 2017). The spectacular harm caused by
napalm became in the United States a cultural touchstone, a synecdoche,
and even, some argue, a cliché for all that was wrong with the war
(McCarthy 2009). Protests against Dow began at its California napalm-
producing facility in 1966 and spread across the country by 1967.[63] The
iconic photograph of nine-year-old Phan Thi Kim Phúc fleeing a friendly-
fire napalm raid by South Vietnamese forces appeared on the *New York
Times* front page on June 9, 1972. Kim Phúc's clothing had burned off by
the time AP photographer Nick Ut captured the Pulitzer Prize–winning
image, now likely seared into the memory of all who have seen it. The
multiple forms of exposure to which Kim Phúc was subjected resonate with

Animal's response to the Australian journalist's visual prosthesis: "Their curiosity feels like acid on my skin" (7).

Given its enduring status an icon of the horrors of Vietnam, Nick Ut's photograph of Kim Phúc evinces a time lag, since US forces in Vietnam had phased out their napalm use by 1972.[64] Military use of herbicides like Agent Orange was slower to elicit widespread public concern in the United States. This gap cannot be attributed solely to the distinction between spectacular and slow violence, since some effects of defoliants were visually striking and immediate: dense green jungle turned to white-coated barren leaves overnight. As the war's proponents and critics both recognized, Operation Ranch Hand was an unprecedented mode of warfare, aimed to destroy entire ecosystems: "Not just humans are targets to be erased by the bombing; even trees become the enemy" (Franklin 2000, 14). Warfare enters a new phase when nature itself becomes a target. Those who saw these "nonlethal" tactics as modern, scientific, even "humane" also invoked this distinction between human and nonhuman targets. The Kennedy, Johnson, and Nixon administrations insisted that the United States was not conducting chemical warfare as proscribed by the Geneva Protocol of 1925 because chemical warfare targeted people, not plants (Zierler 2008, 4; Bonds 2013, 90).[65]

This distinction between people and plants as targets of warfare involved other lethal time lags: not only the chemicals' persistent and/or delayed effects upon ecosystems and organisms (about which more later),[66] but also the fatal disjunctures between innovations in applied chemistry and medicine on the one hand and international law and domestic regulatory regimes on the other. As part of a pivot toward Cold War disarmament and détente, President Nixon announced in 1969 his intention to resubmit the Geneva Protocol to the Senate for ratification, a puzzling move given the controversy regarding the use of chemicals in Vietnam.[67] Nixon miscalculated the domestic politics of his geopolitical gambit: concerned scientists persuaded the Senate Foreign Relations Committee to ratify only if the United States renounced herbicidal warfare—a condition Nixon could not accept, and the Geneva Protocol was not ratified until after his resignation (Zierler 2008). Nonetheless, Nixon's dual role as world statesman and commander-in-chief inadvertently catalyzed international debate about just warfare, the nature of nature, and new threats to life posed by the military-industrial complex in the late twentieth century. As organic chemist J. S. Bellin explained, "When the Geneva Protocol was drawn up, the term 'poisonous' still had the simple connotation of immediate lethality; mutagenic, teratological, and carcinogenic action were as yet unsuspected manifestations, to be elicited by branches of sciences [non-existent] in 1925. Pesticides had not yet been discovered" (1972, 2).

Mid-twentieth-century advances in chemistry distinguish the military use of chemicals after the 1940s from earlier practices of indirect killing—modes of violence against people, waged through nature, including scorched earth policies or strategic clearing of forests as rebel hideouts discussed in Chapter 3. Napalm and Agent Orange were products of World War II–era research undertaken in US universities and military research facilities. Herbicides like Agent Orange were synthetic plant growth regulators (hormones) that could stimulate the growth of beneficial "crops" or manage harmful "weeds" by overstimulating growth to the point of unviability. After 1945, these chemicals were mass-marketed in the United States for civilian use; this "postwar chemicalization of agriculture" (Zierler 2008, 9) also involved synthetic nitrogen fertilizers developed from nitrogen-fixing techniques Germany used to manufacture bombs during World War I. "Ecocide" was the term Yale plant biologist Arthur Galston coined for the US herbicidal strategy in Vietnam, which he opposed because he saw this military experiment as portending the risk of worldwide environmental destruction if inexpensive and easily obtainable substances were deployed as weapons (Zierler 2008, 22–23).

Advances in agrochemistry spurred by the Second World War brought *Silent Spring* to the United States, the Green Revolution and Union Carbide to India, and ecocide to Vietnam. It is another aspect of the Anthropocene: The mid-twentieth-century moment that launched the Great Accelerations of economic growth, greenhouse gas emissions, and global warming also saw an unprecedented anthropogenic rearrangement of molecules at scales both cellular and planetary. Detonations of atomic weapons left their signature in every living thing, and highly dangerous synthetic compounds like dioxins, DDT, PCBs, and other persistent organic pollutants (POPs) became global chemicals, dispersed across the earth. The debate about herbicidal warfare in Vietnam was a watershed moment in environmental discourse and international law. The self-serving distinction between people and plants as military targets was challenged by a more robustly ecological understanding of toxic exposure and what we would now call transcorporeality (Alaimo 2011). Molecules abide neither legal categories nor species distinctions in their movements across cell membranes or up the food chain. Just as the horrors of the Second World War elicited a new international consensus about protecting civilian noncombatants from acts of genocide, the ecocidal use of herbicides in Vietnam spurred efforts to prohibit the environment from being targeted in warfare—a new consensus reflected in the 1977/78 UN Convention on the Prevention of Military or any other Hostile Use of Environmental Modification Techniques and Additional Protocols I and II to the Geneva Conventions (Zierler 2008, 247–48; Rauxloh 2011, 429–31). This is not to say that international law or domestic regulations adequately protect humans or the environment from toxic exposure to synthetic chemicals—which leads us back to stratified vulnerability and the solidarity or sympathy evoked by Bhopal and *Animal's People*.

When the Kennedy administration sought to deflect early concerns about Operation Ranch Hand in 1963, Assistant Defense Secretary William Bundy invoked the commercial availability of the same "weed killers" and their widespread use in the United States to insist, "They are not injurious to man, animals, or the soil" (quoted in Bonds 2013, 90). Bundy sought to domesticate an unprecedented military deployment of these products in concentrations far exceeding their commercial applications. Yet the military-consumer nexus is problematic for reasons more insidious than Bundy's misleading assurances. The repeated shifts between military and domestic uses of synthetic herbicides (and other chemicals) have been described as a "pendulum," swinging between military expediency and commercial imperatives—twin pressures that resulted in the widespread use of chemicals whose safety was never adequately tested (Whiteside 1979, 11–20). Dow Chemical played a crucial role in this history that continues today; the controversy over Agent Orange set a precedent in which toxic substances were regulated in terms of *proof of harm* (to be established after exposure, by individuals or regulators), as opposed to *proof of safety* that companies had to demonstrate before bringing products to market (Doyle 2004, 63–64; Whiteside 1979, 19). This is a crucial example of neoliberalism's socialization of risk and privatization of profits. Only in June 2016 did a revision to the Toxic Substances Control Act of 1976 begin to remedy this regulatory displacement of risk from corporations to individuals and society—a long-awaited accomplishment weakened almost immediately by Trump's EPA.

Thomas Whiteside, author of *The Pendulum and the Toxic Cloud: The Course of Dioxin Contamination* (1979), made one of the earliest attempts to alert the American public to the dangers of Agent Orange.[68] Like Rachel Carson in 1962, Whiteside published an article and series of follow-up "Letters" in the *New Yorker* in 1969–70—a multipart exposé of the hazards of these putatively "safe" and "harmless" chemicals and their domestic ubiquity. Whiteside takes a remarkably stereoscopic or contrapuntal view; the same herbicides increasingly suspected of causing fetal abnormalities in Vietnam were, he observed, widely available on American store shelves.[69] He feared that one consequence of bringing attention to the dangers of the components of Agent Orange would be that as the military scaled back its use of herbicides in response to controversy, more of these substances would be marketed in the United States (75).[70] Whiteside advocated a kind of reading for the planet, urging Americans to connect the dots between the spectacular military use of chemicals in Vietnam and the quotidian dangers lurking in their own medicine cabinets, grocery carts, and garden sheds.

Another kind of pendulum (along with other lethal time lags) is evident in Dow's responses to concerns about Agent Orange. Too long and convoluted to unravel fully here, this is a tale of secrets and lies whose theme is Dow's effort to prevent regulation of dioxin[71]—perhaps the most hazardous chemical known to science, to which there is no demonstrated safe level of exposure (Vallianatos 2014, 63, 252n33). Dioxin is an inevitable byproduct in the manufacture of many organochlorine chemicals, including 2,4,5-T, a component of Agent Orange. Dow was concerned enough about dioxin to hold a secret summit of competitor manufacturers of 2,4,5-T in March 1965, to emphasize its hazards and encourage them to minimize dioxin levels in their products. Dow feared that dioxin exposures during manufacture or use of 2,4,5-T might draw regulatory attention; the company later cited contractually stipulated secrecy to explain why it did not disclose to competitors a low-temperature manufacturing process, aimed to minimize dioxin production, that it acquired for $35,000 from the German firm Boehringer Sohn (Doyle 2004, 83–84; Rempel 1984, 20). When a study commissioned by the National Cancer Institute and undertaken by Bionetics Research Laboratories indicated in 1966 that 2,4,5-T was extremely teratogenic in mice and rats (i.e., it caused fetal abnormalities), Dow was well positioned to point fingers at dioxin and the other suppliers, from whom, Dow argued, Bionetics must have acquired a "dirty sample." (A secret 1965 analysis of competitors' 2,4,5-T found dioxin levels ranging from three to sixteen times its own one part per million [Rempel 1984, 20].) Seeking to protect its military market and market share in the mid-1960s, Dow acknowledged (to the inner circle briefed on the classified Bionetics study) the dangers of dioxin and promised the "purest" 2,4,5-T available.

The pendulum swung the other way in the 1970s when Dow pivoted toward the US domestic market and sought to cast regulatory doubt on the risks of dioxin. As Whiteside feared, the end of Operation Ranch Hand meant the expansion of commercial uses for components of Agent Orange:

"by the mid-1970s, 2,4,5-T spraying across America *exceeded annually* in acreage the total 5 to 6 million acres that had been sprayed in Vietnam over more than eight years" (Doyle 2004, 61; emphasis in original). The beginning of the end of herbicidal warfare came in 1969, when the classified Bionetics study was leaked to a lawyer working with Ralph Nader; in the three-year interim, approximately 15,000 tons of 2,4,5-T were sprayed in Vietnam (Whiteside 1979, 14). This revelation resulted in restrictions upon the approved domestic uses of 2,4,5-T in April 1970 and the cessation of herbicidal warfare in 1971. For over a decade, Dow fought these domestic restrictions at every turn—and reported in 1983 having spent more than $10 million to do so (Stein 1983)—even as the harms inflicted upon US veterans and their children became increasingly evident. The first Agent Orange disability claim was filed with the Veterans Administration in 1977, and veterans' lawsuits were consolidated in 1980 into an unprecedented class-action product liability tort of 2.4 million injured veterans and families claiming damages "in the range of $4 billion to $40 billion" against Dow and other Agent Orange manufacturers (Schuck 1986, 4, 45).

Even after a cluster of miscarriages in Oregon led to a temporary emergency ban in 1979 on using 2,4,5-T for forestry and clearing rights-of-way along highways and power lines (but allowing continued use on rangelands and rice fields), Dow exerted such influence at the EPA that 2,4,5-T was poised for a return to the market in 1983. In *No Margin of Safety*, Oregon resident Carol van Strum and Vietnam veteran Paul Merrell detail Dow's astonishing machinations in the 1970s and 80s to create a "regulatory stalemate" regarding dioxin (1987, III-12). In terms of risk logic and unevenly universal vulnerability to corporate poisons, notice a paradox in this history: The stalemate resulted from an emergent understanding of how dangerous dioxin was, not a failure to recognize its dangers. Studies in the late 1970s—by Dow and EPA scientists—found teratogenic and carcinogenic effects at the lowest possible dose of daily dietary exposure to dioxin: one part per trillion of bodyweight (II-5–6; Valliantos 2014, 41–63). In this sense, there was no demonstrated safe level of exposure to dioxin. But in another sense—as with Wall Street banks deemed too big to fail—dioxin was, in effect, too widespread and dangerous a hazard to regulate.

Without a demonstrated safe dose, any EPA regulation based on safe levels of exposure would "result in economic havoc to a wide range of industries producing dioxin pollution, such as the chemical, pharmaceutical, waste disposal, wood treatment, and leather-tanning industries" (Van Strum and Merrell 1987, III-8). Dioxin is a contaminant produced in the manufacture of many synthetic chemicals besides 2,4,5-T. An additional challenge was municipal waste incineration, which the EPA initially promoted as a two-for-one solution for reducing landfill and generating electricity. Since dioxins are produced under conditions of high heat, any number of otherwise "safe" products containing synthetic chemicals yield dioxins when they are burned (Whiteside 1979, 56). Think plastic—and consider the scale of slow violence inflicted by the military tactic of using herbicides and napalm together (Whiteside 1979, 65). Dioxin is highly persistent in the environment; it has low solubility in water but an affinity for fats, which means that it easily contaminates groundwater and travels up the food chain through bioaccumulation and biomagnification (i.e., when animals eat organisms containing dioxin). Its interaction with other compounds in the environment makes some of them more carcinogenic. It is everywhere, and it does not easily disappear once it appears. Its ubiquity in "modern" industrial life opens up a glimpse of a toxic sublime. Imagine if CO_2 and other greenhouse gases not only changed the earth's chemistry as they accumulated over decades and centuries, but also threatened health at any known exposure.

A more practical pressure that made dioxin troublesome to regulate in the early 1980s was the Agent Orange class action lawsuit, in which manufacturers threatened to sue the US government as an indemnifying third party if the plaintiffs' suit for billions of dollars in damages succeeded (Van Strum and Merrell 1987, III-8). The EPA's first administrator, William Ruckelshaus, reappointed by Ronald Reagan, argued in September 1983 that regulation of such substances was tenable only if scientific standards based on lab-demonstrated levels of safe exposure (which determined much of the EPA's regulatory activity) were replaced by risk-benefit economic standards already mandated for pesticides, which also fell under the jurisdiction of the USDA. (The 1976 Toxic Substances Control Act and the Resource Conservation and Recovery Act, regulating waste disposal, used the risk-benefit model.) For the EPA to attend solely to science without weighing regulation's economic consequences, Ruckelshaus argued, would pose "a grim and unnecessary choice between the fruits of advanced technology and the blessings of democracy" (1983, 1028).

This contest between a safe-dose standard and risk-benefit analysis is a key moment in the emergence of risk logic, following Beck's account of risk society. For Beck, "risk" involves not merely the statistical possibility of harm but the *perception* of hazard, based partly on regulatory pronouncements shot through with scientific uncertainty and/or political and economic expediency to an extent that citizens may not recognize. Dioxin's extreme toxicity and unpredictable interactions with other compounds severely complicate efforts to quantify the risks associated with it. The theoretical (or political) impossibility of calculating risk is too easily transmuted into the spurious notion that hazardous substances whose risks are incalculable are "safe." To invert Zafar's arithmetic in *Animal's People*, risk perceptions can transform everything into nothing. In 2012, the EPA released the first volume of an assessment, more than two decades in the making, that finally set a safe dioxin exposure threshold for noncancer risks (0.7 trillionths of a gram per kilogram of body weight per day). A second volume, on cancer risks, was said to be forthcoming but has not been released. Nonetheless, headlines announced "EPA Sets Safe Dioxin Level" (Trager 2012). This dynamic of risk perception has repeated in the Trump era; a federal study that found hazards posed by two drinking water contaminants at levels significantly below EPA standards was temporarily suppressed because it would be a "public relations nightmare."

In October 1983, Dow abruptly announced it was pulling 2,4,5-T from the US market; the EPA followed its lead by canceling all remaining registered uses of the chemical. Van Strum and Merrell (1987) contend that Dow's sudden capitulation in this years-long battle was spurred by a leaked data table from a 1979 EPA study of dioxin levels in drinking water sediment, wildlife, and miscarried human fetuses in Oregon; they go so far as to suggest that a desire to minimize public attention to this "smoking gun" regarding dioxin's effects on humans (which would bolster the veterans' case) led to the settlement of the Agent Orange lawsuit for $180 million on May 7, 1984. Regardless of the validity of this claim about the Agent Orange settlement, what is inconvertible are the extreme measures Dow took for decades to head off regulation of dioxin, despite early knowledge of its dangers. Even in its final capitulation with 2,4,5-T, Dow maintained in public that "we didn't believe it was harmful in 1979 and we don't believe it is harmful now" (Stein 1983). Like Exxon and American tobacco companies, Dow was a "merchant of doubt" (Oreskes and Conway 2010) in its battle to keep marketing the components of Agent Orange in the United States, partly by keeping its scientists' concerns about dioxin under wraps, except for strategic moments like responding to the Bionetics study in 1966. Despite having been identified as possibly carcinogenic and teratogenic as early as the Bionetics study, 2,4-D (the other component of Agent Orange) remains on the US market; its use has increased with the FDA approval in 2014 of genetically engineered 2,4-D resistant crops, dubbed by environmentalists "Agent Orange corn." Dow has successfully sued to prevent the EPA from withdrawing its 2014 approval of Enlist Duo, a new 2,4-D–glyphosate formulation.

To inhabit the world manufactured by Dow is to confront multiple forms of exposure and persistence that necessitate and complicate attempts to think between places like Bhopal, Vietnam, and the United States. Despite the persistence of its chemicals in the environment and living tissue, and despite the persistent inevitability of disasters associated with such hazardous materials, Dow persists in selling poison—and fighting for lax regulatory regimes that allow it to do so. Giving up on the US market in 1983, Dow continued manufacturing 2,4,5-T in New Zealand and marketing it elsewhere. "We must assume that life now takes place in a minefield of risks from hundreds, perhaps thousands of substances," William Ruckelshaus wrote in 1983, announcing, in effect, a new disposition of nature as a life-world potentially inimical to life (1027). This statement suggests that all of us lead shadow lives as the actuarial subjects, "composed of numbers inside and out," that Reinhold Martin theorized (2010) in describing Bhopalis as chemical subalterns, whose exposure to risk is always-already factored in to make consumer capitalism possible. The "growing empire of toxic capital" (Hanna, Morehouse, and Sarangi 2005, xix) is shaped less by the old hemispheric polarities—East/West, North/South—than by paths of least resistance. The unmapped sacrifice zones of this new empire lie not only in the peripheries of empires past, but also at its very center. Dow's corporate headquarters in Midland, Michigan, is a classic site of slow violence: Routine incineration and dumping of liquid waste from the 1890s to the 1970s contaminated Midland neighborhoods, the Tittabawassee River, and Saginaw Bay in Lake Huron with dioxin. And yet, with Whiteside's pendulum image in mind, it is important to remember that the hard-won 1984 Agent Orange settlement, no matter how inadequate in addressing the needs of US veterans, did absolutely nothing for Vietnamese victims, who, like Bhopalis, still await justice.[72]

When Dow acquired Union Carbide in 2001, investors and activists alike recognized the implications of merging these companies' histories of harm. A 2004 report by Innovest Strategic Value Advisors succinctly mapped Dow's global exposure to liability claims for Agent Orange, the Bhopal leak and site contamination, and dioxin contamination in Michigan, as well as litigation involving silicone breast implants and exposure of Dow and Union Carbide workers to asbestos and other hazardous chemicals involved in semiconductor manufacture. The report also identified the "overall market risk" inherent in Dow's core mission of manufacturing organochlorine chemicals, increasingly shown to be "persistent bioaccumulating toxins" and likely to be phased out or spark new toxic torts (Hanna, Morehouse, and Sarangi 2005, 271). Activists in myriad local

Figure 7. Anti-Dow graffito in Bhopal, India, c. 2009. Joe Muddy.

struggles also perceived that the merger of Dow and Union Carbide could effect "the incidental merger of their opponents' and victims' interests" (Hanna, Morehouse, and Sarangi 2005, 263). With new transnational links forged across these localized sites, the twentieth anniversary of the Bhopal disaster in 2004 exposed Dow to its first student protests since Vietnam, and Bhopal activists have staged demonstrations in support of Agent Orange victims. (See Figure 7.)

Literary comparison organized around the corporation could draw similar links among these instances of harm: spectacular sites on the map of world literature according to Dow. Such a method might identify, juxtapose, and differentiate tropes, genres, rhetorical modes, and patterns of imagery emerging from local literary contexts within these transnational histories. Poetry written by American Vietnam vets, and novels about chemical aspects of the war like Stephen Wright's *Meditations in Green* (where foliage is experienced as an enemy combatant) or Bobbie Ann Mason's *In Country* (featuring Agent Orange–exposed veterans who take jobs at Union Carbide) could be read in tandem with short stories and plays written by Vietnamese survivors and Australian children of veterans.[73] These texts speak back against the ideological obfuscations of 1970s and

1980s Hollywood films, which demonized the "Viet Cong" (the derogatory term for the National Liberation Front) by inaccurately depicting them as perpetrators of tactics (including napalm and Agent Orange) that the US military used against them (Franklin 2000; Nguyen 2015). This refusal and reversal of responsibility is analogous to Union Carbide's spurious, self-serving claim that the gas leak in Bhopal resulted from sabotage by a disgruntled local employee. Exculpatory world-imaginings on offer from corporate media blame distant victims and reinscribe assumptions of American innocence and benevolence. Nonetheless, literary and cultural production spurred by these disasters can also offer alternative maps of vulnerability, exposure, and responsibility, reversing the scope once again. Reading among these bodies of work, literary critics can connect the dots among sites that multinational corporations aim to keep localized and quarantined from one another.

The transnational imaginary charted by such a method could offer a literary corollary to efforts in the legal realm to hold multinational corporations accountable. After the Bhopal disaster, Indian jurists articulated a new doctrine of liability, summarized by Indian Supreme Court Chief Justice P. N. Bhagwati: "where an enterprise is engaged in hazardous or inherently dangerous activities and harm results to anyone on account of an accident in the operation of such hazardous or inherently dangerous activity . . . the enterprise is strictly and absolutely liable to compensate all those who were affected by the accident" (quoted in Rosencranz et al. 1994, 50). This formulation of absolute enterprise liability renders moot defenses like sabotage; damages would be determined by the company's ability to pay, not by calculations of victims' lost wages (50). Bhagwati wrote for the court in *M. C. Mehta v. Union of India*, involving a relatively minor oleum gas leak at the Shriram Food and Fertilizer Company in New Delhi in 1985. His ruling, released in December 1986, was written with an eye toward Bhopal litigation. It directly echoes the Union of India's plaint against UCC (Civil Suit 1113/86), filed in Bhopal District Court in September 1986:

> Multinational corporations by virtue of their global purpose, structure, organization, technology, finances and resources have it within their power to make decisions and take actions that can result in industrial disasters of catastrophic proportion and magnitude. This is particularly true with respect to those activities of the multinationals which are ultrahazardous or inherently dangerous.
>
> Key management personnel of multinationals exercise a closely-held power which is neither restricted by national boundaries nor effectively

controlled by international law. The complex corporate structure of the multinationals, with networks of subsidiaries and divisions, makes it exceedingly difficult or even impossible to pinpoint responsibility for the damages caused by the enterprise to distinct corporate units or individuals. In reality there is but one entity, the monolithic multinational . . . acting through a neatly designed network of interlocking directors, common operating systems. . . . In this manner, the multinational carries out its global purpose through thousands of daily actions, by a multitude of employees and agents. Persons harmed by the acts of [the] multinational corporation are [not] in a position to isolate which unit of the enterprise caused the harm, yet it is evident that the multinational enterprise that caused the harm is liable for such harm. The defendant multinational corporation has to bear this responsibility for it alone had at all material times the means to know and guard against hazards likely to be caused by the operation of the said plant. (Union of India [1986] 1990, 5–6)

This argument *localizes* responsibility in the multinational corporation: liability rests with "one entity," regardless of its legally complex, globe-spanning structure.

Absolute multinational enterprise liability aims to disrupt settled understandings of the legal process of incorporation as a "veil" that delimits liability between human persons and corporate persons and isolates parent companies from local subsidiaries. Responding to the Union of India's plaint, Union Carbide's lawyers questioned its logic on these fundamental grounds: "The defendant submits that there is no concept known to law as 'multinational corporation' or as 'monilithic [*sic*] multinational'" ("Written Statement" [1986] 1990, 61). As with US public discourse surrounding the idea of corporate personhood in the United States after the 2010 *Citizens United* and 2014 *Hobby Lobby* rulings, Union Carbide's statement reveals the gulf between legal doctrine and embodied common sense, which recoils against the notion that a corporation is, in fact, a legal person. The mind boggles at a multinational corporation stating in a legal brief that multinational corporations do not exist, so far as the law is concerned. (The same was true of dioxin until 1985, but its status as a legal nonentity made it no less toxic [Whiteside 1979, 75].) This premise allowed UCC to deny it had "operations" in India for which it could be held liable ("Written Statement" [1986] 1990, 62)—a formulation of corporate personhood that shares the localizing impulse of Gerstacker's Dow island dream.

The out-of-court settlements of the Agent Orange class action and the Union of India's civil suit against Union Carbide effected a foreclosure—not only of greater monetary damages that might have been awarded, but also of opportunities to establish legal precedents regarding corporate liability for mass disasters (Baxi 1990, ix). Judge Bhagwati's ruling in *Mehta*, released ten days after Union Carbide scoffed at the notion of a multinational corporation, affirmed the notion of absolute liability within Indian jurisprudence. There is, however, no such doctrine codified in international law.[74] To use the multinational corporation as an axis of literary comparison might work against quarantines of the imagination enforced by the legal structures for limiting corporate liability. This method could narrow the gap between legal and other kinds of common sense—an amicus brief, of sorts, for efforts to hold multinational corporations more effectively to account for their actions, across time and space, in the era of neoliberal globalization. Without the force of law behind it, the literary imagination is not necessarily constrained by legal niceties: this is both its limitation and the source of its power.

In *Animal's People*, there is a certain genius in Sinha's exclusive, generic use of *the Kampani* to name the corporate entity responsible for decades of harm in Khaufpur. There are many reasons Sinha might not want to name Union Carbide/Dow in the novel, nor include within Khaufpur's history the complications introduced by the acquisition of one multinational by another. As a generic term, "the Kampani" simplifies the plot, gives the narrative an allegorical resonance with the predicament of globalization pitting the power of nothing against the power of Kampanis, and likely keeps the publishers' lawyers happy.[75] "The Kampani" also generates a provocative historical echo with the British East India Company, intimating a continuity between multinational corporations and colonial charter companies in successive waves of a globalizing capitalism. Most significantly, "the Kampani" affirms the premise of absolute multinational enterprise liability: the Kampani is the Kampani is the Kampani. "The Kampani" effects in prose fiction what absolute multinational enterprise liability attempts in the legal arena: It sweeps away corporations' caviling over legal distinctions (and veils of liability) among their various entities.[76] If there is a Kampani responsible for this harm, it is *this*, it is *this*, it is *this*. One Kampani. One world.

EPILOGUE

Fixing the World

Do not be too afraid. Do not be too sad. Do not be too angry.

—LINDA HOGAN, *Mean Spirit*

In a remarkable feat of culture jamming by the prankster activists known as the Yes Men, BBC News viewers on the twentieth anniversary of the Bhopal gas leak in December 2004 saw a representative of Dow Chemical announce that the company would accept responsibility for the disaster and liquidate the recently acquired assets of Union Carbide to compensate survivors. As chronicled in *The Yes Men Fix the World* (2009), Bhopal survivors first wiped away tears of joy at the news, then tears of disappointment upon learning of the hoax. The Yes Men pretended to do what Dow (and Union Carbide) should have done: The "real hoax," they explained in a statement, is the company's long history of claiming there is nothing it can or should do about Bhopal (Hanna, Morehouse, and Sarangi 2005, 276).

The Yes Men's shtick is to marshal the power of satire and counterfactual imagining against abuses of corporate and state power that deny the possibility of alternatives to the status quo and work actively to foreclose them: to make them unimaginable. Another sequence in *The Yes Men Fix the World* features the publication in mid-November 2008 of a fake July 4, 2009, edition of the *New York Times*. The above-the-fold headline announced an immediate end to the Iraq War; other stories in the fourteen-page spoof detailed (according to the actual *New York Times*) "a liberal utopia of national health care, a rebuilt economy, progressive taxation, a national oil fund to study climate change, and other goals of progressive politics" (Chan 2008). Such alternative futures can stretch the imagination, thereby reaching a bit closer to making them a reality. But what's the difference between alternative futures and fake ones? Critics of the Yes Men's Bhopal stunt said it was cruel to offer the victims false hope; I confess to some discomfort about another Yes Men prank in August 2006, when an activist posing as a US Department of Housing and Urban Development (HUD) undersecretary "announced" in post-Katrina New Orleans a new commitment to affordable housing for all and a multibillion-dollar commitment from oil companies to protect wetlands in the Gulf of Mexico.

The uneven vulnerability to risk and harm traced throughout this book demands that we consider the multiple audiences for such interventions—fractured along fault lines of socioeconomic inequality and proximity to disaster—and the possibility that such dream-hacking could register as an additional injury to the most vulnerable, the most exposed. When Ulrich Beck writes that "the *same* pollutants can have quite *different* meanings for *different* people" (1992, 26), he invites us to contemplate the metabolism of toxic substances in terms of *interpretation*: finding meaning in matter.

And yet, the multiple senses of *exposure* traced in Chapter 4 make it unsurprising that those institutions whose policies and practices are exposed as inadequate by the Yes Men (Dow, HUD) are first to invoke concern about the cruelty of offering victims false hope. Dow's stock price plunged after the Bhopal prank; the markets registered the financial exposure to liability that Dow seemed finally to be willing to accept. Dow's concern for Bhopal survivors' feelings seemed like crocodile tears, given the thousands of billable hours spent insulating the company from responsibility for harm—a legal and PR approximation of Gerstacker's island dream. Recall Chimamanda Adichie's observation about the Niger Delta: Hegemonic historical narratives too often begin from "secondly" and obscure seminal acts of dispossession and violence. Or recall the cycle of wasting in which the enclosure of "waste" land yields lands and lives laid waste. "What we're doing is not actually lying. It's actually exposing the lies," explained Andy Bichlbaum, the activist who posed as the HUD undersecretary, to CNN. "All hopes are false until they're realized, and what's an hour of false hope to 20 years of unrealized ones?" the Yes Men asked in their statement about the Bhopal stunt (Hanna, Morehouse, and Sarangi 2005, 276). Such interventions expose the falsity of resigned hopelessness by opening an ironic gap between actuality and possibility. That there might be balm for the injured in such irony is evident in the response to the HUD stunt by the media coordinator of a New Orleans tent city: "Right now, a lie is better than the truth" (CNN 2006).

A similar moment occurs in *Animal's People*, when a secret meeting of politicians and Kampani officials is disrupted by a stink bomb planted by a mysterious burqa-clad woman (possibly Elli) posing as a cleaning woman. The men, conspiring behind closed doors to negotiate a deal to let the Kampani off the hook, emerge from the gas-filled room into a phalanx of tipped-off journalists: "once the secret was out, the deal was dead" (Sinha 2008, 361). The genius of this stunt is that it weds toxic and journalistic exposure. Throats burning, eyes stinging, the men "thought they'd been attacked with the same gas that leaked on that night, and every man there knew exactly how horrible were the deaths of those who breathed the Kampani's poisons" (ibid.). Against the fug of scientific uncertainty that cultivates doubt about the relationship between toxic causes and effects, the stink bomb elicits an embodied certainty of what it feels like to be poisoned. This simulated certainty, an experience of the as-if, is another experiential prosthesis. Animal exults, "It's poetic justice of a fully rhyming kind," which, as Zafar observes soberly, "is not the same as real justice, but being the only kind available to the Khaufpuris was at least better than nothing" (ibid.). A lie is better than the truth.

These acts of counterfactual imagining—whether media-savvy stunts or literary texts like *Animal's People*—can function as an alternative forum that yields poetic justice, as opposed to the "real justice" that courts of law have yet to offer. That poetic justice might also catalyze real justice is the assumption motivating claims like Sheila Jasanoff's about the work that *Animal's People* has done for Bhopal—and, in some way, the work I have done in the preceding chapters. This book has sought to be alert to the kinds of remedy such imaginings can offer—and *how* they work at the level of form—yet also to be circumspect about the limits of such remedies and the solidarities to be forged through imaginative prostheses of the experience of others. After the stink bomb stunt, the Kampani claims to have been a "victim of terrorism" and demands that the culprit be prosecuted, but the journalists observe that "one stink bomb, however disgusting, could not compare to the terror the company had brought on the people of Khaufpur" (361). This comparative logic insists upon proportionality (i.e., *convenience*) and the difference between simulated and actual exposure, as if in rejoinder to Beck's claim that victim and perpetrator eventually become identical in the world that risk makes.

Modes of compensation and redress that occur solely in the realm of the imaginary or the court of public opinion have significant limits—as is evident in the fact that Warren Anderson, CEO of Union Carbide in 1984, acknowledged weeks after the disaster that "Union Carbide has a moral responsibility in this matter, and we are not trying to duck it." Every other kind of responsibility, Anderson and Union Carbide did their best to duck; having arrived back in the United States after posting bail and promising to return to India when summoned, Anderson lived out his days as an "absconder" from the Indian criminal justice system. Insisting upon legal *cordons sanitaires* differentiating it from Union Carbide, Dow refused even this moral responsibility, which, if reckoned in currencies that might make a real difference in the lives of survivors, amounts to "little enough, less than little: nothing" (Coetzee 1999, 220). In what currency would Animal reckon the "fully rhyming" satisfaction of the 2013 Bollywood blockbuster *Dhoom 3* naming its villain, the heartless CEO of "Western Bank" in Chicago, Warren Anderson?

In "The Truth of Fiction," Chinua Achebe extolled the "life of the imagination [as] a vital element" of human existence, yet he also warned against its more sinister aspects. Racism, ethnocentrism, and sexism are among the "fictions generated by the imagination" that he dubbed "malignant," "the cause of all the trouble in the world" ([1978] 1990, 147). For Achebe, the difference between malignant and "beneficent" fictions derives from reflexive self-awareness: Beneficent fiction "never forgets that it is fiction and the other never knows that it is. . . . Beneficent fiction operates within the bounds of imagination; [malignant fiction] breaks the bounds and ravages the real world" (148). "Malignant fictions . . . never say, 'Let us pretend,'" he observes (148). The temptation, I think, in the Nigerian novelist's powerful formulation is to map the help-or-harm binary onto discursive, disciplinary, or vocational differences: to align beneficent fiction with prose fiction and the literary imagination and to dub *malignant* the dangerous nontruths of philistine world-ravagers—with corporations being among the most powerful offenders. Beyond now-ubiquitous cries of "fake news," Exhibit A in this logic could be Dow's Promethean theory, floated in the late 1970s, that dioxin was the naturally occurring result of all combustion and its "trace chemistries of fire"; a malignant fiction in every sense, "God makes dioxin" was the quintessential naturalization of toxic harm (see Bumb et al. 1980; Van Strum and Merrell 1987, 3:3–4). But Achebe himself would surely aver that Joseph Conrad's once-upon-a-time tale spinning in *Heart of Darkness* was shot through with malignant fictions, lethal certainties about the "fact" of European superiority.

The Disposition of Nature is driven by a conviction about the capacity of the imagination to open up alternative possibility in relationships among humans and with a more-than-human world. It has also shown how counterfactual (literary) imagining can entrench habits of mind and modes of being that foster environmental injustice. Adapting Zafar's mantra, I could say that the power of such imagining—its simultaneous vastness and immaterial puniness—is a variant of the *power of nothing*, which nonetheless can make something happen in the world, for better and for worse. Perhaps this quibble with Achebe derives from my being a literary critic rather than a novelist, but I understand the relationship between the "bounds of the imagination" and the "real world" to be more porous and permeable than he allows, along the lines of Alaimo's (2011) notion of transcorporeality as the flows of matter, power, and ideas across living bodies. Violation and ravaging are one mode of interaction between imagination and the real world, but there are others too. Like toxic compounds, their transit obstructed by neither legal distinctions nor cell membranes, cultural logics travel among multiple realms of experience and modes of discourse. They are persistent and volatile, transformed by their circulation and shaped by pressures of mediation, form, genre, and rhetorical situation—as the preceding chapters demonstrated with the cultural logics of consumerism, citizenship, enclosure, and exposure. Words like *nature, community*, and *justice* don't sound or mean the same to everyone or in all contexts. Instead of sorting them out into beneficent or malignant ones, perhaps we should understand all fictions as risky: unpredictable in the ways their causes and effects work themselves out across time and space. Such risks entail not only exposure to the possibility of harm but also leaps of faith into the unknown and as-yet unrealized, and the prospect that the "touch of innocence" (Zinn 1967) that we tend to imagine about ourselves might be countered with a newfound sense of complicity, entanglement, or even self-reflexive solidarity. To attend to risky fictions in this way could align the literary with what Upendra Baxi describes as "histories of people's resistance to . . . the onward march of global capital from Agent Orange and Bhopal to Ogoniland and beyond" (2006, 715).

Fixing the world? I harbor no certainty that reading for the planet is up to the task. But I do believe that the project of environmental justice is impossible without it, and this narrative intelligence is what I know how to offer the future. Let go of hope and keep fighting. Let us pretend and see what happens.

I gratefully acknowledge permission to include here material that appeared in print in earlier versions, including parts of Chapter 1 in "Consumption for the Common Good: Commodity Biography Film in an Era of Post-consumerism" in *Public Culture* 23, no. 3 (2011): 573–602; parts of Chapter 2 in "Petro-Magic-Realism: Towards a Political Ecology of Nigerian Literature" in *Postcolonial Studies* 9, no. 4 (2006): 449–64, and in "Petro-Magic-Realism Revisited: Unimagining and Reimagining the Niger Delta" in *Oil Culture*, edited by Ross Barrett and Daniel Worden (University of Minnesota Press, 2014): 211–25; and parts of Chapter 3 in "Forest Fictions and Ecological Crises: Reading the Politics of Survival in Mahasweta Devi's 'Dhowli.'" in *Postcolonial Ecologies*, edited by Elizabeth DeLoughrey and George Handley (Oxford University Press, 2011), 136–57.

This book has benefited from questions and provocations of audiences at several universities, to whom I acknowledge gratitude for opportunities to share my work: Austin College, University of California at Los Angeles, University of Cape Town, Columbia University, University of Connecticut, Emory University, Goldsmiths/University of London, King's College London, University of Leeds, Manchester Metropolitan University, University of Michigan, University of Montreal, New York University, University of Pennsylvania, Pennsylvania State University, Queen Mary University London, St. Mary-of-the-Woods College, University of Texas at Austin, and Yale University.

This project has been in the making for longer than I would like. In the interim have emerged conversations about postcolonial ecocriticism, the environmental humanities, and the Anthropocene, and my arguments have evolved in concert with those. What has also emerged in the past decade is a sense of just how formidable are the challenges and opponents we are up against. Since 2016, only a fool would confidently posit the nation (or ethnic chauvinism) as a vestige of some pre-global past.

Along the way I have received help and support from innumerable students, colleagues, and friends, a few of whom I want to acknowledge here.

My thinking about the questions in this book was honed in conversation with students in "Postcolonial Theory," "Postcolonial Ecologies," and "The Nature of Imperialism" at the University of Michigan and Columbia University. Research assistance from Cass Adair at Michigan and Veronica Belafi at Columbia was invaluable. I must thank Christi Merrill, Farina Mir, Scotti Parrish, Cathy Sanok, Megan Sweeney, Andrea Zemgulys at Michigan and Brent Edwards, Eleanor Johnson and Rosalind Morris at Columbia for incisive feedback and conversation. Juan Cole, Tom Keenan, and Bridget Hanna helped facilitate a trip to Bhopal. Ben Conisbee Baer generously talked me through aspects of Mahasweta Devi's Bengali and formalized translations of some sections of "Dhowli." I am indebted to Mary Louise Pratt for her enabling affirmations of this work, her timely assistance, and her luminous example and inspiration. I am particularly grateful for Tom Lay's nimbleness in bringing this project to fruition. As ever, Joey Slaughter has been a stalwart support and savvy reader; he is probably even more relieved than I am to see this book off my laptop(s) and into the world.

Although I did not know it at the time, the germinal moment of this book was when one of my graduate school advisors, Barbara Harlow, asked about my dissertation, "Rather than environmental degradation, what if you thought in terms of environmental justice, instead?" More than twenty years later, I'm still at work answering that question. This book, my sequel, is for Barbara.

NOTES

INTRODUCTION: READING FOR THE PLANET

1. See Deckard (2012); Heise (2012).

2. The hundred-year flood is better described as a flood with a 1 percent chance of occurring in any given year, yet it is precisely those probabilities that seem to be shifting in a changing climate. Note, too, a colloquial, scientifically imprecise scaling up of the word *ecology* to describe all issues of environment, climate, and the planet's capacity to support human life.

3. The "Earth system" concept considers interrelated processes through which Earth's various spheres (atmosphere, biosphere, cryosphere, geosphere, hydrosphere, lithosphere, pedosphere, etc.) function.

4. Previous forms of subsidy include the capture of human labor and natural resources and unfavorable terms in international "development" and debt servicing. See Wenzel (2015).

5. See Srinivasan et al. (2008).

6. On the other hand, it aligns with histories of the Anthropocene concept that begin with chemist Paul Crutzen and biologist Eugene Stoermer's 2000 essay.

7. Nixon makes a similar observation (2011, 249).

8. On the multiple frameworks for valuing nonhuman nature, see Martínez-Alier (2002, 149).

9. Postcolonial ecocriticism's "first wave" is arguably the decade between 2001 and 2011, beginning with essays by Susie O'Brien (2001), Graham Huggan (2004), and Rob Nixon (2005), who note the relative absence of attention to environmental concerns in postcolonial studies, and concluding with the publication of books that consolidated the field: Roos and Hunt (2010), Huggan and Tiffin (2010), Mukherjee (2010), DeLoughrey and Handley (2011), and Nixon (2011).

10. On narrative intelligence, see LeMenager (2013) and Ricoeur (1986).

11. See also Keenan (2002).

12. The idiom is ironic here, given its origin in Benjamin Disraeli's 1864 riff on Charles Darwin's disruptive view of the place of humans in the

cosmos. The opposite of angels for Disraeli was not devils, but apes: "Is man an ape or an angel? . . . I am on the side of the angels."

13. For a critique of ecocritics' wariness about acknowledging the literariness of their object of study, see Phillips (2003).

14. See Said (1983). Here I contest the Warwick Research Collective's dismissal: "It is surely a mistake, given its irrecuperable formalism, to attempt to defend the received disciplinary practice of 'close reading' in any strict sense. For the price of the rigorous examination of language and literature in institutionalised 'close reading' has invariably been abstraction from their social determinants and structuring conditions of existence" (2015, 26).

15. *Annals of the Association of American Geographers* (1934), quoted in the *Oxford English Dictionary* definition of "fundament."

16. See Cosgrove (2001) and Robbins (1999). Robbins asks, "What does it mean to take your slant on things from a B-17?" (2).

17. "Global risks activate and connect actors across borders who other-wise don't want to have anything to do with one another" (Beck 2009, 61).

18. "What kind of world does world literature let us imagine?" (Cheah 2016, 43); "what 'world' does world-literature demand be made visible?" (Warwick Research Collective 2015, 48).

19. Marx and Engels recognized dialectical affinities with Darwin's account of natural history, in which organism and environment are mutually determining, even as they modified its Malthusian emphasis on struggle. Tracing their reflections on Darwin and nature as the substrate of the social, Jason Moore concludes, "Nature shapes and is actively shaped by society" (2003, 449–50). Humans make their own history, but not under environmental circumstances of their choosing.

20. Both Casanova and Bruno Latour invoke the French parliamentary system as a model for alternative political arrangements involving a radically different kind of polity—Casanova's "world republic of letters," Latour's "republic of things" in *The Politics of Nature* (2004).

21. See http://www.london-futures.com/postcard_images.

22. In his brilliant critique of "The Coming Anarchy," Simon Dalby juxtaposes Kaplan's *Atlantic Monthly* article with advertisements in the magazine. An ad for Bombay Sapphire Distilled London Dry Gin features Queen Victoria on its label, which "suggests the legacy of colonialism and the commercial advantages gained by European powers in earlier geopolitical arrangements" ignored by Kaplan (1996, 481).

23. On the running-out-of-gas genre, see Wenzel (2017).

24. Compare Berlant's account of the pleasures of the conventional ordinary as dangerous attachment to a situation of "profound threat" (2011, 2); "how best to live on, considering" (3).

25. Lynn's remark about toxic residue "showing up worse on white people" echoes Maureen's observation that the dust and dirt of July's settlement show up worse on her children than on their black playmates.

1. CONSUMPTION FOR THE COMMON GOOD? COMMODITY BIOGRAPHY IN AN ERA OF POSTCONSUMERISM

1. After comparing whales' possible fate with that of North American buffalo (i.e., bison), Ishmael reassures himself with thoughts of the elephant's survival despite millennia of hunting (Melville [1851] 1993, 381). On shifts in the representation of whales, see Lawrence Buell (2001, 196–223).

2. See Lynn (1997) and Law (1995).

3. The *Pequod*'s "quaintness of both material and device" is described in terms of the grotesque and compared to a legendary bedstead upon which a medieval Icelandic hero carved images of his exploits (Melville [1851] 1993, 59). Queequeg's tattoos are revealed to be the archive of a cosmology, which he begins retranscribing on his unused coffin (396); Ishmael recorded the measurements of a whale skeleton in a tattoo on his arm, but he was sparing with the details in order to save room for a poem he was composing (373).

4. In an earlier guise, tusks did speak. Art historians surmise that tusks carved for Europeans evolved out of an earlier practice of carving tusks as oliphants, side-blown horns with holes carved for use in Kongo royal courts. See Bridges (2009).

5. My view is that both modes of reading are available; the syntagmatic, narrative relationship among figures along the spiral seems primary to the paradigmatic/juxtaposed relationship along the vertical axis, even if, from a single vantage point, the narrative can be read only in fragments. That Strother's view is not unanimous among art historians is evident in the National Museum for African Art's title for an online exhibit of a Loango tusk: "A Spiral of History." See National Museum for African Art (1998). Carvers elsewhere in Africa chose to align their figures along the tusks' vertical axis rather than carving in a spiral; see the Nigerian altar tusks held by the Metropolitan Museum of Art in New York.

6. Imre Szeman observes a similar dynamic in documentary films about oil, in which he finds a "blockage that seemingly no amount of conceptual thought *or* political activity looks likely to undo" (2012, 14). These films "proceed with the awareness that the importance of oil to social life is already well known, that publics have yet to adequately respond . . . [and] may be entirely unable to respond even if they believe once they see" (10).

7. Until the Chiquita-led challenge at the WTO, Jamaican bananas were exported under favorable terms stipulated by the Lomé Conventions,

trade and aid agreements between former European imperial states and African, Caribbean, and Pacific Countries (ACP).

8. See Nichols (1983).

9. See Spivak (1990, 163).

10. The motto "Trenton Makes, the World Takes" has been inscribed in neon on the Delaware River Bridge in Trenton, New Jersey, since 1935. The Chamber of Commerce adopted this motto in 1910, asserting Trenton's prominence in a phase of global capitalism that preceded the deindustrialization of the Global North. Once upon a time, Europe would "take" natural resources from its colonies with which to "make" consumer goods in its factories while suppressing industrialization elsewhere.

11. Commodity chain analysis tracks value creation through differentiated stages of production, often globally dispersed (Ramamurthy 2004, 739). Such analyses tend to be linear and unidirectional, "with an identifiable beginning from raw material to finished product and the orderly transmission of value from labor to capital" (747). Their narrative structure echoes Fordist logics of assembly: from cotton seed to camp shirt, or cocoa pod to chocolate bar.

12. This allegation is at the heart of the controversy surrounding *Darwin's Nightmare*, which elicited a furious backlash from the Tanzanian government. The "truth" about Mwanza, to the extent that a single truth exists, must lie somewhere between Sauper's atmospheric, suggestive documentary style and this heavy-handed response (including the alleged torture and documented threats of deportation against Sauper's journalist informant, Richard Mgamba). I do not disagree with social scientists Thomas Molony, Lisa Ann Richey, and Stefano Ponte that *Darwin's Nightmare* might reinforce "the power imbalances it claims to critique"; however, the same can be said of their "critical assessment" of the film (2007, 599). Their argument is not that no evidence exists of illicit arms traffic in Tanzania but that Sauper does not cite it in his film. Seeking to discredit Sauper, Molony et al. cite statements made by the film's informants about having been paid by Sauper and asked to "act" (600); however, they do not make clear that these statements were elicited in the state-organized backlash, an endeavor that (as they acknowledge later in their review) also disseminated "a couple of doctored images of Sauper posing with Saddam Hussein and Osama Bin Laden" (605). They indict Sauper for "speaking from the safety of Europe" (leaving his informants vulnerable to state pressure) while not acknowledging that the "evidence" they use against Sauper might have been produced under duress (606). Aside from their troubling use of what in US jurisprudence is called "fruit of the poisonous tree," their reductive reading of the film exemplifies one peril of

reading for the planet: seeking (or finding) transparent truth in a text whose logic eschews simple sentences in the declarative mood. To anticipate a Conradian metaphor later in this chapter, such readings only muddy the waters.

13. For invaluable perspective on the history of Nile perch and the social relations constellated around foodscapes and fisheries in the Great Lakes region, see Jennifer Lee Johnson (2017).

14. The credits identify this film as *Invaders: Animal Invaders/The Fresh Water Killers* (2000).

15. See Rivoli (2014) and Hansen (2000).

16. For an indispensable account of the aesthetic and economic aspects of coffee as commodity, twinned like the halves of a coffee bean, see Hitchcock (2003, 165–83).

17. The sacks and wheat are supplied by the United States Agency for International Development; a small USAID logo on the bottom of the sacks is dwarfed by "USA" printed in outsized letters.

18. *Black Gold*'s directors note that the 2002 Ethiopian famine spurred their interest; they included shots of Ethiopia's lush scenery in order to counter the dusty, flyblown image of Ethiopia established in 1980s international media coverage of famine.

19. Pollan describes industrial food production as "a journey of forgetting" (2006, 10), which echoes in synchronic terms what Robbins describes as a diachronic "forgetting" (2005, 460n10) of violent histories of colonial exploitation that put sugar in English (i.e., Chinese) tea, tobacco in European pipes, and enslaved Africans on New World plantations.

20. On "beautiful soul," see Timothy Morton (2007).

21. Alaimo analyzes a genre she calls "material memoir": narratives of environmental risk and toxic exposure that focus on *involuntary* "consumption" of harmful substances. Like commodity biographies, material memoirs situate protagonists within complex global webs of interrelation and demonstrate how "the very substance of the self is interconnected with vast biological, economic, and industrial systems that can never be entirely mapped or understood" (2011, 23).

22. Lizbeth Cohen (2003) argues that an ideology of mass consumption as an egalitarian project became synonymous with and thus eclipsed the ideal of citizenship in the United States after World War II, generating new class, gender, and race inequalities and evacuating the sphere of politics.

23. "The market that supposedly gives us 'free' choices . . . [has] been depriving us of the most important ones all along: choices about aggregate distribution of resources, of sustainability, of health and taste. . . . The conditions in which choices are made must be equalized more fully so that

'choice' is a more fair and meaningful indicator of actual desire" (Bartolovich 2010, 59, 49).

24. Abolitionist Thomas Clarkson linked consumer culture and activism in his remarks about the "am I not a man and a brother?" medallion that English potter Josiah Wedgwood produced for the Society for the Abolition of the Slave Trade's late eighteenth-century publicity campaign. The medallion became a fashion craze, inlaid with precious metals into gentlemen's snuffboxes and ladies' hairpins and jewelry, prompting Clarkson to articulate the possibilities of consumption for the common good: "At length the taste for wearing them became general; and thus fashion, which usually confines itself to worthless things, was seen for once in the honorable office of promoting the cause of justice, humanity and freedom" (1839, 417).

25. Raymond Williams quipped that the notion of human-as-consumer "is a way of seeing people as though they are either stomachs or furnaces. 'And what sort of effect will this have on the consumer?,' politicians ask, the consumer then being a very specialized variety of human being with no brain, no eyes, no senses, but who can gulp" (1989, 216).

26. This information appears on an eight-pack of Seventh Generation (emphasis in original).

2. HIJACKING THE IMAGINATION: HOW TO TELL THE STORY OF THE NIGER DELTA

1. I refer to Christopher Brown's illustration for the Heinemann's African Writers Series 1988 edition.

2. Davis cites Trefon (2004, 1).

3. Ferguson's argument hinges on a paradox of underdevelopment: "to say that people live lives that are structured by a modern capitalist world system or that they inhabit a social landscape shaped by modernist projects does not imply that they enjoy conditions of life that they themselves would recognize as modern" (2006, 168).

4. Consider the differences between the 1972 and 2004 editions of *Limits to Growth*, a landmark analysis that pioneered computer modeling to warn against "overshooting" the planet's carrying capacity. Since the first edition, the authors have acknowledged the dangers posed by overconsumption in the Global North, as opposed to their initial focus on anticipated population growth in the Global South. Even in 1972, they recognized that if developed nations proposed to "freeze the status quo of economic development . . . it would be taken as a final act of neocolonialism" (Meadows et al. 2004, 194). See also Harvey (1996); Curtin (1999).

5. The 1960 and 1963 constitutions mandated that the federal government share 50 percent of mineral royalties and rents with the relevant states.

However, this derivation formula was a casualty of Nigeria's protracted periods of military rule, during which miniscule percentages (1.5–3%) were allotted to oil-producing areas and considerable amounts disappeared into individual overseas accounts. In 2000, the derivation to Niger Delta states increased to 13 percent, but many argue that this increased revenue has lined the pockets of state governors rather than benefiting communities in the region.

6. The Niger Delta region encompasses several distinct ecosystems of significant biodiversity: coastal islands, brackish creeks and mangrove swamps, rainforest, and agricultural lands formerly so productive that the region was dubbed Nigeria's breadbasket.

7. In a secret 1994 memo to the governor of Rivers State, Internal Security Task Force commander Lt. Col. Paul Olusola Okuntimo wrote that "Shell's operations still impossible unless ruthless military operations are undertaken for smooth economic activities to commence" (quoted in Rowell, Marriott, and Stockman 2005, 15).

8. Adam Nossiter (2010) does the math: Every year, the equivalent of one *Exxon Valdez* (11 million gallons) spills in the Niger Delta; the BP spill was estimated at 2.5 million gallons a day.

9. I use *hospitality* in Edward Said's sense of a "profound humanistic spirit deployed with generosity . . . [in which] the interpreter's mind actively makes a place in it for a foreign Other" (2003, xxv).

10. Some secrets of the slick alliance hide in plain sight. A 2009 classified US diplomatic cable disseminated by WikiLeaks has Shell's Ann Pickard boasting that the company "had seconded people to all of the relevant [Nigerian] ministries . . . and consequently had access to everything that was being done in those ministries"—a fact Pickard says the Nigerian government "had forgotten." This amnesia turns on its head Sir John Robert Seeley's infamous quip about empire and fits of absentmindedness. See Dearing (2010).

11. On the vexed question of a Nigerian national literature, see Lindfors (1975) and Sullivan (2001).

12. See Wenzel (2006). I stumbled into political ecology around 2003, when literary studies offered little help in making sense of Nigerian texts about petroleum and palm wine. In their 2015 preface to the second edition of *Postcolonial Ecocriticism*, Graham Huggan and Helen Tiffin write, "Postcolonial ecocriticism might be best described today as a branch of environmental humanities that is heavily influenced by, but non-identical with, political ecology."

13. Writing of spatial, social, and ideological displacements caused by megadams, Nixon describes "unimagined communities" as those who are

left out in the imagining of Andersonian national community (2011, 150–74). I use *unimagining* in a more transitive sense to name how a socio-ecological polity is *unmade*, or a crisis is made to exceed the capacity to be imagined.

14. The shale gas revolution in the United States was enabled by technological innovations (e.g., horizontal drilling and hydraulic fracturing, or "fracking") that outpaced the regulatory and infrastructural capacity to capture natural gas.

15. *Petro-naira* refers to oil money in Nigeria, whose currency is the naira. In 1966, Nigeria had three states and fifty local governments; by 2004, there were thirty-six states and nearly one thousand local governments (Watts 2004, 292).

16. "Youth" movements are relevant to Saro-Wiwa's death. His Movement for the Survival of the Ogoni People challenged traditional forms of leadership; this intergenerational power struggle and the deaths of several elders sparked the charges of instigating murder that led to his execution.

17. Fanon's insistence that the anticolonial violence is a dialectical response to colonial violence resonates with Adichie's observation that stories of injustice too often begin from "secondly."

18. Watts and Kashi spoke at the University of Michigan in March 2009. I initially misheard Watts worrying that the book was a "promo for men"—a legitimate concern, given the book's scopic attention to laboring or militant male bodies. Cioffi's *Sweet Crude* (2010) offers an important corrective: It eschews masculinist militant heroism and details how women and men, mothers and sons grapple with violence and nonviolence as responses to dispossession and repression.

19. This statement also appears in Sebastian Junger's 2007 *Vanity Fair* profile of MEND.

20. A devastating anatomy of an ABC News interview with a MEND militant who is quizzed incessantly about Jomo Gbomo (whom he says he's never heard of) demonstrates how the region's complexities are reduced to a ridiculous narrative of MEND as "terrorists," in the post-9/11 sense of al-Qaeda sympathizers posing a direct threat to the United States. The genius of Cioffi's media critique is her juxtaposition of the brief, sensationalist story that ABC viewers saw with footage of the tense interview that ended up on the cutting room floor, inconvenient to the story ABC wanted to tell. Cioffi expresses bitter disappointment over the lost opportunity for media exposure. Nigeria briefly became the face of foreign oil in the United States, but this act of reimagining was constrained by the media's dominant narrative templates.

21. My point is not that communism no longer exists, but that this statement responds to an implicit imputation of communism by the interna-

tional media or the Nigerian state that is strange and anachronistic, not least because Nigeria lacks a strong socialist or communist tradition.

22. In a 2009 review article, Adam Groves examines the paradox that Shell's post-1995 turn to corporate social responsibility and community engagement led to cooperation with "those actors which pose a tangible threat to its interests." In other words, Shell recognizes men with guns—or even arms them in an attempt to co-opt resistance by hiring local groups on "surveillance contracts."

23. Note that both senses are implicit in the English word *thug*, which derives from Hindi and bears traces of British colonial anxiety about the menace of "thuggee," described as organized gangs of bandits and thief-assassins.

24. In Ifowodo's *The Oil Lamp*, government officials use radio and newspaper to cast blame for the Jese explosion upon "a dangerous band of youths sworn to sabotage / for redress of perceived wrongs" (2005, 15).

25. The Odi massacre occurred shortly after the death of General Sani Abacha in 1998 and the restoration of civilian rule in May 1999, when Olusegun Obasanjo was elected president; the massacre and the spokesman's invocation of human rights occurred at a moment when Nigeria sought to redeem its image as a democracy after fifteen years of military rule.

26. A counterexample of mobilization across ethnic lines was the Chicoco Movement of the late 1990s, which opposed the proliferation of new local governments based on ethnicity. Founder Oronto Douglas described Chicoco [also Chikoko] as a "Pan Niger Delta Resistance move-ment committed to reclaiming our humanity." Its charter dedicated the movement to the "struggling unity of these ethnic minority nationalities against our common oppressors," which included the Nigerian state and elites and the oil multinationals (quoted in Ukeje 2001, 29). *Chicoco* refers to the soil of mangrove swamps, which fosters aquatic life, prevents erosion, and can be used in building dwellings and land reclamation: "To the people of the Niger Delta, Chicoco is a balm" (36n35).

27. See Wenzel (2017, 5–7).

28. Fanon's discussion of natural resources in *The Wretched of the Earth* resonates with the efforts of newly independent nation-states to establish in international law the principle of Permanent Sovereignty over Natural Resources. See Anghie (2004) and Wenzel (2015).

29. See Mamdani (1996) and Comaroff and Comaroff (1991).

30. *Curse of the Black Gold* documents relationships between particular companies and local/ethnic formations: King Egi of Ogbaland in his reception room funded by Total/Elf (2008, 106–7); a maternity clinic in Nkoro built by Total, which the photo's caption commends as a model

community/infrastructural development project (176–77). *Sweet Crude*
originated as a commissioned documentary on the 2005 opening of the
Niger Delta Friendship Library in the Delta State village of Oporoza, which
marked the cessation of hostilities between rival Ijaw factions. The library
was funded by Chevron and the US NGO Global Citizen Journey. Oporoza
was bombed by the Nigerian Joint Task Force in May 2009, after production
of *Sweet Crude* concluded.

    31. See the SPDC (Shell) internal working paper, "Peace and Security in
the Niger Delta," by WAC Global Services (2003).

    32. "If under 'colonial globalization' . . . direct political control was needed
to organize primary commodity production and trade within restricted
markets, then under neoliberal globalization, the unregulated production and
free circulation of primary commodities in the open market requires a
significant dismantling of state controls previously oriented toward the
protection of national industries. Before, the exploitation of primary commodities took place through the visible hand of politics; now it is organized by
the ostensibly invisible hand of the market in combination with the less
prominent, but no less necessary, helping hand of the state" (Coronil 2001, 75).

    33. Ukeje argued that even rhetorical flirtation with secession became
politically untenable after the early trauma of Igbo secession in Biafra
during the first decade of independence (2001). The Niger Delta region (and
its oil) was contained within the territory declared as the Republic of Biafra;
the Biafra secession of 1967–70 was immediately preceded by the brief
secession of ethnic minorities who proclaimed a Niger Delta Republic.
Secessionist impulses have reemerged in the twenty-first century: for
example, in 2011, the Niger Delta Liberation Force cited the example of
South Sudan as a precedent for a revived Niger Delta Republic—an aspiration also voiced in 2016 by the Niger Delta Avengers. See Amaize (2011).

    34. Ferguson argues, "popular legitimacy in Africa requires a perception
not simply of *'good government'* (efficient and technically functional institutions) but of *a government that is 'good'* (morally benevolent and protective of
its people). . . . Africans continue to regard the state largely as a malevolent
and ever hungry predator and to perceive it not as an expression of their
collective will but as an instrument of the exploiters" (2006, 85).

    35. Figures vary and oil prices are volatile, but a 2014 Nigerian Extractive
Industries Transparency Initiative audit published in 2016 found that
77 percent of revenues collected by the state were from oil and gas (Malden
2017, 2). See also https://eiti.org/nigeria#eiti-reports-and-other-key
-documents.

    36. Reno distinguishes between internal and external sovereignty:
"Weak state–foreign firm partnerships benefit from *international order* that

international norms create. Thus armed, these partners exploit *internal disorder* to manipulate sovereign prerogatives to exclude commercial and political rivals, violently appropriate resources, and shield transactions from the eyes of outsiders. . . . Their actual exercise of power strays from conventional norms of internal state sovereignty, but conforms outwardly to outsiders' expectations that a state system exists everywhere in the world" (2001, 199). Some "failed" states have no difficulty achieving what international capital requires: "the biggest 'failures' have been among the *most* successful at developing capital-attracting enclaves" (Ferguson 2006, 40). Other states are declared failures to pave the way for neocolonial intervention, "as globalization interpellates and mediates the viability of states according to value extraction and trade" (Hitchcock 2007, 746).

37. Nigerian political scientist Claude Ake dubbed this dynamic the "privatization of the state" (1996, 42).

38. Note also the coincidence in 1958 of the first oil exported from Nigeria to England, the opening of the first British motorway (the M6), and the first transatlantic passenger flights from London to New York (Rowell, Marriott, and Stockman 2005, 66–67).

39. This palimpsest of resource frontiers in the Niger Delta is legible in the Escravos export terminal, whose name derives from the Portuguese word for slaves.

40. Consider, for example, how topographical differences shaped the Ogoni and Ijaw movements: "the Ogoni territory is located on an easily accessible, land-based hinterland, while much of the Ijaw areas are tucked within thick mangroves, swampy areas and poorly demarcated creeks and rivers that serve as strong barriers to effective policing" (Ukeje 2001, 26).

41. In her contribution to *Curse of the Black Gold*, "My Blessing, My Curse," novelist Kaine Agary depicts the Niger Delta as a beautiful woman with a succession of "lovers from foreign lands" (i.e., Arabs, Portuguese, and a last one "whiter than white"). Within this bodyscape/landscape, petroleum is eroticized: "From my head grew great big bunches of plantain; out of my pores oozed palm oil; my legs stood long and strong, the healthiest of rubber trees; in my mouth swam schools of fish to feed my grown children; between my legs was a secret treasure buried so deep that as many times as they were with me, my early lovers didn't find it" (2008, 152).

42. An alternative bodily metaphor for petro-modernity was offered in 1939 by Paul W. Litchfield, president of Goodyear Tire & Rubber: "Think of our industrial structure as a living thing, the skeleton of which is composed of metal and cement, the arterial system of which carries a life stream of oil, and the flexing muscles and sinews of which are of rubber." See Tully (2011, 17).

43. Hardin invokes Alfred North Whitehead's account of dramatic tragedy as "the solemnity of the remorseless working of things" (1968, 1244): Hardin's "tragedy of the commons" is a drama of remorseless exploitation and using-up. Whitehead's definition resonates with that compiled by Ato Quayson, who contemplates the relationship between historical event and classical dramatic form in reading Saro-Wiwa's struggle and death through the lens of tragedy: "Saro-Wiwa is a tragic hero because he committed himself to his people but could not possibly have controlled all the forces he unleashed" (2003, 75). In Chapter 3, I consider the relationship between colonial designations of "waste" (or unproductive) lands, and the historical creation of wasted lands, laid waste through overexploitation. For Hardin, the "commons" is something like waste land inevitably transformed into wasted land. Given the scorn with which Hardin is greeted in progressive environmental circles, it is worth noting that he worries about pollution in the industrial, chemical, nuclear era as a problem of not having closed "the commons . . . as a place for waste disposal" (Hardin 1968, 1248)—an urgent issue in the Anthropocene.

44. Additional relevant legislation included the Oil in Navigable Waters Act of 1968 and the Exclusive Economic Zone (EEZ) Decree of 1978. See Obi (2010, 223). These laws reconfigure for the postcolonial era the British colonial legal framework, which, as discussed below, guaranteed a monopoly to Shell-BP that facilitated the discovery and early development of commercial oil deposits.

45. Compare Saro-Wiwa's imputation of *international* criminality resulting from the state's expropriation of oil: "the 'Nigerian' oil which the Americans, Europeans and Japanese buy is stolen property: it has been seized from its owners by force of arms and has not been paid for" (1992, 8).

46. The District Commissioner and his book *The Pacification of the Primitive Tribes of the Lower Niger* reappear in Achebe's *Arrow of God*. One likely historical target of Achebe's (and Ifowodo's) parody is Arthur Glyn Leonard's *The Lower Niger and Its Tribes* (1906), which explains the ethnology and religion of inhabitants (what Leonard terms "naturism") in terms of the environment of the Niger Delta. The discussion of imperialism and the pathetic fallacy in Chapter 3 returns to Leonard's text.

47. Major Kitemo is based on Paul Olusola Okuntimo, commander of the Rivers State Internal Security Task Force who has been identified as a liaison between Shell and the Nigerian military in the 1990s repression of the Ogoni. Okuntimo wrote the Wiki-leaked memo urging "ruthless military operations" to "smooth" Shell's operations; he also recommended "wasting operations during MOSOP and other gatherings, making constant military presence justifiable," as well as "wasting targets cutting across

communities and leadership cadres, especially vocal individuals in various groups." (Here *wasting* denotes rapid gunfire.) Evidence from the *Wiwa et al., vs. Royal Dutch Petroleum et al.* cluster of lawsuits, filed in 1996 and settled for $15.5 million in 2009, implicates Okuntimo in the murders of four Ogoni elders which Saro-Wiwa was executed for allegedly inciting.

48. In "On National Culture," Fanon writes, "National consciousness, which is not nationalism, is the only thing that will give us an international dimension" (1968, 247).

49. "Baptizing the Gun" was Akpan's first published story, which was published in Kenya mere days after he submitted it to the *Hekima Review* in 2000; it appeared in the *New Yorker* in 2010.

50. There are suggestive resonances between Akpan's "Luxurious Hearses" and the literature of Partition in South Asia—particularly Khuswant Singh's *Mano Majra* (Train to Pakistan) and the short stories of Saadat Hasan Manto that deal with mass migrations across the newly drawn border. Akpan's novella can also be juxtaposed with the bus journey of concerned citizens that structures Karen King-Aribisala's *Kicking Tongues* (1998), which stages a mobile national allegory by borrowing the conceit of pilgrimage as frame narrative from Chaucer's *Canterbury Tales*.

51. Nigerian literary critics Ikenna Kamalu and Isaiah Fortress demonstrate how Akpan stages these divides at the linguistic level, making audible/legible in English his characters' various accents (Hausa/Fulani; Igbo; Niger Delta Urhobo and Calabar) and dialects (Standard Nigerian Pidgin English) (2011, 214–17).

52. In *Imagined Communities*, Anderson observes that "advances in communications technology, especially radio and television, give print allies unavailable a century ago. Multilingual broadcasting can conjure up the imagined community to illiterates and populations with different mother-tongues" (1991, 135).

53. The narrative compression of Jibreel's execution contrasts with the interminable journey and dilatory narrative of "Luxurious Hearses"—a tension that feels related to the disjunct timescales of fossil fuels. If, as Timothy Mitchell writes, "the equivalent of the earth's entire production of plant and animal life for 400 years was required to produce the fossil fuels we burn in a single year," and that organic matter had to fossilize over millions of years, then to combust fossil fuels is to consume time itself (2009, 402).

54. During the transition to independence, a British colonial commission headed by Sir Henry Willink was charged with addressing concerns expressed at the 1954 Constitutional Convention that Nigeria's majority ethnic groups would dominate the hundreds of minority groups in the three

proposed regions of the independent Nigerian federation. The Willink Commission Report (1958) recommended constitutional protections of individual rights at the federal level rather than a system of smaller states charged with representing minority and regional interests.

55. The gap between these images—an internal wrong turning, and an external assault—reflect the nuance in Achebe's account of colonialism, which insists on recognizing "our own sins and blasphemies," most notably, the acceptance of racial inferiority (43).

56. The first discovery of commercially viable oil deposits in the Niger Delta, at Oloibiri in 1956, was facilitated by the British colonial legal framework, which allowed only British firms to prospect for oil in the Nigerian colonies and thus guaranteed Shell-BP's monopoly in a colonial version of the petro-state: "to Shell-BP, the colonial government was more than just a favourable government: Shell-BP's interests in Nigeria and those of the British state were completely intertwined" (Rowell et al. 2005, 54–59). Shell-BP lost its monopoly in 1959, at the beginning of a decade of largely unregulated development of the oil industry in Nigeria (Obi 2010, 229–30).

57. "Petro-magic" is Watts's felicitous paraphrase of Coronil's argument about the magical aspects of the oil state; see Watts (1999, 7).

58. Apter links the magical aspects of oil to occult practices of "money magic" in southern Nigeria, whereby human blood and body parts are illicitly transmuted into currency (2005, 50). He cites Karin Barber's classic essay, "Popular Reactions to the Petro-Naira."

59. The emphasis on the number 1,001 in Ifowodo's dedication and epigraph recurs at the end of *The Oil Lamp*, in a couplet "copied" from a poem being written by Major Kitemo's "nemesis," the schoolboy-turned-law-student (and poet): "*I remember the dew, / the one thousand and one gone, and what will remain true*" (2005, 56).

60. Relevant here are philosophical treatments of nonhuman external nature transformed by human activity, ranging in the Western tradition from Cicero through Kant, Hegel, and Karl Marx, to Leo Marx and the Frankfurt School. Neil Smith reviews this tradition in his account of the "production of nature" (2008). Arturo Escobar's (2008) *technonature* reso-nates with my interest in material landscapes and ecosystems, as opposed to the human subjectivities and social institutions of *second nature*.

61. Marx demonstrates how the short-term rhythms of capitalist produc-tion disregard slower, longer organic cycles of growth and renewal, thereby "robbing the soil" of fertility and making sustainable forestry "an industry of little attraction to capitalist enterprise" (1977, 1:637–38, 2:244).

62. These rust flakes link Ifowodo's infernal landscape to "flakes of fire" in Dante's *Inferno*, another epigraph in *The Oil Lamp*.

63. The African oil palm, *Elaeis guineensis*, yields wine, oil, and kernels. Unlike palm wine, which spoils quickly and does not travel well, palm oil and palm kernel were drawn into global circuits of exchange. The European trade in palm oil and palm kernel in West Africa dates back to the 1480s and was worth a million pounds by 1840. In the colonial era, Nigeria's Oil Rivers region was named for palm oil, not petroleum, and palm oil was as indispensable for nineteenth-century industry as petroleum was for twentieth-century industry: palm oil (known as "Lagos oil") was used as an industrial lubricant, an edible oil, and in the making of soap, tin, and candles. Beyond their significance as exportable commodities, palm oil and palm kernel have been used locally for edible oil, food, and lighting; the tree yields materials for building, roofing, and other household uses. Within the riverine economy of the Oil Rivers region, jars of palm oil functioned as currency. See Lynn (1997).

64. For a reading of *The Palm-Wine Drinkard* in terms of petro-magic and the political ecology of oil and literature in Nigeria, see Wenzel (2006).

65. There are echoes of Okri's story in a field report circulated by the Nigerian NGO Environmental Rights Action, which opens with testimony from John Erakpoke, a palm wine tapper whose business disintegrated after a December 1999 pipeline rupture in Adeje. Erakpoke laments, "Nobody wants to drink palm wine again, they say it is poisoned." The report does not specify whether he joined those who began collecting and selling the spilled premium motor spirit after it ruined their farms. See Raphael (2000).

66. Ato Quayson argues that, since Okri is Urhobo rather than Yoruba, his allusions to Fagunwa and his deployment of Yoruba narrative and cosmological traditions reflect the "development of a broadly Nigerian consciousness," intimating the possibility of a national literature produced through "strategic filiation with a specific discursive field irrespective of ethnic identity" (1997, 101–2). In this view, interethnic intertextuality fosters reimagining of national community.

67. See Faris (2004) and Cooper (1998). Gaylard (2006) offers a more expansive view of this mode of writing on the continent.

68. Carpentier's first articulation of "lo real maravilloso Americano" was in the prologue to his novel *El reino de este mundo* (1949). He returned to the question in an afterword to *Los pasos perdidos* (1953). See Roh (1923) and Carpentier (1949).

69. Magical (or animist) realism reinvigorates what John Ruskin, in 1856, called the "pathetic fallacy"—a literary-critical intervention articulated at a moment when perceptions of the relationships among (human) sentience and affect, natural landscapes, and inanimate objects were a crucial axis for producing colonial difference. Chapter 3 considers further the literary and ideological stakes of personifying nature.

70. For analyses of postcolonial literature as the marketing of cultural difference, see Huggan (2001) and Brouillette (2007). Anatomizing the sociology of global literary circulation, they argue that marketing and other editorial pressures not only determine what gets published, but also shape what gets written. In this context, representation and reception are not easily separated.

71. Bissoondath is less interested in Okri's engagement with contemporary Nigeria than his evocation of "truths" about "what, for want of a better term, we call the third world" (1989).

72. This chapter aims to create a stereoscopic view from what Coronil called the "split vision" distinguishing South American novelists from social scientists: "On one side we would see an elusive continent where history unfolds as the wild offspring of a unique merger of the real and the magical. On the other we would recognize pale replicas of canonical first-world nations, societies not so much different as incomplete, whose history, while traversing thwarted paths, is supposed to evolve toward familiar ends" (1997, 122).

73. BP blocked the attempted rescue of endangered sea turtles from contaminated areas, even though turtles and other wildlife were obviously trapped in "corral areas" or "burn boxes" where BP was burning off spilled oil. Some commentators suggest that BP intentionally burned the turtles, to destroy evidence of their deaths. Under the Endangered Species Act, the death of each protected turtle carries a $50,000 fine (Murphy 2010).

74. The Ijaw god of war, Egbesu, offers invincibility to those fighting a just war. See Pratten (2008).

75. For analysis of bulletproof claims in terms of "magic," "superstition," and various forms of Christianity in colonial contexts, see Wenzel (2009).

76. Habila broke onto the international scene in 2001 with a short story in which his aspiring writer-protagonist is advised, "The quickest way to make it as a poet [in Nigeria] is to get arrested": the resulting visibility will mean an end to visa troubles and maybe even "an international award." To adapt this critique of the curious economy of domestic political repression and international literary prestige, *Oil on Water* implies that the "quickest way to make it" as a journalist in Nigeria might be to scoop an interview with a missing white woman.

77. A more interesting intertext for *Oil on Water* is Cyprian Ekwensi's *People of the City* (1954), whose young journalist character Amusa Sango is a forebear of Rufus, also concerned with the contradictory intersections of journalistic careerism and nation-building. *Oil on Water* can also be juxtaposed with Chris Cleave's bestseller *Little Bee* (2009; published in the UK as *The Other Hand*)—whose protagonist is a Nigerian adolescent in London fleeing what she calls the "African oil wars." Both novels combine mid-

market appeal with media critique. It overstates their literary ambitions to call this pair a latter-day version of *Heart of Darkness* meets *Season of Migration to the North*; as with Conrad's and Salih's novels, however, their characters' trajectories are complementary—white woman in the Niger Delta, Nigerian girl in London.

78. Huggan and Tiffin worry about politically engaged literature and criticism instrumentalizing the aesthetic and reducing the literary, "as if transparent messages were all that were contained within even the most factual of non-fictional reports" (2010, 41). This chapter attends to questions of form across genres and media in order to challenge the assumption that "transparency" is a necessary corollary of political commitment.

79. See Obi (2001, 177, 181) and Nixon (2011, 111–12, 234–35). Quayson argues for Saro-Wiwa's "world-historical significance. The fight for a right to a clean earth, the struggle against a negating totalitarianism and the predatory privations unleashed by international capital, and the effort to arouse a silent people into an engagement with their history are all values that give his activism a resonance beyond Ogoniland" (2003, 74).

80. Polycyclic aromatic hydrocarbons (PAH) are associated with respiratory and skin problems, infertility, cancer, and genotoxic effects. Studies of PAH found in air, sediment, and soil in the Niger Delta investigate its sources (petroleum extraction, gas flaring, natural occurrence) and implications for human health. See, for example, Ana, Shridar, and Emerole (2012).

81. In "Imperial Debris," Ann Laura Stoler writes, "how easy it is to slip between metaphor and material object, between infrastructure and imagery, between remnants of matter and mind. The point of critical analysis is not to look 'underneath' or 'beyond' that slippage but to understand what work that slippage does and the political traffic it harbors" (2008, 203).

82. The frisson of Detroit ruins porn derives partly from the cognitive dissonance of First World third nature: trees and grasses reclaim abandoned neighborhoods, urban monuments, and rust-ruined industrial sites as the afterlife of deindustrialization. As I discuss in Chapter 3, the abandoned site of the Union Carbide factory in Bhopal looks similar: a poisonous nature preserve amid cramped urban settlement, with trees growing up through the machinery of destruction.

83. "The sale of stolen oil from the Niger Delta has had the same pernicious influence on that region's conflict as diamonds did in the wars in Angola and Sierra Leone. The proceeds from oil theft are used to buy weapons and ammunition, helping to sustain the armed groups that are fighting the federal government" (US Institute for Peace 2009, 2).

84. In an assessment more sober and sympathetic to the causes of Niger Delta resistance, Cyril Obi estimates that the Nigerian oil industry lost

10 percent of its capacity in 2009 to bunkering, in addition to a shutdown of between 25 and 40 percent of production capacity resulting from attacks on oil installations in the 2005–9 spike in militant insurgency (2010, 220).

85. In the forgotten annals of corporate history lies the ironic fact that the entity granted a concession in the Niger Delta in the 1950s was the Shell-BP Petroleum Development Company.

86. Shell's PR efforts after Saro-Wiwa's execution involved then-innovative mechanisms to create the illusion of interactivity and consumer-citizen participation. The 1998 print publication *Profits and Principles* included postcards for readers to mail back to the company, and the website (which briefly featured a short story by Saro-Wiwa) invited visitors to "'Tell-Shell' what you think" (Rowell, Marriott, and Stockman 2005, 120–24).

3. FROM WASTE LANDS TO WASTED LIVES: ENCLOSURE AS AESTHETIC REGIME AND PROPERTY REGIME

1. See Johnson (2012) on waste in medieval England, which entailed *overuse* and despoliation of land and a refusal to labor. Cronon (1995) historicizes wilderness and its cultural logics: Whereas Lockean waste awaits the infusion of labor, post-nineteenth-century wilderness awaits the infusion of leisure.

2. Locke's argument-by-encroachment does acknowledge a difference between the constraints of his seventeenth century present and the "first peopling of the great common of the world," when "it was quite otherwise" (2:35). However, the American continent functions as deus ex machina, reopening the earth to limitless enclosure. There is so much land in America that without others to trade with, "It would not be worth the enclosing" (2:48). As if performing Locke's logic of surplus, this rhetorical sleight-of-hand happens twice in "Of Property." See 2:36 and 2:45.

3. Hardin makes a fundamental category error, confusing a "commons" for open access or *terra nullius* and failing to recognize that common property *is* a property regime, subject to social norms and regulations. Hardin acknowledged as much in 1991, clarifying that his concern was an *unmanaged* commons. Locke made a similar distinction, in suspect civilizational and geographic terms: He distinguished commons-by-compact in England from the unclaimed wastes of America.

4. Bartolovich asks: "What if private property produces what it proposes to cure?" noting "the curious return of resource crises at ever expanding scales following the enclosure that is supposed to prevent it" (2010, 46).

5. In "Searching the World for Timber," in his *Forests and Sea Power* (1926), R. G. Albion traces how the British frantically sought to secure timber in Canada, the Baltic, Brazil, the Cape Colony in southern Africa,

Madagascar, and New Zealand. Indian teak provided an alternative, although competition in extraction and shipbuilding from the French, Dutch and Portuguese had to be dispatched. Grove identifies this historical moment as the first recognition of "the global strategic value of a raw material" (1996, 391)—a precursor to the geopolitical centrality of oil.

6. Preston writes that a hundred-year-old oak tree worth £5 "has at that Age done Ten Pounds worth of Mischief" (quoted in Albion 1926, 119).

7. Jones also advocated the professionalization of science (particularly botany) in India. He read Linnaeus; his correspondence with imperial botanist Sir Joseph Banks shaped the establishment of botanical gardens in India, connected with those in other British colonies and the Royal Botanical Gardens at Kew (Grove 1996, 340–41). EIC sponsorship of scientific inquiry facilitated botanist/surgeons' observations of changes in precipitation and soil and atmospheric conditions, discussed below.

8. A sly parody of Macaulay's ostentatiously ignorant judgment and belittling ratios appears in Salman Rushdie's introduction to *Mirrorwork: 50 Years of Indian Writing 1947–1997*. After admitting (like Macaulay) that he doesn't read the relevant languages, Rushdie declares, "the prose writing . . . in this period by Indian writers *working in English*, is proving to be a stronger and more important body of work than most of what has been produced in the 16 'official languages' of India . . . during the same time, and indeed, this new, and still burgeoning, 'Indo-Anglian' literature represents perhaps the most valuable contribution India has yet made to the world of books" (1997, viii). Rushdie made this assertion to justify his inclusion of only one translated text (Saadat Hasan Manto's Urdu masterpiece, "Toba Tek Singh") in his 550-page anthology. Rushdie's judgment elevates a few decades of postcolonial Indian writing in English over millennia of Indian texts championed by Jones.

9. As discussed later in this chapter, "jungle," as a misleading English cognate and translation of the Sanskrit word *jāṅgala*, can describe areas of secondary growth where agriculture has been abandoned.

10. On Pattullo, see Guha 1963, 42–49.

11. Nicholson's *The Forests from Within* was a pamphlet for a popular audience. Dedicated to "the people of Bihar and Orissa," it repeatedly addresses "you"—owners of forests for which the Forest Departments are "custodians of a great State property" (1926, 30, 65).

12. See also McCay and Acheson: "the tragedy of the commons is not only one of destruction by self-interested exploitation. It is a tragedy of rural impoverishment and agrarian crisis caused by the loss of common rights" (1987, 24). They cite Ciriacy-Wantrup and Bishop's 1975 formulation, "tragedy of the commoners."

13. In other words, forests reserved by the state and barred to local users can exclude even without enclosure as private property—a process Vandergeest and Peluso (1995) theorize as territorialization. For an account of Anderson's report and his conflict with the Forest Department, see Chhatre (2003). On rivalries between foresters and other colonial officials, see Rajan (2006, 97–100).

14. On the other hand, the 1997 Indian Supreme Court decision in *M. C. Mehta v. Kamal Nath et al.* held that the public trust doctrine from Roman and English common law applied to India: "The Public Trust Doctrine primarily rests on the principle that certain resources like air, sea, waters and the forests have such a great importance to the people as a whole that it would be wholly unjustified to make them a subject of private ownership. The said resources being a gift of nature, they should be made freely available to everyone irrespective of the status in life. The doctrine enjoins upon the Government to protect the resources for the enjoyment of the general public rather than to permit their use for private ownership or commercial purposes. . . . Every generation owes a duty to all succeeding generations to develop and conserve the natural resources of the nation in the best possible way. It is in the interest of mankind. It is in the interest of the nation" (quoted in Singh 2012). *Public trust* is a rather different orientation toward nature than Locke's "common stock."

15. See Martínez-Alier (2002).

16. *Adivasi* is the aggregate name for India's diverse indigenous peoples (also known as "tribals"); it means "first inhabitant."

17. Bonded labor is a form of indebted servitude outlawed in India in 1976 but widely practiced nonetheless. Gyan Prakash (1990) argues that "bonded labor" as a category emerged through British colonial misrecognition of seasonal labor relations between landowners and tenants in southern Bihar. In Mahasweta's story, Dhowli's father became his landlord's bondservant after borrowing money for Dhowli's wedding, but, unlike in Mahasweta's other fiction, this detail does not drive the plot.

18. Mahasweta's use of multiple registers of Bengali (and English), and the politics of her writer-advocacy, pose challenges for her translators. The only published English translation of "Dhowli" is by Kalpana Bardhan, whom Minoli Salgado argues takes a "liberal feminist," intersubjective and individualizing approach, in comparison with the intersectional granularity of social critique emphasized by Pinaki Bhattacharya, whose translations of "Shishu" she compares (2000, 139). Salgado situates her analysis of Mahasweta's translators within a broader account of the pressures on translation within a global literary marketplace. I have discussed this problem with Ben Conisbee Baer, and later in the chapter I use his unpublished translation of

the end of "Dhowli" in order to get somewhat closer to the starkness of Mahasweta's language.

19. Mahasweta's "Douloti the Bountiful," a story about bonded prostitution, describes female bodies similarly: "the boss has turned them into land,/The boss ploughs and ploughs their land and raises the crop" (1995, 59). These indictments of women treated as agricultural land contrast with the metonymic association between Mary Oraon and the forest in Mahasweta's "The Hunt." Indeed, "Dhowli" reverses the plot of "The Hunt"; whereas Mary slyly arranges to tryst with her tormentor in the forest and slays him with a machete, Dhowli fends off the forest contractor at her hut by mentioning a knife. "The Hunt" valorizes a link between women and nature in Mary's defense of herself in the forest. Dhowli's relation to the forest, by contrast, is self-consciously mediated through the cultural tradition of forest tales she imagines herself into.

20. Historically, the Dusad *jati* (caste) would have been deemed "untouchable," at the bottom of the Hindu social order. Constitutionally protected (as Scheduled Castes), such communities now tend to identify as Dalits. By "ritual ecology," I mean everyday practices regulating caste purity and pollution, with consequences at scales ranging from the body to the cosmos. The relationship between ritual ecology and ecology *an sich* is not necessarily metaphorical. Gadgil and Guha argue that traditional intercaste divisions of labor and nature play a role in managing human impacts on the environment (1993, 91–110)—a view challenged by Guha (2001). U. R. Ananthamurty's Kannada-language novel *Samskara* (1965) examines the relationship between Hindu ritual ecology and environmental health and pollution.

21. Another name for the grounds for claiming the right to survival is *commons*; Bartolovich identifies the symbolic and social role of commons in early modern England, as sites where the rural population negotiated the distribution of resources and set limits to their "own exclusion from control over access to food, fuel, and other means of subsistence" (2010, 56).

22. Here I draw on an unpublished translation by Ben Conisbee Baer, because of the interpretive pressure I put on this passage. See note 18 on the problems of translating Mahasweta's prose. Bardan's translation reads: "The bus starts speeding, and her village recedes. The sun rises, and Dhowli watches the sky, blue as in other days, and the trees, as green as ever. She feels hurt, wounded by nature's indifference to her plight. Tears finally run from her eyes with the pain of this new injury. She never expected that the sky and the greens would be so impervious on the day of turning Dhowli into a public whore. Nothing in nature seems to be at all moved by the monstrosity of what is done to her. Has nature then accepted the disgracing of the Dhowlis as a matter of course? Has nature too gotten used to the

Dhowlis being branded as whores and forced to leave home? Or is it that even the earth and the sky and the trees, the nature that was not made by the Misras, have now become their private property?" (Devi 1990a, 205).

23. Roads and road-building are multivalent tropes in Mahasweta's writing: roads linking remote rural and tribal areas to the "outside world" offer an expanded horizon of opportunity to escape or counter local dynamics of exploitation, but also portend intensified exploitation of people and resources through the penetration of commercial, state, and international forces. This tension manifests when Dhowli and her mother consider working on road construction as they struggle to survive.

24. Miles's *Pathetic Fallacy in the Nineteenth Century* retains interest not least for its quantitative methodology. Without the assistance of electronic distant reading technologies, Miles compiled statistics on the frequency of use of the pathetic fallacy in twenty-four poets, from Collins to T. S. Eliot.

25. See, for example, Garuba (2003), Escobar (2008), and Kohn (2013).

26. See LeMenager's brilliant analysis of the "creaky magic" and "scalar epiphany" offered by lenticular images, which "have a philosophical if not a technical genealogy in Victorian-era spirit photography and its revelations of the 'soul' of matter. They are the visual equivalent of the 'aha' moment" (2013, 174).

27. For an extended discussion of this discursive tradition and its significance to Mahasweta's oeuvre, see Wenzel (1998).

28. Cf. Bhattacharya on "the romantic generation of British Indian officials": "In this pastoral imagination, the pastoralists did not figure" (1998, 74).

29. Ecofeminist Vandana Shiva frequently invokes the idea of *aranya sanskriti*; see, for example, her citation of Rabindranath Tagore's *Tapovan* in *Staying Alive*: "Indian civilization has been distinctive in locating its source of regeneration, material and intellectual, in the forest, not the city. India's best ideas have come where man was in communion with trees and rivers and lakes, away from the crowds. The peace of the forest has helped the intellectual evolution of man. The culture of the forest has fuelled the culture of Indian society. The culture that has arisen from the forest has been influenced by the diverse processes of renewal of life which are always at play in the forest, varying from species to species, from season to season, in sight and sound and smell. The unifying principle of life in diversity, of democratic pluralism, thus became the principle of Indian civilization" (1988, 55).

30. J. Hillis Miller might describe this scandalousness as monstrosity, given his discussion of divine inspiration in Ruskin's "Of the Pathetic Fallacy," which he sees as chafing against the proposopoeia/personification

at work in all language (1986, 405–6). Perhaps the possibility raised at the end of "Dhowli" is that capital replaces the divine as the transcendent force or spirit of nature.

31. One trace of the epic association between nature and justice in "Dhowli" is Sanichari, the lone character who speaks truth to the Misras' power. She is an herbalist, and they are dependent upon her expertise. Her understanding of the uses of plants for healing also makes her a counterpart of the EIC surgeon-naturalists who worried about deforestation.

32. Mahasweta's "Salt" also raises questions about the correspondence between landscape aesthetics and characters' inner states. As the problem elephant stands at a riverbank piecing together who is responsible for stealing his salt, we read, "An inspiring scene. The river, sand, sky, night, silhouette of the Palamau Fort, the lone elephant. Peaceful and timeless. The only difference was that in the brains of the said elephant were thoughts quite unsuited to the flutter of white doves" (1981, 34).

33. Timothy Morton wonders whether "the extent to which literary history condemns anthropomorphism and the pathetic fallacy [is] the extent to which the society in which it exists is imperialist" (2001).

34. See Slaughter (2018).

35. Regarding parsimony in descriptions of nonhuman nature, see Phillips (2010) and Miles (1965, 96).

36. On Anthropocene reading, see Menely and Taylor (2017).

4. HOW FAR IS BHOPAL? INCONVENIENT FORUMS AND CORPORATE COMPARISON

1. These figures are uncertain, and the number of "gas-affected" survivors has been a matter of litigation for decades. This uncertainty began immediately after the disaster: "no attempt was made to properly count the number of the dead; the emphasis was on getting rid of the bodies as quickly as possible," so that victims who were merely unconscious were gathered for burial (Rajagopal 1987, 134–35).

2. Union Carbide ceased operations at the Bhopal factory in July 1985, when the government of Madhya Pradesh refused to renew its license. Since 1998, the government of Madhya Pradesh has controlled the ninety-acre Union Carbide facility. Union Carbide claimed to have spent $2 million cleaning up the site, but an estimated 350 tons of toxic waste aboveground, and up to a million tons of contaminated soil, still require disposal. Stock-piled chemicals reportedly still fill warehouses on site. Dow maintains that remediation should be the government's responsibility, since it no longer controls the site. I visited the site nearly three decades after the disaster and saw laboratories looking as if they were hastily abandoned in the middle of

the night. This "abandoned" industrial site is surrounded by dense settlements a stone's throw away. The poisons continue their work while litigation drags on.

3. Numerous critics, beginning with Robert Reich in 1973, quote Gerstacker's statement. Even though the remark about paying natives makes little sense without it, the sentence about attacking the United States—an astonishing thing to say in the White House—is not quoted by a single critic I have found.

4. Gerstacker's May 1966 internal memo became Dow's standard PR statement on napalm during the controversy (Brandt 1997, 353).

5. Even *One Water*'s focus on Haiti implies the nation-state's irrelevance. The 2010 earthquake was only the most recent of a series of challenges, dating back to France's 1825 demand for 150 million francs as compensation for recognizing Haiti's independence. From a Eurocentric perspective, Haiti is the epitome of a failed state.

6. US District Court, May 1986, 25 I. L. M. 771 (Keenan 1986).

7. I use "narrative jurisdiction" as a literary term provoked by, but not identical to, the legal concepts of jurisdiction, standing, and *forum non conveniens*—which pertain to law's spatiality and its narratives' sociological dynamics.

8. Union Carbide's 1985 motion to dismiss also argued that the 200,000 plaintiffs lacked standing to bring suit in the United States and that the lawyers lacked authority to represent them (Kelley Drye & Warren [1985] 1986, 25). Their *forum non conveniens* argument cites *Harrison v. Wyeth Laboratories*, in which residents of the United Kingdom sued the American drug manufacturer for injuries resulting from oral contraceptives. Union Carbide's lawyers write: "It would be inappropriate for this Court to set standards in a foreign forum, particularly one where the economic and social norms are so enormously disparate. Indeed, speaking specifically of India, the court in the *Wyeth* case wrote, in words especially apt here: 'The impropriety of such an approach would be even more clearly seen if the foreign country involved was, for example, India, a country with a vastly different standard of living, wealth, resources, level of health care and services, values, morals and beliefs than our own. Most significantly, our two societies must deal with entirely different and highly complex problems of population growth and control. Faced with different needs, problems and resources in our example India may, in balancing the pros and cons . . . give different weight to various factors than would our society. . . . Should we impose our standards upon them in spite of such differences? We think not'" (44–45). This extraterritorializing thought-experiment in *Wyeth*—which had nothing to do with India—informs Carbide's argument about

Indian values; the quoted language from *Wyeth* reveals that Union Carbide's claim of "incomprehensibility" depends on a belief in the differential and relative value of human life, weighed against poverty and underdevelopment.

9. See Slaughter (2008, 104–5).

10. Compare Gerstacker's argument for the anational company: in "corporate structure today," following US law while operating abroad means that the corporation is "through no choice of its own . . . an instrument of American policy. In many nations the American corporation is seen therefore as an arm of what is called American 'imperialism' . . . The truly anational company is possible only if it can be divorced from its mother country and thus no longer is a part of one culture or one nation. It is not possible if it is seen by any nation as forcing one nation's customs, mores, and politics upon other countries around the world" (1972, 103).

11. In March 1985, the Bhopal Gas Leak Disaster (Processing of Claims) Act, known as the "Bhopal Act," used the legal principle of *parens patriae* to designate the Union of India as the plaintiff in any case, in India or abroad, connected to the incident. Ostensibly this move was to simplify litigation (by consolidating 145 cases filed in US courts) and to put the power of the state behind the victims, many of them poor and illiterate. However, the Indian government was potentially implicated in the case, for its regulatory regime and its role as 22 percent shareholder in Union Carbide India Limited—just one of the complications of this legal maneuver.

12. Galanter's affidavit ((1985) 1986) noted deficiencies including incomplete emergence from colonial rule, lack of a robust class action or mass tort provision in Indian law, insufficient provisions for pretrial discovery, chronic backlogs and delays, and, most crucially, lack of jurisdiction over US-based Union Carbide.

13. In their motion to dismiss, Union Carbide's lawyers noted that "virtually all proceedings and communications would be severely handicapped by language problems" because "English is spoken only by educated persons" and "the number of illiterates and degree of illiteracy among the claimants are unprecedented for a U.S. court" (Kelley Drye & Warren [1985] 1986, 47). Their doubts about American jurors' capacity to understand Bhopal were preceded by a more pernicious argument that the plaintiffs' illiteracy (and consequent lack of understanding) invalidated "the affidavits on which they have placed their thumb prints" (47).

14. Adeno Addis (2009) makes an analogous point about universal jurisdiction, invoking Benedict Anderson's notion of imagined communities to consider how law contributes to the work of transnational imagining.

15. Anderson retired from Union Carbide in 1986 and lived out his life in Florida, Connecticut, and the Hamptons. He, along with other executives

and the company itself, was charged by the Indian Criminal Bureau of Investigation with culpable homicide, grievous hurt, and the death of animals; Anderson was officially an absconder from justice until his death. Arrested in Bhopal on December 7, 1984, Anderson posted bail, left India that day, and never returned. Additional warrants for his arrest were filed, most recently in 2009, by the Chief Judicial Magistrate in Bhopal. Charges were also filed in 1987 against Keshub Mahindra, chairman of Union Carbide India Limited (UCIL), and six other Indian employees. In 2010, convicted of a lesser charge of death by negligence, these employees were sentenced to two years' imprisonment and a fine of approximately $2,000. They were released on bail and served no time.

16. Discussing the irrelevance of "advantages in law" in one forum over the other in *forum non conveniens*, Keenan cites *Piper Aircraft Co. v. Reyno*: "The possibility of an unfavorable change in law should never be a relevant consideration in a forum non conveniens inquiry. Of course, if the remedy provided by the alternative forum is so clearly inadequate or unsatisfactory that it is no remedy at all, the unfavorable change in law may be given substantial weight; the district court may conclude that dismissal would not be in the interests of justice" (1986, 11–12).

17. Union Carbide internal documents from 1972–84, produced during legal discovery in 2002, state: "The comparative risk of poor performance and of consequent need for further investment to correct it, is considerably higher in the UCIL operation than it would be had proven technology [like that at the Institute site] been followed throughout" (Hanna, Morehouse, and Sarangi 2005, 19–21). On the other hand, when UCIL personnel in Bhopal argued that MIC was too dangerous and volatile to store in large quantities, they were overruled by American UCC management who favored the Institute design (Plaintiffs' Executive Committee [1985] 1986, 67–68).

18. This is a close paraphrase from Union Carbide's motion to dismiss (see Kelley Drye & Warren [1985] 1986, 25). Having won this argument, Union Carbide complained about an Indian lack of due process! Appealing the conditions Judge Keenan placed upon his 1986 ruling, Union Carbide asked for US District Court supervision of litigation in India; the company cited the freezing of $2 billion in assets by Bhopal District Judge G. S. Patel as evidence of lack of due process. The US court of appeals (1987, 809 F.2d 195) found this motion "impractical," reflecting "an abysmal ignorance of basic jurisdictional principles, so much so that it borders on the frivolous." Nonetheless, the court sided with Union Carbide in deciding that the language regarding due process in the 1986 ruling introduced problematic ambiguities. The sequester of assets by Judge Patel was thrown out when it was discovered that he was a plaintiff in the case.

19. So claimed Jackson Browning, UCC's Vice-President for Health, Safety, and Environmental Affairs, at a March 1985 press conference. See "Excerpts from Report" (1985).

20. Jack Doyle begins to connect the dots in his encyclopedic *Trespass Against Us: Dow Chemical & The Toxic Century* (2004), tracing Dow's history from humble origins making bleach in Michigan to its arrival as the world's largest chemical corporation. See also Public Citizen's "The Union Carbide Record," a 1985 *amicus* brief. The composite map of Union Carbide and Dow industrial production casualties includes sites in Arkansas, California, Colorado, Florida, Louisiana, Michigan, New York, Ohio, Oregon, Tennessee, Texas, West Virginia, and Puerto Rico, as well as Canada, Belgium, India, and Indonesia. As discussed later in this chapter, napalm and Agent Orange created their own geographies, linking sites in Vietnam (and Cambodia and Laos) where Dow's products were used to sites in Australia, New Zealand, and the United States, where they were manufactured and carried home in the bodies of returning veterans.

21. Although Sinha is cagey about the relationship between Khaufpur and Bhopal, the urban space and history of disaster described in the novel are recognizable as those of Bhopal. For example, a case number in the novel—RT 8460/96 (Sinha 2008, 189)—is the number of the criminal case in the Bhopal Chief Judicial Magistrate's court against Warren Anderson, UCC, and UCIL employees, which lasted from 1987–2010. See note 15.

22. As gas victims sought emergency care, factory officials claimed that MIC was an "irritant" rather than toxic (Everest 1986, 14, 53). Thus began what activist Satinath Sarangi describes as the persistent "medical disaster that followed" the gas leak (Hanna, Morehouse, and Sarangi 2005, 246), involving a lack of information about the components of the gas, its health effects, and effective treatments. Such information was actively suppressed, by Union Carbide (citing "trade secrets") and the Government of India (the 1985 Bhopal Act classified "Official Secrets"). Government-funded studies by the Indian Council for Medical Research were abruptly halted in 1994, possibly because they began to demonstrate second-generation effects (Hanna, Morehouse, and Sarangi 2005, 126). Consequently, care providers have tended to treat symptoms (often ineffectively) rather than identify—and cure—a syndrome (164). See Rajagopal (1987).

23. "Vilayat" is a Hindi/Urdu word that here denotes England, Europe, or "foreign" more broadly.

24. See Doniger (1999, 88–109).

25. This sentence features the trilingual reduplication of phrases in Hindi, French, and English discussed in the next section; *ous raat* is Hindi for "that night."

26. In 1989, the Union Carbide Corporation and the Government of India reached a controversial $470 million settlement, protested by survivors and activist groups as financially inadequate and bureaucratically problematic. This settlement is not part of Khaufpur's history in *Animal's People*; instead, the community organizes against a prospective settlement that would halt litigation.

27. See Luc Boltanski: "Around each unfortunate brought forward crowds a host of replacements. The sufferings made manifest and touching through the accumulation of details must also be able to merge into a unified representation. Although singular, they are nonetheless exemplary" (1999, 12).

28. Animal offers Eyes a tour of the factory site that is his home and an eerie font of death, reclaimed by vegetation growing up through abandoned machinery. In his dismissal, Judge Keenan determined that the "possibility of view . . . of the plant and hutments" was more easily undertaken in an Indian juridical forum (1986, 57). Animal approximates this "view" here and throughout the novel.

29. Compare Boltanski's notion of the "pure spectator," whose totalizing gaze and unseen seeing make him "completely independent of the scene he views" (1999, 24–27).

30. The analogies among Watt's jurisprudential theory of narrative, Animal's narration, and Bhopal litigation are qualified by the fact that India abolished jury trials in 1960.

31. As Antony Anghie argues (2015), "transnational" law was innovated in the mid-twentieth century era of decolonization to protect corporations from the sovereignty of postcolonial nation-states; the forum imagined by *Animal's People* is therefore aptly described as transnational rather than international.

32. As Baxi (among others) observes, among the most disturbing elements of Keenan's 1986 dismissal was his rejection of the plaintiff's argument (supported by amicus briefs from US environmental and social justice NGOs), that, given its import for how multinational corporations operate domestically and abroad, the case was relevant to the public interest in the United States (with public and private interest among the considerations in *forum non conveniens*) (Baxi 1986b, 27–30; "Brief Amicus Curiae" [1985] 1986).

33. "Thus, the cities of the future, rather than being made out of glass and steel as envisioned by earlier generations of urbanists, are instead largely constructed out of crude brick, straw, recycled plastic, cement blocks, and scrap wood. Instead of cities of light soaring toward heaven, much of the twenty-first century urban world squats in squalor, surrounded by pollution, excrement, and decay" (Davis 2006, 19).

34. See Huggan (1997); Moore (2012); Cheele (2013).

35. An unfortunate example of this reading practice is Evelyn Ch'ien's *Weird English* (2004), a study of multilingualism in the postcolonial Anglophone novel. Without knowledge of the languages informing her primary texts, Ch'ien dubs their traces "weird" and nonsensical rather than meaningful to readers who understand them.

36. The woman's speech may draw from *Regiment of Lyfe*, Thomas Phaer's 1544 translation of a medical text by Jehan Goeurot; the OED entry for *yex* cites Phaer as an example. Phaer published his translation of Goeurot with three of his own medical tracts (including one on pediatrics) in "one of the most widely read and frequently reprinted medical texts of the Tudor era," realizing his desire that medical knowledge be a thing available "to the use of the many, which ought not be secrete for the lucre of a fewe." Phaer was first to attempt a complete English translation of Virgil's *Aeneid*; he died with only nine books completed (Schwyzer 2009). It is not hard to see Phaer and Animal as kindred spirits.

37. Animal does not use the Hindi word for English, *Angrezi*, which is a cognate but not a homophone.

38. Defined most narrowly, *alphabet* denotes the script used to write Greek; its extension to Latin makes sense because the two systems share similar initial letters. Although *alphabet* is now used to describe any writing system, the absurdity of this locution in many cases ("Hindi alphabet," "Chinese alphabet") evidences ethnocentrism and blindness to the historical role of European imperial languages that use Roman scripts.

39. The history of Coca-Cola's presence in India intersects with that of Union Carbide. Coca-Cola chose to leave the Indian market in 1977 rather than disclose its formula and reduce its equity stake, as required by the Foreign Exchange Regulation Act, which also determined the equity structure of UCC in relation to UCIL. UCC is thought to have reduced investments in safety at the Bhopal plant in response to these stipulations. Coke returned with an Indian subsidiary in 1993, during economic liberalization led by Manmohan Singh (then Finance Minister, later Prime Minister). Coca-Cola has been criticized for depleting and contaminating groundwater in India. In a 2003 report, the Center for Science and the Environment found significant contamination of Coca-Cola products by pesticides and other toxic chemicals. As with Bhopal, anti-Coca-Cola activism has pressed for absolute multinational enterprise liability. See Shankar (2010).

40. "FUCK YOU WICKED CUNTS I HOPE YOU DIE PAINFULLY FOR THE HORRIBLE THINGS YOU DID TO US AND THE ARROGANT FUCKING CRUELTY YOU'VE DISPLAYED EVER SINCE" (Sinha 2008, 177).

41. This history is complex; what we now call "imperial languages" were not always and everywhere imposed unilaterally, but often used, to varying degrees in various aspects and modes of rule, in tandem with local languages. Viswanathan (1989) analyzes the classic debate between Anglicists and Orientalists in early nineteenth century India, about whether imperial power is best exercised through knowing local languages or not deigning to know them. See also Cohn (1996).

42. *Animal's People* stomps all over the ideal of "invisibility" dominant in English-language translation, which Lawrence Venuti identifies as the "illusion" that "the translated text is not in fact a translation, but the 'original' . . . The more fluent the translation," this model holds, "the more invisible the translator, and, presumably, the more visible the writer or meaning of the foreign language text" (1995, 1–2). Venuti deems this ideal "a mystification of troubling proportions" that conceals hierarchies shaping the one-way traffic or "trade imbalance" of translation, from English into other languages (16, 14).

43. "Modernist" is the qualifier that makes Walkowitz's argument perhaps narrowly true but more troubling, for taking that version of modernism as the measure from which all writing "veers." Although it is beyond the scope of my argument, I disagree with Walkowitz that Coetzee (whose oeuvre I know best, among her examples) eschews "stylistic marking . . . that would remind readers of a specific original language" (2009, 570). Coetzee's focalizing characters often have grammarian tendencies, and large structures of meaning are built around fine points of language. Walkowitz expands and complicates her arguments in *Born Translated* (2015), which nonetheless identifies as an aesthetic program ("what the born-translated novel is trying to do" [33]) what Huggan (2001) and Brouillette (2007) more convincingly analyze as commercial exigencies in the global publishing industry.

44. To describe someone's use of language as unaccented partakes of what linguists call "standard language ideology," the linguistic version of a subtle ethnocentric blindness that takes one's experience as a norm without recognizing it as a norm; every speaker of a language has an accent.

45. See Anna Tsing: "Translations across sites of difference *are* capitalism: they make it possible for investors to accumulate wealth" (2015, 62). Translation is connected to "scalability," "the ability to make projects expand without changing their framing assumptions," which "banishes meaningful diversity . . . that might change things" (38).

46. Salman Rushdie uses a similar strategy in *Midnight's Children*: lines from the morning prayer of Saleem Sinai's grandfather Aadam Aziz are interwoven with his thoughts about returning to Kashmir; later in the novel,

lines from Jawaharlal Nehru's speech marking India's independence are juxtaposed with an account of Saleem's birth at that moment (1982, 11–12, 116–17). These episodes reflect the novel's contest between secular national imagining and religious devotion: can the mythology of the new nation, called into being in Nehru's speech, take the place of or coexist with religious affiliation? In *Animal's People*, marsiyas serve as a vehicle of understanding across multiple divides.

47. It is unclear whether hearing the marsiya's lament for suffering orphans directly elicits Elli's thoughts of the infant Animal, or whether the echo between Elli's thoughts and the ambient chants is ironic because she cannot understand them yet nonetheless thinks (so Animal tells us) in counterpoint with them.

48. In the confusing tumult roiling Khaufpur, Animal assumes, it turns out wrongly, that Zafar fasts unto death; the novel's focalization through Animal effects a narrative "resurrection" when Zafar reappears and explains what really happened.

49. This contest between nothing and everything has echoes in the struggle between Bhopal survivors and Union Carbide/Dow. Declared one woman activist in 2004, "We will continue to fight for justice till the day we die. We lost everything on that night, we have nothing else to lose, so we have no fear" (quoted in Mukherjee 2004, 11). Dow espoused its own "vision of zero": in an open letter to employees on the eve of the disaster's eighteenth anniversary, CEO Michael Parker described the company's "vision of zero harm to the environment, to our people or to anyone we touch in the value chain." He urged employees to mark the anniversary by "doing your part to moving our company every closer to that vision of zero" (Hanna, Morehouse, and Sarangi 2005, 249).

50. The use of *zero* rather than *nothing* may invoke the advanced thinking about zero in early Hindu and Arabic mathematics; India's status as the place that invented zero works against notions of the West and its Kampani as the origin of scientific knowledge. The reduplication of words for zero/nothing conveys the aggregate force of the polyglot global majority constituted by those who have nothing.

51. I am grateful to Nasia Anam for noting this connection.

52. Sinha is having another joke: within the moral geography charted in the novel, *Jehannum* is an apt pun for the Jehan Numa Palace, now a luxury hotel on a hill over Bhopal's Upper Lake.

53. This implicit exhortation echoes Sinha's 1980s and 1990s copywriting work for Amnesty International. Sinha wrote a series of full-page print ads that included a tear-out membership coupon in the bottom corner. The final paragraph of these ads addressed the reader directly, as in "Should We

Give Up?": "The strongest voice on earth belongs to you. Use it. Join us." Sinha used a similar strategy in ads for the Bhopal Medical Appeal (SOFII 2008).

54. Animal makes a similar point while railing against the Australian journalist's arrogance: "For his sort we are not really people. . . . Extras we're, in his movie. Well bollocks to that. Tell mister cunt big shot that this is my movie he's in and in my movie there is only one star and it's me" (Sinha 2008, 9).

55. The 1999 film *Bhopal Express* emphasizes the significance of poetry as a mode of private conversation and public performance; the citation and invention of poetic couplets establish relationships between characters and introduces the film's themes. *Bhopal Express* was a transnational venture (with support from David Lynch and Bhopal activist Satinath Sarangi) that used the mass appeal of feature film and a bourgeois love story to re-awaken awareness of justice yet undone for Bhopal. Its Hindu protagonist (a Union Carbide employee, scapegoated as a saboteur) bonds with his Muslim best friend (a fierce critic of the company, even before the disaster) in part through the exchange of Urdu couplets.

56. This statement is not empirically true of MIC, but it is true of dioxin, possibly the most toxic substance on earth and now a global chemical, disseminated across the planet. As discussed below, Dow has been the largest source of dioxin.

57. Note the temporal/historical contradictions: For Beck, the Third World simultaneously inhabits the equivalent of early and late industrial society, losing out in the distribution of both wealth and risk. More satisfying is Neil Smith's (2008) account of the tendency of capital to move from place to place, navigating gaps among regulatory regimes.

58. See Rajagopal's account (1987) of postdisaster Bhopal as a place riven by suspicion.

59. Napalm B was Dow's reformulation of the jellied gasoline first used as an incendiary weapon in World War II. Dow developed napalm B by adding polystyrene to the gasoline/benzene mix to increase adhesion and burn time. Agent White contained picloram, a Dow-manufactured chemical that is highly persistent in the environment (i.e., it does not easily break down into less harmful components).

60. These figures come from the Herbs Tape, an unclassified US Air Force computerized record of herbicidal aerial spraying missions from 1965 to 1971. This record does not include truck or hand spraying and was estimated by the Veterans Education Project in 2000 to include only 86 percent of actual missions; more recent scholarship on Agent Orange suggests that official figures significantly underestimate actual quantities of

herbicides used in Vietnam (see Stellman et al. 2003; National Institute of Medicine 2014). Because individual spraying missions are recorded by date and province, the Veterans Education Project advised veterans to use the Herbs Tape to ascertain their possible exposures.

61. In Tim O'Brien's Vietnam memoir, the Zippo appears in a catalog of weapons: "In the years preceding the murders at My Lai, more than 70 percent of the villages in this province had been destroyed by air strikes, artillery fire, Zippo lighters, napalm, white phosphorus, bulldozers, gunships and other such means" (1994, 53). The use of Zippos in Vietnam returned to public consciousness in the United States in 2004, as part of the Swift Boat attacks on presidential candidate John Kerry. See also Fiorella (1998).

62. Herbicidal air missions were quite dangerous, the largest source of Air Force fatalities in Vietnam, because pilots could not fly C-132s at the Apollonian altitudes of distant warfare associated with other forms of aerial bombardment.

63. Military use of napalm and herbicides catalyzed political divides within American academic professional organizations in the late 1960s. At the American Anthropological Association, a 1967 resolution condemning the use of napalm was opposed by Margaret Mead but approved by the membership (Gough 1968). A heated forum at the 1969 Modern Language Association convention opened with Frederick Crews's "Do Literary Studies Have an Ideology?" which argued that notions of literary studies as apolitical and value-free (compared against natural and social scientists' aid to the war effort) were accommodations to a militarist state, itself handmaiden to global capitalism (Crews 1970). The American Association for the Advancement of Science (AAAS) conducted fieldwork to document the toxic effects of Agent Orange and first publicly reported its results at its December 1970 convention. On the AAAS's convention's first day, the White House announced a phase-out of military herbicides. That AAAS opinion was not unanimous is evident in board member Kenneth V. Thimann's reaffirmation of his 1968 position that herbicidal "defoliation of forest cover probably represents a military device for saving lives that has an unprecedented degree of harmlessness to the environment" (Boffey 1971, 43–44). For a detailed account of conflicts in the AAAS and negotiations that led to the study, see Neilands (1970).

64. Pentagon estimates suggest that more than 100,000 tons of napalm were used by 1968, and an additional 125,000 tons between January 1969 and June 1971 (Neilands [1971] 1972, 34).

65. The Geneva Protocol of 1925 prohibited "asphyxiating, poisonous, or other gases, . . . all analogous liquids, materials, or devices . . . [and]

bacteriological methods of warfare" (quoted in Jones 1980, 430–31). As interpreted by the Kennedy administration, "chemical warfare as defined by international law requires injury to the physical person of the enemy," Assistant Defense Secretary William Bundy wrote in response to a 1963 letter by US Congressman Robert Kastenmeier protesting herbicidal warfare (quoted in Bonds 2013, 90). At the United Nations, Hungary raised the issue of US military herbicide use in 1966. In 1969, the General Assembly passed Resolution 2603 (XXIV), a nonbinding statement rejecting the people vs. plants distinction by defining chemical warfare as the use of substances "employed because of the direct toxic effects on man, animals, or plants" (quoted in Zierler 2008, 246–47). In US jurisprudence, however, a 2004 suit against manufacturers brought by the Vietnam Association for Victims of Agent Orange was dismissed on the grounds that Agent Orange was not used with the intent to poison humans; therefore, it was not a chemical weapon and its use not a war crime. The inventor of napalm, Harvard chemist Louis Fieser, said he intended it for use upon things rather than people—or "babies and Buddhists," as he said in a 1967 interview with John Lannan.

66. As early as 1968, a study commissioned by the State Department and conducted by USDA ecologist Fred Tschirley showed that defoliants in Vietnam caused long-term ecological changes. The penetration of wind and sunlight to the forest floor caused soil laterization and erosion and encouraged the growth of bamboo and invasive grasses, preventing forest regeneration (Zierler 2008, 199–200). Tschirley's carefully qualified findings were euphemistically summarized and reported in the *Washington Post* with the misleading, consent-manufacturing front page headline, "U.S. Study Finds Defoliant Harmless; Defoliants Claimed Viet Life Saver" (Lescaze 1968).

67. In the aftermath of World War I, the United States led an effort to prohibit military use of poison gas, which culminated in the Geneva Protocol of 1925. The Senate, yielding to lobbying by the US Army Chemical Warfare Service and the American Chemical Society, failed to ratify the treaty: "many chemical warfare agents were common industrial chemicals, whose strict control would interfere with the growth of chemical industry in the United States" (Jones 1980, 433).

68. See also an essay in *New Republic* by scientists Robert E. Cook, William Haseltine, and Arthur Galston (1970).

69. Whiteside worried about the ubiquity of polychlorinated phenolic compounds like 2,4,5-T in "such common products as paper, paints, varnishes, timber, soaps, hair shampoos, and laundry starches" that "had never been adequately studied, either singly or as a class, for their potential harmfulness to humans." Tracing a regulatory failure, Whiteside further

documents the failure of government agencies to share with each other data about possible hazards (1979, 12–13).

70. Congressman Bertram Podell made this connection between military demand and commercial availability in a May 1968 statement: "It is ironic that the plans to drop ten million gallons of vegetation and crop-killing poisons will cause a shortage of garden and weed killers. This circumstance demonstrates how dangerously free we have been using chemical and biological poisons for domestic purposes, including DDT and other pesticides, without knowing how serious their long-range impact may be" (Neilands 1970, 225).

71. By *dioxin*, I mean 2,3,7,8-tetrachlorodibenzo-*p*-dioxin (2,3,7,8-TCDD), the most studied and most toxic of the chlorinated dioxins.

72. In 2017, US Representative Barbara Lee introduced a bill, "Victims of Agent Orange Relief Act," that would provide funds for remediation of sites in Vietnam and for medical treatment for victims.

73. See Waugh (2010) and Waugh and Lien (2010).

74. See Dearborn (2009) and Joseph (2004).

75. "Hang Peterson," a graffito on the wall outside the Kampani's factory (Sinha 2008, 178), is a thinly veiled reference to Warren Anderson, CEO of UCC in 1984.

76. See Dow's detailed 2004 brief explaining to the Bhopal Chief Magistrate why it is not even the corporate equivalent of a distant cousin to UCIL (Hanna, Morehouse, and Sarangi 2005, 101–6).

Achebe, Chinua. 1958. *Things Fall Apart*. London: Heinemann.

———. (1965) 1990. "The Novelist as Teacher." In Achebe 1990, 40–46.

———. (1975) 1990. "An Image of Africa: Racism in Conrad's *Heart of Darkness*." In Achebe 1990, 1–20.

———. (1978) 1990. "The Truth of Fiction." In Achebe 1990, 138–53.

———. 1990. *Hopes and Impediments: Selected Essays*. New York: Anchor.

Addis, Adeno. 2009. "Imagining the International Community: The Constitutive Dimension of Universal Jurisdiction." *Human Rights Quarterly* 31, no. 1: 129–62.

Adichie, Chimamanda Ngozi. 2008. "Memoire." In Kashi and Watts 2008, 102–3.

"Affidavit of Marc S. Galanter." (1985) 1986. In Baxi and Paul 1986, 161–221.

"Affidavit of N. A. Palkhivala." (1985) 1986. In Baxi and Paul 1986, 222–30.

Agary, Kaine. 2008. "My Blessing, My Curse." In Kashi and Watts 2008, 152–53.

Ake, Claude. 1996. *Democracy and Development in Africa*. Washington, DC: Brookings Institution Press.

Akpan, Uwem. 2000. "Baptizing the Gun." *Hekima Review* 24 (December): 65–79.

———. 2008. *Say You're One of Them*. New York: Little, Brown.

Alaimo, Stacy. 2011. *Bodily Natures: Science, Environment, and the Material Self*. Bloomington: Indiana University Press.

Albion, Robert Greenhalgh. 1926. *Forests and Sea Power: The Timber Problem of the Royal Navy, 1652–1862*. Cambridge, MA: Harvard University Press.

Althusser, Louis. (1970) 2001. "Ideology and Ideological State Apparatuses." In *The Norton Anthology of Theory and Criticism*, ed. Vincent B. Leitch et al., 1483–1509. New York: Norton.

Amaize, Emma. 2011. "Militant Group Demands Republic of Niger Delta." *Vanguard*, July 12.

Ana, G. R., M. K. Shridar, and G. O. Emerole. 2012. "Polycyclic Aromatic Hydrocarbon Burden in Ambient Air in Selected Niger Delta Communities in Nigeria." *Journal of Air Waste Management Association* 62, no. 1 (January): 18–25.

Anderson, Benedict. 1991. *Imagined Communities: Reflections on the Origin and Spread of Nationalism.* New York: Verso.

Anderson, Daniel Gustav. 2012. "Accumulating-Capital, Accumulating-Carbon, and the Very Big Ecological Body: An Object of Responsibility for Ecocriticism." *Public Knowledge Journal* 3 (S1).

Anghie, Antony. 2015. "Legal Aspects of the New International Economic Order." *Humanity* 6, no. 1 (Spring): 145–58.

Appadurai, Arjun. 2004. "The Capacity to Aspire: Culture and the Terms of Recognition." In *Culture and Public Action*, edited by Vijayendra Rao and Michael Valton, 59–84. Stanford: Stanford University Press.

Appleton, Jay. 1974. *The Experience of Landscape.* London: Wiley.

Apter, Andrew H. 2005. *The Pan-African Nation: Oil and the Spectacle of Culture in Nigeria.* Chicago: University of Chicago Press.

Apter, Emily. 2013. *Against World Literature: On the Politics of Untranslatability.* New York: Verso.

Armah, Ayi Kwei. 1969. *The Beautyful Ones Are Not Yet Born.* London: Heinemann.

Balfour, Edward. 1849. *On the Influence Exercised by Trees on the Climate of a Country.* Madras: Reuben Twigg.

Barnard, Rita. 2007. *Apartheid and Beyond: South African Writers and the Politics of Place.* New York: Oxford University Press.

Bassey, Nnimo. 2008. "Oil Fever." In Kashi and Watts 2008, 90–91.

Bartlet, Olivier. 2006. "The Ambiguity of Darwin's Nightmare." Translated by Kyana LeMaitre. *Africultures*, April 1, 2006. http://www.africultures .com/php/index.php?nav=article&no=5745.

Bartolovich, Crystal. 2010. "A Natural History of 'Food Riots.'" *New Formations* 69 (Summer): 42–61.

Baucom, Ian. 2012. "The Human Shore: Postcolonial Studies in an Age of Natural Science." *History in the Present* 2 (1): 1–23.

Bauman, Zygmunt. 2003. *Wasted Lives: Modernity and Its Outcasts.* New York: Polity.

Baxi, Upendra, ed. 1986a. *Inconvenient Forum and Convenient Catastrophe: The Bhopal Case.* New Delhi: Indian Law Institute.

———. 1986b. "Introduction." In Baxi and Paul 1986, i–xi.

———. 1990. "The Bhopal Victims in the Labyrinth of the Law: An Introduction." In Baxi and Dhanda 1990, i–lxix.

———. 2006. "What May the 'Third World' Expect from International Law?" *Third World Quarterly* 27 (5): 713–25.

Baxi, Upendra, and Amita Dhanda, eds. 1990. *Valiant Victims and Lethal Litigation: The Bhopal Case*. New Delhi: Indian Law Institute.

Baxi, Upendra, and Thomas Paul, eds. 1986. *Mass Disasters and Multinational Liability: The Bhopal Case*. New Delhi: Indian Law Institute.

Beck, Ulrich. 1992. *Risk Society: Towards a New Modernity*. Translated by Mark Ritter. London: Sage.

———. 1999. *World Risk Society*. Cambridge: Polity.

———. 2009. *World at Risk*. Translated by Ciaran Cronin. Cambridge: Polity.

Bellamy, Brent, and Imre Szeman. 2014. "Life after People: Science Fiction and Ecological Futures." In *Green Planets: Ecology and Science Fiction*, edited by Gerry Canavan and Kim Stanley Robinson, 192–205. Middletown, CT: Wesleyan University Press.

Bellin, J. S. 1972. "CBW and Geneva Protocol." *Science and Public Affairs: Bulletin of the Atomic Scientists* 28, no. 1 (January): 2.

Benjamin, Walter. 1969. "Theses on the Philosophy of History." In *Illuminations*, translated by Harry Zohn, edited by Hannah Arendt, 253–64. New York: Schocken.

———. 1999. *The Arcades Project*. Translated by Howard Eiland and Kevin McLaughlin. Cambridge, MA: Harvard University Press.

Berlant, Lauren. 2011. *Cruel Optimism*. Durham, NC: Duke University Press.

Bhattacharya, Neeladri. 1998. "Pastoralists in a Colonial World." In *Nature, Culture, Imperialism: Essays on the Environmental History of South Asia*, edited by David Arnold and Ramachandra Guha, 49–85. Delhi: Oxford University Press.

Bichlbaum, Andy, Mike Bonanno, and Kurt Engfehr, dirs. 2009. *The Yes Men Fix the World*. HBO.

Bissoondath, Neil. 1989. "Rage and Sadness in Nigeria." *New York Times*, August 13, 1989.

Black, Stephanie, dir. 2001. *Life and Debt*. Tuff Gong Pictures.

Bloch, Ernst. 1986. *Principle of Hope*. Translated by Neville Plaice, Stephen Plaice, and Paul Knight. Cambridge, MA: MIT Press.

Boffey, Phillip M. 1971. "Herbicides in Vietnam: AAAS Study Finds Widespread Devastation." *Science* 171, no. 3966 (January 9): 43–47.

Boltanski, Luc. 1999. *Distant Suffering: Morality, Media, and Politics*. Translated by Graham D. Burchell. Cambridge: Cambridge University Press.

Bonds, Eric. 2013. "Hegemony and Humanitarian Norms: The US Legitimation of Toxic Hegemony." *Journal of World-Systems Research* 19, no. 1: 82–107.

Bose, Purnima, and Laura E. Lyons, eds. 2010. *Cultural Critique and the Global Corporation*. Bloomington: Indiana University Press.

Bradford, George. (1985) 2005. "We All Live in Bhopal." In Hanna, Morehouse, and Sarangi 2005, 283–86.

Brandt, E. N. 1997. *Growth Company: Dow Chemical's First Century*. Lansing:
Michigan State University Press.

Braun, Daniel Rafael. 2009. "Economies of Looking." Unpublished manu-
script, University of Michigan.

Bridges, Nichole. 2009. "Kongo Ivories." Heilbrunn Timeline of Art
History, The Metropolitan Museum of Art. https://metmuseum.org/toah
/hd/kong/hd_kong.htm.

"Brief Amicus Curiae of Citizens Commission et al." (1985) 1986. In Baxi
1986a, 278–98.

Brouillette, Sarah. 2007. *Postcolonial Writers in the Global Literary Marketplace*. Basingstoke: Palgrave Macmillan.

Buchanan, Sherry. 2007. *Vietnam Zippos: American Soldiers' Engravings and
Stories, 1965–73*. Chicago: University of Chicago Press.

Buell, Frederick. 2003. *From Apocalypse to Way of Life: Environmental Crisis in
the American Century*. New York: Routledge.

Buell, Lawrence. 1995. *The Environmental Imagination: Thoreau, Nature
Writing, and the Formation of American Culture*. Cambridge, MA: Belknap
Press of Harvard University Press.

———. 2001. *Writing for an Endangered World: Literature, Culture, and
Environment in the U.S. and Beyond*. Cambridge, MA: Belknap Press of
Harvard University Press.

Bumb, R. R. et al. 1980. "Trace Chemistries of Fire: A Source of Chlorinated Dioxins." *Science* 210, no. 4468 (October 24): 385–90.

Butter, Donald. 1839. *Outlines of the Topography and Statistics of the Southern
Districts of Oudh, and of the Cantonment of Sultanpur-Oudh*. Oudh, India:
Huttman.

Caffentzis, George. 2010. "The Future of 'The Commons': Neoliberalism's
'Plan B' or the Original Disaccumulation of Capital?" *New Formations* 69
(Summer): 23–41.

Callaghy, Thomas M., Ronald Kassimir, and Robert Latham, eds. 2001.
Intervention and Transnationalism in Africa: Global-Local Networks of Power.
Cambridge: Cambridge University Press.

Carpentier, Alejo. (1949). "On the Marvelous Real in America." In Zamora
and Faris 1995, 75–88.

Carson, Rachel. 1962. *Silent Spring*. Boston: Houghton Mifflin.

Casanova, Pascale. 2004. *The World Republic of Letters*. Cambridge, MA:
Harvard University Press.

Cazdyn, Eric. 2007. "Disaster, Crisis, Revolution." *South Atlantic Quarterly*
106, no. 4: 647–62.

Chakrabarty, Dipesh. 2009. "The Climate of History: Four Theses." *Critical Inquiry* 35 (Winter): 197–222.

Chan, Sewell. 2008. "Liberal Pranksters Hand out Times Spoof." *New York Times*, November 12, 2008.

Cheah, Pheng. 2016. *What Is a World? On Postcolonial Literature as World Literature*. Durham, NC: Duke University Press.

Cheele, Ellie. 2013. "The Booker Prize: Scandal, Controversy and Marketing Tool." *Journal of Publishing Culture* (April): 1–7.

Chhatre, Ashwini. 2003. "The Mirage of Permanent Boundaries: Politics of Forest Reservation in the Western Himalayas, 1875–97." *Conservation and Society* 1, no. 1 (June): 137–59.

Ch'ien, E. Nien-Ming. 2004. *Weird English*. Cambridge, MA: Harvard University Press.

Cioffi, Sandy, dir. 2010. *Sweet Crude*. Cinema Guild, New York.

Clapp, Jennifer. 2010. "Global Mechanisms for Greening TNCs: Inching Towards Corporate Accountability?" In *Handbook on Trade and the Environment*, edited by Kevin Gallagher, 159–70. Cheltenham, UK: Edward Elgar.

Clarkson, Thomas. 1839. *History of the Rise, Progress, and Accomplishment of the Abolition of the African Slave Trade*. London: Parker.

Cleghorn, Hugh, et al. 1860. "Report of the Committee Appointed by the British Association to Consider the Probable Effects in an Economic and Physical Point of View of the Destruction of Tropical Forests." *Proceedings of the British Association for the Advancement of Science*, 78–102.

CNN. 2006. "Oops: Impostor Scams HUD Officials." *CNN*, August 28. http://www.cnn.com/2006/POLITICS/08/28/hud.hoax.

Coetzee, J. M. 1988. *White Writing: On the Culture of Letters in South Africa*. New Haven: Yale University Press.

———. 1999. *Disgrace*. New York: Penguin.

Cohen, Lizbeth. 2003. *A Consumer's Republic: The Politics of Mass Consumption in Postwar America*. New York: Vintage.

Cohn, Bernard. 1996. *Colonialism and Its Forms of Knowledge: The British in India*. Princeton: Princeton University Press.

Columbus, Christopher. 1998. *Journal of the First Voyage to America, 1492–1493*. In *The Heath Anthology of American Literature*, 3rd ed, edited by Paul Lauter, 1:117–25. Boston: Houghton Mifflin.

Comaroff, Jean, and John L. Comaroff. 1991. *Of Revelation and Revolution: Christianity, Colonialism, and Consciousness in South Africa*. Chicago: University of Chicago Press.

———. 2000. "Millennial Capitalism: First Thoughts on a Second Coming." *Public Culture* 12, no. 2: 291–343.

Conrad, Joseph. (1902) 2006. *Heart of Darkness.* Edited by Paul B. Armstrong. New York: Norton.

Cook, Ian, and Peter Crang. 1996. "The World on a Plate: Culinary Culture, Displacement and Geographical Knowledge." *Journal of Material Culture* 1: 131–53.

Cook, Robert E., William Haseltine, and Arthur Galston. 1970. "Deliberate Destruction of the Environment: What Have We Done to Vietnam?" *New Republic* 162, no. 2: 18–21.

Cooper, Brenda. 1998. *Magical Realism in West African Fiction: Seeing with a Third Eye.* London: Routledge.

Coronil, Fernando. 1997. *The Magical State: Nature, Money, and Modernity in Venezuela.* Chicago: University of Chicago Press.

———. 2001. "Towards a Critique of Globalcentrism: Speculations on Capitalism's Nature." In *Millennial Capitalism and the Culture of Neoliberalism,* edited by Jean Comaroff and John L. Comaroff, 63–87. Durham, NC: Duke University Press.

Cosgrove, Denis. 2001. *Apollo's Eye: A Cartographic Genealogy of the Earth in the Western Imagination.* Baltimore: Johns Hopkins University Press.

Crews, Frederick. 1970. "Do Literary Studies Have an Ideology?" *PMLA* 85, no. 3 (May): 423–28.

Cronon, William. 1995. "The Trouble with Wilderness; or, Getting Back to the Wrong Nature." In *Uncommon Ground: Rethinking the Human Place in Nature,* edited by William Cronon, 69–90. New York: Norton.

Curtin, Deane. 2005. *Environmental Ethics for a Postcolonial World.* Lanham, MD: Rowman & Littlefield.

Dalby, Simon. 1996. "The Environment as Geopolitical Threat: Reading Robert Kaplan's 'Coming Anarchy.'" *Cultural Geographies* 3, no. 4 (October): 472–96.

Dalzell, N.A. 1869. "The Influence of Trees on Climate." In *Extracts on Forests and Forestry,* 22–23. Bombay: Education Society's Press, Byculla.

Daminabo, Ferdinand, and Owajionyi Lysias Frank. 2015. "The Curse of Oil." *Journal of Sciences and Multidisciplinary Research* 7, no. 1: 44–51.

Damrosch, David. 2003. *What Is World Literature?* Princeton: Princeton University Press.

Dasgupta, Subhachari. 1986. *Forest, Ecology, and the Oppressed: A Study from the Point of View of the Forest Dwellers.* New Delhi: People's Institute for Development & Training.

Davis, Mike. 1998. *Ecology of Fear: Los Angeles and the Imagination of Disaster.* New York: Metropolitan.

———. 2006. *Planet of Slums.* London: Verso.

Dawson, Ashley. 2010. "Introduction: New Enclosures." *New Formations* 69: 8–22.

Dearborn, Meredith. 2009. "Enterprise Liability: Reviewing and Revitalizing Liability for Corporate Groups." *California Law Review* 97, no. 1: 195–262.

Dearing, Stephanie. 2010. "Wikileaks: Royal Dutch Shell Infiltrated Nigerian Government." *Digital Journal*, December 9, 2010. http://www.digitaljournal.com/article/301254.

Deckard, Sharae. 2012. "Editorial: Reading the World-Ecology." *Green Letters* 16, no. 1: 5–14.

DeLoughrey, Elizabeth, and George B. Handley. 2011. *Postcolonial Ecologies: Literatures of the Environment*. Oxford: Oxford University Press.

Devi, Mahasweta. (1978) 1995. "Shishu" (Children). Translated by Pinaki Bhattacharya. In *Women Writing in India: 600 B. C. to the Present*, Vol. II: *The Twentieth Century*, edited by Susie Tharu and K. Lalita, 236–51. Delhi: Oxford University Press.

———. 1981. "Salt." In *Protest: An Anthology of Bengali Short Stories of the 70's*, translated by Tapan Mitra, edited by Partha Chatterjee, 21–38. Calcutta: Srijani.

———. 1990a. "Dhowli." In *Of Women, Outcastes, Peasants, and Rebels: A Selection of Bengali Short Stories*, edited and translated by Kalpana Bardhan, 185–205. Berkeley: University of California Press.

———. 1990b. "Draupadi." In *Bashai Tudu*, translated by Gayatri Chakravorty Spivak, edited by Samik Bandyopadhyay, 149–62. Calcutta: Thema.

———. 1995. *Imaginary Maps: Three Stories by Mahasweta Devi*. Translated by Gayatri Chakravorty Spivak. New York: Routledge.

———. n.d. "Dhowli." Unpublished translation by Ben Conisbee Baer.

Dimock, Edward. 1974. *The Literatures of India: An Introduction*. Chicago: University of Chicago Press.

Doan, H. H. 1967. "Why Does Dow Chemical Make Napalm?" *Wall Street Journal*, December 8, 1967.

Doniger, Wendy. 1999. *Splitting the Difference: Gender and Myth in Ancient Greece and India*. Chicago: University of Chicago Press.

Douglas, Oronto. 2008. "Now Is the Time." In Kashi and Watts 2008, 142–43.

Dove, Michael R. 1992. "The Dialectical History of 'Jungle' in Pakistan: An Examination of the Relationship between Nature and Culture." *Journal of Anthropological Research* 48, no. 3: 231–53.

"Dow Chemical to Quit Selling 2 Herbicides, Ending EPA Battle." *Wall Street Journal*, October 17, 1983.

Doyle, Jack. 2004. *Trespass Against Us: Dow Chemical & The Toxic Century*. Monroe: Common Courage.

Edwards, Paul N. 2010. *A Vast Machine: Computer Models, Climate Data, and the Politics of Global Warming.* Cambridge, MA: MIT Press.

Emerson, Ralph Waldo. 1836. *Nature.* Boston: James Monroe.

Enzensberger, Hans. 1974. "A Critique of Political Ecology." *New Left Review* 84 (March–April): 3–31.

Equiano, Olaudah. (1789) 2001. *The Interesting Narrative of the Life of Olaudah Equiano, or Gustavus Vassa, the African, Written by Himself.* Edited by Werner Sollors. New York: Norton.

Escobar, Arturo. 2008. *Territories of Difference: Place, Movements, Life.* Durham, NC: Duke University Press.

Everest, Larry. 1986. *Behind the Poison Cloud: Union Carbide's Bhopal Massacre.* Chicago: Banner.

"Excerpts from Report and Comments on Company's Inquiry." 1985. *New York Times,* March 21.

Fagunwa, D. O. (1938) 1968. *The Forest of a Thousand Daemons: A Hunter's Saga.* Translated by Wole Soyinka. London: Nelson.

Fanon, Frantz. (1961) 1968. *The Wretched of the Earth.* Translated by Constance Farrington. New York: Grove.

Farah, Nuruddin. 1996. "Highway to Hell: The Travel-Writing of the Disaster," *Transition* 70: 62.

Faris, Wendy B. 2004. *Ordinary Enchantments: Magical Realism and the Remystification of Narrative.* Nashville: Vanderbilt University Press.

Ferguson, James. 2006. *Global Shadows: Africa in the Neoliberal World Order.* Durham, NC: Duke University Press.

Fiorella, Jim. 1998. *The Viet Nam Zippo Cigarette Lighters 1933–1975.* Atglen, PA: Schiffer.

Fortun, Kim. 2001. *Advocacy after Bhopal: Environmentalism, Disaster, New Global Orders.* Chicago: University of Chicago Press.

Fox, Diane Niblack. 2003. "Chemical Politics and the Hazards of Modern Warfare: Agent Orange." In *Synthetic Planet: Chemical Politics and the Hazards of Modern Life,* edited by Monica J. Casper, 73–90. New York: Routledge.

Francis, Marc, and Nick Francis, dirs. 2006. *Black Gold.* Fulcrum Productions.

Franklin, Bruce H. 2000. *Vietnam and Other American Fantasies.* Amherst: University of Massachusetts Press.

Gadgil, Madhav, and Ramachandra Guha. 1993. *This Fissured Land: An Ecological History of India.* Delhi: Oxford University Press.

Garuba, Harry. 2003. "Explorations in Animist Materialism: Notes on Reading/Writing African Literature, Culture, and Society." *Public Culture* 15, no. 2: 261–85.

Gaylard, Gerald. 2005. *After Colonialism: African Postmodernism and Magical Realism*. Johannesburg: University of the Witwatersrand Press.

Gerstacker, Carl A. 1972. "The Structure of the Corporation." Paper presented at the White House Conference on the Industrial World Ahead, February 7–9.

Ghotge, Nitya. 2011. "How Grazing Lands Became 'Waste' Lands." *InfoChange Agenda* 21: 16–20. http://www.infochangeindia.org/downloads /agenda_21.pdf?

Gidwani, Vinay. 1992. "'Waste' and the Permanent Settlement in Bengal." *Economic and Political Weekly*, January 25: 39–46.

———. 2008. *Capital, Interrupted: Agrarian Development and the Politics of Work in India*. Minneapolis: University of Minnesota Press.

Gordimer, Nadine. 1989. "Living in the Interregnum." In *The Essential Gesture: Writing, Politics and Places*, edited by Stephen Clingman, 261–84. New York: Penguin.

Gough, Kathleen. 1968. "Anthropology and Imperialism." *Monthly Review* 19, no. 11 (April): 12–27.

———. 1990. "'Anthropology and Imperialism' Revisited." *Economic and Political Weekly* 25, no. 31 (4 August): 1705–8.

Graves, Robert, and Didier-Madoc Jones. *Postcards from the Future*. 2010. http://www.postcardsfromthefuture.co.uk.

Grbic, Jovana. 2010. "Selling Science Smartly: Dow Human Element Campaign." *ScriptPhD*, February 18, 2010. http://scriptphd.com /advertising/2010/02/18/selling-science-smartly-dow-human-element -campaign.

Griswold, Wendy. 2000. *Bearing Witness: Readers, Writers, and the Novel in Nigeria*. Princeton: Princeton University Press.

Grove, Richard. 1996. *Green Imperialism: Colonial Expansion, Tropical Island Edens and the Origins of Environmentalism, 1600–1860*. Cambridge: Cambridge University Press.

Groves, Adam. 2009. "Shell and Society: Securing the Niger Delta?" *E-International Relations Students*, June 10, 2009. http://www.e-ir.info /2009/06/10/shell-and-society-securing-the-niger-delta.

Guha, Ramachandra, and Juan Martinez-Alier. 1998. *Varieties of Environmentalism: Essays North and South*. Delhi: Oxford University Press.

Guha, Ranajit. 1963. *A Rule of Property for Bengal: An Essay on the Idea of Permanent Settlement*. Paris: Mouton.

Guha, Sumit. 2001. "Economic Rents and Natural Resources: Commons and Conflicts in Premodern India." In *Social Nature: Resources, Representations, and Rule in India*, edited by Arun Agrawal and K. Sivaramakrishnan, 132–46. New Delhi: Oxford University Press.

Habila, Helon. 2010. *Oil on Water.* New York: Norton.

Halhed, Nathaniel Brassey, trans. (1781) 2013. *A Code of Gentoo Laws, or, Ordinations of the Pundits. From a Persian translation, made from the original, written in the Shanscrit language.* Cambridge: Cambridge University Press.

Hanna, Bridget, Ward Morehouse, and Satinath Sarangi, eds. 2005. *The Bhopal Reader: Remembering Twenty Years of the World's Worst Industrial Disaster.* New York: Apex.

Hansen, Karen Tranberg. 2000. *Salaula: The World of Secondhand Clothing and Zambia.* Chicago: University of Chicago Press.

Haraway, Donna. 1988. "Situated Knowledges: The Science Question in Feminism and the Privilege of Partial Perspective." *Feminist Studies* 14, no. 3: 575–99.

Hardin, Garrett. 1968. "The Tragedy of the Commons." *Science* 162 (3859): 1243–48.

———. 1991. "The Tragedy of the *Unmanaged* Commons: Population and the Disguises of Providence." In *Commons without Tragedy: Protecting the Environment from Overpopulation—A New Approach,* edited by Robert V. Andelson, 162–85. London: Shepheard-Walwyn.

Hartman, Geoffrey H. 1997. *The Fateful Question of Culture.* New York: Columbia University Press.

Harvey, David. 1990. "Between Space and Time: Reflections on the Geographical Imagination." *Annals of the Association of American Geographers* 80, no. 3 (September): 418–34.

———. 1996. *Justice, Nature, and the Geography of Difference.* Malden, MA: Blackwell.

———. 2003. *The New Imperialism.* Oxford: Oxford University Press.

Heede, Richard. 2014. "Tracing Anthropogenic Carbon Dioxide and Methane Emissions to Fossil Fuel and Cement Producers, 1854–2010." *Climatic Change* 122: 229–41.

Heise, Ursula. 2008. *Sense of Place and Sense of Planet: The Environmental Imagination of the Global.* New York: Oxford University Press.

———. 2012. "World Literature and the Environment." In *The Routledge Companion to World Literature,* edited by Theo D'Haen, David Damrosch, and Djelal Kadir, 404–12. Oxford: Routledge.

Hitchcock, Peter. 2003. *Imaginary States: Studies in Cultural Transnationalism.* Urbana: University of Illinois Press.

———. 2007. "Postcolonial Failure and the Politics of Nation." *South Atlantic Quarterly* 106, no. 4: 727–52.

Hogan, Linda. 1992. *Mean Spirit.* New York: Ballantine.

Hollander, Gail M. 2003. "Re-Naturalizing Sugar: Narratives of Place, Production and Consumption." *Social and Cultural Geography* 4, no. 1: 59–74.

Hsu, Hsuan L. 2011. "Fatal Contiguities: Metonymy and Environmental Justice." *New Literary History* 42, no. 1: 147–68.

Huggan, Graham. 1997. "Prizing 'Otherness': A Short History of the Booker." *Studies in the Novel* 29, no. 3 (September): 412–33.

———. 2001. *The Postcolonial Exotic: Marketing the Margins*. New York: Routledge.

———. 2004. "'Greening' Postcolonialism: Ecocritical Perspectives." *Modern Fiction Studies* 50, no. 3: 701–33.

Huggan, Graham, and Helen Tiffin. 2010. *Postcolonial Ecocriticism: Literature, Animals, Environment*. London: Routledge.

Ifowodo, Ogaga. 2005. *The Oil Lamp*. Trenton, NJ: Africa World Press.

Iheka, Cajetan. 2018. *Naturalizing Africa: Ecological Violence, Agency, and Postcolonial Resistance in African Literature*. Cambridge: Cambridge University Press.

Ince, Onur Ulas. 2018. *Colonial Capitalism and the Dilemmas of Liberalism*. Oxford: Oxford University Press.

Jameson, Fredric. 1986. "On Magic Realism in Film." *Critical Inquiry* 12, no. 2: 301–25.

———. 2012. "Antinomies of the Realism-Modernism Debate." *Modern Language Quarterly* 73, no. 3 (September): 475–85.

Jasanoff, Sheila. 2008. "Bhopal's Trials of Knowledge and Ignorance," *New England Law Review* 42, no. 4 (Summer): 679–92.

Jodha, N. S. 1986. "Common Property Resources and the Rural Poor in Dry Regions of India." *Economic and Political Weekly* 21, no. 27 (July 5): 1169–81.

Johnson, Eleanor. 2012. "The Poetics of Waste: Medieval English Ecocriticism." *PMLA* 127, no. 3: 460–76.

Johnson, Jennifer Lee. 2017. "Eating and Existence on an Island in Southern Uganda." *Comparative Studies in South Asia, Africa and the Middle East* 37, no. 1: 1–22.

Jones, Daniel P. 1980. "American Chemists and the Geneva Protocol." *Isis* 71, no. 3 (September): 426–40.

Joseph, Sarah. 2004. *Corporations and International Human Rights Litigation*. Oxford: Hart.

Kamalu, Ikenna, and Isaiah Fortress. 2011. "The Discursive Construction of Identity and Religious Fundamentalism in Uwem Akpan's Luxurious Hearses." In *From Boom to Doom: Protest and Conflict Resolution in the*

Literature of the Niger Delta, edited by Chinyere Nwahunanya, 210–24. New Owerri, Nigeria: Springfield.

Kaplan, Robert. 1994. "The Coming Anarchy." *Atlantic Monthly* 273, no. 2 (February): 44–76.

Kapuściński, Ryszard. 1992. *Shah of Shahs*. New York: Vintage International.

Karve, Iravati. 1969. *Yuganta: The End of an Epoch*. Poona: Deshmukh Prakashan.

Kashi, Ed. 2008. "Shadows and Light in the Niger Delta." In Kashi and Watts 2008, 24–27.

Kashi, Ed, and Michael Watts, eds. 2008. *Curse of the Black Gold: 50 Years of Oil in the Niger Delta*. New York: PowerHouse Books.

Kasturi, Kannan. 2008. "Whose Land Is Waste Land?" *InfoChange Agenda* 11: 47–50. http://www.infochangeindia.org/downloads/agenda_11.pdf.

Kazeem, Yomi. 2018. "A Legal Loophole Has Enabled Years of Environmental Damage by Global Oil Companies in Nigeria." *Quartz Africa*, January 30, 2018. https://qz.com/1192558.

Keenan, John F. 1986. Opinion and Order. US District Court Southern District of New York. In Re: Union Carbide Corporation Gas Leak Disaster at Bhopal, India in December 1984. In Baxi 1986a, 35–69.

Keenan, Thomas. 2002. "Publicity and Indifference (Sarajevo on Television)." *PMLA* 117, no. 1: 104–16.

Kelley Drye & Warren. (1985) 1986. "Memorandum in Support of Union Carbide's Motion to Dismiss," July 31, 1985. In Baxi and Paul 1986, 17–58.

Kermode, Frank. 1967. *The Sense of an Ending: Studies in the Theory of Fiction*. New York: Oxford University Press.

Kerridge, Richard, and Neil Sammells, eds. 1998. *Writing the Environment: Ecocriticism and Literature*. London: Zed.

Kincaid, Jamaica. 1988. *A Small Place*. New York: Plume.

———. 1999. *My Garden (Book)*. Illustrated by Jill Fox. New York: Farrar, Straus and Giroux.

Klein, Naomi. 2014. *This Changes Everything: Capitalism vs. the Climate*. New York: Simon & Schuster.

Lanchester, John. 2007. "Warmer, Warmer." *London Review of Books* 29, no. 6 (March 22): 3–9.

Lappé, Anne. 2011. "What Dow Chemical Doesn't Want You to Know About Your Water." *CSRwire*, June 7. http://www.csrwire.com/csrlive/commentary_detail/4646.

Latour, Bruno. 2004. *Politics of Nature: How to Bring the Sciences into Democracy*. Cambridge, MA: Harvard University Press.

Law, Robin, ed. 1995. *From Slave Trade to "Legitimate Commerce": The Commercial Transition in Nineteenth-Century West Africa.* Cambridge: Cambridge University Press.

Lawall, Sarah. 1994. *Reading World Literature: Theory, History, Practice.* Austin: University of Texas Press.

Lazarus, Neil. 2011. *The Postcolonial Unconscious.* Cambridge: Cambridge University Press.

LeMenager, Stephanie. 2013. *Living Oil: Petroleum Culture in the American Century.* Oxford: Oxford University Press.

Leonard, Arthur Glyn. 1906. *The Lower Niger and Its Tribes.* London: Macmillan.

Leopold, Aldo. (1932) 1991. "Game and Wild Life Conservation." In *The River of the Mother of God: And other Essays by Leopold,* edited by Susan L. Flader and J. Baird Caldicott, 164–68. Madison: University of Wisconsin Press.

Lescaze. Lee. 1968. "U.S. Study Finds Defoliant Harmless; Defoliants Claimed Viet Life Saver." *Washington Post,* September 21.

Lesjak, Carolyn. 2013. "Reading Dialectically." *Criticism* 55, no. 2: 233–77.

Lewis, Simon L., and Mark A. Maslin. 2015. "Defining the Anthropocene." *Nature* 519 (7542): 171–80.

Lindfors, Bernth. 1975. "Are There Any National Literatures in Sub-Saharan Black Africa Yet?" *English in Africa* 2, no. 2: 1–9.

Locke, John. 1988. *Two Treatises of Government: A Critical Edition with an Introduction and Apparatus Criticus.* Edited by Peter Laslett. Cambridge: Cambridge University Press.

Lynn, Martin. 1997. *Commerce and Economic Change in West Africa: The Palm Oil Trade in the Nineteenth Century.* New York: Cambridge University Press.

Macaulay, Thomas Babington. (1835) 1969. "Minute on Education." In *Sources of Indian Tradition,* general editor Wm. Theodore de Bary. Compiled by Stephen N. Hay and I. H. Qureshi, 2:44–49. New York: Columbia University Press.

MacCannell, Dean. 1976. *The Tourist: A New Theory of the Leisure Class.* Berkeley: University of California Press.

Macdonald, Graeme. 2017. "Fiction." In *Fueling Culture: 101 Words for Energy and Environment,* edited by Imre Szeman, Jennifer Wenzel, and Patricia Yaeger, 162–65. New York: Fordham University Press.

Macklem, Patrick. 2005. "Corporate Accountability under International Law: The Misguided Quest for Universal Jurisdiction." *International Law Forum* 7, no. 4: 281.

Malden, Alexander. 2017. *Nigeria's Oil and Gas Revenues: Insights from Company Disclosures.* New York: Natural Resource Governance Institute.

Mamdani, Mahmood. 1996. *Citizen and Subject: Contemporary Africa and the Legacy of Late Colonialism.* Princeton: Princeton University Press.

Marsh, George Perkins. 1864. *Man and Nature: Or, Physical Geography as Modified by Human Action.* New York: Scribner.

Martin, Reinhold. 2010. *Utopia's Ghost: Architecture and Postmodernism, Again.* Minneapolis: University of Minnesota Press.

Martínez-Alier, Joan. 2002. *The Environmentalism of the Poor: A Study of Ecological Conflicts and Valuation.* Cheltenham: Edward Elgar.

Marx, Karl. (1852) 1959. "The Eighteenth Brumaire of Napoleon Bonaparte." In *Marx and Engels: Basic Writings on Politics and Philosophy,* edited by L. S. Feuer, 318–48. New York: Anchor.

———. (1867) 1967. *Capital: A Critical Analysis of Capitalist Production.* 3 vols. edited by Frederick Engels, translated by Samuel Moore and Edward Aveling. New York: International.

———. 1977. *Capital: A Critique of Political Economy,* Vol. 1. Translated by Ben Fowkes. New York: Vintage.

Mazel, David. 1996. "American Literary Environmentalism as Domestic Orientalism." In *The Ecocriticism Reader,* edited by Cheryll Glotfelty and Harold Fromm, 137–46. Athens: University of Georgia Press.

McCarthy, David. 2009. "Dirty Freaks and High School Punks: Peter Saul's Critique of the Vietnam War." *American Art* 23, no. 1 (Spring): 78–103.

McCay, Bonnie J., and James M. Acheson. 1987. "Human Ecology of the Commons." In *The Question of the Commons: The Culture and Ecology of Communal Resources,* edited by Bonnie J. McCay and James M. Acheson, 1–36. Tucson: University of Arizona Press.

Meadows, Donella H., and Club of Rome. 1972. *The Limits to Growth: A Report for the Club of Rome's Project on the Predicament of Mankind.* New York: Universe Books.

Meadows, Donella H., Jørgen Randers, and Dennis L. Meadows. 2004. *The Limits to Growth: The 30-Year Update.* White River Junction, VT: Chelsea Green.

Medovoi, Leerom. 2009. "The Biopolitical Unconscious: Toward an Eco-Marxist Literary Theory." *Mediations* 24, no. 2 (Spring): 122–38.

———. 2010. "A Contribution to the Critique of Political Ecology: Sustainability as Disavowal." *New Formations* 69 (Summer): 129–43.

Melville, Herman. *Moby-Dick.* (1851) 1993. London: Wordsworth.

Menely, Tobias, and Jesse O. Taylor, eds. 2017. *Anthropocene Reading: Literary History in Geologic Times.* University Park: Pennsylvania State University Press.

Miles, Josephine. (1942) 1965. *Pathetic Fallacy in the Nineteenth Century: A Study of a Changing Relation between Object and Emotion.* New York: Octagon.

Miller, J. Hillis. 1986. "Catachresis, Prosopopoeia, and the Pathetic Fallacy in the Rhetoric of Ruskin." In *Poetry and Epistemology: Turning Points in the History of Poetic Knowledge*, edited by Roland Hagenbuche and Laura Skandera, 398–407. Regensburg: Pustet.

Mitchell, Timothy. 2009. "Carbon Democracy." *Economy and Society* 38, no. 3: 399–432.

Mitchell, W. J. T. 2002. "Imperial Landscape." In *Landscape and Power*, edited by W. J. T. Mitchell, 5–34. Chicago: University of Chicago Press.

Mitee, Ledum. 1999. "Oil, Arms and Terror—The Ogoni Experience." *Interventions* 1, no. 3: 430–38.

———. 2008. "Twelve Years Later." In Kashi and Watts 2008, 162–64.

Molony, Thomas, Lisa Ann Richey, and Stefano Ponte. 2007. "'Darwin's Nightmare': A Critical Assessment." *Review of African Political Economy* 34, no. 113 (September): 598–608.

Moore, Alexandra Schulteis. 2012. "'Disaster Capitalism' and Human Rights: Embodiment and Subalternity in Indra Sinha's *Animal's People*." In *Theoretical Perspectives on Human Rights and Literature*, edited by Elizabeth Swanson Goldberg and Alexandra Schultheis Moore, 231–46. New York: Routledge.

———. 2015. *Vulnerability and Security in Human Rights Literature and Culture*. New York: Routledge.

Moore, Jason W. 2003. "Capitalism as World-Ecology: Braudel and Marx on Environmental History." *Organization & Environment* 16, no. 4: 431–58.

Moretti, Franco. 2000. "Conjectures on World Literature." *New Left Review* 1 (January–February): 54–68.

———. 2003. "More Conjectures." *New Left Review* 20 (March–April): 73–81.

———. 2007. *Graphs, Maps, Trees: Abstract Models for a Literary History*. New York: Verso.

Morton, Timothy. 2001. "'Twinkle, Twinkle, Little Star' as an Ambient Poem; a Study of a Dialectical Image; with Some Remarks on Coleridge and Wordsworth." Romantic Circles. https://www.rc.umd.edu/praxis/ecology/morton/morton.html.

———. 2007. *Ecology without Nature: Rethinking Environmental Aesthetics*. Cambridge, MA: Harvard University Press.

Moses, Michael Valdez. 2001. "Magical Realism at World's End." *Literary Imagination: The Review of the Association of Literary Scholars and Critics* 3: 105–33.

Mufti, Aamir R. 2016. *Forget English! Orientalism and World Literatures*. Cambridge, MA: Harvard University Press.

Mukherjee, Suroopa. 2004. "Anger and Denial on the Streets of Bhopal." *InfoChange Agenda* 1: 8–11.

Mukherjee, Upamanyu Pablo. 2010. *Postcolonial Environments: Nature, Culture, and the Contemporary Indian Novel in English.* Basingstoke, UK: Palgrave Macmillan.

Murphy, John. 1993. *Harvest of Fear: Australia's Vietnam War.* St. Leonards, NSW: Allen & Unwin.

Murphy, Kim. 2010. "Death by Fire in the Gulf." *Los Angeles Times,* June 17.

National Institute of Medicine. 2014. *Veterans and Agent Orange: Update 2012.* Washington, DC: The National Academies Press.

National Museum of African Art. 1998. "The Tusk." *A Spiral of History.* February 1–April 26. https://africa.si.edu/exhibits/loango/ltusk.htm.

Neilands, J. B. 1970. "Vietnam: Progress of the Chemical War." *Asian Survey* 10, no. 3: 209–29.

———. 1972. "Napalm Survey." In *The Wasted Nations: Report of the International Commission of Enquiry into United States Crimes in Indochina, June 20–25, 1971,* edited by Frank Browning and Dorothy Forman, 26–37. New York: Harper & Row.

Neumann, Roderick P. 2004. "Nature-State-Territory: Toward a Critical Theorization of Conservation Enclosures." In Watts and Peet 2004, 195–217.

Newton, John. 1999. "Colonialism above the Snowline: Baughan, Ruskin and the South Island Myth." *Journal of Commonwealth Literature* 34, no. 2: 85–96.

Nichols, Bill. 1983. "The Voice of Documentary." *Film Quarterly* 36, no. 3: 17–30.

Nicholson, J. W. 1926. *The Forests from Within: Bihar and Orissa.* Patna: Bihar and Orissa Government Printing.

Nixon, Rob. 2005. "Environmentalism and Postcolonialism." In *Postcolonial Studies and Beyond,* edited by Ania Loomba et al., 233–51. Durham, NC: Duke University Press.

———. 2011. *Slow Violence and the Environmentalism of the Poor.* Cambridge, MA: Harvard University Press.

Nossiter, Adam. 2010. "Far from Gulf, a Spill Scourge 5 Decades Old." *New York Times,* June 16.

Nwokeji, G. Ugo. 2008. "Slave Ships to Oil Tankers." In Kashi and Watts 2008, 62–65.

Obi, Cyril I. 2001. "Global, State, and Local Intersections: Power, Authority, and Conflict in the Niger Delta Oil Communities." In Callaghy, Kassimir, and Latham 2001, 173–193.

———. 2010. "Oil Extraction, Dispossession, Resistance, and Conflict in Nigeria's Oil-Rich Niger Delta." *Canadian Journal of Development Studies/ Revue canadienne d'études du développement* 30, nos. 1–2: 219–36.

O'Brien, Susie. 2001. "Articulating a World of Difference: Ecocriticism, Postcolonialism and Globalization." *Canadian Literature* 170–71: 140–58.

O'Brien, Tim. 1994. "The Vietnam in Me." *New York Times*, October 2.

Okonta, Ike. 2008. *When Citizens Revolt: Nigerian Elites, Big Oil, and the Ogoni Struggle for Self-Determination.* Trenton, NJ: Africa World Press.

Okonta, Ike, and Oronto Douglas. 2001. *Where Vultures Feast: Shell, Human Rights, and Oil in the Niger Delta.* San Francisco: Sierra Club Books.

Okri, Ben. 1988. *Stars of the New Curfew.* London: Secker & Warburg.

Ola, Doifie, and David Eighemhenrio. 1998. *Wasting Lives: Official Negligence Results in Grave Tragedy at Idjehe, Niger Delta, Nigeria: ERA Field Report #17.* Benin City, Nigeria: Environmental Rights Action.

Oliver, Kelly. 2015. *Earth and World: Philosophy after the Apollo Missions.* New York: Columbia University Press.

"One World." 2011. Dow Chemical Company. YouTube, March 30, 2011. https://www.youtube.com/playlist?list=PL54B4D115DC28325A.

Open Society Justice Initiative. 2005. *Legal Remedies for the Resource Curse: A Digest of Experience in Using Law to Combat Natural Resource Corruption.* New York: Open Society Institute.

Oreskes, Naomi, and Erik M. Conway. 2010. *Merchants of Doubt: How a Handful of Scientists Obscured the Truth on Issues from Tobacco Smoke to Global Warming.* New York: Bloomsbury.

Owuor, Yvonne. 2016. "Reading Our Ruins: Postcolonial Stories that Float from Afar." Keynote Address, Association for Commonwealth Literature and Language Studies. Stellenbosch University. Available at https://www.theelephant.info/features/2018/03/022/reading-our-ruins-postcolonial-stories-that-float-from-afar.

Pattullo, Henry. 1772. *An Essay on the Cultivation of the Lands, and Improvement of the Revenues of Bengal.* London: Becket and DeHondt.

Peluso, Nancy, and Michael Watts. 2001. "Violent Environments." In *Violent Environments*, edited by Nancy Lee Peluso and Michael Watts, 3–38. Ithaca, NY: Cornell University Press.

Phillips, Dana. 2003. *The Truth of Ecology: Nature, Culture, and Literature in America.* Oxford: Oxford University Press.

———. 2010. "Weeping Elephants, Sensitive Men." *Safundi* 11, nos. 1–2: 19–47.

Plaintiffs' Executive Committee. (1985) 1986. "Memorandum in Opposition to UCC's Motion." In Baxi and Paul 1986, 59–107.

Pollan, Michael. 2001. "Produce Politics," *New York Times*, January 14.

———. 2006. *The Omnivore's Dilemma: A Natural History of Four Meals.* New York: Penguin.

Pontecorvo, Gillo, dir. (1966) 2004. *La bataille d'Alger/The Battle of Algiers.* Criterion Collection/Home Vision Entertainment, Irvington, NY.

Prakash, Gyan. 1990. *Bonded Histories: Genealogies of Labor Servitude in Colonial India.* Cambridge: Cambridge University Press.

Pratt, Mary Louise. 1992. *Imperial Eyes: Travel Writing and Transculturation.* New York: Routledge.

———. 2008. "Planetary Longings: Sitting in the Light of the Great Solar TV." In *World Writing: Poetics, Ethics, Globalization,* edited by Mary Gallagher, 207–22. Toronto: University of Toronto Press.

Pratten, David. 2008. "Masking Youth: Transformation and Transgression in Annang Performance." *African Arts* 41, no. 4: 44–60.

Public Citizen. (1985) 1986. "The Union Carbide Record." In Baxi 1986a, 299–302.

Quayson, Ato. 1997. *Strategic Transformations in Nigerian Writing: Orality & History in the Work of Rev. Samuel Johnson, Amos Tutuola, Wole Soyinka & Ben Okri.* Oxford: Currey.

———. 2003. *Calibrations: Reading for the Social.* Minneapolis: University of Minnesota Press.

Rajagopal, Arvind. 1987. "And the Poor Get Gassed: Multinational Aided Development and the State—the Case of Bhopal." *Berkeley Journal of Sociology* 32: 129–52.

Ramamurthy, Priti. 2004. "Why Is Buying a 'Madras' Cotton Shirt a Political Act? A Feminist Commodity Chain Analysis." *Feminist Studies* 30, no. 3 (Fall): 734–69.

Rangarajan, Mahesh. 1996. *Fencing the Forest: Conservation and Ecological Change in India's Central Provinces, 1860–1914.* Delhi: Oxford University Press.

Raphael, Victor. 2000. "ERA Field Report #51: Spewing Premium Motor Spirit From NNPC Pipelines Around Adeje." Environmental Rights Action, January 11, 2000, http://www.waado.org/Environment/OilSpills/OillSpills_Urhobo/Adeje.html.

Rauxloh, Regina. 2011. "The Role of International Criminal Law in Environmental Protection." In *Natural Resource Investment and Africa's Development,* edited by Francis N. Botchway, 423–61. Cheltenham, UK: Edward Elgar.

Reich, Robert. 1973. "Global Social Responsibility for the Multinationals." *Texas International Law Journal* 8, no. 187: 187–217.

Rempel, William. 1984. "Agent Orange Makers: Dioxin Peril; Memos tell Inside Story." *Los Angeles Times,* May 19.

Reno, William. 2001. "How Sovereignty Matters: International Markets and the Political Economy of Local Politics in Weak States." In Callaghy, Kassimir, and Latham 2001, 197–215.

———. 2004. "Order and Commerce in Turbulent Areas: 19th Century Lessons, 21st Century Practice." *Third World Quarterly* 25, no. 4: 607–25.

Rich, B. Ruby. 2006. "Documentary Disciplines: An Introduction." *Cinema Journal* 46, no. 1 (Fall): 108–15.

Richey, Lisa Ann. 2007. "Better (RED) Than Dead: Celebrities and the New Frontier of Development Assistance." Paper presented at Africa Workshop, University of Michigan, October 16.

Ricoeur, Paul. 1986. "Life: A Story in Search of a Narrator." In *Facts and Values,* edited by M. C. Doeser, 121–32. Dordrecht: Springer.

Rivoli, Pietra. 2014. *The Travels of a T-Shirt in the Global Economy: An Economist Examines the Markets, Power, and Politics of World Trade.* Hoboken, NJ: John Wiley.

Robbins, Bruce. 1999. *Feeling Global: Internationalism in Distress.* New York: NYU Press.

———. 2005. "Commodity Histories." *PMLA* 120, no. 2: 454–63.

Roberts, David. "Climate Change and 'Environmental Journalism." *Grist* 21, August 2013. http://grist.org/climate-energy/climate-change-and -environmental-journalism.

Roh, Franz. (1923). "Magical Realism: Post-Expressionism." In Zamora and Faris 1995, 15–31.

Roos, Bonnie, and Alex Hunt, eds. 2010. *Postcolonial Green: Environmental Politics and World Narratives.* Charlottesville: University of Virginia Press.

Rose-Innes, Henrietta. 2007. "Poison." In *African Pens: New Writing from Southern Africa 2007,* 1–10. Claremont, South Africa: Spearhead.

Rosencranz, Armin, Shyam Divan, and Antony Scott. 1994. "Legal and Political Repercussions in India." In *Learning from Disaster: Risk Management after Bhopal,* edited by Sheila Jasanoff, 44–65. Philadelphia: University of Pennsylvania Press.

Rowell, Andrew, James Marriott, and Lorne Stockman. 2005. *The Next Gulf: London, Washington and Oil Conflict in Nigeria.* London: Constable.

Rowell, Andy. 1995. "Shell Shocked." *Village Voice,* November 21.

Ruckelshaus, William D. 1983. "Science, Risk, and Public Policy." *Science* 221, no. 4615 (September 9): 1026–28.

Rukeyser, Muriel. (1938) 2005. "The Book of the Dead." In *The Collected Poems of Muriel Rukeyser,* edited by Janet E. Kaufman and Anne F. Herzog. Pittsburgh: University of Pittsburgh Press.

Rushdie, Salman. 1982. *Midnight's Children.* New York: Avon.

———. 1997. "Introduction." In *Mirrorwork: 50 Years of Indian Writing, 1947–1997,* edited by Salman Rushdie and Elizabeth J. West. New York: Henry Holt.

Ruskin, John. 1849. *The Seven Lamps of Architecture.* London: Smith, Elder.

———. 1888. *Modern Painters, Vols. 2 and 3*. London: George Allen.

Said, Edward W. (1978) 2003. *Orientalism*. New York: Pantheon.

———. 1983. *The World, The Text, and the Critic*. Cambridge, MA: Harvard University Press.

———. 1993. *Culture and Imperialism*. New York: Vintage Books.

Sagoff, Mark. 1988. *The Economy of the Earth: Philosophy, Law, and the Environment*. Cambridge: Cambridge University Press.

Salgado, Minoli. 2000. "Tribal Stories, Scribal Worlds: Mahasweta Devi and the Unreliable Translator." *Journal of Commonwealth Literature* 35, no. 1: 131–45.

Saro-Wiwa, Ken. 1992. *Genocide in Nigeria: The Ogoni Tragedy*. London: Saros.

Sauper, Hubert, dir. 2004. *Darwin's Nightmare*. Mille et Une Productions.

———. n.d. "Filming in the Heart of Darkness." https://www.darwinsnightmare.com/darwin/html/film3.htm.

Schuck, Peter H. 1986. *Agent Orange on Trial: Mass Toxic Disasters in the Courts*. Cambridge, MA: Belknap Press of Harvard University Press.

Schwyzer, Philip. 2009. "Phaer [Phayer], Thomas." Oxford Dictionary of National Biography. https://doi.org/10.1093/ref:odnb/22085.

Shankar, S. 2010. "Necessity and Desire: Water and Coca-Cola in India." In Bose and Lyons 2010, 151–81.

Shiva, Vandana. 1988. *Staying Alive: Women, Ecology and Development in India*. Delhi: Kali for Women.

———. 1991. *Ecology and the Politics of Survival: Conflicts over Natural Resources in India*. New Delhi: Sage.

"Silicosis Deaths Assailed in House." 1936. *New York Times*, February 8.

Simon & Schuster. 2018. "Corporate Overview." http://about.simonandschuster.biz/corporate-overview.

Singh, Subrata. 2012. "Common Lands Made 'Wastelands': Making of the 'Wastelands' into Common Lands." Working Paper 32. Foundation for Ecological Security.

Sinha, Indra. 2008. *Animal's People*. New York: Simon & Schuster.

Slaughter, Joseph R. 2007. *Human Rights, Inc.: The World Novel, Narrative Form, and International Law*. New York: Fordham University Press.

———. 2008. "Humanitarian Reading." In *Humanitarianism and Suffering: The Mobilization of Empathy*, edited by Richard A. Wilson and Richard D. Brown. Cambridge: Cambridge University Press.

———. 2018. "Images That Resemble Us Too Much: Natives, Corporations, Humans, and Other Personified Creatures of International Law." Annual *London Review of International Law* Lecture, London School of Economics, London. http://www.lse.ac.uk/website-archive/newsAndMedia

/videoAndAudio/channels/publicLecturesAndEvents/player.aspx?id
=4037.

Slemon, Stephen. 1995. "Magic Realism as Postcolonial Discourse." In
Zamora and Faris 1995, 407–26.

Smith, Neil. 2008. *Uneven Development: Nature, Capital, and the Production of
Space.* Athens: University of Georgia Press.

SOFII. 2008. "Amnesty International UK: Press Ads That Shook a Nation."
SOFII. http://newsofii.org/case-study/amnesty-international-uk-press-ads
-that-shook-a-nation.

Sontag, Susan. 2003. *Regarding the Pain of Others.* New York: Farrar, Straus
and Giroux.

SPDC (Shell). 2003. "Peace and Security in the Niger Delta: Conflict Expert
Group Baseline Report" Working Paper, prepared by WAC Global
Services. www.shell2004.com/2007/shell_wac_report_2004.pdf.

Spivak, Gayatri Chakravorty. 1990. "Criticism, Feminism, and the
Institution." Interview by Elizabeth Grosz. In *Intellectuals: Aesthetics,
Politics, and Academics*, 153–71. Minneapolis: University of Minnesota
Press.

Srinivasan, U. Thara, et al. 2008. "The Debt of Nations and the Distribution
of Ecological Impacts from Human Activities." *PNAS* 105, no. 5: 1768–73.

Stebbing, Edward Percy. (1922) 2010. *The Forests of India and the Neighboring
Countries, Volume 1.* Delhi: Asiatic Publishing House.

Stein, Mark. 1983. "Dow Ends Bid." *LA Times*, October 15.

Stellman, J. M., et al. 2003. "The Extent and Patterns of Usage of Agent
Orange and Other Herbicides in Vietnam." *Nature* 422, no. 6933
(April 17): 681–87.

Stoler, Ann Laura. 2008. "Imperial Debris: Reflections on Ruins and
Ruination." *Cultural Anthropology* 23, no. 2: 191–219.

Strother, Z. S. 2010. "Dancing on the Knife of Power: Comedy, Narcissism,
and Subversion in the Portrayals of Europeans and Americans by Central
Africans." In *Through African Eyes*, ed. Nii O. Quarpocoome, 49–59.
Detroit: Detroit Institute of the Arts.

Sullivan, Joanna. 2001. "The Question of a National Literature for Nigeria."
Research in African Literatures 32, no. 3: 71–85.

Szeman, Imre. 2007. "System Failure: Oil, Futurity, and the Imagination of
Disaster." *SAQ* 106, no. 4: 805–23.

———. 2012. "Crude Aesthetics: The Politics of Oil Documentaries."
Journal of American Studies 46, no. 2: 423–39.

Tattersall, Nick. 2007. "Mali Film puts West's Blueprint for Africa on
Trial." *Washington Post*, January 12.

Trager, Rebecca. 2012. "EPA Sets Safe Dioxin Level." *Chemistry World*, February 12. https://www.chemistryworld.com/news/epa-sets-safe-dioxin -level/3001482.article.

Trefon, Theodore. 2004. *Reinventing Order in the Congo: How People Respond to State Failure in Kinshasa*. London: Zed Books.

Trotsky, Leon. (1914) 1996. *The War and the International*. Trotsky Internet Archive. https://www.marxists.org/archive/trotsky/1914/war/part3 .htm#ch11.

Tsing, Anna Lowenhaupt. 2005. *Friction: An Ethnography of Global Connection*. Princeton: Princeton University Press.

———. 2015. *The Mushroom at the End of the World: On the Possibility of Life in Capitalist Ruins*. Princeton: Princeton University Press.

Tully, John. 2011. *The Devil's Milk: A Social History of Rubber*. New York: Monthly Review Press.

Tuodolo, Felix. 2008. "Generation." In Kashi and Watts 2008, 114–15.

Tutuola, Amos. 1952. *The Palm-Wine Drinkard and His Dead Palm-Wine Tapster in the Dead's Town*. London: Faber and Faber.

Ukeje, Charles. 2001. "Oil Communities and Political Violence: The Case of Ethnic Ijaws in Nigeria's Delta Region." *Terrorism and Political Violence* 13, no. 4: 15–36.

Ukiwo, Ukoha. 2008. "Empire of Commodities." In Kashi and Watts 2008, 70–73.

Union of India v. Union Carbide Corporation, Suit for Damages. (1986) 1990. Civil Suit 1113/86, Bhopal District Court. September 5. In Baxi and Dhanda 1990, 3–12.

US Air Force Communications. 1965–1971. "Herbs Tape: Defoliation Missions in South Vietnam, 1965–71. Data by Province." From Special Collections of the National Agricultural Library, Alvin Young Collection on Agent Orange. https://www.nal.usda.gov/exhibits/speccoll/items/show /1257.

US Court of Appeals, Second Circuit, 809 F.2d 195 (2d Cir. 1987). 14 January 1987. Questia US Law.

US Environmental Protection Agency. 2012. *Reanalysis of Key Issues Related to Dioxin Toxicity and Response to NAS Comments, Volume 1*. Washington, DC. https://cfpub.epa.gov/ncea/iris/iris_documents/documents/subst /1024_summary.pdf.

US Institute for Peace. 2009. "Blood Oil in the Niger Delta." Special Report on the Niger Delta. https://www.usip.org/sites/default/files/blood_oil _nigerdelta_0.pdf.

Valliantos, John, with McKay Jenkins. 2014. *Poison Spring: The Secret History of Pollution and the EPA*. New York: Bloomsbury.

Van Strum, Carol, and Paul Merrell. 1987. *No Margin of Safety: A Preliminary Report on Dioxin Pollution and the Need for Emergency Action in the Pulp and Paper Industry.* Toronto: Greenpeace Great Lakes Toxics Campaign.

Vandergeest, Peter, and Nancy Peluso. 1995. "Territorialization and State Power in Thailand." *Theory and Society* 24, no. 3: 385–426.

Venuti, Lawrence. 1995. *The Translator's Invisibility: A History of Translation.* London: Routledge.

Viswanathan, Gauri. 1989. *Masks of Conquest: Literary Study and British Rule in India.* New York: Columbia University Press.

Wald, George. 1970. "Corporate Responsibility for War Crimes." *New York Review of Books*, February 2.

Walkowitz, Rebecca. 2009. "Comparison Literature." *New Literary History* 40, no. 3: 567–82.

———. 2015. *Born Translated: The Contemporary Novel in an Age of World Literature.* New York: Columbia University Press.

Wallerstein, Immanuel Maurice. 2004. *World-Systems Analysis: An Introduction.* Durham, NC: Duke University Press.

Warwick Research Collective (WReC). 2015. *Combined and Uneven Development: Towards a New Theory of World-Literature.* Liverpool: Liverpool University Press.

Watt, Ian. 1957. *The Rise of the Novel.* Berkeley: University of California Press.

Watts, Michael. 1999. "Petro-Violence: Some Thoughts on Community, Extraction, and Political Ecology." Working Paper 99-1. Berkeley Workshop on Environmental Politics, Institute of International Studies.

———. 2001. "Petro-Violence: Community, Extraction, and Political Ecology of a Mythic Commodity." In *Violent Environments*, edited by Nancy Lee Peluso and Michael Watts, 189–212. Ithaca, NY: Cornell University Press.

———. 2004. "Violent Environments." In Watts and Peet 2004, 273–99.

———. 2008. "Sweet and Sour." In Kashi and Watts 2008, 36–47.

Watts, Michael, and Richard Peet. 2004. *Liberation Ecologies: Environment, Development, Social Movements.* London: Routledge.

Waugh, Charles. 2010. "'Only You Can Prevent a Forest': Agent Orange, Ecocide, and Environmental Justice." *ISLE* 17, no. 1: 113–32.

Waugh, Charles, and Huy Lien, eds. 2010. *Family of Fallen Leaves: Stories of Agent Orange by Vietnamese Writers.* Athens: University of Georgia Press.

Wenzel, Jennifer. 1998. "Epic Struggles over India's Forests in Mahasweta Devi's Short Fiction." *Alif: Journal of Comparative Poetics* 18: 127–58.

———. 2006. "Petro-Magic-Realism: Toward a Political Ecology of Nigerian Literature." *Postcolonial Studies* 9, no. 4: 449–64.

————. 2009. *Bulletproof: Afterlives of Anticolonial Prophecy in South Africa and Beyond*. Chicago: University of Chicago Press.

————. 2015. "Reading Fanon Reading Nature." In *What Postcolonial Theory Doesn't Say*, edited by Ziad Elmarsafy, Anna Bernard, and Stuart Murray, 185–201. New York: Routledge.

————. 2017. "Introduction." In *Fueling Culture: 101 Words for Energy and Environment*, edited by Imre Szeman, Jennifer Wenzel, and Patricia Yaeger, 1–16. New York: Fordham University Press.

White, Hayden. 1980. "The Value of Narrativity in the Representation of Reality." *Critical Inquiry* 7, no. 1: 5–27.

Whitehead, Judith. 2012. "John Locke, Accumulation by Dispossession and the Governance of Colonial India." *Journal of Contemporary Asia* 42, no. 1: 1–21.

Whiteside, Thomas. 1979. *The Pendulum and the Toxic Cloud*. New Haven: Yale University Press.

Williams, Raymond. 1973. *The Country and the City*. New York: Oxford University Press.

————. 1989. *Resources of Hope: Culture, Democracy, Socialism*. London: Verso.

Wilson, J. Spotswood. 1859. "On the General and Gradual Desiccation of the Earth and Atmosphere." *Report of the Twenty-Eight Meeting of the British Association for the Advancement of Science*, 155–56. London: John Murray.

Wordsworth, William. 1974. *The Prose Works of William Wordsworth*, vol. 1. Edited by W. J. B. Owen and Jane Worthington Smyser. Oxford: Clarendon.

World Bank. 1995. "Defining an Environmental Development Strategy for the Niger Delta." May 25.

"Written Statement of Union Carbide." (1986) 1990. Civil Suit 1113/86, Bhopal District Court, 10 December 1986. In Baxi and Dhanda, 33–107.

Yaeger, Patricia, et al. 2011. "Editor's Column: Literature in the Ages of Wood, Tallow, Coal, Whale Oil, Gasoline, Atomic Power, and Other Energy Sources." *PMLA* 126, no. 2: 305–25.

Zamora, Lois Parkinson, and Wendy B. Faris, eds. 1995. *Magical Realism: Theory, History, Community*. Durham, NC: Duke University Press.

Zierler, David. 2008. "Inventing Ecocide: Agent Orange, Antiwar Protest, and Environmental Destruction in Vietnam." PhD dissertation, Temple University.

Zimmermann, Francis. 1987. *The Jungle and the Aroma of Meats: An Ecological Theme in Hindu Medicine*. Berkeley: University of California Press.

Zinn, Howard. 1967. "Dow Shalt Not Kill." *The Idler*, December 1967: 7–11.

Page numbers in italics indicate an illustration.

First World and Third World, 35–36, 37, 60, 191, 202–3, 239
flaring. *See* gas flaring
focalization. *See* point of view
food aid, 69, 271n17
foreclosure, 37, 134, 159, 167, 171–72, 257–59. *See also* quarantines of imagination; unimagining
foreign aid, 68–69, 271n17
Foreign Exchange Regulation Act (India), 295n39
Forest Acts (India), 150, 152
Forest Department, India, 152, 153–54, 285n11
forests, 45, 120–21, 122, 280n61; India, 141, 143, 148–67, 172–77, 190, 286n13, 288n29. *See also* jungle; trees; waste; wilderness
Forests and Sea Power (Albion), 150, 284n5
Forests from Within, The (Nicholson), 174, 285n11
Forget English! (Mufti), 6
forgetting, 7, 34, 37, 43, 76, 131, 262, 271n19
form, 19–20, 26, 86 89, 115, 181, 229, 261; cultural, 15–21, 34, 55; narrative, 32–33, 41, 46, 148, 159, 164, 238–40
Fortress, Isaiah, 279n51
forum non conveniens, 46, 201, 202–6, 230, 290n8, 292n16
forums, alternative. *See* alternative forums
fossil fuels, 18, 28, 31, 92, 186, 194, 279n53; imagination and, 119, 126. *See also* oil; petro-magic-realism
Francis, Marc. *See Black Gold* (Marc and Nick Francis)
Francis, Nick. *See Black Gold* (Marc and Nick Francis)
Francis, Philip, 151
fundament, 21
fundamentalism: climate, 20–21; market, 21, 145–48, 162; religious, 21, 111, 133. *See also* resource logic
future inferior, 35, 37
future perfect, 129, 139, 148
futures, 1–3, 21, 30–42, 129, 147–49, 153–54, 175, 187, 189, 192, 236, 259–61, 263; climate change as theft of, 5, 144, 186; fake, 1, 260. *See also* improvement

Gadgil, Madhav, 151, 174, 287n20
Galanter, Marc, 204, 291n12
Galston, Arthur, 248
gardens, European imperial, 13–14, 170, 285n7
Garuba, Harry, 124–25, 129
gas flaring, 85, 91–92, 92, 121, 123, 130, 205, 283n80
gasoline prices, 93
Gbokoo, Daniel, 131
Gbomo, Jomo, 96–98, 274n20
gender: activism and, 81, 242, 261, 274n18, 286n18; relations to nature and, 38, 64, 177, 277n41, 287n19; social exploitation and, 67, 113, 160–64
Geneva Conventions: Protocol 1925, 247, 299n65; 300n67; Additional Protocols I and II, 249
genres, literary, 26, 30, 38, 114, 130, 169, 177, 224, 230, 263
gentrification of imagination, 9, 33, 57, 244
geographies, elastic. *See* elastic geographies
geopolitics, 7–8, 26, 35, 50, 247, 268n22, 285n5
Gerstacker, Carl, 197–98, 205, 209, 257, 260, 290nn3–4, 291n10
Gibson, Alexander, 151, 154, 192
Gidwani, Vinay, 150
global bestsellers, 8, 114
global chemicals, 5, 40, 210, 248
global culture industry, 33, 114, 130, 220–21
Global Fund to Fight AIDS, Tuberculosis, and Malaria, 78
Global North, 4, 5, 83, 267n4, 272n4
global scale, 3, 7–8, 22, 30, 148, 189–90, 243. *See also* worldwide
Global Shadows (Ferguson), 82, 83
Global South, 4, 36, 114, 144, 267n4, 272n4. *See also* Third World
Global Stratotype Section and Point (GSSP), 193
global warming, 3, 17, 30, 143–44
globalization, 3–5, 25, 30, 42, 102, 230, 241; backside, 62–63; capitalism and, 29, 50, 68, 134, 192, 230, 263, 299n63; contradictions, 33, 67; corporate, 199; knowledge and, 56, 73–74, 82;

local leaders and oil companies, 101,
  275n30
local subsistence users: colonialism and,
  60, 146, 179, 192, 284n3; India, 143,
  144, 149, 151–56, 174–75, 191, 286n13;
  Lake Victoria, Africa, 62, 63–64;
  Niger Delta, 84–85
localization, 42–43, 198–200, 202, 206,
  210, 214, 219, 230, 241
Locke, John, 45, 151, 154, 167, 180, 186,
  194, 284nn1–3. *See also* "Of Property"
  (Locke)
looking, 14, 94, 171, 211–14. *See also*
  reflexivity; seeing; spectatorship
looking for labor, 184, 186
Lower Niger and Its Tribes, The
  (Leonard), 179, 278n46
"Luxurious Hearses" (Akpan), 111–16,
  118, 279nn50–51,53
Lyons, Laura, 9
Lyrical Ballads (Wordsworth), 181–82

M. C. Mehta v. Kamal Nath et al., 286n14
M. C. Mehta v. Union of India, 256, 258
Macaulay, Thomas Babington, 151, 172
MacCannell, Dean, 57
Macdonald, Graeme, 29, 189
Macklem, Patrick, 208
Madhya Pradesh, India, 289n2
Madoc-Jones, Didier, 33–36, 41
magic, 88, 126–27, 282n75. *See also* oil:
  magical aspects; petro-magic;
  petro-magic-realism
magical realism, 120, 121, 124, 126–29,
  281n69. *See also* petro-magic-realism
Mahabharata, 174, 177
Mahasweta Devi, 156–57, 164, 177–78,
  286n18, 287n19, 288n23. *See also*
  "Dhowli" (Mahasweta Devi); "Salt"
  (Mahasweta Devi)
Mahindra, Keshub, 292n15
malignant fictions, 262
Malm, Andreas, 192
Mamdani, Mahmood, 101
Man Booker Prize, 220
Man with a Movie Camera (Vertov),
  74–75
Manto, Saadat Hasan, 279n50, 285n8
maps, 4, 8, 23, 26, 28, 35, 50, 81, 108–9,
  173, 206, 207, 245, 254–55, 293n20. *See
  also* Mercator projection

Maps, Graphs, and Trees (Moretti), 6
margins, 5, 9, 89, 157–67, 173; as
  possibility, 158–59, 162–64
marginalization, 164, 177–78, 191
markets, 11, 25–26, 57, 60, 66–70, 77, 85,
  121, 144, 194, 228, 271n23, 276n32;
  fundamentalism, 21; literary, 24–26,
  114, 126, 228, 282n70, 286n18;
  rationality of, 77, 147, 162; as world,
  24–25. *See also* neoliberalism; resource
  logic
marsiyas, 11–12, 231–32, 297nn46–47
Martin, Reinhold, 198, 243, 254
marvelous real, American, 124, 281n68
Marx, Karl, 25, 35, 49, 51, 64, 112,
  268n19, 280n61; commodities, 49, 51,
  54, 70, 79; personification, 70;
  primitive accumulation, 143
Marxism, 5, 25, 27–28, 112, 125, 237
Maslin, Mark, 193–94
Mason, Bobbie Ann, 255
materialism, 77, 124–25, 271n21; animist,
  124–25, 127; planetary, 210. *See also*
  new materialism
materiality, 3, 5, 88–90, 112–13, 116, 119,
  133, 142, 207, 210, 260, 263, 283n81
mattering, 16–18, 112. *See also* counting
Mazel, David, 16
McCay, Bonnie J., 285n12
McCurry, Steve, 195
Mead, Margaret, 299n63
media consumption, 33, 56, 64–65,
  74–76, 84
media exposure, 14, 33, 36, 46, 86–87,
  96, 200, 207, 216–17
mediation, literary, 8, 12, 15–19, 41, 263,
  287n19
Meditations in Green (Wright), 255
Medovoi, Lee, 7, 8, 17, 31, 188
Mehta, M. C., v. Kamal Nath et al.,
  286n14
Mehta, M. C., v. Union of India, 256,
  258
Mehta, Suketu, 218–19
Melville, Herman. See *Moby-Dick*
  (Melville)
memory, 31, 34, 94, 180–82, 187. *See also*
  forgetting
MEND (Movement for the
  Emancipation of the Niger Delta),
  95–96, 100, 274nn19–20

JENNIFER WENZEL is Associate Professor of English and Comparative Literature and of Middle Eastern, South Asian, and African Studies at Columbia University. She is the author of *Bulletproof: Afterlives of Anticolonial Prophecy in South Africa and Beyond* (Chicago and KwaZulu-Natal, 2009). With Imre Szeman and Patricia Yaeger, she co-edited *Fueling Culture: 101 Words for Energy and Environment* (Fordham, 2017).

CPSIA information can be obtained
at www.ICGtesting.com
Printed in the USA
JSHW031611200820
7398JS00001B/63